March 27, 1999

To Diane
With best wishes

Give Us Credit

GIVE
US
CREDIT

▲

ALEX COUNTS

TIMES BOOKS

RANDOM HOUSE

All rights reserved under International and Pan-American Copyright Conventions. Published in the United States by Times Books, a division of Random House, Inc., New York, and simultaneously in Canada by Random House of Canada Limited, Toronto.

Library of Congress Cataloging-in-Publication data is available.
ISBN 0-8129-2464-9

Printed in the United States of America on acid-free paper
24689753

Book design by Mina Greenstein

For Gail Lawler

CONTENTS

Epilogue   342

INTRODUCTION

I first heard of Muhammad Yunus and his Grameen Bank in Bangladesh when I was at college, studying economics and the causes of world poverty. My activism to date had consisted of tutoring poor children from the Bronx, raising money for overseas charities, and educating students on the causes of world hunger, but I had come to realize that Western attempts to stem hunger and poverty were piecemeal and ineffective; I was applying Band-Aids rather than finding permanent solutions to these problems. As I read about Yunus, I saw that he had found a way of profoundly changing the lives of people in his country, without advice or technology from the West. Eventually, I learned that we had very little to teach him and that he had some important insights into the issue of poverty in wealthy nations like the United States.

Over time, my interest in Grameen grew. At the end of my junior year of college, I wrote a letter to Muhammad Yunus and asked if I could come to Bangladesh to spend a year working for the Grameen Bank. His reply was characteristically blunt: I was allowed to come, but I would have to bear all my own expenses. "If you don't like the work, you can leave," he wrote. "If we don't like you, we will not be able to use you." After a long delay in getting my visa—caused by the disastrous flood that struck Bangladesh in August—I arrived in December 1988, full of wonder and fear.

Muhammad Yunus and I left Dhaka at six on the morning of January 4, 1989, and drove for two hours until we arrived at a gathering of several thousand borrowers, an "anniversary celebration" marking the month when the local Grameen Bank branch office had given out its first loan nine years earlier. I spent the next five days going to three or four of these events each day.

These celebrations surpassed anything I had imagined I would see in Bangladesh—a country where the per capita income is two hundred times less than in the United States. Reflecting my state of mind at the time, I wrote in a personal letter on January 11:

> Grameen Bank borrowers come out of the closet society puts them in. Seeing them come out is an awesome spectacle.
>
> Each year, Yunus comes to huge gatherings of centers, which is to say groups of borrowers within the branch. One such celebration last week consisted of more than 2,000 borrowers, hundreds of their children, and the local Grameen employees—people as far as the eye could see. Thousands more had gathered just to see what all the fuss was about.
>
> When Yunus arrived, we walked to an arch built of painted vases piled on top of each other, with a sign on top announcing the occasion in Bengali with appropriate exclamations. Two children walked forward, saluted Yunus, and handed him flowers. Bouquet in hand, he walked down a roped-off path while children on either side of him threw flower petals at his feet. At the end of the procession, two women borrowers saluted him, put garlands around his neck, and followed him to a small platform.
>
> At this point, the crowd stood and shouted slogans in Bengali—one translates as "Unity, hard work, and discipline, that is our creed"—and cheered. If you're wondering, three thousand landless Bengalis are LOUD.
>
> Then came Yunus's speech, which was terrific. In Jesse Jackson–like cadence he said, "And when our children finish pri-

mary school, they will *not* be finished with their education. We will send them to high school. And when they graduate from high school, we *still* won't be finished—we'll send them to college. But we *still* won't be finished then. Only when they graduate from university will we be finished." The crowd roared in approval.

After the speech, Yunus walked among the borrowers for an hour, greeting everyone. Once, after such a celebration, I said to Yunus, "I was so moved seeing all those women in that crowd as we walked around. They seemed so proud of what they've accomplished." He looked at me and said slowly, "You know, one of them showed me something she'd made with a loan, and I asked her how much money she took out. She couldn't even answer, but spontaneously burst into tears." When he finished speaking, Yunus leaned back in his chair as we both sat silently, overcome with emotion.

I concluded the letter by relating a conversation with Yunus that put these gatherings in perspective:

Yunus describes these occasions as times when the poor can show off, be heard, be loud, make a stir. The slogans, the fanfare—it's all part of a process of overcoming the shame and isolation of poverty and expressing what he calls "disciplined energy." Society tells the poor: "Stay in your cruddy houses; you are neither to be seen nor heard." Grameen invites them: "Come together, hold your head up high, be seen, be heard."

Those five days left a deep impression on me. I had come to Bangladesh expecting to see the teeming humanity of Calcutta with the sunken faces and bloated stomachs of the Ethiopian famines. Indeed, over the ten months I would spend in Bangladesh that year, I would see some of that. For many weeks I continued writing and thinking about the anniversary celebrations. Some months later, a friend forwarded one of my letters to *60 Minutes* after they had expressed interest in doing a segment on Grameen; the images I had described seemed to grab their imagination as well. In May,

Morley Safer and his entourage arrived and asked if any anniversary celebrations were planned for the coming weeks. Yunus, knowing that they weren't, said he didn't know but he'd check. Within twenty-four hours a branch in Tangail—chosen by *60 Minutes* largely because I had written my letters from there—was preparing a program.

When Yunus returned to Dhaka during the second week in January, I asked him if I could spend a few weeks at a local branch office, preferably one that was situated in a remote and backward area. He agreed. I told him I was determined to find out what all this celebrating was about, what had made so many thousands of people joyous in a nation that was among the most downtrodden in the world.

In creating the Grameen Bank, Muhammad Yunus turned the conventional wisdom of traditional financial institutions on its head. Banks seek out wealthy people with collateral, and exclude the poor. Yunus sought out the impoverished, and excluded the rich. The worse the financial straits a person was in, the more welcome she was in his bank. Banks had incentives to disburse large loans, while Yunus, in testimony before the United States Congress, bragged about his smallest loan ever—for \$1.

Yunus broke all these rules while maintaining high repayment rates and recording a modest profit most years. Yunus succeeded by finding a fertile middle ground between rugged capitalism and ragged socialism, between lending to individuals and lending to cooperatives. He would lend to poor people on an individual basis, but only after they had joined a group.

A woman who wants to borrow from Grameen must therefore find four other friends who are eligible for membership. That is, they must also be poor. None of the women can be a blood relation to anyone else in the group, and they must agree to help each other succeed in their businesses. In the event one of the five falls into difficulty, the others are obliged to assist her and, in the event of default, work to repay her loan or risk having their line of credit reduced. Thus, along with peer *support* comes peer *pressure*.

After five women have declared their intention to form a group,

they undergo seven days of "group training" in which they learn *establishing a group*
the rules of the bank and memorize a social contract called the
Sixteen Decisions. To become a recognized group, they must pass
an oral examination administered by a senior bank official that
tests their understanding of the rules and decisions. That way, no
one can say they didn't understand the rules of the bank later on.
After recognition, two members are allowed to submit loan proposals. A typical amount would be 1,000 to 3,000 taka ($25 to
$75). After these first two women, normally the poorest in the
group, receive their loans and pay their first five (of a total of fifty)
weekly installments, two others become eligible to apply for loans.
When those two repay for four or five weeks, the final member is
allowed to submit her proposal. After making fifty installments,
the borrower pays her interest* and a small contribution into a life
insurance fund. Then she is eligible to apply for a larger loan, sometimes as much as double the original amount. This cycle continues
as long as she and her group members are borrowers in good standing with the bank.

The bank's motto is "We don't ask the people to come to the
bank, we bring the bank to the people." Loan payments are made
in weekly center meetings held in the village where the women live.
A center consists of six to eight groups of five borrowers, and often
they pool their resources to build a "center house" so that they can
meet in a dignified fashion during the rainy season. After center
meetings, bank employees often visit individual borrowers' houses
to inspect their businesses—such as cow fattening, weaving, poul-
try farming, food processing, and shopkeeping—and to discuss any
problems that have arisen, such as a borrower's illness. The meetings are opened and closed by rituals that are meant to symbolize
the discipline and unity of the groups. Loan proposals are made at
the meetings, but loans are disbursed at the branch office, for security reasons.

In the mid-1970s Yunus had only a few hundred borrowers as
he went through a process of trial and error. Initially he combined
men and women in the same groups, but over time decided to form

---

*Twenty percent simple interest charged on a declining balance.

only all-male and all-female centers, with strong preference given to the latter. Women borrowers proved to be more disciplined and resourceful—their payments came in more regularly and the profits they earned benefited the entire family. (Men, it was discovered, tended to spend their profits on themselves.) By 1993, Grameen's membership had swelled to 1.6 million borrowers spread throughout 25,000 villages nationwide, and 93 percent of these members were women. On an average working *day,* the bank was disbursing 40 million taka, or $1 million. Over the next two years, those figures grew to two million borrowers in 34,000 villages and daily disbursements of $1.5 million. Grameen employed some 11,000 young men and women, and the loans they sanctioned generated enough interest income to pay their salaries.

In March 1993, an independent evaluation conducted by Professor David Gibbons of the impact of Grameen's lending program on its borrowers was completed. Among women who had been borrowing from Grameen for eight or more years, 46 percent had crossed above the poverty line and had accumulated enough assets to be unlikely to fall back below it. Another 34 percent were close to coming out of poverty, while the remaining 20 percent remained mired in extreme poverty, mostly due to the chronic illness of one or more family members. When additional data were included, the measured impact was even greater. Among non-Grameen families, only 4 percent had come out of poverty over the same period of time.

After the bank's eighteen years in business, one could conservatively estimate that half a million families were able to throw off a life of destitution and begin living with a modicum of honor and dignity as a result of intervention from the Grameen Bank. Many hundreds of thousands more are likely to do so in the months and years ahead.

Muhammad Yunus had intended to run his program as a pilot project for a few years and then turn it over to banking professionals. He thought that all he would need to do was prove that his system could recover a percentage of its loans that was equal to or greater than that recovered by traditional banks, and do so at an acceptable cost. He came to realize, however, that no matter how successful his program became, the bankers would remain unwilling to adopt it themselves. By then, he had staked out an even more radical position, regularly stating in public fora that "credit is a fundamental human right."

"The financial institutions' contention that they can deal only on the basis of collateral," he said in a 1984 speech, "is merely a device to deceive the poor. To say that there can be no banking without collateral is like saying men will not be able to fly unless they have wings. . . . To suggest that human beings were incapable of devising any other form of banking except with provision of collateral would be quite ridiculous." But that, of course, is what the bankers had been arguing since the early days of Grameen— and for the most part what they continue to argue to this day.

Such was Grameen's success that efforts began in the mid-1980s to replicate it in other developing countries. It took more time for the idea that Yunus's brainchild might have relevance for poverty in the United States or other developed nations to be taken seriously. On the surface, the idea seemed ludicrous. If technology from rich countries couldn't help poor ones, why was there any reason to think the opposite could be true? If anything had been learned over the preceding decades, it was that the socioeconomic and cultural differences between rich and poor nations were so profound as to incapacitate most efforts at collaborative problem-solving. Nevertheless, the idea intrigued some antipoverty specialists in the U.S. philanthropic and nonprofit communities.

The success of the Grameen Bank in rural, impoverished Bangladesh demonstrated that access to investment capital can make a tremendous difference in people's lives, despite the obstacles that may face them. Prey to the vagaries of a monsoon climate, in a country with virtually no infrastructure, the main focus of the lives of the rural poor is to grow enough food to be able to survive. Grameen has provided many people with a means of raising themselves above subsistence. In America, famine is not the enemy. Yet there is, in the richest nation on earth, a huge gulf between the richest and the poorest, between the disadvantaged and the privileged, that sees the worst-off unable to break out of low standards of living in dangerous and unhealthy environments. The barriers to economic self-improvement are as daunting in America as in Bangladesh, if different in appearance. And Yunus's idea that access to credit could empower an individual and allow him or her the chance to scale some of these barriers is as applicable in North America as in the Indian subcontinent.

Yunus, it turns out, has discovered something that has nearly universal applicability. Banks in both Bangladesh and the United States demand collateral before they consider sanctioning a loan; the principal difference is that in rural Bangladesh, there are at least branch offices to tell the poor they were ineligible to borrow. There was a need in both countries for financial institutions that were tailored to the needs of low-income people and did not exclude those who lacked collateral.

Inspired by Yunus's example, a handful of mavericks in the nonprofit sector set out to replicate his experiment on the South Side of Chicago, a place that could serve as a paradigm for inner-city deprivation.

Experiments in providing banking services in inner-city Chicago neighborhoods had a history dating back to the early 1970s, when the South Shore Bank—then on the verge of failure—was bought by a group of young idealists and turned into a profit-making success story. Their achievement suggested that banking in poor neighborhoods was possible, but few heeded the example. Nationwide, banks were fleeing the ghettos; the few that remained only did so to siphon the savings of the urban poor and channel it into investment schemes in more prosperous neighborhoods. By the 1980s, lending in inner-city neighborhoods—whether for buying a home or starting or expanding a business—had all but stopped.

South Shore Bank succeeded in making and recovering loans for housing redevelopment and for certain types of commercial ventures. Occasionally, local residents emboldened by the bank's work in the community would ask for business loans of only a few thousand dollars. These amounts were but small fractions of the smallest commercial loans most banks sanction for businesses, and

South Shore's management was puzzled as it tried to respond to the requests.

When Mary Houghton, one of the founders of South Shore, visited Bangladesh in the early 1980s and learned about Grameen, she felt that she had stumbled onto a strategy that might be of help in meeting the needs of entrepreneurs who wanted infusions of tiny amounts of capital. She decided that it would be better to serve these clients through a separate nonprofit organization than through South Shore itself, and with Yunus's blessing the Women's Self-Employment Project (WSEP) was founded in 1986, and its first executive director, Connie Evans, was hired. Two years later, WSEP's Full Circle Fund (FCF), based on the Grameen Bank, was inaugurated.

It took some time for Evans, a bright and energetic black woman in her mid-twenties, to come to believe that adapting a Bangladeshi development strategy made sense for the problems of poor women in Chicago. A meeting with Yunus in Chicago helped, but it was not until she visited Bangladesh in November 1988 that she was convinced. After returning to the Windy City, she and Susan Matteucci, a recent MIT graduate and a gifted organizer and activist, began working day and night to make the Full Circle Fund a success.

Persuading low-income women, many on public aid, to join groups in order to take out tiny commercial loans was difficult. Many prospective borrowers suspected that the FCF was a scam to cheat poor people out of their money. The idea that an organization was willing to lend them small amounts of money without reference to their credit histories seemed ludicrous. And forming groups didn't initially appeal to people. Susan, a white woman trying to recruit black and Hispanic women, aroused suspicion at first. But her hard work and remarkable ability to transcend the barriers of race and class paid off. In 1989 and 1990, the number of groups was expanded, scores of loans were sanctioned, and business began to grow. Connie provided Susan and the borrowers with friendship, moral support, and, most important, a steady stream of foundation grants that allowed them to expand the FCF's staff, membership, and loan portfolio.

On the whole, Grameen's group structure and lending methodology translated surprisingly well to Chicago. Various aspects of the process were slightly altered for American sensitivities. Orientations, group training sessions, and repayment meetings were held fortnightly in concrete buildings (usually community centers), rather than weekly and outdoors. Weekly saving was made voluntary and was deposited into personal rather than group accounts. Another change was the "fifteen-minute rule" that required that a training session be canceled if any member of the group failed to arrive at the meeting within a quarter of an hour of the starting time. Loans were repaid over periods ranging from three to eighteen months, depending on the needs of the borrower (rather than over one year for all loans, as is the case with Grameen). Loans were disbursed, and often collected, as checks or money orders rather than cash. But the essential idea remained the same.

As the FCF was established, other projects grew up elsewhere. The Good Faith Fund provided loans to fledgling entrepreneurs in some of rural Arkansas's poorest counties. The South Dakota–based Lakota Fund reached out to Native Americans. Accion International, a nonprofit organization with more than two decades of experience lending to poor entrepreneurs in Latin America, opened up shop in a low-income, Hispanic neighborhood in Brooklyn. The Coalition for Women's Economic Development began extending credit to African Americans and Mexican Americans in south-central Los Angeles. Working Capital took up the charge in inner-city Boston as well as in poor rural areas in several New England states. By 1994, more than two dozen nonprofit organizations in the United States were operating lending programs based on the Grameen methodology, and many others had incorporated the approach in some form. Pilot projects had also been established in France, Canada, and Norway. Together, they served the complete spectrum of disadvantage in the developed world—from African American mothers and Sioux Indians on welfare to immigrants from Southeast Asia, Latin America, and North Africa to poor white men and women in the American South to unemployed college graduates in Scandinavia.

These programs challenged entrenched beliefs about poor people in rich countries. The idea that a welfare recipient might prefer the risk and hard work inherent in running a business to living off the dole struck many people as absurd. But when the pilot projects began to grow in the early 1990s to the point where their combined efforts were reaching tens of thousands of people and lending millions of dollars, they began being recognized by a growing number of opinion-makers as an enlightened alternative to both handouts that required nothing in return and proposals to leave the poor to fend for themselves without any support from government.

As the FCF entered its seventh year of operations in 1995, it continued to confront doubters among groups as diverse as potential borrowers, philanthropic foundations, and members of the media. Yet the progress its borrowers were making was giving even a skeptic reason to hope that the program was onto something important.

The idea of writing a book on Grameen dates back to 1989, but gained momentum when people in the publishing industry began expressing interest in it in 1990. When I presented my first outline of a book, the response was that it was too dry. The Grameen story needed a human face; if possible, I was told, it should be told largely from the borrower's perspective. Another idea was to include the stories of women in the United States who were borrowing from nonprofit organizations that were Grameen spin-offs. At first I resisted these suggestions, but ultimately I saw the wisdom of them. When I agreed to write the book in this manner, I realized that doing the research for it would be a major undertaking—so much so that the actual writing of it would be something of an afterthought by comparison. Resigning from my job in Washington, D.C., and moving to Bangladesh was my only real option.

In order to capture the drama of low-income women in Bangladesh and South Chicago improving their conditions through access to loans, I needed to immerse myself in their lives. That required a remarkable degree of trust from the women who are the subjects of this book. They allowed me to share their most private thoughts and experiences, their successes and failures in business, their joy and despair. For that trust, I am deeply grateful and humbled. Their honesty and openness, no less than the improvements they made in their lives by taking out loans from Grameen and the FCF, was and remains an inspiration. Taken together, their stories are compelling evidence that poverty can and must be taken off the global stage and placed where it belongs—in museums, for future generations to ponder.

Give Us Credit

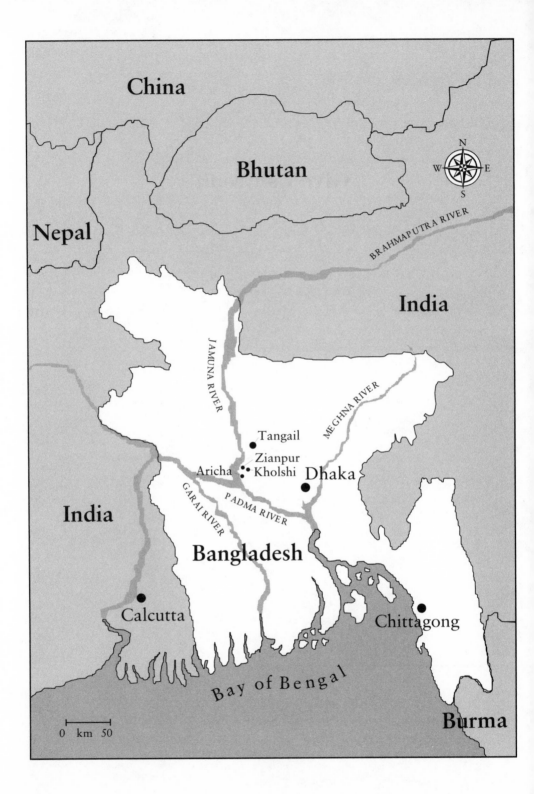

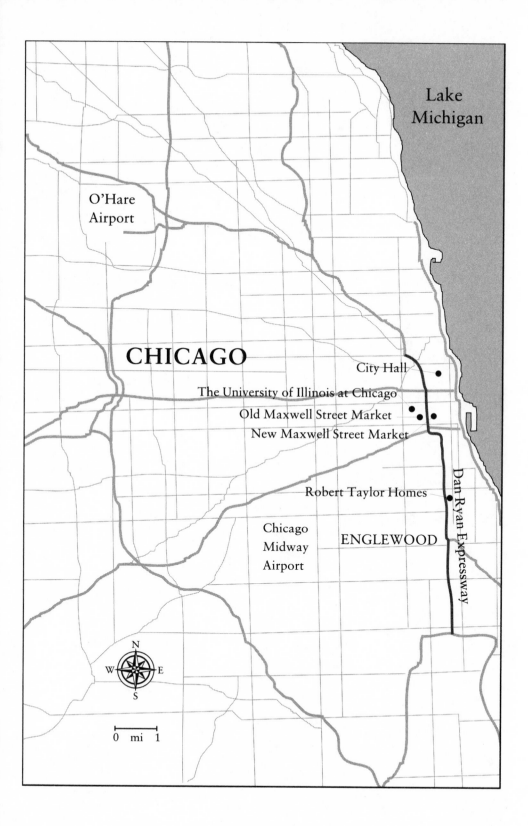

Lake
Michigan

O'Hare
Airport

CHICAGO

City Hall
The University of Illinois at Chicago
Old Maxwell Street Market
New Maxwell Street Market

Robert Taylor Homes

Chicago
Midway
Airport

ENGLEWOOD

Dan Ryan Expressway

N
W E
S

0   mi   1

1

▲

Muhammad Yunus

From Vanderbilt to Chittagong

It began as one stubborn man's desperate attempt to make sense of his life in a country racked by famine. In 1974 Bangladeshis were dying by the thousands for lack of even the meager nourishment to which they had grown accustomed. The skies blackened with vultures in search of another corpse to devour.

Three years removed from the glorious war of liberation, the country's dreams of freedom had been cruelly broken, transformed into a nightmare of hunger, wanton violence, and despair. U.S. secretary of state Henry Kissinger called Bangladesh "the world's basket case."

On the streets of this poor nation, human beings walked around like zombies, waiting to die. Some had only a touch of life left in them, yet still they breathed, at least for one more day. On a village path, one starving man would eat for the first time in days, only to vomit what he consumed because it left his system in shock. An hour later, another person would come across the vomit and, after hesitating briefly, begin to eat it.

For one Bangladeshi, this was intolerable. He had to do something, even if it could only begin as a small gesture. Exactly what, he didn't have the faintest idea. Still, there was one thing he understood: the economic theories he had mastered at American universities while earning his PhD would be of little use. Professor Muhammad Yunus would have to mix with the poor and see what he could think up after immersing himself in their reality. He hardly had grand illusions about what one man could do, working alone. But he had to act.

That is how it began.

As he emerged from his ground-floor apartment in the Grameen Bank living quarters, a small, redbrick building behind the training institute, Muhammad Yunus strode forward with a purposeful gait. It was 8:05 A.M. on a hot summer morning in 1993. He was unencumbered by the stacks of files he had pored over the previous evening; a junior staff person had carried them to his office fifteen minutes earlier.

Yunus turned a corner, following a narrow brick road that connects the back of the two-acre complex to the five-story main building, and passed a new structure under noisy, round-the-clock construction. The jarring sound of metal striking metal rang out in the air, muffled briefly by several loud thumps.

Three laborers spotted him as he passed the construction site. They immediately alerted each other, stood stiffly at attention, and saluted, military style. Yunus returned the salute in a casual yet respectful manner. Some of his junior colleagues, he knew, looked down on laborers in their longhis (simple skirts worn by men) and tattered T-shirts, and either failed to salute them or performed the ritual perfunctorily. But it wasn't Yunus's style to upbraid his staff for acting that way; he merely tried to lead by example.

As he approached the front door of the complex's main office building, several more staff stiffened as they saluted the managing director. When he looked at them, he didn't smile—he knew it would most likely confuse them if he did—but he wanted to. This was the time of day when he was most relaxed and cheerful. Yet when you run an organization with eleven thousand employees, you have to keep up appearances by maintaining a professional demeanor. Sometimes he yearned for the days when he knew the name of every person who worked for him.

It had been nineteen years since famine had stalked the Bangladesh countryside, and Yunus was shepherding the organization he'd created to relieve hunger and poverty through a major turning point in its history. While for many years his venture had been known simply as a pilot project making tiny loans to destitute women, it was finally gaining recognition in Bangladeshi financial circles for its ability to disburse more than $1 million in loans each working day and earn a modest profit doing so. Later in 1993, the nation's finance minister, who had long been a critic of Yunus's work, would agree to lend his program millions of dollars. At the same time, Grameen Bank was becoming recognized as a model for poverty alleviation programs in Southeast Asia, Africa, North America, and beyond.

As Yunus climbed the stairs to his fourth-floor office, he reflected on the new era that was dawning for his organization. He sometimes thought it was approaching a "critical mass" that would allow Grameen to conquer problems that had previously stymied it. Yet he knew that getting big and famous held its own dangers. He often warned his staff about getting complacent, about "basking in their worldwide glory." The job, he told them, would not be finished until poverty had been eliminated from Bangladesh, once and for all, and the only place one could find destitution was in history books.

He entered his office at 8:11, before most of his four hundred Dhaka employees had arrived. Three of his four personal staff, who had long since become used to the hours he kept, were there to greet him in the waiting room outside his office where they worked. He turned on the lights and an overhead fan, sat down behind his desk, and read the newspapers for a few minutes, looking for any signs that Bangladesh's emerging political crisis was ebbing. A few minutes later, he began receiving a steady stream of guests. They sat in front or at the side of his simple, sturdy wooden table. It has no drawers, symbolizing his commitment to conducting all business openly.

The first to come in were Khalid Shams and Muzammel Huq, his two senior deputies. The men shared tea, reviewed the previous day's developments, and looked ahead. All three had well-cultivated senses of humor and liked to laugh when they huddled together; it provided balance to the rest of their day, when uptight, often humorless junior personnel would meet with them. After the two men left, others in Yunus's inner circle, many of them students from the time when he was a university professor, began parading in and out of his office. A handful of foreign guests, including a journalist, were able to have a word with him. In between the meetings, he read letters, drafted responses, and made notes to himself in his diary.

Yunus owns a rounded, even pudgy face highlighted by expressive—some say magical—eyes and an eager smile. Visitors get the sense that their host is a jolly man, someone who takes his work considerably more seriously than he does himself. Quick with a witty remark in any of the several languages he speaks, Yunus has that rare ability to make nervous strangers feel like long-lost friends in a matter of minutes. Even when under stress himself, Yunus is known for giving guests his undivided attention. Akhtar Hossain, the managing director's unflappable personal secretary, often remarks that every visitor seems to emerge with an expression that says, "I must have been the most important person he met with today."

It has been a long and improbable road to building the Grameen empire to where it is today, reaching into remote villages of Bangladesh, poverty-stricken islands in the Philippine archipelago, clusters of mud huts in Malawi, and decrepit slums in Chicago, Los Angeles, and Paris. Sometimes he pauses between appointments to marvel at what he and his colleagues have accomplished and to wonder about what the years ahead have in store for his movement.

At ten minutes before six o'clock, after nearly everyone had left, Yunus piled his files on his desk, tidied up the remaining papers, and checked his calendar for the following day. The sun was setting, and young boys were playing soccer on a grassy field adjacent to the complex, their screams and cheers drowned out by the relentless clanking and scraping at the construction site. As Muhammad Yunus left his office, his personal staff rose and saluted him, saying "As Salaam o Aleikum, sir" in unison. He returned the traditional Muslim greeting and headed toward the stairs. Several minutes later, a messenger carried the pending files to his residence and stacked them on the floor, near the telephone. After eating dinner, catching up with his wife, and playing with his seven-year-old daughter Dina, he began reading the files, making comments in red ink, followed by his initials. Most often, he wrote the words "*Tai houk*" in Bengali script when a subordinate asked for his permission to move ahead on a project. The words meant "let it be." He believed in allowing people to make their own mistakes.

At ten-thirty, he retired for the evening, even as work continued apace at the construction site, located less than fifty yards from his bedroom.

In 1961, Muhammad Yunus, the son of a prosperous Muslim jeweler, was fresh from earning a master's degree at Dhaka University, Bangladesh's most prestigious seat of higher education. After graduation, he accepted a position as an economics instructor at Chittagong College. Yunus, just twenty-one, was an impatient young man brimming with self-confidence, optimism, and ambition. The first phase of his training complete, he felt it was time to launch one of the many projects he had toyed with during his student days.

While at Dhaka University, he had founded a nationally circulated literary magazine called *Uttaran* (Advancement). In the process of putting out the publication, he was surprised to learn that virtually all local packaging, up to and including the printing on cigarette packets, was being done in West Pakistan. It occurred to him that opening a printing and packaging plant in East Pakistan could be lucrative, and he promised himself to try to do so someday.

Soon after settling in Chittagong, Bangladesh's commercial capital and main port city, he began researching how he might follow through on the idea. With financial support from his father, Yunus made a fact-finding trip to West Pakistan and had the good fortune to meet a Bengali who was involved in a Swedish-Pakistani packaging venture. The man showed Yunus the ropes of the business and provided some tips on how to get started. By the time the next year rolled around, the long process of buying the necessary machinery—accomplished with the help of a half-million-taka ($12,500) loan from the Industrial Development Bank—and receiving government clearance was complete. In due course, the presses began to roll, providing gainful employment to one hundred people and within two years turning a small profit. Yunus, responding to pressure from his father, repaid the loan to the Industrial Bank ahead of time, with interest. So rare was it that the bank had its loan repaid early and in full that it offered Yunus a 10-million-taka ($250,000) loan to finance the expansion of the operation.

After dividing his time between teaching and running the factory, Yunus realized that his first love was teaching. To get on the fast track required a PhD from abroad. In 1964 he applied for and received a Fulbright scholarship to study in the United States. Having expressed a preference on his application form for studying "development economics," Yunus was rather improbably placed at Vanderbilt University in Nashville, Tennessee. He had never heard of Vanderbilt before, but when he located it on a globe he noticed that Tennessee had the distinction of being almost exactly halfway around the world from Bangladesh.

Already an experienced traveler, Yunus relished the opportunity to expand his horizons again. The only anxiety related to what he'd read about the civil rights movement in the southern United States. Yunus was concerned that he'd be considered "black" and be subjected to harassment. The fear, as it turned out, was unfounded: white classmates would inform him that only Negroes were at risk; brown fellows like him, he was assured, had nothing to fear. Much to his disappointment, Vanderbilt's one-year master's program turned out to be something of a bore. Yunus applied for the university's PhD program, and when he scored in the ninety-eighth percentile on the Graduate Record Exam, his acceptance was assured.

In his second year, Yunus enrolled in a statistics course taught by Professor Nicholas Georgescu-Roegen, a Romanian immigrant trained at the Sorbonne in France. Yunus found himself mesmerized by Georgescu's lectures. By the second week of classes he realized that despite having taken three statistics courses previously, he barely understood anything about the subject. The elegance of Georgescu's two-and-a-half-hour orations touched something deep inside him; he and other admirers compared them to performances of a symphony orchestra. To Yunus, Georgescu's genius was in reducing statistics to its essence, breathing life into vapid concepts using storytelling and simple mathematics. Never had Yunus been in the presence of a master teacher, the kind who leads students down the long road to independent thought punctuated by "Aha!" realizations that are never forgotten. Now that he was under the wing of such a person, he couldn't get enough of it.

Georgescu's reputation as a difficult grader was, by all accounts, well earned. He was rumored to give no grade higher than a C. Most students, trained to memorize and regurgitate information, would do poorly on his exams, which tested understanding of the fundamentals of statistical theory. Yunus, determined to beat the odds, immersed himself in his mentor's approach and received an A-plus for his efforts. He would go on to take Georgescu's Economic Theory class and, later, become his teaching assistant.

Georgescu's influence on the young Yunus was profound. Never was he to forget the distinction between a mere conveyor of information and a master teacher. As he saw it, the former informs while the latter empowers. Twenty years after first coming in contact with Georgescu, Yunus would write, "All human problems in their basic manifestation are quite simple. [It is merely our] arrogance [that] prompts us to put these problems in more and more complicated formulations." On many occasions during the intervening two decades, he left learned audiences puzzled, unsure why they had been addressed in a manner a seventh-grade student could have understood.

With the exception of Georgescu and a computer center that, at the time, was state of the art, Vanderbilt had little of interest to offer Yunus as he pursued his PhD. By the time he completed his dissertation on "Intertemporal Allocation of Resources—A Dynamic Programming Model," he had already moved on and was teaching economics at Middle Tennessee State University in Murfreesboro.

Yunus happily passed his days in classrooms. By this time he had married an American woman named Vera Forostenko and was preparing to wind down his life in Tennessee and begin anew in Bangladesh. Suddenly, his nation called. In March 1971, the West Pakistani armed forces took control of Dhaka, the capital of East Pakistan, following public calls for regional autonomy and independence by Bengali political leaders. A full-scale civil war was suddenly a distinct possibility. On March 26, Maj. Zia Ur Rahman defiantly declared Bangladesh an independent nation, and the war of liberation, in which more than three million Bengalis were to die, began. Yunus, hearing all of this over the radio in Nashville, immediately joined with five other Bengalis living there to form the Bangladesh Citizens' Committee and began to visit local radio and television stations and newspapers to explain the Bangladeshi cause.

On March 27, Yunus left for Washington, D.C., to attend a pro-Bangladeshi rally and seek out other Bengali patriots. He met with Enayet Karim, a Bengali who at the time was the second-ranking official in the Pakistani embassy and who would later become the foreign secretary of independent Bangladesh. Karim and other Bengalis in the embassy were working secretly with the Bengali American community while they planned to form a separate Bangladesh embassy with the support of the Indian government.

For the first three days after Yunus arrived in Washington, he and other activists lived with Karim. On one of those evenings, the Pakistani ambassador paid an unannounced visit to Karim's apartment, ostensibly to convey his sympathy for the loss of life in East Pakistan. Horrified at the prospect of his boss's discovering Yunus and other activists living with him, Karim ordered his guests to grab the food they had been eating and flee into a room upstairs, where they had to remain completely still during the entire discussion. That was enough; Yunus moved into new living quarters the next day.

Yunus stayed in Washington to help run the Bangladesh Information Center. He relentlessly lobbied the U.S. Congress, particularly the Senate, and foreign embassies, hoping to win diplomatic recognition for the emerging nation. He organized an aggressive grassroots lobbying effort, principally by encouraging Bengali Americans to educate their senators about the cause of liberation. Colleagues recall a young man who combined zeal and impressive organizational skills with the temperament of a diplomat.

The center's principal goal was to alter the Nixon administration's strong support of West Pakistan, to which it continued to send arms after the civil war began. Henry Kissinger was especially pro-Pakistani. Yunus and his colleagues worked around the clock in an effort to counter Dr. Kissinger's exercise in realpolitik. But they failed to sway him, despite the support they received from a vocal minority in the State Department, including a small number of Dhaka-based diplomats who backed the Bengali cause.

When Bangladesh achieved its independence in December 1971, the young economist, swept up in the euphoria of victory and the prospect of helping to build a new nation, was eager to return to Bangladesh for good.

As Yunus prepared to leave the States, a fourteen-year-old African American girl named Connie Evans was living with her mother and siblings in Franklin, Tennessee (a town just outside of Nashville), and going to high school. She was being brought up to be independent, self-assured, and achievement-oriented by a mother who supported the family as a self-employed caterer. While Connie understood what racism was, she knew little about conditions in Chicago, where she would move years later. She certainly didn't know much, if anything, about Bangladesh, and had never had occasion to meet Muhammad Yunus, though it is possible that they passed each other on the street, since Connie had traveled alone to school in Nashville from the age of six.

It would be nearly twenty years later that the two would be introduced. What Connie and Yunus would discuss in 1987 would be an approach to empowering the inner-city poor that few had ever heard of and fewer still believed would work. But that was later, much later.

. . .

Yunus and Vera arrived in Dhaka in June 1972. To his dismay, the only job he was offered at Dhaka University was a junior position in the Economics Department—an offer he declined. He was recruited by Nurul Islam, a former teacher who was the chief of the government's Planning Commission. When Yunus said he had no intentions of working for the postliberation government, Islam refused to take no for an answer and pressed upon Yunus the contributions he could make to the process of nation-building from inside the commission.

While he reconsidered the job offer, Yunus pondered the massive task of rebuilding the world's 139th independent nation. Despite the obstacles, he was far from discouraged. To the contrary, he felt that building the Bangladesh of his dreams, virtually from scratch, was the ultimate challenge. If Japan could become a powerhouse within a few decades of defeat in World War II, he reasoned, then surely Bangladesh could reclaim its ancient glory and assume a dignified place among the nations of the world.

In the end, Yunus overcame his doubts and decided to work for the government; his title was deputy chief of the General Economics Division of the Planning Commission, but his responsibilities were left unclear. Yunus was naturally anxious to get busy, but he waited for days, and then weeks, for someone to give him work to do. For reasons he never completely understood, nobody obliged. He collected a paycheck and spent his days reading newspapers. Disturbingly, his situation was far from unique. Throughout the government, officials sat about drinking tea and basking in their self-importance while millions of people tried desperately to put their lives back together in the wake of the war with little or no outside assistance.

Yunus realized that before there could be any "economic development" as described in the computer models he had studied in Tennessee, a transformation in the mentality of thousands of bureaucrats, indeed the entire government, was necessary. A sense of urgency and responsibility had to be developed.

Even though he would later meet dedicated civil servants, he came to believe that they were exceptions to a pervasive rule. In

Yunus's view, bureaucrats seldom had any notion of serving the nation. Anyone who proposed new ideas was seen as someone likely to show up his boss; people learned to keep their mouths shut and to shower their superiors with compliments and gifts whenever possible. Most of those who figured out how to manipulate the system would use their positions primarily for personal aggrandizement. Meanwhile, Bangladesh languished while neighbors like South Korea, Malaysia, Sri Lanka, and India progressed.

Not surprisingly, in his brief time in the civil service Yunus developed a lifelong mistrust of government. He saw that without firm political leadership, bureaucratic inertia was inevitable and expensive programs and schemes were rendered useless, mired in red tape. After two months of government work, Yunus left a note of resignation on his desk and departed for his home district in southeastern Bangladesh, where he took a job as an associate professor of economics at Chittagong University.

In Chittagong, Professor Yunus was relieved to have some work to do: classes to teach, articles to write, cultural events to participate in and organize. Yunus was named head of the Economics Department based on his credentials as a PhD from America with teaching experience. He began talking to his colleagues about his interest in incorporating an aggressive program of "action-research" into the curriculum. His argument was that a more practical and interactive curriculum would help break down some of the covert hostility between the university and nearby communities while tapping into the experience of those villages for conducting original research. In addition, it would give the students who were involved a grounding in real-life rural development that their peers at Dhaka University would only read about in books.

Most of his colleagues responded coolly to the proposals. Indeed, the idea that generated the most discussion was his proposition to vacate the large office reserved for the department head so that his twelve staff members, until then crammed into an office fit for one or two people, could have something approaching a dignified place to work. He constructed partitions for his staff with his own money and began to work in the office into which they had been squeezed. Nobody could quite understand why he was willing to forgo his privileges, and even several junior faculty members who stood to benefit from his plan tried to talk him out of it.

Faced with the unexpected reluctance of his staff to embrace his ideas, Yunus decided he needed an institutional base outside of the department to build the program he envisioned. In 1973, after he had tried to resuscitate the university's moribund Rural Development Program, he established his own Rural Studies Program (RSP). The RSP had no budget, no permission from the university to operate, and no staff. What it had, simply, was its founder's enthusiasm and some stationery he had printed up at his own expense.

As part of the "curriculum" offered by the program, Yunus developed a course called Issues in Rural Development in which students would do original field research in the neighboring villages of Jobra and Fatehpur. His aim was to break the tradition in higher education, particularly prevalent in Bangladesh, of merely expecting people to read scholarly works and then repackage those views in their own papers. Rural development was happening right at the university's doorstep, he figured, so why should they all rely on books?

Students initially responded slowly. Many were clumsy interviewers, eager to retreat back into the world of books. After a few semesters, however, a small number started to catch on. Over time, the courses offered by the program became more popular, and by the late 1970s enrollment was high. The Rural Economics Program (REP), as it was renamed, also began putting out research reports on issues such as agricultural development and community organization.

One of the program's earliest initiatives was to encourage farmers in Jobra to adopt high-yielding varieties (HYVs) of rice.* Students, together with Yunus and H. I. Latifee, one of the few departmental colleagues who had shared Yunus's enthusiasm, went into the fields to work with cultivators to grow rice using modern methods. The farmers were initially amused, but in a short

---

*Traditional varieties yield less per acre but do not need the constant attention that the HYVs do.

time Yunus and Latifee struck up warm friendships with many villagers; people were impressed at how the two men were developing an encyclopedic knowledge of Jobra, including the names of hundreds of farmers and their family members.

Unfortunately, most of the students dropped out of the program within weeks. Many were uneasy doing farmwork, feeling that the reason they were at university in the first place was to ensure that they never had to stand knee-deep in mud planting rice seedlings. A university publication put it bluntly: ". . . the program was not a success. . . . Compared to the cost incurred the achievement was negligible. Many students joined this program just as a fad to show off." The education of the professor had begun.

Another program that Yunus inaugurated was the designation of plots of land on campus as student vegetable gardens. To spur some friendly competition, close attention was paid to whose plot was the most productive. The program, established in the famine year of 1974, initially set aside one-third of an acre to be cultivated by thirty first-year students. All but five of them, however, commuted from the city of Chittagong and were usually gone by noon (prompting Yunus to once write a report in which he criticized C.U. for being a "part-time university"). Dipal Chandra Barua, a member of Bangladesh's tiny Buddhist minority who bicycled to class each day from his home in Jobra, was asked by his peers to look after their plot. When Yunus noticed that the vegetable garden was thriving under Dipal's meticulous care, he invited the young economics student to get involved in the REP. At the time, Dipal was something of a Bangladeshi hippie—skinny with long hair and eager to try new things. He easily fit into the offbeat rhythms of the Rural Economics Program, and Yunus was quick to take him under his wing.

While he worked on the REP, Yunus kept abreast of the floundering efforts to jump-start the nation's economy. National politics, in particular, sapped his optimism. Yunus became increasingly frustrated by how little he was able to do that could bring tangible benefits to Bangladesh's poverty-stricken populace. Years later he would say, "After a few years at the university, I felt the classroom was like a movie house, where professors have all the answers and the tale works out so neatly at the end of the day. But it's make-believe. When you turn on the lights and go outside, it's a completely different world, with problems about which professors have nothing much useful to say."

The region that had become Bangladesh had not always been the famine-ravaged shambles it had become by 1974. The historian Pliny commented in the second century A.D. that dresses made from muslin fabrics imported from Bengal were in such demand among wealthy ladies in Rome that unthinkable amounts of precious metals were flowing from the coffers of the empire to Bengali traders and weavers. In the sixteenth century, Bengal was renowned around the world as "the Paradise of Nations." When the traders came, merchants in Dhaka dictated their terms, not the other way around. During the seventeenth century, Bengal—made up of present-day Bangladesh and the Indian state of West Bengal—was an important part of the vast Mughal empire and known for its booming textile trade and agriculture. Most historians agree that the average Bengali during this period was somewhat better nourished than his counterpart in Europe. Indeed, Bengal was known to be among the most prosperous regions in the world. A European visitor wrote, "Money is so plentiful in Dhaka that it is seldom counted, but always weighed. There is a profusion of food and other articles in the numerous bazaars of the city. The vastness of the wealth is stupefying."

For centuries, economic activity in the rural areas was conducted principally at the level of the household, with complex supply networks based largely on the barter system linking cotton and silk cultivators with spinners, weavers, and traders. A British traveler touring Bengal during the Mughal period wrote, "When at some distance from the high road, or a principal town, it is difficult to find a village in which every man, woman, and child is not employed in making a piece of cloth. . . ."

The eighteenth century marked the gradual dissolution of the Mughal empire in India and the establishment of British rule, initially under the auspices of the East India Company. The company, in search of quick profits, assumed control of Bengal's lucrative textile industry, which produced one-third of all cotton textiles used in Europe at the time. It appointed its own network of much-hated middlemen, the most important of whom were called *gomastas,* under the "Agency System" of 1753. In the words of a former company employee, ". . . [the *gomasta*] makes [the weavers] sign a bond for the delivery of a certain quantity of goods, at a certain time and price, and pays them part of the money in advance. The assent of the poor weavers is in general not deemed necessary. . . ." Rights to the production of individual weavers were freely traded among the *gomastas* as if their clients were slaves. Those who refused to participate in the system were flogged, and on occasion killed. The prices the weavers received were, by one estimate, 20 to 40 percent less than they could have got in the marketplace.

This progressive impoverishment led directly to several famines during the next two decades, one of which killed one in three people living in Bengal. By the last quarter of the eighteenth century, many weavers faced with a declining revenue that barely covered their costs had given up the trade and taken up day-laboring, fishing, and other work.

While it was developing its own textile industry during the early nineteenth century, Britain began pricing Bengali textiles out of its domestic market through high tariffs, while at the same time making a handsome profit trading them with the rest of the world. By the 1820s, a series of technological innovations, including the spinning jenny, the power loom, and the use of chlorine for bleaching had made the north of England the foremost producer of textiles in the world.

Soon, British yarn was being spun at less than half the cost of Indian yarn, and the drive to aggressively market British textile goods in Bengal and throughout India virtually finished off the indigenous industry. Between 1824 and 1837, the value of yarn imports from England increased fifty-five-fold. Bengal's silk industry lasted somewhat longer, but by 1876 the value of silk exports had declined to less than 3 percent of what it was at the turn of the century. It would take Mahatma Gandhi's campaign in the early twentieth century to shame people of the Indian subcontinent into wearing cloth spun at home to make any dent in this historic reversal.

By the second half of the nineteenth century, famines had become so common in Bengal that the British regime was pressed by growing unrest in the countryside into passing a series of reforms, including the creation of representative government at the village level and the promulgation of a famine code that was effective enough to prevent mass death from hunger for more than fifty years. But the province often teetered on the brink of starvation, and in 1943, with the British Empire focused on the Second World War and Japanese aggression in Asia, a famine killed three million people in eastern India.

When India gained independence from Britain in 1947, the colony became two separate sovereign nations—India and Pakistan. As part of the complex and improbable agreement negotiated among the British, Indian Hindus, and Indian Muslims, the regions where there was a Hindu majority became India and the remaining Muslim-dominated areas, with the exception of Kashmir, became Pakistan.

Of the many problems this compromise presented, the most obvious was that West Pakistan (known today simply as Pakistan) and East Pakistan (present-day Bangladesh) had no common border and were more than one thousand miles apart. It was as if California and Pennsylvania constituted one country and the rest of the United States a second, hostile nation. Furthermore, the two provinces of East and West Pakistan (or "wings," as they were called), despite sharing a common faith, had profound cultural and economic differences. Most fundamentally, East Pakistan was made up of Bengali speakers, while most West Pakistanis spoke Urdu.

The Bengalis were initially pleased to be part of Muslim-dominated Pakistan, their political leaders having been among the most vocal pro-Pakistan partisans during the negotiations with the British. But within a decade after partition, many Bengalis had come to feel betrayed. Their motherland, it seemed, had once again come under foreign domination, this time by the arrogant West Pakistanis.

Upon independence, East Pakistan was separated from Calcutta, its former capital, whose jute mills were essential to the production of its primary cash crop.* It was this division that prompted Muhammad Ali Jinnah, the man whose efforts led to the creation of Pakistan, to complain that he had been given a "moth-eaten" state. The sudden separation of Bengal's head from its body plunged East Pakistan's already precarious economic situation into dire straits. Sir Frederick Burrows, the last British governor in Bengal, assessed these conditions and predicted that East Pakistan would become "the greatest rural slum in history."

After partition, East Pakistan slowly resumed exporting jute, though the money thus earned largely flowed to the coffers of West Pakistan. By and large, East Pakistan's "gold fibre" financed West Pakistan's rapid postindependence industrialization. Ultimately, East Pakistan became little more than a colony of West Pakistan.

Tensions mounted during the 1950s and 1960s over calls in the Bengali-speaking East for regional autonomy. Bengali anger was ignited by proposals to have Urdu, the predominant language in West Pakistan but virtually unknown in the East, adopted as the national language. Shortly before his death, Jinnah came to Dhaka for the only time in his life and, to the dismay of Bengalis, declared, "The state language of Pakistan is going to be Urdu and no other language. Anyone who tries to mislead you [on this issue] is really an enemy of Pakistan."

The West Pakistanis feared that the numerically superior but economically backward Bengalis of East Pakistan would create a single political party and gain control of the Parliament. They worked to ensure that positions of influence were held by West Pakistanis while largely ceremonial ones were occupied by Bengalis. During the fifties and sixties, the West Pakistani elite tried to institutionalize a civilian government that would be more responsive to Bengali aspirations while ensuring that West Pakistanis re-

---

*Jute is the raw material from which gunnysacks are made.

tained most of the power. Their efforts, however, were too little, too late. By 1971, negotiations between Sheikh Mujib, a charismatic Bengali political leader, and West Pakistani politicians had failed to produce a compromise on the issue of regional autonomy, and Mujib declared Bangladesh an independent nation. Upon doing so, he was arrested, the military took control of Dhaka, and what is known in Bangladesh as "The Independence War" began.

A campaign of genocide was unleashed by the Pakistani (almost entirely *West* Pakistani) armed forces, assisted by an influential minority of Bengalis who stayed loyal to the regime. In the spring of 1971, the Mukti Bahini (Bangladeshi Freedom Fighters) began filtering back into the country after receiving training and arms in India, and full-scale war was under way by June, with napalm supplied by the United States government being used on recalcitrant Bengali villages in East Pakistan.

After the monsoon subsided, the pace of the battles picked up, with outgunned Mukti Bahini divisions often retreating into India when they were on the run. As Pakistani forces followed them, there were a series of escalating border clashes between Indian and Pakistani troops, culminated by a preemptive strike by the Pakistani air force in early December. Indian forces joined the conflict and helped the freedom fighters rout the Pakistani forces, leading to the signing of a peace treaty on December 16 in Dhaka and the birth of Bangladesh.

The new nation had its work cut out for itself. The communications and transportation networks, and hundreds of thousands of acres of standing crops, had been destroyed during the war, and more than 20 percent of the nation's food had to be imported. A black market in weapons that had accumulated during the conflict developed, and armed gangs settled old scores, with real or imagined collaborators of the Pakistanis being slaughtered.

In January 1972, Mujib, who had been hours away from being executed when the cease-fire was declared, triumphantly returned to the new nation and become its first prime minister. Overwhelmed by the task in front of him, Mujib lamented to a friend shortly after his return, "[When I returned] I was brought face-to-face with the greatest man-made disaster in history. I could never imagine the magnitude of the catastrophe. They have killed more than three million of my people. They have raped our mothers and our sisters and have butchered our children. More than thirty percent of all houses have been destroyed. . . . What do you do about currency? Where do you get food? Industry is dead. Commerce is dead. How do you start them again? What do you do about defense? I have no administration. Where do I get one? Tell me, how do you start a country?"

Mujib was a better rhetorician than administrator, and had only limited success in dealing with these challenges. By 1973, frustrations with his inept leadership were being vented in public protests. Attempting to retain control of the fragile and violent nation, Mujib, the once-beloved "Bangabandhu" (Friend of the Bengalis), created the Jatiyo Rakhi Bahini, a shadowy paramilitary force directly responsible to him. Violence begot violence, with more than two thousand politically motivated murders occurring in 1973 alone. Among the victims were several members of Parliament. In May of 1974, after the country's Supreme Court reprimanded the Rakhi Bahini for having tortured and killed a seventeen-year-old boy, Mujib stripped the court of its powers to pass judgment over his personal terror force.

If 1973 was the year of violence, 1974 was the year of famine. As thousands of people died, the prime minister's party, the Awami League, disintegrated into warring factions. To impose order, Mujib declared a state of emergency in late December. His famine relief effort was poorly conceived and executed. Among the more odious aspects of the relief program was the herding of fifty thousand Bangladeshi destitutes who had migrated to Dhaka into a camp bordered by a barbed-wire fence and bereft of any medical or sanitation facilities. One unfortunate resident told a visiting journalist, perhaps mistaking him for an aid worker, "Either feed us or shoot us."

In June, Mujib moved decisively toward a one-party state. He wanted to create a leftist government of national unity in which all power would be vested in a single authority—namely, him. As for an economic program, Mujib declared his intention to create compulsory rural cooperatives in every village. The system was to take effect on September 1.

Two weeks before his sweeping reforms were to come into force, Mujib and virtually his entire family were assassinated in his home in Dhanmondhi on the orders of a group of army officers. The plotters announced over Radio Bangladesh that Mujib was dead, martial law was in force, and Khondokar Mushtaq, one of Mujib's ministers, was to be sworn in as president. The senior commanders of the armed forces went along with the coup and initially recognized the legitimacy of Mushtaq, even attending his swearing-in ceremony.

The brief embers of democracy had been snuffed out; it would be sixteen years before they would begin to glow again. During those intervening years, great damage was done to the country and its people. Yet, at the same time, there were several remarkable success stories, prompting people the world over to take notice of a country known to many in South Asia as "the land of poets and lovers."

As Muhammad Yunus contemplated the famine of 1974, he wondered what he should do. He recalled how aggressively American intellectuals spoke out on controversial social, political, and economic matters. Yet his colleagues at Chittagong University were unwilling to break the conspiracy of silence concerning Mujib's disastrous policies and his maddening unwillingness to even admit that there was a famine.

Yunus approached Abul Fazal, the university vice-chancellor, and suggested that he publish a formal statement to the press criticizing the government's role in creating and prolonging the crisis. Fazal was a well-known writer with a close personal relationship to Mujib. To the young professor's surprise, the vice-chancellor agreed, provided that Yunus draft the statement and join him in signing it.

Within days, other faculty members signed, and the harshly worded antigovernment statement was sent off to the newspapers, where it was printed and widely commented on. In the following weeks, groups of academics at other leading universities followed suit and presented their own critiques. In subsequent years, as histories were written of Bangladesh in the mid-1970s, the statement was frequently mentioned as the one that stimulated a robust public debate about the causes of the famine.

Yunus decided that another opportunity to speak out publicly would be the occasion of Ekushey (literally, "on the twenty-first")—the annual remembrance of the martyrs who had died on February 21, 1952, while protesting Pakistani government efforts to make Urdu the single national language.

Each year, Shaheed Dibosh (Martyrs' Day) is observed in a diverse manner typical of Bengali culture. At dawn, wreaths are laid on *shaheed minars* (martyrs' monuments), citizens are expected to walk barefoot out of respect to the martyrs, festive book fairs are held, and pledges are made to ensure that "the Bengali language is used in all walks of life."

After the emergence of Bangladesh as an independent nation with Bengali as its language, continuing to observe Martyrs' Day in the traditional manner seemed to Yunus somewhat like observing the Fourth of July in the United States by having people take a pledge to continue resisting British rule. With so many other challenges facing the country, Yunus thought that the martyrs should be remembered as people willing to die to ensure that Bangladesh actualized itself as a nation, rather than simply as supporters of the Bengali language. He submitted an article to a local newspaper proposing that Shaheed Dibosh be made more relevant to the contemporary reality. He proposed, for example, that Martyrs' Day be a time to honor the farmers coming in with sheaths of paddy and scientists improving agricultural yields.

His article was roundly criticized for being unfaithful to the legacy of the martyrs. Bangladeshi politicians, then as now feeling safer fighting yesterday's battles than today's, dismissed the idea out of hand.

During his first few months on the Chittagong University faculty, Yunus had noticed that farmland adjacent to the university campus lay fallow during the dry season, and he joined his local member of Parliament in petitioning the government to sink an irrigation tube well—a driven well—in Jobra. Their lobbying was successful, and Yunus felt that this was one instance where the government had been responsive and would make a difference in the lives of the rural people.

Yunus was surprised to find out that only nine of sixty acres were irrigated during the first cropping season. Local farmers assured him that utilization would improve once kinks in the management system were worked out. But the second season was hardly any better, with barely ten acres receiving water. As the third year approached, Yunus was informed that there were no plans to operate the tube well at all.

Partly out of his frustration with the misutilization of the tube well in Jobra, Yunus researched the state of irrigation nationwide. By the early 1970s, a significant number of irrigation pumps called deep tube wells (DTWs) had been sunk with foreign-aid funds to irrigate a dry-season rice crop using modern, high-yielding seeds developed in the Philippines. It was hoped that this would bring the nation's chronic food deficits under control.

Unfortunately, it turned out to be far easier for the government to sink a tube well capable of irrigating sixty acres than to find an institutional mechanism ensuring that it actually irrigated five. The management structure for the tube wells was supposed to be a cooperative that local farmers would join to ensure fair and judicious use of the machinery. In practice, within a short time most tube wells fell under the control of the wealthiest person within its command area. In most instances, the cooperatives existed only on paper. Often, huge bribes were given to ensure that the DTW was sunk on a politically well connected person's property. Worse still, slivers of poor people's land were often seized in order to build the canals that would carry the water to the wealthy farmer's fields. Over time, most of the pumps fell into disuse. Without maintenance of the machinery and the use of fertilizers in the paddy fields, irrigated agriculture is a risky venture.

On a fall day in 1975, Yunus asked Dipal Chandra Barua to find out why the irrigation pump in his village was not going to be used during the upcoming season. Dipal reported that over the two and a half years since it was sunk, the farmers had been unable to afford the diesel fuel and parts to keep it running. Those who had contributed toward the cost complained that because others refused to pay their share, the water had been shut off during critical periods. Rice harvests had been ruined, and participating farmers were sometimes worse off than if they had simply left their land fallow. On several occasions, unhappiness about mismanagement had boiled over into violence.

Yunus studied the problem, talking to farmers in the fields and at his home. He decided to convene a meeting of farmers whose land fell within the pump's command area. His aim was to persuade them to work together to ensure that there was a dry-season crop in the coming months. The gathering was held outdoors, in front of a tea stall in Jobra. As is customary in Bangladesh, most of the farmers who attended arrived late, and it was past midnight when Yunus interrupted the shouting matches that had broken out, and presented a plan.

Under it, Yunus and people he appointed to a management committee would run the tube well and supply all the seeds, fertilizer, and insecticide. In exchange, Yunus would receive one-third of all the crops harvested. The other two-thirds would be split equally between the owner and the cultivator of the land. Yunus would sell his share to recover the costs of running the program, and any surplus would be reinvested into the upkeep and improvement of the tube well. He liked the simplicity of *tehbhaga* (three share)—three parties shared the work, and the same three parties shared the fruits of that work. Each had incentives to make the initiative a success, and the farmers had the rare opportunity to cultivate under a scheme in which someone else bore most of the risk of crop failure.

When Yunus opened the meeting up for questions, he felt a strong undercurrent of hostility. Old wounds and jealousies from earlier efforts to manage the tube well had been reopened. The larger farmers seemed particularly mistrustful. They were interested in increasing their yields, but resisted the idea of receiving only one-third of the harvest as opposed to the traditional one-half. They suggested that Yunus accept one-sixth of the crop instead. In addition, they wanted no part of any loss the scheme might generate. If the government could sink the tube well without charging the villagers anything, why couldn't the university put together a management plan for free as well?

Yunus announced that he was willing to make up any loss with his own money, figuring it was the only way to gain everyone's agreement, but he stood firm on the issue of his share. He announced a cooling-off period of a week, during which several of Yunus's students aggressively talked up the program in the village. A procession of small farmers and sharecroppers called on Yunus at the university. Many of those who came had not even attended the original meeting, but had got word of the proposal and were eager to get involved. The elites in the village, eager to maintain their positions of influence, requested that they be given special status by being included on a largely symbolic advisory committee. Yunus agreed. When it was time to make a formal decision on whether to agree to the proposal, it was adopted nearly unanimously.

Yunus named the project the Nabajug Tehbhaga Khamar (New Era Three Share Cultivation Scheme), divided the participating farms into four blocks, and assigned a student to manage each. Assaduzzaman, a recent graduate of the Economics Department whom Yunus had hired to be the secretary of the Rural Economics Program, was named the project coordinator. Yunus and Assad (as Assaduzzaman is commonly known) began procuring the necessary seeds, fertilizer, diesel fuel, and insecticide with a 40,000-taka ($1,000) loan from a local branch of Janata Bank.

During the management and advisory committee meetings that were held soon after the water began flowing, farmers who had originally declined to participate asked to join in. Yunus resisted, fearing that if the command area was expanded too much, the pump might run dry toward the end of the season. Yet the farmers persisted. Finally, someone suggested that additional irrigation could be arranged by building an inexpensive cross dam in a nearby stream and digging a canal through which the water could flow to the rice fields. When objections were raised by farmers who lived seven miles downstream, it was agreed that Tehbhaga would divert water only two days during the week. To finance the expansion, Yunus took out an additional 25,000-taka loan from Janata Bank.

Nearly everyone associated with the project was impressed by the degree of Yunus's personal involvement. The expectation was that he would have his students organize everything and simply come back after the harvest to inspect the results. Instead, he attended every committee meeting and spent considerable time in the fields talking to the farmers. His and Latifee's familiarity with every aspect of life in Jobra grew.

When the harvest was completed in early June 1976, the results were impressive. The land under cultivation had ended up reaching eighty-five acres, and the yield exceeded 1.2 tons per acre, double the national average. Yet as a result of an unexpected drop in the price of rice, the high cost of overseeing the program, storage problems, and some pilferage, the program posted a 13,405-taka ($335) loss after the bank loan was repaid. Yunus, refusing to go back on his word, went ahead and covered the amount out of his own pocket. When word leaked to the village that the professor had absorbed the loss, many farmers were surprised and distraught. Some expressed a feeling of shame at having six months' worth of rice in their houses while the man who'd organized the program was out thousands of taka.

When the 1976–77 dry season began, the farmers begged Yunus to reorganize the program. The professor refused, but agreed to advise the farmers as they worked out their own management system and to provide the necessary introductions to the bankers and the wholesalers from whom he had bought the agricultural inputs. Yunus argued that he was a professor, not an irrigation specialist, and that his job was merely to demonstrate what was possible. It was now their job to institutionalize the program, or, if they so chose, to discontinue it.

In the second year, under the farmers' direction, overall production rose an additional nine tons. This time, however, the program recorded a profit of 8,522 taka, or about $210. By the fifth cropping season, the harvest reached 235 tons, more than double the inaugural year, and its profit exceeded 39,000 taka. Yunus never considered asking to be repaid his loss during the first year from the surplus generated later on.

In 1977, while Yunus was out of the country, a senior civil

servant asked Dipal to draft a nomination that he would submit so that Yunus could receive the President's Award for his involvement with Tehbhaga. Not only did Yunus receive the award, but a nationwide government initiative called the Package Inputs Program (PIP), designed on the Tehbhaga experience, was being planned.*

By the late 1970s, Yunus kept himself apprised of the developments of Tehbhaga and PIP, but he was by then deeply involved in another demonstration project from which it was proving much harder to extricate himself.

The interrelated problems of poverty and misutilization of resources were not unique to Jobra; if anything, conditions there were somewhat better than those in far-flung villages in the western half of the country. For the most part, however, as control of the central government changed hands during the second half of the twentieth century, conditions in the rural areas worsened as the politicians in Dhaka squabbled. On more than one occasion, Yunus said he believed Dhaka to be virtually a foreign country. He would tell people that he would never agree to be based in Dhaka; he felt that people who lived and worked there got hopelessly out of touch with their countrymen.

As the years passed, the situation outside the urban centers was becoming progressively more desperate. Periodic famines, chronic ill health, and uncertain food-grain prices that punished marginal farmers and rewarded speculators combined to ensure that the numbers of landless poor families steadily increased. In the process, small farmers became sharecroppers, sharecroppers became day laborers, and, as the pool of day laborers grew, their wages were forced lower. Even such traditional work as raising livestock and manufacturing handicrafts was done on the basis of sharecropping, in which middlemen reaped the lion's share of the benefits produced by someone else's labor.

By 1983, despite nearly ten years of an "assault on poverty"

---

*Sadly, it was imposed from above, without the active involvement of the farmers it was supposed to benefit, and as a result, it failed.

declared in the wake of the 1974 famine, real wages were 23 percent lower than in the last year of Pakistani rule, and a day's work in the fields bought a laborer three kilograms of rice instead of the four it had fetched in 1970. At the same time, the nation had three million new mouths to feed every twelve months. By the mid-1980s, per capita consumption reached an all-time low of 1,943 calories and 48.9 grams of protein; according to the Food and Agriculture Organization, the minimum daily requirement to sustain sedentary life is 2,150 calories and 65 grams of protein.

Under the stress of this impoverishment, the Bangladeshi family unit began to disintegrate. Deprivation drove fathers to abandon their wives and children in previously unheard-of numbers. It was no longer routine for sons and daughters to take care of their parents when they became old and infirm. In a society historically characterized by strong ties between the generations, it became increasingly common for parents to spend their final days in a state of semistarvation, with their children, living only a few yards away, refusing to deplete what little cushion they had against destitution. Fathers were often bullied into handing over their inheritance to their grown children as early as possible, and often after doing so any assistance they had been promised by their offspring was cut off.

The glory of independence wore thin, and many tea stall conversations in the rural areas centered on the strengths of the British and Pakistani regimes, perceived deficiencies of the Bengali race, and people's dreams of sending their sons to America, Europe, or the Middle East. A growing cottage industry of "agents" claiming to be able to place young men in jobs abroad came to cheat thousands of poor families out of millions of taka.

As people searched for answers to these vexing problems, Islamic fundamentalism gained ground, and although this was a people long known throughout Asia for their tolerance, relations between the Muslim majority and the nation's Hindus, Buddhists, Christians, and animists deteriorated. Politicians fanned ethnic and religious hatred and used student-front organizations as pawns in their quest for power. Violence, politically inspired or otherwise, became commonplace, and thievery a popular profession. Prostitution and abuse of drugs and alcohol were on the rise, and gambling, an old problem, was reaching epidemic proportions.

The plight of women in rural Bangladesh became increasingly severe. Even in good times, women prepare the feasts but are only permitted to eat the leftovers after the men are finished; they wash their husband's new clothes while wearing their old saris; and they hope, often in vain, that the money their guardians earn is being saved or productively invested instead of being gambled away. In bad times, women go the hungriest, work the hardest, and have to stand by helplessly while their children cry out for food. All year round, in good times and bad, women suffer constant humiliations. They are unable to initiate a legal divorce, though their husbands need only say "I divorce you" three times to end their marriage. They cannot travel outside their immediate home after puberty without the risk of becoming the subject of lurid rumors; they are the victims of frequent beatings and verbal abuse by husbands and in-laws, and against all reason, are blamed for floods, droughts, and disappointing harvests.

Life for a Bangladeshi woman is, more than anything else, one of isolation. In certain parts of the country, it is common to find women who have not strayed from an area smaller than two hundred square yards for decades at a time; who have never held currency in their hand or seen a market; who have no friends; who have never played any meaningful role in the politics of their family, their village, or their country.

With an annual per capita income of around $200, and a population of roughly 115 million packed into 68,000 villages in a country the size of the state of Wisconsin, the fundamental problems in the political and economic management of Bangladesh are manifest. Blame can be liberally spread amongst the government, the private sector, and the foreign aid agencies. But to understand the depth of the sorrow this nation has suffered, one need not open a single history book or read a fancy economic printout. One need only stand in a village for a few hours and look around at all the frail women with sunken, toothless faces hunching over earthen stoves or carrying water on one hip and a child in their arms as they walk barefoot down muddy village paths strewn with animal and human feces.

Particularly striking will be the moment a woman in rural Bangladesh realizes you're looking at her; reflexively, she will pull her sari over her face in shame. A brief conversation with any of these women is almost too much for those unaccustomed to life in rural Bangladesh—a lesson of what life is like when it is nasty, brutish, and short and when the only legacy you can leave any of your offspring who survive childhood is a life of poverty deeper than you inherited at birth.

2

▲

The Birth of the Grameen Bank

Surprisingly few people mourned the violent passing of Sheikh Mujib in 1975. For many, in fact, the founding father's death came as something of a relief. Mujib's successor, Khondokar Mushtaq, chose Mahabub Alam Chashee, a colleague and acquaintance of Yunus's, as his principal secretary.* One of Mushtaq's first acts was to call a conference whose purpose was to reflect on the idea of *swanirvar Bangladesh* (self-reliant Bangladesh). People were concerned about becoming overly dependent on other nations, often citing the example of how the United States government had cut off aid to Bangladesh after it exported some jute to Cuba in 1973. Many claimed, in fact, that this action was a contributing factor to the 1974 famine.†

The mood of the conference, held in September 1975, was tense, as it was the first major gathering since Mujib's assassination. The army generals were conspicuous by their presence from

---

*A post roughly equivalent to a White House chief of staff.
†Later research, however, revealed that despite the sanctions there was plenty of food in the country; the famine came, in fact, on the heels of a record harvest. The real villain was an inadequate distribution system.

beginning to end, and no one mentioned Sheikh Mujib for fear of their reaction.

Muhammad Yunus delivered a paper to the conference. Chashee had chosen him because he admired, even envied, Yunus's ability to weave diverse concepts, objectives, and strategies into coherent theoretical frameworks. He wanted to hear what the PhD from America had to say about self-reliance.

In his presentation, Yunus defined the concept of self-reliance as a state in which a nation or region is not involved in any dependent relationship. This did not, he emphasized, preclude the possibility of mutually beneficial trade.

Before Bangladesh could be self-reliant, he said, there had to be self-reliant Bangladeshi families. Building up independence was not something done from the top down, he said, but rather from the bottom up.

Yunus gave the example of a farmer who feels helpless when he hears a government proclamation stating that there is a national rice shortfall of several million tons. The farmer believes that he, or for that matter any individual, is powerless to solve such a huge problem. He is left believing that the answer can only come from the government. But if that farmer can be told instead that in his own village there is a shortfall of fifty tons, the problem immediately becomes easy to grasp and, more important, solvable.

Goals and strategies, Yunus went on to assert, must be broken down to the family and village level, and then solved from there, with supplementary assistance from the central government. The entire exercise in planning, he added, should be turned upside down so that the national plan is mainly the sum of thousands of smaller plans developed at the village level.

The challenge facing the nation, as he saw it, was to tap into the idealism and willingness to sacrifice that had characterized the liberation struggle and to channel these attitudes toward the awesome task of economic and social development. The framework that would stimulate this vision, he told his audience, would be *gram sorkar* (village government).

"Sheikh Mujib was right in that the village must have its own institutions," Yunus said. "But he called for *compulsory* village cooperatives. This was his mistake—cooperation cannot be mandatory." *Gram sorkar,* a system in which the bulk of the nation's political decisions would devolve to the villages, was the way to fulfill the martyred leader's vision, Yunus concluded. For perhaps the first but certainly not the last time in his public career, he then relinquished the podium and listened as his idea was dismissed by most present at the meeting before the conference's focus shifted to other issues.

Yet a change in government soon gave *gram sorkar* a friend in a high place. Gen. Zia Ur Rahman, the chief of staff, seized power in a bloodless coup in late 1975, ending the fiction of civilian government that Musthaq represented. After taking over, Zia discussed the matter with Yunus and indicated that he, with the help of Mahabub Alam Chashee, intended to implement *gram sorkar* nationwide. Many Bangladeshi intellectuals were outraged that the proposal was being taken seriously, perhaps because it valued the knowledge of semiliterate villagers more than theirs.

In March 1976, Yunus was invited to elaborate his idea of *gram sorkar* at the national convention of the Bangladesh Economic Association (BEA), a group, then as now, dominated by utopian socialist intellectuals. Yunus's paper was titled "Institutional Framework for Swanirvar Bangladesh," and after he presented it the attack was immediate and fierce. The assembled economists and politicians were contemptuous of the idea of organizations in which the poor, and women, would have a central role. (In Yunus's revised proposal, the poor, who constituted the majority in nearly every village, would be assured a strong voice in the running of *gram sorkar* through a system of proportional representation based on social classes.) The election of *gram montri* (village ministers) was criticized as being insulting to the national ministers. One prominent participant commented, "You cannot have an organization made up of poor people. Look at the history of poor people's organizations—they never amount to anything. Remember, if you add zero to zero to zero to zero, no matter how many times you do it, you still end up with zero."

Yunus responded by asserting that if you had a national minister and a village minister, and asked them both about the socio-economic condition under their jurisdiction, he would bet on the village minister to give the right answer every time. To try to rule entirely from the center, he suggested, is like groping in the dark. Second, he countered that the estimate of the poor being "zeros" may be *close* to the truth, but not the entire truth. The whole truth is that each one is a very small positive number *near* zero. But using that slightly different approximation, millions of very small numbers added together will amount to a very large number.

Finally, addressing his more vociferous critics, he added, "Let's be honest. I have not organized a poor man's organization, and neither have you. We are talking without experience. Let us go back to our campuses and actually organize poor people's organizations, and report back next year about what we found. That way, we can have a real discussion."

Yunus was working on the Tehbhaga tube well project at the time, and was thinking about what he could learn from its successes and shortcomings as he planned to establish a poor people's organization. One lesson was that government solutions, such as the sinking of the tube well, rarely worked by themselves. By donating expensive machinery like the irrigation pump outright, without asking for anything from the community in return, the government was sowing the seeds of underutilization, mismanagement, and graft. Local problems needed to be solved by local people and organizations in which they actively participated. Government, he and his colleagues felt, could play a supportive role and even be a catalyst, but it had to be recognized that the responsibility for success or failure rested solely with the people. Any program failing to recognize this was doomed to end in disappointment.

He and his colleagues who worked on the project felt that while poor sharecroppers had, relatively speaking, gained the least from the program, it was their willingness to try something new that had turned the tide of opinion that had been running against the initial proposal. They decided that future efforts spearheaded by the Rural Economics Program would try to take advantage of the unexpected eagerness of the poor to participate in community reform by ensuring that the bulk of the benefits accrued to them directly.

Yunus recalled a conversation with a woman in Jobra who complained that the recently completed Tehbhaga program had not helped her very much. In response, Yunus had asked whether she had got additional work. Yes, the woman replied, but only for two weeks. After the postharvest processing was complete, the farmers had half a year's worth of rice while the women had only gained a few days of backbreaking work at low wages. Yunus recalled how the laborers threshed the rice in the traditional manner, dancing on the stalks until the individual grains came loose. The image of women fighting each morning for a shady place where they could perform this hard labor, for which they would receive one kilogram of rice per day, was seared into his memory, a reminder that his program had brought disproportionate benefits to wealthy farmers while creating grueling, low-wage work for the poor. Yunus was determined that he not make the same mistake again.

Still, Yunus and his colleagues in the REP felt that Tehbhaga was an early success about which they could feel proud; indeed, many professors would take such an achievement and spend the next ten years lecturing and writing about it. But Yunus wasn't that type of person. Instead, he began walking through Jobra and the nearby village of Fatehpur in search of the issue around which he could organize his next project. From the beginning, he felt he should again try to involve the bank that had underwritten the tube well. Otherwise, he had few concrete ideas of how it should look.

Progress in developing the new project was slow. On occasions when he wanted to talk with poor women in the Muslim *paras* (neighborhoods), he often had to conduct the dialogue with a bamboo wall separating him and the women to whom he was talking. The Muslim custom of *purdah*,* the practice of keeping married women in a state of virtual seclusion from the outside world, was strictly observed in Chittagong. When Yunus's or the women's voices could not carry through the fence, a female intermediary (usually a student in the Economics Department or a local schoolgirl) would run back and forth with messages.

---

*Literally, "curtain" or "veil."

After several weeks of talking with poor men and women, Yunus asked two students from the REP to conduct a survey in which families would be classified into several categories—those producing enough food for the entire year, for nine months, for six months, for one month, and finally, those living hand-to-mouth. Yunus then began a series of in-depth interviews with those who fell into the final group.

Yunus became intrigued when he saw many of the women in the poorest families making *mora* (finely woven bamboo stools). Because they lacked money, the women were forced to deal with *paikars* (middlemen) who sold them raw materials on credit and bought the stools for a pittance. The women's effective daily wage was 8 anna, or half a taka ($0.02). Yunus had several of his students find out how many people in the village were working under this type of arrangement. It turned out that there were forty-two people who worked for roughly two pennies a day because they collectively lacked capital amounting to 856 taka ($21). Some needed only 10 or 20 taka, and the greatest amount any one person needed was 65 taka.

Yunus was flabbergasted. Years later he would say that as he tried to reconcile himself with this information, he "felt ashamed to be part of a society which could not make $21 available to forty-two hardworking, skilled human beings so that they could make a decent living." This lack of investment capital, he came to believe, was one of the root causes of the poverty that blighted the villages he saw.

Yunus quickly gave the stool-makers loans from his own pocket. Meanwhile, he approached the bank manager and asked if the bank could make loans to poor craftspeople. The professor explained how he had done so in Jobra, and argued that if a bank would agree to do it, it would represent a permanent solution to the problem of exploitation by village moneylenders.

The economics professor was politely received, but his proposal was firmly rejected. He was told that if the poor wanted to borrow, they had to provide collateral. Moreover, the manager explained, the kinds of loans Yunus was talking about were so small they were hardly worth the paper on which the proposals would be written. And who would write the proposals, Yunus was asked, since the people he was talking about were illiterate?

Yunus tried his luck next with R. A. Howlader, a regional manager for Janata Bank who was based in the city of Chittagong. Howlader responded warmly to Yunus's proposal, but he saw obstacles to actually implementing it. The main problem was the poor people's lack of collateral. Howlader told Yunus he could sanction the loans if every borrower could identify a wealthy person in the village to serve as a guarantor. Yunus knew that was unworkable—potential guarantors would exact a high price from the poor for helping them—but the proposal gave him an idea. Yunus suggested that *he* be the guarantor of *all* the loans. Howlader couldn't find a valid reason to reject the proposal and accepted it, provided that total loans advanced under this program would be initially limited to 10,000 taka.

Yunus agreed, but added that if the people defaulted, Janata Bank would have to take him to court in order to get its money back. He said he'd be willing to accept any consequences the court imposed on him, including jail. Howlader laughed at that one. What bank, he asked Yunus, would want the negative public relations of bringing to court a professor who didn't take any money for himself, but gave it all to the poor? At meeting's end, Howlader simply wished Yunus success in his endeavor.

It took four months to work out the formalities with Janata Bank. The first loans were released in early January 1977, and as the borrowers received their precious taka, others began to come forward with their own ideas and proposals. Both men and women were eager to borrow. The project, at long last, had been launched.

As the first loans were disbursed in Jobra, Vera was in her seventh month of pregnancy. In March, she gave birth to a girl. Yunus and Vera named their daughter Monica, one of the few names that was common for girls in both America and Bangladesh. But almost immediately after the birth, the family became engulfed in a crisis.

Vera had been growing progressively more unhappy in the years after the move to Bangladesh. She felt isolated and bored, as the house the university provided Yunus was in a remote area surrounded by hills on all sides. She became a voracious reader, and tried to get out when she could, but her husband was first and foremost obsessed with his work. Immediately after Monica's birth, Vera insisted that they return to the United States. Bangladesh, she felt, was the wrong place to raise their child. To his dismay, Yunus discovered that his wife no longer shared his optimism for the country in which they were living.

In July, at Dhaka's old international airport, Vera and Monica boarded a flight bound for the United States. Yunus, who would never emigrate, as his wife had hoped, was only able to see his daughter sporadically over the next twenty years, and always in the United States.

As destiny would have it, Monica Yunus and Grameen Bank were born within three months of each other. One would have only intermittent contact with Muhammad Yunus over the following two decades, while the other would receive his constant attention. In his quiet moments, Yunus longed to be able to nurture both of his creations.

As the date for the first loan disbursement came and went, Yunus decided that the safest way to ensure timely repayment of the loans was to mandate repayment on a daily basis. For the first months of 1977, loans were made individually and installments were collected by a shopkeeper who sold *paan* (spiced supari nuts wrapped in betel leaf) at a central point in the village. After a time, it was decided that weekly repayments were more practical for borrowers whose businesses did not yield daily income. Continuing to rely on one shopkeeper to collect payments proved unworkable and Yunus decided that there would be regular, weekly meetings during which installments would be collected.

Over time, all the daily installments were converted into weekly payments, and everyone was required to come to the meetings. Yet there was little continuity and discipline at the gatherings. One borrower would come to the meeting place, drop off his installment, and rush off before the next person came.

Later in 1977, Yunus decided to organize groups of borrowers according to the purposes for which they took out their loans.

Consequently, there were "cow groups," "rickshaw groups," "puffed rice groups," and so on. These so-called activity groups began meeting separately, on particular days, to make their payments. But groups made up of people taking loans for the most popular activities started becoming unwieldy as their numbers grew, while other activity groups remained stuck at two and three members. Moreover, there was no force bonding these groups together; rickshaw owners, for example, competed fiercely on the streets, and this often spilled over into the meetings. Finally, Yunus decided that groups would be limited to between five and ten members who selected one another.

As he moved from an individual- to a group-based lending strategy, Yunus felt that he had an opportunity to demonstrate how a cooperative organization could be successfully run. Since his return from the United States, he had been a leading critic of the cooperative movement, and particularly of cooperatives run by the government. He believed that one of the principal reasons for their failure was that they were too large. Yunus's five-to-ten-member groups were far more manageable than the thirty-or-more-strong cooperatives. The larger the number of members, he believed, the less likely it was that the poor would participate in any meaningful way and that money would be handled with integrity.

Some cooperatives required members to save money that could be mobilized for investment. Yunus liked this idea in principle and wanted to adopt it in some form, but feared that if the savings requirement was too large, poorer borrowers would be unable to participate. Ultimately, each group was asked to identify the person for whom weekly savings would be the biggest hardship. Whatever that person was able to pay would be the amount everyone in the center would contribute into their respective group's fund. In most cases, the amount was set at 1 taka, though in a few cases it was 25 or 50 poysha.* Later on, Yunus became frustrated with the slow growth in savings and wanted to link it to the size of the loans people were receiving. With that in mind, a group tax of 5 percent of the loan amount was charged at the time of dis-

---

* 100 poysha is equal to 1 taka.

bursement. This was also deposited in the group fund, from which loans could be taken by individual members of the group, provided that everyone agreed.

In explaining to borrowers the rationale for the group tax, Yunus likened it to the traditional practice of *mushti chaal* (literally, "a handful of rice"), in which a mother puts aside a small amount of rice every night to build up a stock for a rainy day. By her putting it away a little at a time, the rice is not missed, but as it accumulates it provides a cushion against food shortages and famines.

In the months following the first disbursement of loans, the repayment rate was perfect, and the male rickshaw pullers who plied the roads from the university gate to the classrooms became the proud standard-bearers of the new project. In time, they began putting signs on the rear of their rickshaws that identified them as part of the project and had the words *"maleek-chalok"* (owner-driver) prominently displayed. Many of the borrowers had spent years renting the rickshaws they peddled in exchange for a daily fee. Even though the total amount a puller would pay the owner over the years could easily surpass the value of ten rickshaws, the puller could barely dream of ever owning a single rickshaw for lack of the investment capital to purchase one. Loans from the project changed all that.

As 1977 progressed, meetings were held regularly and were well attended, and new loan proposals were coming in at an accelerating rate. Unfortunately, it turned out that Janata Bank, whose local staff members were far from enthusiastic about administering the project, was unable to process all of the paperwork. Each proposal, no matter how small, had to be sent to Dhaka for approval, where it had to compete for the attention of bank officials with loans that were thousands of times larger. During all of 1977, only sixty-five people were able to take out loans, and hundreds of others to whom Yunus had promised loans were becoming restless. He needed to find a more flexible sponsor than Janata.

In April 1977, Yunus paid a courtesy call on A. M. Anisuzzaman, a senior civil servant and the managing director of Bangladesh Krishi (Agriculture) Bank, in his office in Dhaka. The professor had planned on briefing his host about the progress of his project, but instead found himself on the receiving end of a long monologue about how useless academics were because they never had proposals that were of any practical value. Yunus countered that he *did* have a practical proposal.

Yunus argued that the entire concept of a Krishi Bank was wrong, since many of the people in the rural areas, particularly the landless, were not involved in agriculture, or at least not the whole year round. Krishi Bank should strive to be a "rural bank" or "village bank" (in Bengali, *grameen* bank) that would make loans for *all* of the productive activities in which villagers were involved, instead of simply for agriculture.

Yunus spelled out his specific proposal. Krishi Bank should put an entire branch at his disposal, a branch where he would make the rules, deciding who borrows and on what terms. If he demonstrated that lending to the poor was viable, Krishi Bank could replicate the program in other areas, and ultimately rename itself as Grameen Bank. To test out this idea on a practical level, Yunus's branch would be called the Poreekkhamulak Grameen Shakha (Experimental Rural Branch) of Bangladesh Krishi Bank. Despite the boldness of Yunus's idea, the managing director was receptive and said that when Yunus returned home, he would tell his top man in Chittagong to meet Yunus to work out the details.

And indeed, there he was the next day. He and Yunus drafted a proposal and sent it to Dhaka, where Anisuzzaman was having problems selling the idea of an experimental branch under the direction of an outsider to his colleagues and to the government-appointed directors of the bank. He began looking for some way that would allow him to follow through on his commitment to Yunus. Finally, it was decided that Yunus would be given an office that would technically be a "mini-branch" or "outpost," formally under control of the Krishi Bank branch in the city of Chittagong, but in practice enjoying a high degree of independence.

As these negotiations proceeded, operations continued, albeit at a snail's pace, with Janata Bank. Frustration set in among prospective borrowers and the people who administered the project— mostly young villagers with a little bit of education who received a small stipend from Yunus, and a few university students. When

Yunus spent three months at the end of 1977 in the United States as part of the Bangladesh delegation to the United Nations General Assembly, he was forced to make arrangements so that the individual loan proposals were sent to him in New York, where he would sign them in his hotel room and hurriedly send them back to Chittagong by airmail.

The mini–branch office under Krishi Bank was opened in April 1978. Yunus received an appointment letter as project director, and Assad, the project coordinator of the Tehbhaga initiative, was named to that position again. Nurjahan Begum and Jannat-i-Quanine, two unemployed female students who had recently completed their master's degrees, were given jobs as bank workers. Within two months, more loans were made under this format than had been made during fifteen months with Janata Bank. By September 1978, credit had been extended to 398 people, amounting to almost half a million taka ($12,500).

As the project grew, Yunus was forced to formalize its regulations and set up a staff training program. Yunus and his staff quickly drew up a *bidhimala* (constitution) that finally laid down a set of uniform written rules. The *bidhimala* included several of the innovations that had emerged in the project's second year. The most important was the idea that the groups should federate into centers that in turn select a "center chief" from among the group chairpersons. The centers would in turn federate into a village association of the landless. If the other social groupings, such as the landowners, youth, and so on, could be organized into their own village associations, the foundation for Yunus's *gram sorkar* would be laid. Since the major argument against *gram sorkar* was the difficulties his colleagues had seen in forming an organization of the poor, if he could scale that hurdle through his lending program, the case for *gram sorkar* would be considerably stronger. As it turned out in practice, however, the idea of a village association of the poor was unwieldy, and it was later dropped.

The *bidhimala* also incorporated a rigorous definition of who was "poor" and thus eligible to join a group. On several occasions, Yunus had met borrowers who had been allowed to join a group despite being fairly prosperous. The professor soon recognized that a villager might seem to one staff member to fall into the target group of "the poor" or "the landless" while clearly being outside that group in the eyes of someone else associated with the program. In a few cases, families that were clearly poor had been excluded because they owned a few hundredths of an acre of land; in others, a wealthy merchant who had given up farming was included when he claimed to be "landless."

A more flexible formula was agreed upon and included in *bidhimala*. To join a group, a person's household had to be "functionally landless," which was defined as cultivating less than one *kani* of land. One *kani,* a common measure in Chittagong, amounted to four-tenths of an acre. If someone owned a plot but had leased it out, or was sharecropping some land, it was not counted in the total. Conversely, if someone had leased and was cultivating land owned by another household, it was counted in the total. In addition, to be eligible the value of a household's assets could not exceed the value of one acre of medium-quality land. This definition remains essentially intact to this day.

By the end of 1978, Yunus felt confident that his mechanism for ensuring the recovery of his loans was working. Peer support and peer pressure had replaced traditional collateral requirements. In his mind, the poor had demonstrated that they were creditworthy and that reducing hard-core poverty was possible, even simple. Yet there were problems nonetheless. Recruiting women, who formed their own women's associations after some initial experiments with mixing men and women in the same groups and centers, proved difficult. Yunus's goal was to keep the number of female borrowers at least equal to that of male borrowers. But by September 1978 they constituted barely one-quarter of the project's membership. During the third year, some problems with repayment and with borrowers dropping out of the program began to surface.

Yet visitors from Dhaka rarely got deeply enough into the project to see its weaknesses. In a country conditioned to failure, they latched onto the dramatic effect the loans were having on many borrowers. Joshsan ara Rahman of the United Nations Children's Fund visited in 1979 and wrote about her experience in UNICEF's national journal *Shishu Diganta* (Children's Horizons). She described the plight of Zorina Begum, a beggar woman thrice deserted by husbands. "[Zorina] came to know about the bank loan. Initially she was afraid to even think about taking a loan. . . . [Overcoming her fears, Zorina] took a loan of 250 taka [$6]. She invested the money in trading grocery goods in the neighborhood. She paid off the entire loan in weekly installments. She did not have any problem. As soon as the first loan was repaid she took a second loan. This time she was bold. She borrowed 1,000 taka [$25]. Now she is an independent businesswoman. . . .

"Zorina now finds no problem feeding all the mouths [in her family]. She has repaired the roof of her hut. She is dreaming of a new life for herself, her children and her grandchildren. . . ."

In 1978, as the project neared the completion of its second year, Bangladesh Bank, the nation's central bank, held a seminar on "Financing the Rural Poor" that was funded and dominated by bureaucrats, academics, and consultants connected with the U.S. Agency for International Development (AID), the arm of the State Department responsible for disbursing foreign aid. Anticipating a hostile reaction to a presentation about his pilot project, Yunus decided to write and deliver a two-page paper about the Experimental Grameen Branch, to be followed by nearly fifteen pages of tables and charts detailing how much money had been taken out and paid back, who had taken it out, and for what purposes. He ended his presentation by asking those in attendance to "tell me what our experience means."

His audience was skeptical. Several people expressed the belief that the project's impressive-looking statistics were the result of a onetime miracle that was dependent on the charisma of a well-respected local university professor. The obvious implication was that it could not be replicated anywhere else. Other participants argued on more technical grounds. Some felt that the project should be run as a business, and that for it to be profitable Yunus would have to charge a higher interest rate than 13 percent. The consensus was that 36 percent—the rate being charged by the AID-funded Experimental Rural Finance Project—would be the right amount. Such a high rate, it was argued, would cover the greater risks that were thought to be associated with lending to the land-less. It would force poor people, who were assumed to be reckless, to carefully scrutinize their loan proposals. And it would be near the "market rate"—that is, the rate that would generate income sufficient to cover the costs of administering the project.

In reply, Yunus said he believed that, over time, his program could recover its costs while charging the same interest rate levied by the government banks, which at the time was 13 percent. The main thing, Yunus argued, was the *recovery* rate, not the *interest* rate. The corruption-plagued government banks were known to have repayment rates in the range of 40 to 60 percent. The Indus-trial Bank, serving the nation's elite, had a *default* rate in excess of 85 percent. If a program charged negative 5 percent interest, and actually got *repaid* 95 taka for every 100 taka it lent, it would be doing far better than any real or hypothetical bank that charged 36 percent interest but failed to get back even half the principal of its loans.

At the end of the day, Yunus was challenged by a banker to demonstrate that his methodology could work over an entire dis-trict—a challenge that he accepted on the spot. Yet there was the question of who would provide him with the resources necessary to do the work.

As luck would have it, one person who had listened sympa-thetically to the debate was in a position to let Yunus try his hand at transforming his small project into a much more serious enter-prise. Toward the end of the seminar, Yunus was invited to meet with A.K.M. Gangopadaya, the deputy governor of Bangladesh Bank and a widely admired figure in financial circles.

Gangopadaya was impressed with Yunus and promised to bring up the subject of expanding his project at an upcoming meet-ing with the managing directors of the nationalized commercial banks. When that meeting was held, Yunus argued that he had demonstrated that the poor could borrow, invest, and repay better than the wealthy, and hoped that the banks would take it from there, freeing him to return to teaching full-time.

The bankers were skeptical. One participant said he would sup-port the expansion of the project if Yunus resigned from the university and if it were carried out in a district other than Chittagong. Yunus countered that he would be willing to take leave from the university for two years, as long as the bankers agreed that if the project succeeded he could return to teaching and Bangladesh Bank would expand the program elsewhere. He readily agreed to conduct this two-year experiment in any district. The meeting ended inconclusively, but Gangopadaya was slowly softening his people up.

When the issue was discussed at a Bangladesh Bank board meeting, Mafuzul Huq, a former minister of the Central Government of Pakistan, spoke up in support of the idea and suggested that the board members take a field trip to Jobra to visit the project. Huq was something of an anomaly in government circles; long a champion of cooperatives and agricultural development programs, he always came to Bangladesh Bank meetings dressed in a traditional longhi.* He claimed to be an authentic rural Bangladeshi farmer, and looked forward to the excursion to Jobra as an opportunity to entertain his colleagues at his ancestral home in Mirsharai district, north of Chittagong. With Huq's support, the trip was arranged for December 1978.

Several board members, joined by the managing directors of the Janata, Krishi, and Sonali banks, made the trip to Jobra. During a discussion held at Yunus's residence after a tour of the villages, the managing director of Sonali Bank suggested Yunus open an experimental branch in a nearby subdistrict. The managing director of Janata Bank, feeling that his bank had started the project but was now out of the picture, expressed interest in getting involved again. And Anisuzzaman said that Krishi Bank was keen on expanding its existing collaborative operation with Yunus's program.

But the Bangladesh Bank took the lead and Gangopadaya began formalizing the role it would play in the project's expansion. He approved a budget of 1.3 million taka for the expenses of expanding the project, just a quarter of what Yunus asked for but more than enough to get started. The site of the project was iden-

---

*This would be like the secretary of agriculture coming to cabinet meetings in overalls.

tified—the troubled district of Tangail, some seventy miles north of Dhaka. On June 8, 1978, Yunus, Assad, and Dipal officially began work for Bangladesh Bank.

After completing formalities in Dhaka, the three men moved to Tangail. Yunus found office space and began discussing with local officials how many project offices there would be and where they would be located. It was finally agreed that there would be nineteen. Negotiations often bogged down, since so many institutions were involved in the project. Bangladesh Bank provided the funds for the head office, while six banks, including Janata, Krishi, and Sonali, each agreed to host three project offices and another agreed to house one. Later, a United Nations agency got involved and further complicated matters. Something as trivial as the way the head office's signboard was written—"Grameen Bank Prakalpa: A Project of Bangladesh Bank" or "Bangladesh Bank: Grameen Bank Prakalpa"—stirred people up.

It was decided that Yunus's star pupils would be "project officers" responsible for overseeing the day-to-day operations of the project; Dipal was responsible for nine offices, Assad the remaining ten. Yunus asked Sheikh Abdud Daiyan, a young statistician, to come on board as a research officer. In order to give Daiyan some field experience, he was given the additional responsibility of supervising one of Assad's project offices. A few months later Nurjahan, later to become Assad's wife, and Jannat turned over their responsibilities in Jobra and joined the group in Tangail. Yunus assigned them responsibilities for designing a series of social development workshops for female borrowers, and their salaries were paid not by Bangladesh Bank but by UNICEF.

Before the project could get going, several issues needed to be resolved. The first was the recruiting and training of staff from the nineteen project offices. In Bangladesh, the process of hiring is usually done so as to ensure that the power, stature, and financial position of the recruiter is enhanced. Jobs often go to relatives of the ultimate decision-maker, sometimes in exchange for some sort of social obligation, such as marrying someone's daughter or sister. In other instances, the job goes to the person who pays the largest bribe. The suitability of someone for a particular post is, at best, a secondary consideration. It is even more rare for a person, once hired, to be expected to do much work, and training is provided only in exceptional cases. Yunus, however, was committed to selecting employees on the basis of their qualifications. The recruitment process was designed to be simple and free of bribes.

By the beginning of October, Yunus began hiring the "boys and girls" who would be the first field managers and bank workers. To be selected, applicants, who usually responded to advertisements in newspapers, needed to have scored reasonably well on their secondary school and, in the case of prospective field managers, university examinations, and not raise any red flags during a brief interview and written examination. Salaries were set at 500 taka ($12.50) per month for bank workers and 1,200 taka ($30) for field managers.

Several staff members were recruited in unusual ways. Abdul Mannan Talukdar was a frequent companion of Yunus's in a tea stall near the project office in Tangail. The project director would occasionally hear this robust young man with long, curly black hair spinning stories of how he'd helped win the country's liberation as a freedom fighter. One day Yunus asked Mannan what he was doing with himself during the rare moments when he was not in the tea stall. It turned out he was managing a sawmill owned by some of his relatives and earning 150 taka per month for his efforts. Yunus suggested that he apply for work with the Grameen Bank Project, where he could earn 500 taka per month. Within a few weeks, Mannan had applied for the position of bank worker and was appointed to a GBP office in the Narandia bazaar. Among Mannan's colleagues there was a high school graduate who until recently had been plying a rickshaw on the streets of Tangail.

In another instance, dozens of interviews had been scheduled on a day that a transport strike had been called. Sitting in his office on that quiet day, Yunus was stunned to meet a young woman named Asma Siddika who had walked twenty-one miles in the scorching heat to make sure she arrived at her appointed time. Yunus told her no interview was necessary; she was given a job on the spot.

The new staff members were given some instruction on a slightly revised *bidhimala*—the number of borrowers in each group was, for example, set at five rather than allowed to vary between five and ten—and were told to come to Tangail once a week for a training seminar at which the project director would preside. So advised, these new recruits headed to their host branches with many unanswered questions floating around in their minds. Why didn't I have to give a bribe? Am I really expected to work hard? After arriving at the branch, they had even more questions. Why are the local bank staff members with whom I am supposed to work so hostile? Since this work is temporary, should I keep looking for a permanent job? By March 1980, forty-nine staff members had been hired and fifteen of the nineteen planned project offices had been opened.

The second problem facing Yunus was the local bureaucrats, who took themselves and their status, though not necessarily their work, very seriously. When Yunus arrived, there was immediate confusion over his rank. Bangladesh Bank referred to him as a project director, which was not very helpful. Nobody could find mention in government manuals of where a "project director" fit into the rigid hierarchy of the Bangladesh civil service.

In Bangladesh, before people want to know anything about a new colleague's work or ability, they want to know his rank. For Bengali bureaucrats, talking to someone without knowing whether he is junior or senior to you can be a disorienting experience. No one was sure whether Yunus should have to call on the local bank and government officials or whether they should go to him. Yunus decided to break the tension by paying courtesy calls on all the relevant officials. When he described what the GBP was trying to do, and failed to even attempt to pull rank on them, all that registered in their minds was how they could use the program to expand their influence. Within weeks, requests began coming from various local bureaucrats, by way of their PAs (their personal assistants, or male secretaries), asking Yunus to sit on this or that committee or to set up a branch in such and such village. Yunus, busy with his project, rejected most of the invitations as soon as he realized that the bureaucrats' sole purpose in extending them was to show off that the new "project director" was at their beck and call. As a result, throughout the early months of the project Yunus was frequently interrupted by hostile phone calls from the PAs of stuffed shirts throughout Tangail.

In one case, Abur Rahman, one of President Zia's ministers whose home district happened to be Tangail, stormed into the GBP office with a considerable retinue and began shouting at Yunus for not having hired a boy he had recommended for employment in the project. The project director kept his cool, politely asking his enraged guest to have a seat and join him for tea. Surprised by the reaction, Rahman stormed out as quickly as he had come in, saying, "I have not come here to talk with you. I have come here to find out who it is that is willing to defy me!"

Recruiting staff and dealing with people like Abur Rahman were time-consuming and often tedious. But figuring out what to do about the campaign of terror being carried out by the violent left-wing group called the Gonobahini (People's Army) was probably Yunus's most pressing concern.

By the time of Yunus's arrival in Tangail, most wealthy families with large tracts of land in the rural areas had fled to the city for fear of their lives. Rarely did a day pass when the professor and his students were not confronted by dead bodies strung from trees or lying in the gutter, the latest victims of the People's Army terror campaign. For a time, Yunus considered calling off the entire project for fear for his staff's safety.

Frantically, Yunus tried to make contacts with people reported to have ties to the Gonobahini; usually these contacts were recently graduated students who had been involved with radical politics at the university level. On a few occasions, they assured Yunus that he and his staff were not at risk. But Yunus had no way of knowing how close these young men were to the terrorists or if they were telling him the truth. He nonetheless forged ahead and recommended that everyone be cautious and keep a low profile.

By the time the project entered its second year in Tangail, Yunus had learned that several members of the Gonobahini had joined the project as staff members. On several occasions, Yunus was startled to see members of his staff toting machine guns under their shawls when he paid unannounced visits to project offices. In one instance, he confronted an armed bank worker and ordered him to put the weapon away. The young man resisted, saying defiantly that he was a *mukti judda* (freedom fighter). Yunus responded firmly, saying that the war of liberation was over, and that now it was time for the liberators to work for a living and build up their country. GBP staff, he said, do not carry guns—ever.

At one branch, this volatile mix of politics, action-research, and guns boiled over. The local Krishi Bank manager, like many of his colleagues annoyed at having to take on additional responsibilities serving the GBP without an increase in salary or bribes, continually tried to humiliate Yunus's local staff. One evening, as the manager was returning home, he was ambushed by the local field manager and a bank worker. He was pinned to the ground, nearly suffocating as one gun was pressed against his throat and the barrel of another pointed at his chest. Before they let him go, the bank manager was forced to promise that he would treat the GBP staff with more respect.

Despite Yunus's ministrations, the manager, fearing another encounter with the GBP staff, left his branch. Yunus quickly fired the bank worker and demoted the field manager, who subsequently quit. But the damage had been done. Rumors circulated among government bank staff in Tangail about GBP workers being terrorists. Relations with Krishi Bank, historically the most cooperative of the banks with which GBP worked, took months, even years, to heal.

Amid all the commotion, the work of forming groups and disbursing loans was progressing well. Yunus spent most of his days moving from branch to branch, sitting in on center meetings and group training sessions or simply talking to borrowers in their homes about the progress they were making. When his staff learned of his personal sacrifices—eating in a communal mess, living alone in a dingy apartment, forgoing a pay increase—many were willing to put in the long hours needed to ensure that the project worked.

The diversity of skills that the poor could capitalize on with loans from GBP impressed Yunus and his staff. There were the weavers of Deojan Delduar, the confectionery makers of Rokkhitbelta, the puffed rice fryers of Narandia, and the mustard oil crushers of Ghatail. More than ever, he was becoming confident that the approach worked. The effects on people's lives were often dramatic. A *dakat* (mugger), who was known to have killed several people and who had escaped death by evading angry mobs on several occasions, was petitioning his local branch manager, Dulal Chandra Kor, to allow him to form a GBP group so he could borrow. "What am I supposed to do?" Dulal asked Yunus. "If I don't let him in, he may kill me; if I let him in he will certainly default, as no bank worker will have the courage to demand payment from him. And then people will think Grameen Bank is a bunch of *dakats*." Dulal, a hulking young man with curly hair and an infectious smile, had spent his first night at his branch sleeping on a primitive bed he had retrieved out of a pond. Yunus considered him among the more promising new managers, and had entrusted him with training more than his share of new managerial recruits. With Yunus's help, he had transformed the local political boss from an enemy into an ally. But in the case of the *dakat,* Dulal thought he had met his match.

Against the advice of his staff, Yunus suggested allowing the *dakat* to form a center, agreeing to take full responsibility in the event he became a defaulter. Dulal agreed to go along. The *dakat* quickly formed a group and a center and became a strong center chief, and for many years was among the most successful borrowers in his area. By the time Dulal was transferred, the *dakat* had become very religious, wearing a beard and *tupi* (Muslim hat) everywhere he went. There was talk of the village pooling its resources to allow him to perform hajj (make a pilgrimage to Mecca during the festival of Eid-ul-Azha).*

Despite the project's successes, there were concerns about how much it was costing to run. Sonali Bank started claiming in 1981 that its new Sonali Bank—Krishi Shakha (Golden Bank—Agriculture Branch) was accomplishing the same objectives as the Grameen Bank Project at considerably lower cost. This was at a time

---

*Years later, the *dakat*'s past caught up with him, and he was imprisoned for crimes committed before his conversion. But he repaid his Grameen Bank loan in full, sending his final installments from his jail cell.

that Yunus was petitioning the bankers to allow him to expand to three new districts in order to prove that the program could thrive without his close supervision. Field trips to Ghatail, where Grameen Bank and Sonali Bank were operating side by side, were arranged for senior people in the banking community. The trip was a success for Sonali Bank; the senior banking officials who visited were suitably impressed. But the GBP branch there was under instructions from its director to not try to match the elaborate tour that was arranged by its rival.

Yunus was concerned. The statistics provided by Sonali Bank, if true, made a strong case for the expansion of the competing program instead of his own. He soon discovered, however, that someone in the Sonali Bank—Krishi Shaleha (SBKS) branch in Ghatail was cooking the books. The manager was transferred, but Sonali Bank argued that other branches were performing well. After this disgrace, however, people no longer made the argument that SBKS was superior to GBP. This helped pave the way for the expansion of the project in 1982 to Dhaka, Rangpur, and Patuakhali districts.

While he was working to establish his ideas at the local level, Yunus continued to be involved with national political figures. He had a warmer and more complex relationship with President Zia Ur Rahman than he'd had with Sheikh Mujib. The two had first come into contact in 1977 when Yunus received the President's Award on behalf of Tehbhaga Khamar. On several occasions, Zia called on Yunus as a representative of the younger generation of academics to speak out on subjects ranging from the wisdom of conducting state planning on two-year cycles (rather than the traditional five) to the proposal for beginning to transmit television signals in color as opposed to black and white. Yunus usually argued the minority view while the other side carried the day, but important people in government circles noticed his ability as a debater.

By 1978, Zia was trying to institutionalize his regime by creating a political party, the Bangladesh Nationalist Party (BNP). In April 1978, soon after Krishi Bank had opened the experimental

Grameen branch run by Yunus, a close political advisor to Zia called the professor to Dhaka to meet with the president. The discussions were supposed to be about *gram sorkar,* which at the time was the subject of vigorous debate. But the conversation soon turned to politics. Yunus was invited to continue his development work, but instead of doing it while based at Chittagong University, he would become a salaried employee of the BNP. It was intimated that were he to join the party, in due time he would be made a minister. Yunus resisted the offer, but when the president asked Yunus to join him on an upcoming field trip to the drought-ravaged district of Pabna, he agreed to go.

Zia will be remembered, if for nothing else, as being one of the most energetic leaders of modern times. When he went on his frequent visits to the rural areas, he would insist on traveling by foot, marking his path through the villages on maps provided by the military. He wanted to be close to his countrymen. In addition, he refused to accept any fancy meals. Plain rice, simple *dal* (lentils), and a modest portion of either fish or chicken (but never both) were the most he or anyone in his party would accept.

On that hot Friday in April, Yunus followed Zia and his entourage for seven miles. On two occasions, he listened to the president's speeches, and both times Zia made sure that Yunus was sitting next to him when he delivered his remarks. After the second speech, Zia and the people traveling with him stopped for lunch. After he finished eating, he began the thirty-minute rest that he was under doctor's orders to take each afternoon. Soon after Yunus had retired, presidential assistants came running in search of him. The president wanted to speak to him. When Yunus, still drenched with sweat from all the walking, entered the room where Zia was resting, he was ushered into a chair by the president's bedside. Zia looked up at his guest and said, "So, what did you think?"

Taken aback, Yunus innocently asked, "About what?"

"About my speech."

Measuring his words carefully, Yunus said, "Well, I think people were very inspired to hear from you." He paused, and began again. "But there is one thing I would have changed. You see, people are talking about how bad this drought is, but I saw a lot of water in the river we passed over in the helicopter. If some of that water was diverted to the fields by canals or even lifted by hand, then we would be seeing some green fields instead of brown ones. And that's something people can make a beginning on right now.

"What I'm trying to say, Mr. President, is that in your speech you kept telling people what you are going to do for them. I think it would be much more useful if you talked about what they could do for themselves."

By 1983 Yunus's main preoccupation was addressing concerns of his staff that were forcing some of them to leave. These included low pay, lack of job security, and the abuse they continued to suffer at the hands of the government bank employees with whom they were forced to work. It was time to find a permanent solution that would address these problems while at the same time allowing for expansion.

Yunus asked Gangopadaya and the managing directors of the banks participating in the project to consider a proposal that would transform Grameen Bank into an independent financial institution specializing in bringing banking services to the poor. This bank, he proposed, would be owned by the poor people who borrowed from it. As Yunus would recall years later, "The assembled bankers spoke in one voice against the absurdity of the idea." Yunus looked for allies and began discussing various organizational structures for his proposed Grameen Bank.

Yunus's investigations were interrupted by another change of government in Dhaka. Gen. Hossain Muhammad Ershad, the army chief of staff, staged a coup d'etat and declared martial law. Ershad named M. A. Muhith, a participant in the bank's reorganization discussions, as finance minister. Yunus knew Muhith from his days running the Bangladesh Information Center in Washington in 1971 when he had been the most openly pro-Bengali Pakistani embassy official. When Yunus pressed his case to Muhith, he found the new minister receptive but unable to build any support in the banking community for the proposal to create an independent Grameen Bank. Muhith decided to directly approach Ershad, who threw his support behind the idea and ordered Muhith to draft an ordinance that would establish Grameen as an independent bank. Kamal Hossain, a onetime Awami League presidential candidate and a leading legal scholar, recommended that Yunus and Muhith propose that the government own a 40 percent share in Grameen Bank. Such an institution, Hossain argued, would be more palatable than one completely owned by the borrower-shareholders. Hossain and Yunus finalized the text of the proposed ordinance.

The ordinance was issued by Ershad on September 30, 1983, and became effective on October 2. To Yunus's surprise, however, the ownership provisions had been reversed in the final document. The government's share was set at 60 percent instead of 40. Yunus was furious at first, but when he calmed down he asked Muhith if, at some later date, the borrowers would be able to buy up the government's shares. Muhith said he thought it would be possible. (This did, in fact, occur—over the next ten years the government's share was gradually reduced to less than 10 percent.) And the disagreement did not prevent a joyous celebration at the formal launching of Grameen Bank as an independent financial institution at Jamurki branch in Tangail, at which both Yunus and Muhith spoke.

Upon achieving independence, some Grameen Bank Project employees were faced with the choice of staying with the participating government bank (Krishi, Sonali, Rupali, etc.) that had appointed them or joining Grameen Bank. For many, this was a difficult decision, as there were still fears that a change in government or substantial loan losses could lead to the dissolution of Grameen. Others were attracted by the bribes and other benefits (such as pensions) that government bank employees received. In the end, however, most threw their lot with Yunus, though one notable exception was Assad, the original Jobra project coordinator. One day, Assad came into the director's office and handed him a letter stating that he wished to become a permanent employee of Bangladesh Krishi Bank. Although surprised and taken aback, Yunus accepted the letter immediately, without any discussion. In later years, colleagues would blame the managing director for failing to try to talk Assad out of leaving. But that wasn't his style. Had Assad come to talk, his mentor would have been more than willing; but Assad's coming to him with letter in hand signaled to Yunus that he had already made his decision—without ever having consulted the man who had put so much trust in him.

By the end of 1983, the long process of transferring all the accounts and loan ledgers over to the new Grameen Bank was nearing an end. The number of borrowers had swelled to nearly a hundred thousand across five districts, and the number of staff members was nearing a thousand. In a small country that was home to eighty million poor people, ruled by a military dictator, and repeatedly thrashed by tornadoes, floods, tidal waves, and droughts, this was a modest beginning. Still, there was no denying that Yunus, based in the Dhaka suburb of Shymoli by this time, had already beaten long odds.

3

▲

Zianpur Bazaar

As an incoming plane approaches Zia International Airport in Dhaka, a passenger can see rice fields and tiny thatch huts dotting a vast marshy swampland that extends for miles in all directions during the monsoon season.

A burst of hot air greets passengers as they exit the plane and walk a short distance to a waiting bus that makes a wide loop and ends up at the terminal, often no more than twenty-five yards from where the plane came to rest. Skinny soldiers with World War I–style rifles slung over their shoulders direct the weary travelers into an arrival lounge. Bangladeshis will form a dense line as they wait at the immigration counter, while foreigners pass quickly through the formalities and await their luggage on one of three baggage belts. Once the luggage arrives—rarely, if ever, on the designated belt—foreigners speed through the customs area into waiting vehicles. The locals, many of whom are returning from the Middle East, where they are employed as drivers, cooks, construction workers, and servants, expect delays that can be considerably shortened by greasing the right palms.

Dhaka is a crowded, ugly city, but it wasn't always that way.

Its streets and alleys reek of urine and feces, its roads are pock-marked with gaping potholes, and the major intersections are congested with motorized vehicles belching clouds of black exhaust. Beggars with unspeakable deformities are everywhere.

Apart from a few neighborhoods reserved for diplomats, foreign aid workers, and the small but growing class of superrich Bangladeshis, Dhaka is an overpopulated, dirty, slum-ridden city of seven million people whose rapid horizontal and vertical expansion shows few signs of proceeding according to any plan. Cows, bullock carts, bicycle and motorized rickshaws, cars, and buses so overcrowded that they are on the verge of tipping over compete for narrow lanes on streets dotted with stoplights that nobody pays any attention to.

Families for whom serfdom in the countryside had become unbearable live virtually on top of each other in wretched squatter settlements, often using the putrid liquid in sewers that run through the heart of their makeshift neighborhoods for bathing, drinking, and defecation. A popular game among the naked children who run riot through the slums is to put wayward infants on creaky wooden carts, wheel them to the edge of the sewer, and, after a suspense-filled interval, push them into the shit. Practically none of these children receive any form of schooling.

Dhaka is not, however, without a few redeeming features. It is cleaner and more spacious than Calcutta or Katmandu. While many policemen extort small bribes, they are rarely menacing; indeed, they are likely to ask for money while holding hands with a male colleague. One can usually stay out of the way of armed gangs, unless one intends to purchase land or a building. Common people, despite conventional wisdom to the contrary, are remarkably honest. More likely than not, a shopkeeper or bus conductor will return money if a customer overpays. And above all there is work, either in construction, rickshaw-pulling, garment-making, or, for hundreds of others, crafts; artisans make and sell their wares out in the open, so that customers can watch the products they buy being made.

From the Gabtoli bus station in Dhaka's northwestern edge, a region that less than a generation earlier was farmland, buses leave every few minutes for Aricha, a small port city on the edge of the huge Jamuna River, known to many simply as "the Dancing River." (Together with the Meghna and Ganges, the Jamuna makes this tiny nation home to three of the world's ten largest rivers.) Passengers wearing shirts and pants pay the full fare and pass their bags to those on top, who are clad in tank-top T-shirts and longhis and pay half price. A bus will lurch forward and then stop, and prospective passengers who have waited to see which bus will leave first will jump aboard. An animated conductor will chant his final destination—*"Man-eek-ganj, Man-eek-ganj, Man-eek-gaaanj"*—to the beat of the engine, often grabbing people with luggage and refusing to release his grip until they have heard his pitch for his particular carrier.

Twenty-five taka is enough to get a ticket to Aricha, though for most this town is simply where their bus boards a ferry headed for western Bangladesh, whence travelers can continue their journeys to the northwestern cities of Rangpur, Pabna, Rajshahi, and Dinajpur. The sheer volume of vehicles going to and from the port makes for deadly games of chicken on the narrow Dhaka-Aricha highway that result in hundreds of fatalities each year.

Roughly ten miles north of Aricha lies the Zianpur bazaar, which consists of two tea stalls, three tailors, two general stores (each about the size of a small bedroom), a fertilizer retailer, and the union *porishod* (council)* building, the only concrete structure in the marketplace. Travel between Zianpur and Aricha is primarily by bicycle and rickshaw along a single jagged road composed of dirt and sand that at times runs along a cliff on the edge of a tributary of the Jamuna and at others crisscrosses fields sown with peanuts, rice, and jute. Bamboo jungles in which villagers have erected tiny thatch huts line both sides of the road for much of the way.

Travel to and from Zianpur—or Shaymganj, as it is also called—used to be by boat, but on an angry night in the summer of 1991, the Jamuna burst through a dike in the village of Bagutia

---

*A union is an administrative unit composed of roughly ten to twenty villages. It selects its leaders, one chairman and several members, by direct election. Zianpur is the name of both a union and of one of its constituent villages.

and a new tributary began slicing its way through a landmass that had contained five hamlets. Four of the villages survived in truncated form, while one was completely swallowed up, and the destruction the river wrought left hundreds of families homeless. With the violent creation of this new tributary, the competing river that had flowed by the western edge of the Zianpur bazaar, and was thought to threaten its very existence, began to wither, and within three months it died.

Bordering the bazaar to the east is the Zianpur high school and the field on which its students take recess. The school is composed of three rectangular tin sheds filled with weathered wooden benches behind long tables on which the students work. The only concrete structure in the school complex is the science laboratory. For lack of supplies, the lab is hardly ever used, and starting in 1988 the school rented out half of the building to Zianpur's newest organization—the Grameen Bank. For the right to use half the building, Grameen pays a monthly rent of 500 taka ($12).

For the thirty thousand inhabitants of the two dozen villages that fall within a five-kilometer radius of Zianpur, the bazaar is the principal market and meeting place. It lacks running water, modern medical facilities, electricity, a public pit latrine, and a restaurant. If any of the people in the area get seriously ill, their likely fate is to die on the two-to-three-hour rickshaw ride to understaffed hospitals located in Aricha, Daulatpur, or Ghior. Complicated pregnancies, rarely detected until the mother is about to go into labor, usually result in the death of infant and mother. Common and serious illnesses alike are treated by traditional healers or with medicine purchased from one of two pharmacies located in the bazaar. Neither the healers nor the pharmacists have any training in modern medicine.

Thursdays and Sundays mark the *haat* (twice-weekly market), during which wandering vendors roll out tattered bedsheets and sell their wares from four in the afternoon until seven-thirty in the evening. Hundreds of men (and virtually no women) jam the market on these days, making their weekly purchases, exchanging gossip, and trying to line up work for the coming week. The unemployed or the simply curious wander among the stalls, inquiring about the prices of essential goods.

A rusting signboard with a gaping hole in the lower-right-hand corner is propped precariously on a ledge outside the western wall of the science lab building, identifying it as the local Grameen Bank office. The name of the branch, Shaymganj Daulatpur, is written in Bengali alongside the code number, 393-0188, signifying that this was the 393rd branch opened by the bank and that the first loan disbursement was made in January 1988. The signboard is an island in a sea of political graffiti that covers the building from top to bottom.

On a hot summer day, the eight-hundred-square-foot office is dark and musty. Most of the windows are closed to keep the dust and sand in the air from settling on the tables and in the employees' eyes and lungs. The manager, Muhammad Jobbar Ali, sits at his table with the door to his immediate right and the bazaar visible through the window behind him. He is in a commanding position, overlooking smartly dressed bank assistants sitting behind tables to his left and in the rear, and bony female borrowers wearing colorful saris sitting on benches that are placed against the southern wall.

The bank's three steel cabinets and safe are in advanced stages of rust and decay. Neatly arranged piles of loan ledgers line the walls behind the chairs where the assistants sit and do their paperwork each afternoon. Molding ledgers that have been closed are bundled together and stacked on top of the cabinets. The only decorations are a few sayings of Grameen's managing director, written on plain white paper with marking pens imported from China. One, faded to the point of being virtually unreadable, says in Bengali, "Credit is a fundamental human right."

When Muhammad Abdul Rohim opened his eyes one morning in April 1993, they fixed briefly on the top of his mosquito net, and then on his black digital watch. Even after all these years, it still amazed him that his biological clock woke him at precisely six in the morning, day after day. Rohim put both hands over his face, rubbed hard, and released. As he sat up, he swiveled his torso so that his muscular legs dangled off the side of the bed, just above the floor, where they could feel around for his rubber sandals.

Rohim was one of seven men, all in their early thirties, who were housed in a small shed composed of four walls and a sloping roof made of flimsy corrugated tin. On both the northern and southern ends of the shed, two *choukis* (simple bedsteads) were jammed together. A six-inch gap separated those beds from a third that ran north-south along the shed's western wall, giving the living quarters six beds in all. A small open space, in which the men took their meals in shifts sitting on mats woven from thin strips of bamboo, was left in between the two sleeping areas. Above the beds and the mosquito nets, thin ropes on which each man's wardrobe hung crisscrossed the shed. A set of chess pieces, a deck of ragged playing cards, and two tiny radios, the men's entertainment, were carefully stored away in well-worn cardboard boxes.

Rohim slid out from his bed, grabbed an extra longhi, his *gamchha* (a thin towel), and a bar of soap, and stepped outside the shed into the early-morning sun. He paused for a moment, took a deep breath, and looked back to see if any of his colleagues would join him. When he saw that they were only beginning to stir, he started walking toward a nearby pond.

On his way, he walked past Aklima, the cook, who was in a straw hut that functioned as a kitchen; she had begun boiling the morning rice and cooking the vegetable gruel for which Rohim had long since lost his taste. In exchange for preparing three meals a day, Aklima, abandoned two years ago by her husband, was paid 15 taka (37 cents), with which she tried to feed herself, her two children, and her mother. Rohim grunted as he passed her and continued down a gentle, grassy slope that led to the pond.

In rural Bangladesh, all bathing is done outdoors, requiring strenuous and at times comic efforts to preserve the local concept of modesty. Public bathing is a ritual performed fully or partially clothed, and it requires the simultaneous use of the arms, legs, and mouth to hold clothing in place so that one does not become exposed.

When Rohim returned from the murky pond, he rang out his wet longhi and hung it to dry on the main clothesline just outside the shed's entrance, where it would stay until Aklima folded it and put it on his bed before lunch. Then he unrolled a mat, crouched down on it, scooped some rice onto an aluminum plate, and poured one ladle of vegetable curry on top of it. Rohim ate with his right hand, rolling the rice and curry into balls and pushing them from his palm into his mouth with his thumb. He had never eaten a meal with a fork in his life, though he had read about the practice in books.

After finishing his meal, he brushed his teeth and put on a white dress shirt and gray slacks. At 6:40 he left for the branch office, just seventy yards away from the living quarters (or "mess," one of many English words in use in modern spoken Bengali) on the other side of the bazaar, where he collected two piles of paper, stuffed them into a small bag, and strapped the bag onto a storage rack on the rear of his bicycle. The first bunch of blue and white papers had a huge "2" written on it in Bengali, while the second wad was labeled "42."

Before departing, Rohim double-checked his bag to make sure he had his calculator and two pens, one filled with black ink, the other with red. His bag had become disorderly since his transfer to Shaymganj, and as he rustled through its contents he decided that he would clean it out that night. At 6:50 he departed for the village of Kholshi.

Becoming a Grameen Bank employee in 1987 had been an improbable blessing for Muhammad Abdul Rohim. The year before, he had completed his intermediate (high school) degree—the first person in his family ever to do so—with dreams of going to college and university. But his father became ill and the medical treatment absorbed a large chunk of the family's savings. Suddenly, it became a priority for Rohim to get a job. After several months of frustration, Rohim responded to a Grameen newspaper advertisement and sent an application to Dhaka. A month later, he received an "interview card" assigning him a time and date to appear at Grameen's head office.

Rohim's trip to Dhaka was the first visit there for anybody in his family, and he had no idea what to expect. The magnitude of the capital overwhelmed him, but not as much as what he saw when he arrived at Grameen—nearly six hundred other applicants who had formed long lines to sign in and await their interview. Rohim felt sure that he had no chance at being selected from such a large pool, but after he had his five-minute interview with a panel that included Yunus and Muzammel Huq he felt more confident. After the interview, he headed home. Three weeks later, he received a letter informing him that he was being offered a job—setting off several days of celebrations in his family's small compound.

Rohim performed well during his six-month training period and his first few years as a bank worker. He received two quick promotions, outperforming virtually all of his peers. He worked hard and lived frugally, enabling him to send as much as half of his monthly salary of 2,100 taka ($52) to his parents. But in 1991, things began to go awry. He asked for a transfer to a branch that was closer to home, but when he arrived his new manager was abusive and prone to giving poor evaluations to the half dozen bank workers he supervised, causing him to fall behind his peers at other branches.

Rohim greeted his transfer to Shaymganj in 1993 with relief; he knew he would enjoy a good relationship with his manager, since he had worked with him previously. Krishna Das Bala, a colleague who would take over some of Rohim's responsibilities in Kholshi some months later, had the opposite reaction to being posted there—it annoyed him. Bank workers tend to want access to a bustling market, electricity, running water, and a main road serviced by buses. Shaymganj was the kind of place that many Grameen employees would consider a "punishment branch." But he resolved to make the best of it.

In many respects, Rohim and Krishna, a Muslim and a Hindu respectively, hailing from southwestern Bangladesh, are typical of the eight thousand men and women who travel to center meetings every morning. They share the first trip to Dhaka, the shock at getting work without a bribe, the unfamiliarity with Grameen when they applied (though this became less common), and the financial hardship that prevented them from pursuing higher education. Most employees sign up not out of idealism but because they have few other choices. Only after joining and seeing the impact that can be made on poverty through the Grameen approach does the commitment to the poor and the willingness to work long hours come.

April is among the cruelest months in rural Bangladesh. It marks the end of winter and the beginning of a brief summer that is soon overtaken by the annual monsoon rains. Temperatures in the shade are routinely above a hundred degrees; the heat causes dirt roads to become so parched that they are soon covered in several inches of loose dirt and sand. Tornadoes wreak havoc throughout the country during the summer, killing hundreds and flattening entire villages. Even the wind provides little relief, as it tends to whip up sandstorms in which it becomes impossible to see farther than six feet in any direction. The inhaling of sand and dust leads to widespread respiratory problems that, along with fevers and stomach ailments, cause many Bangladeshis to spend long stretches of the summer ill.

April is also a month of hunger, as families agonize over whether their irrigated rice harvest, still four to six weeks away, will be large enough to meet the needs of their aching stomachs during the coming monsoon. With each passing day from mid-March until mid-May, thousands of rural Bangladeshi families consume the last of their household stock of food grains from the previous harvest and join the millions of others who must buy their rice. Each new entrant into the market nudges the price of rice up a little more, pushing millions from two meals a day to one, from 90 percent of the minimal caloric intake that nutritionists believe is needed to sustain life to 70 percent.

The chronic malnutrition this causes leads not just to death but to widespread stunting. Bangladesh, health officials claim, is the only country on earth where each successive generation is getting smaller and lighter than the one before it—meanwhile, the rest of mankind gets heavier and taller. It is no wonder, then, that one out of ten severely underweight children in the world is a citizen of this tiny, beleaguered nation.

As Rohim weaved his way between trees, around potholes, and through sand traps, he was often forced to grimace, and briefly close his eyes, as the wind whipped up a foul combination of dirt and sand that only a few months back had been submerged in inches of rainwater. The gravelly dirt road on which he pedaled his bicycle was raised six to eight feet above the rice fields on either side of it, having been built so as to ensure that even during floods, communications with the larger townships of Zianpur, Ghior, and Daulatpur would not be completely severed and there would be some place for families whose homes were inundated to take refuge. Beads of dusty sweat began to form on Rohim's face as he entered the homestretch of his three-mile journey.

Roughly one hundred feet before reaching the Kholshi bazaar, Rohim steered his bicycle down a steep slope onto a thin strip of land raised six inches above two rice fields on either side of it, serving as a pathway connecting the road to a Hindu *para*. When he reached the first of the homesteads in the *para*, he dismounted and walked his bike up the slope, put down the kickstand, locked the back wheel, and dislodged his bag. Rohim ducked as he walked into a small hut with a tin roof, a bamboo frame, and no walls. Inside, thirty-five women sat in rows of five on bamboo mats, perched in those awkward-looking deep crouches that people of the Indian subcontinent apparently find so comfortable.

Each had her eyes fixed on Rohim, and as he moved toward a weathered chair placed in front of the first row of women, Amodini Rani Haldar called out the Bengali word for one, *"Aek."* On her command, the women stood up in unison; as they did, the air was pierced by the sound of dozens of knee joints cracking. Then Amodini shouted *"Dui"* (two), precipitating a coordinated military salute, the making of which required some agility, since perhaps one in three of the women had a baby in her arms. Rohim stood at attention in front of the first row of five, surveying the group without looking at anyone in particular, and finally nodded his head slightly, which Amodini took as a cue to call out *"Teen"* (three) and *"Char"* (four). Hearing those orders, the women first put their arms at their sides and then reassumed their crouches.

This was Rohim's first day servicing this center, and the look on his face suggested that he was already impressed. "You are the center chief?" he asked Amodini.

"Yes, sir," she replied firmly. Rohim was slightly startled by the way Amodini looked him directly in the eye when she spoke, and he self-consciously averted his gaze before reaching into his bag for his collection sheet, pens, and calculator.

Amodini, dressed in a patterned pink sari with a red blouse underneath, has piercing eyes, a skinny face highlighted by slightly raised cheekbones, and a facial expression that wanders between anger and hilarity. Her jet-black hair, parted in the middle and pulled back tightly, glistened as the sunlight reflected off the thin layer of coconut oil she had applied earlier in the morning. As she spoke, her hands gestured wildly, pointing at real and imaginary figures, slicing through the air with high intention and, on occasion, fury. On this day, at least, Amodini was in charge.

Rohim laid his supplies on his lap and put his bag on the ground so that it leaned on one of the legs of the chair. He looked up and counted the number of rows of women, noting that although there were only six groups on his collection sheet, there were seven in the hut. Good, he thought, all five women in the new group have come. I'll need to talk to them after all the installments are collected.

When he'd arrived at the branch two weeks earlier, Rohim had presented himself and his transfer order to Jobbar Ali, the manager, and arranged to be briefed on each of the nine centers he would service. Reports about center number two, the Kholshi landless women's association, were mixed but generally positive. This center, he had been told, was like premodern Bangladesh—Hindus and Muslims coexisting peacefully, with the former being in the minority but nonetheless exercising power disproportionate to their numbers.

Rohim unfolded the large wad of papers marked "2," revealing a large grid with Bengali-language headings in black type identifying the columns and the names of each member in the row. He made a few initial markings on the sheet, looked at Amodini, and said, *"Pash boi den"* (Give the passbooks). The center chief lifted up the edge of the mat with her right hand, clenched the booklets, and thrust them in front of Rohim.

Inside each passbook was detailed information about a loan

taken out by one of the five members of Amodini's group. Shandha Rani Haldar, Amodini's predecessor as center chief, who sat immediately to her left in the first row, had taken out a 6,000-taka "general loan" for weaving fishing nets. This week she gave back 120 taka, her thirty-ninth of fifty installments.

Four of the five women in Amodini's group had used their loan capital to buy the expensive thread for weaving fishing nets. Before joining the bank, they were forced to weave nets on a contract basis for others, arrangements under which they earned next to nothing for their efforts. Rasheda Begum, the only Muslim in the group, invested her 5,000 taka ($125) in a grocery store she ran from her home. When her group had been formed six years earlier, the four other original members wanted no part of Rasheda, until the branch manager who founded their branch told them sternly, "Grameen Bank was created for people like Rasheda, the dirt poor. If you do not take her, there will be no group here."

Many of the women were making payments on two or three different types of loans, each with its own skinny passbook in which repayments and a running balance were recorded weekly. Brown passbooks were used for general loans (given for off-farm enterprises such as livestock-raising, trading, and net-weaving) and newer seasonal loans (sanctioned for borrowers whose families were involved in agriculture, usually on a sharecropper basis). General loans were normally in the range of 5,000 to 6,000 taka ($125 to $150) for fifth- and sixth-time borrowers. Seasonal loans tended to be half that amount.

Much-coveted pink books signified housing loans given to borrowers able to demonstrate a strong need for a new house and a dependable income source capable of paying a loan back in weekly installments of at least 40 taka. Blue and yellow passbooks were for recording savings in accounts that were managed by the entire center or individual groups. Each borrower in the center deposited 3 taka of savings per week, one into the special savings fund, one into the children's welfare fund, and one into the group fund.

It took forty-five minutes for Rohim to mark up all the passbooks. In each case, he took the booklets from the group chairperson, who sat on the extreme right-hand side of her row. Rohim first counted the money from each group, making sure it matched the amount due, which he had calculated the day before. Then he deducted the installment from the previous week's balance in the passbook and made a corresponding mark on his collection sheet. After all that was complete, he handed a ragged wad of bills to Shandha, who placed them in piles according to their denominations. Ten-taka notes were the most common, though there were quite a few 100s, 50s, and 20s.

As Rohim went through his paperwork, he occasionally looked up, trying to get a sense of how the women interacted with one another. He noticed a lot of touching, giggling, gossiping. Some seemed to talk primarily with members of their row, while others were more ambitious, carrying on animated dialogues with women from several different groups at once. A few were preoccupied with their children, who lay asleep in their laps; Khulsum Begum, a member of the fourth group, spent the entire meeting breast-feeding her young son. Those who expended more energy in their conversations were, by the end of the meeting, drenched in sweat. The quieter ones were able to keep dry by wiping their faces with their saris.

Rohim noticed the one piece that was out of place in this sweaty mosaic of weathered faces, skinny arms, and colorful saris—Devi Rani Haldar, a proficient fishnet weaver and influential borrower in the fourth group. She sat outside the center hut on a bamboo mat. Rohim wondered why, but decided not to ask. Several weeks later he heard Devi's story. Three years before, a traditional healer in the village had given Devi some advice on how to overcome infertility. She was told she would be more likely to conceive if she kept a greater distance from groups of people; this would give a baby "space" to be created and grow inside her womb. From that day forward, she sat outside the center hut rather than huddling with her group and center members. After following this advice for eighteen months, Devi became pregnant and in due course delivered a healthy baby girl. She continued sitting outside in hopes of getting pregnant a second time.

When all the preliminary computing was complete, Rohim began a series of cross-checks to make sure the figures and the cash he had collected added up. (Were he to fall short once he arrived back at the office, he would have to make up the difference from his own meager salary.) Finally he counted all the stacks of bills, and when that sum came out to 6,400 taka, the accounting was finished.

Rohim turned his attention to the five women sitting in the seventh row. Throughout the meeting they had remained quiet, and had not forwarded any passbooks or money; this last group was still in its training period.

Diverting his gaze to the center chief, he asked, "Amodini, you know that today is the day for the group *shikriti* [recognition]?"

"Yes, sir."

The five women were now staring directly at him, each looking like a deer caught in a set of oncoming headlights.

"Group number seven, stand up," Rohim barked. The women briefly looked at one another before rising in unison. "I'll be coming here at four-thirty this afternoon. With me will be the manager and a senior manager from the area office in Tepra. He will test you on all that you have learned in your group training." Rohim paused, studying the women as they began, one by one, to divert their eyes from his. "Are you ready?" Three of the women adjusted their saris, covering more than half their faces in the process.

Nobirun Begum, the group chairman,* volunteered a feeble "Yes, sir" in a barely audible whisper. Rohim lifted his eyebrows in mock anger and looked at Amodini, who immediately stood up and shouted, "Speak up." As she spoke, her long bony arms pointed threateningly toward the women six rows behind her. Several drops of perspiration dripped from Amodini's forehead onto Bedana, one of her group members, who was crouching below.

"Yes, sir," the women repeated in unison.

"Are they going to pass?" Rohim asked Amodini.

"Yes, sir," she replied firmly. "We've worked hard training them. They'll be ready."

"Make sure to get them here by four o'clock."

---

*Modern colloquial Bengali uses many English words. In referring to the woman who is the elected leader of each group, Grameen staff and borrowers use the word "chairman."

Rohim bundled together the wad of bills with four rubber bands, sticking them and the collection sheet in his bag. Looking at Amodini, and then at his watch, he said, "End the meeting."

"*Kendro . . . Aram . . . Kendro . . . Aram . . . Kendro.*" With each instruction, the women changed the position of their arms, stretching them forward with their elbows touching their knees on the first command and folding them across their knees on the second.

"May I have permission to end the meeting, sir," Amodini asked in a firm but respectful voice.

"End it."

When he called out "*Aek,*" the women stood up, again causing a chorus of cracking knee joints and a few poorly suppressed sighs. On "*Dui,*" the women resumed their crouch. After repeating the standing and crouching once more, they were called to their feet and ordered to prepare to give the salute meant to symbolize the Muslim farewell greeting of "*Salaam,*" short for "*As Salaam o Aleikum,*" meaning "May peace be with you" in Arabic.

On the count of "*Aek,*" the women saluted Rohim and he returned the gesture. On the count of "*Dui*" they put their arms at their sides, and on "*Teen*" they resumed their crouch.

The meeting over, Rohim exchanged a few words with Amodini in private, then rushed off to center number forty-two. After he left, many of the women lingered for a while, savoring a brief respite from their work and the opportunity it presented for gossip. The five women in group number seven huddled with Shandha and Amodini, discussing how to make sure that they all arrived at the center house on time. When that was settled, each of the trainees grabbed a stick from a pile of firewood Shandha had collected, knelt down, and began carving her signature in the dirt. Shandha and Amodini stood over the women, holding hands as they inspected the prospective borrowers' work.

Nonibala Ghosh, the perennial chairman of group number two, was long since gone. She and her family had a massive job ahead of them that day—procuring more than seventy gallons of milk, turning it into *chhana* (cottage cheese), and delivering it by dusk to a confectionery shop in Dhaka more than sixty miles away.

To accomplish this, all they had at their disposal was a few thousand taka in working capital, an industrial-size tin pan, a clay oven, and two rickety bicycles. Nonibala would have liked to gossip and help train the new group, but the clock was ticking. She had no time to lose.

Except on national holidays, every weekday* some 6,000 Grameen Bank employees set off by foot, bicycle, or boat to take part in 10,000 meetings attended by more than 300,000 poor women living in tiny hamlets scattered across Bangladesh. By noon, the bank workers travel a combined distance exceeding one and a half times the circumference of the globe and collect, count, and deposit millions of taka in small bills—all without turning on a single car, motorcycle, or computer.

The women and men they meet with in cramped bamboo houses are taking part in one of the world's most daring experiments in rural development; they are borrowers and owners of the Grameen Bank, and by 1993 their numbers had swelled to 1.5 million and their combined monthly credit requirement to the equivalent of $20 million. Loans they receive are invested in more than five hundred income-generating enterprises as diverse as cow-fattening, rice-husking, trading, tailoring, and weaving.

When Rohim returned to the branch office from his first meeting with the women, he parked his bicycle outside with the others and took his seat behind a wooden table that he shared with Abdul Mustafiz, another bank employee. As he began the long process of entering all the installments into their respective ledgers by hand, a task that would take nearly two hours, Rohim was startled by a scream. Abdul Ahlim, a fellow bank worker, had been hit by a small chunk of concrete that had fallen from the office's crumbling ceiling as he was walking to his desk. Seven women sitting on a long bench, waiting for loans they would receive later that day, looked on in dismay. Several inspected the ceiling above where they were sitting, apparently trying to anticipate any debris that might

---

*In Bangladesh, the workweek is Saturday through Wednesday, with a half day on Thursday, which, in the Grameen Bank, is reserved for clearing the weekly accounts.

fall on them. As the office boy began sweeping up the debris, Ah-lim, apparently unhurt, brushed himself off, and Rohim and the others returned to their paperwork.

A smell of dried sweat filled the air, and dust that the hot summer wind was whipping up had begun to enter from the two windows facing east. Rohim took his handkerchief, wiped his face, and scanned the room. Never before had he been posted at such a remote and backward branch office. Damn it, he thought to himself, whatever possessed me to take this job in the first place? Without pausing to answer his own question, Rohim dipped his right forefinger into a small damp sponge in a plastic tray given to all Grameen Bank employees as a work aid, flipped the page in the loan ledger, and began entering another loan payment he had collected from center number two.

Founding a branch in Zianpur had not been an easy task. In 1987, Shah Alam was the zonal manager in charge of some one hundred branches. He is a brusque man—most who work for him simply call him "the big sir." Founding a branch in Zianpur was his personal project, a bold statement that he had the nerve to open an office in a place so poor and remote that most of his colleagues wouldn't go anywhere near it. The area included *chars* (large silt sandbars that shift every few years) to the west where people were forced to move periodically to stay a step ahead of the river. (Grameen employees are told in their training period to avoid recruiting *aosthayee*—transitory—people as members, as they are the most likely to take a loan and disappear before repaying it.) The people there lived in grinding poverty reinforced by superstition, lawlessness, and a near-complete lack of government services. Some thought that the area was too backward even for Grameen.

After one candidate fled at the sight of the place, Shah Alam chose Abdul Mannan Talukdar for the job. Mannan was one of the first Grameen employees to rise from the position of bank worker to become a manager. Shah Alam knew that Mannan came from Sirajganj, where there were similar problems of migration from shifting rivers, and figured that he would be less intimidated than most of his peers in such an environment. When Shah Alam picked him up in a far-flung area of southern Sylhet and dropped him near Zianpur, the local managers didn't think he had a chance.

Mannan's first night in the Zianpur bazaar was spent in an abandoned room of the union *porishod* building, with only a thin mattress and bedsheet he had brought with him separating his body from the cement floor. Some biscuits he had bought from the only tea stall in the bazaar served as dinner.

The next morning he began a hastily arranged series of more than a hundred meetings in fifteen villages. People doubted what he said about the Grameen Bank program he was going to bring to the area. Loans to women? Loans to the poor? One rumor suggested that this "bank" was a front for an organization that would kidnap women and send them to the Chittagong Hill Tracts, a jungle that the government was trying to colonize with ethnic Bengalis. Another asserted that Grameen Bank was a Christian missionary organization.

Mannan's one request at the end of his meetings was that anyone who had even the slightest bit of interest come to an open-air meeting on the field in front of the Zianpur high school. He tried to encourage the villagers, saying that in some nearby districts Grameen Bank had been established and poor people were prospering; if the meeting in Zianpur was well attended, they could have a branch too. He mentioned that a high-ranking official of Grameen Bank would come that day to explain the rules of the bank, and if the crowd was too small he might call off the preparations. Mannan remained confident in public, but he was very anxious.

On the morning of December 5, the appointed day of the meeting, Mannan rolled out of bed after a restless night's sleep. The meeting was to begin at ten o'clock; when the field lay empty at eight-thirty, Mannan began to worry. At nine-thirty, a few people started to trickle in. By this stage, Mannan was in a panic. Would Shah Alam arrive to see a small, uninterested crowd? If he did, would Mannan ever receive another promotion? Little did Mannan know that huge processions of men and women of all ages were, at that very moment, converging on the bazaar from all four corners.

Thirty minutes earlier, Nonibala Ghosh had emerged from her house with the intention of going to the meeting. She was scared, as this was the first time in her life, at age thirty-seven, that she would be going to the Zianpur bazaar. She was relieved to see so many other people heading in the same direction, and set off on the three-mile trek with Zomella, a Muslim neighbor with whom she was friendly.

Back on the field, the zonal manager's car arrived, pushing its way through the crowds that had suddenly descended on the sleepy bazaar. Wave after wave arrived, forcing those who had arrived earlier into an ever-smaller space. Later, shopkeepers claimed it was the largest crowd ever to gather at the bazaar.

Shah Alam was worried that the crowd was too large. At the time, the country was under martial law that prohibited meetings at which more than five people participated, and here were at least five thousand people waiting to hear him speak. He took the microphone and begged the latest arrivals to turn around and go home. Students who had agreed to help Mannan were instructed to form human barricades at all entrances to the field.

Desperate to get the crowd to disperse, he gave only a perfunctory description of the bank and promised that a branch would be created. Slowly, and after considerable exhortation, the crowd began to break up.

Nonibala Ghosh remembered well the walk home. Some were still convinced that the bank would never sanction a single taka to lend to any poor person in the area. Others took Mannan and the zonal manager at their word. Still others continued to circulate the rumors about Grameen being a missionary organization.

Nonibala paid attention to the discussions swirling around her as she walked. Yet her main preoccupation centered on a single question: How could she get into a Grameen Bank group as soon as possible?

Rukia Begum, a member of the seventh group-in-formation, stuck her head out of her tiny, rotting thatch hut, squinted, and looked at the sun. From its position in the sky she realized it was time to leave for her group recognition test, an oral exam given to prospective Grameen Bank members after their training period. Fixing her sari, she contemplated the nausea she felt and the volume of material she and the other members of her group had memorized. For a moment, she thought she was going to vomit.

The purpose in giving an oral exam to all prospective members of Grameen Bank is twofold. First, it requires them to demonstrate that they understand the rules of the bank, making it more difficult for an unscrupulous bank employee to take advantage of them. It also makes it easier for them to recruit new members once they begin borrowing. The idea is that this is their bank and they must assume their ownership role with eyes open, understanding each and every rule.

An integral part of the bank's regulations is the social constitution known as the Sixteen Decisions, which was drawn up by a meeting of center chiefs in 1984. It was the bank's attempt to respond to the social dimensions of poverty, a series of rules to ease the workings of the bank and help borrowers help themselves out of poverty. They included limiting the size of the family, educating children, not accepting or giving dowry, planting vegetable gardens and fruit-bearing trees, and building sanitary pit latrines. Other decisions were more philosophical; for instance, members pledged to help one another and not let anyone do injustice to them. Borrowers were required to memorize these commitments as part of their group training, the staff was urged to motivate members to implement them, and a special programs division that received funding from UNICEF organized workshops and delivered supplies (such as iodized salt and vegetable seeds) in hopes of speeding their realization.

Perhaps the most important purpose of the recognition test is to allow the area manager or his assistant to observe how new members respond to a demanding male authority figure. Can a woman speak loudly and clearly while looking an area manager in the eye? When pushed by a male authority figure, does it seem that she will agree to *anything*, or can she stand up for herself? In short, the bank wants to know whether a lifetime of oppression by the dominant gender has left a prospective member so pliant that she would turn over money she had received from the bank to a male without raising a fuss. The bank leaders want to have some confidence that in such a case, the woman would alert her group members and center chief and ask them to intervene. With the exception of ill health, the most frequent cause of missed installments and default among Grameen Bank members is male relatives forcing borrowers to disinvest in their business venture and hand over their money.

With her daughter hoisted on her hip, Rukia looked briefly at her niece's son, closed her eyes, and said a prayer. "I'm coming back," she said softly. It was not clear anyone was listening.

Rukia began walking on a narrow village path strewn with animal and human excrement, which after an eighth of a mile joined up with the raised dirt road that cut through the heart of Kholshi. She quickened her pace, not wanting to be the last to arrive at the center house. As it turned out, she was the fourth to arrive, with Nobirun being the last.

At 4:25, Rohim walked briskly into the center house. Three chairs were already arranged in the front end of the hut, one for Rohim, one for Jobbar Ali, the manager, and one for the area manager, Siraj-ul Islam Bhuyian. Before Rohim could lose his temper about Nobirun being late, the group chairman arrived and assumed her position on the end of her row. Outside the house, Shandha and Amodini crouched down, their knees barely touching as they sat.

In February 1988, the first two groups of Shandha's center had been recognized and had begun meeting every Tuesday morning at eight o'clock. During the next twelve months, another four were added. In April 1993, a seventh group was finally being prepared for group recognition. Rohim's job was to ensure that this group was trained the right way and made progress out of poverty in the coming year. It was a challenge he had met elsewhere, but it still thrilled and frightened him.

Rohim turned his attention to the chairs. Which one would he sit on? Which one would the area manager sit on? Suddenly, the sound of a motorcycle engine was audible, and in a moment the vehicle was visible. Some fifty children from all over the village chased the motorcycle as it approached Shandha's home, carefully negotiating the narrow pathway through a field of shimmering paddy.

In an act of bravado, Siraj drove up the slope leading to Shandha's courtyard, almost losing balance halfway there. As he turned off the engine, put down the kickstand, and removed his helmet, he looked behind him at the advancing army of children for whom this was the closest they had ever gotten to motorized transport. Jobbar Ali, who had been sitting in back of the area manager, ran his fingers through his hair nervously and scanned the scene, checking that all the pieces were in place.

Rohim saluted the area manager, who returned the greeting casually as he entered the center house. As Siraj took a step toward the chair reserved for him, Amodini poked another member of the group, Korimun, in the ribs with her finger and Nobirun called out, *"Aek."* The five women stood up together, their eyes trained on the man they had never seen before.

Siraj sat down in the chair, his puffy face trying to restrain a trademark smile. "Sit down," he said to the women. Everyone in the hut, including Jobbar and Rohim, took their seats. Rukia began looking at the ground, her lips moving slowly as she repeated something to herself.

"Begin the meeting," Siraj said.

Nothing happened. Korimun Begum, sitting next to Nobirun, grabbed her chairman's foot with her right hand and squeezed. Nobirun, startled, jumped to her feet.

"Are you feeling sleepy? Perhaps we should come back another time?" Siraj had decided that the time for good humor was past.

"Kendro . . . Aram . . . Kendro . . . Aram . . . Kendro . . ." At each command, the women repeated the ritual movements of their arms that had been performed at the center meeting that morning.

"May we begin this special meeting, sir?" Nobirun asked.

"Begin the meeting."

"Aek." The four women stood up. On *"Dui,"* they reassumed their crouches. *"Aek . . . Dui . . . Aek . . . Dui . . . Aram."* The women assumed a relaxed crouch, and several looked at the children, many of whom were giggling. Amodini, with a wild look in

her eyes, stood up and began shooing away the youngsters. Many would flee, then return minutes later.

"May I sit down, sir?"

Siraj frowned as he studied Nobirun and then the other four women, all crouching five feet in front of him. "Sit down," he said flatly after a long pause.

After introducing himself to the women as the local area manager who supervised their branch and eight others like it, he called Nobirun to her feet and asked her to tell him her name and that of the center and group she was hoping to become a member of. Then he asked her to recite the responsibilities of being a group chairman. Slowly, with her eyes trained on the roof of the hut, she told him what he already knew: that a group chairman was elected each year in the month of Choitro and was responsible for every aspect of the group's performance—utilization of the loan for the stated purpose, attendance at weekly meetings (including signing the attendance register), and, of course, timely payment of installments.

"What is the eleventh decision?" he asked finally.

Nobirun began covering her sad-looking, weathered face with her sari, then resisted the urge and let it drop. "Decision number eleven . . . We shall neither take nor receive dowry in our children's weddings. We shall eliminate the curse of dowry from our center. We shall also not engage in child marriage."

Siraj crossed his legs, sighed, and asked Nobirun to sit down. After asking Korimun, Zorina, and Alow a few questions, he turned to Rukia. As she stood, her child woke up and began to cry. Before Siraj could say anything, Amodini grabbed the little boy and put him in her lap as she reassumed a crouch outside the hut. Looking Rukia in the eye, the area manager asked, "In what different ways is money deposited in the group fund?"

Rukia opened her mouth slightly, but nothing came out. Thirty seconds passed, then a minute. Terror spread among the squatting women as Rukia's eyes glazed over.

"Don't you understand the question?" Siraj tried. Silence. "Well, tell me decision number six."

Zorina covered her mouth and began reciting it softly, so that

Rukia would hear and be reminded. "We shall keep our families small, we shall . . ."

Jobbar Ali's face flushed as he said to Zorina, "The question was for *her,* not *you!*"

Another minute passed, and Rukia began crying softly. Her legs became unsteady, and without warning she reassumed her crouch.

By then, it was over. They had failed the group recognition test.

Word spread quickly through the village that Nobirun's group had failed, and within a few days three of the women—Korimun, Zorina, and the unfortunate Rukia—were wavering on whether they wanted to go through with it a second time. Apparently, they felt that they had been humiliated enough already. Eager to have their center rebound from such a setback, older members began spreading the word that there were openings for as many as three new members in the seventh group.

Amena Begum heard the news from her Hindu neighbor Oloka Ghosh, a borrower who had joined Nonibala Ghosh's group in 1990. Oloka had used her loans to build up a business making sweets (the livelihood assigned to those in her caste), trading milk, and raising cows. Three years and thousands of taka later, she wanted to encourage Amena to get involved. Oloka knew that Amena's son had recently been ill, and that the family had been forced to disinvest from its business to pay for medical treatment. She had also heard the rumors that Amena's husband beat her.

Amena Begum, a relatively tall Muslim woman with a slight build and a nervous smile, had arrived in Kholshi three years earlier. She had taken refuge at her grandfather's homestead land after the place she had been staying with her husband and in-laws had been swallowed up by the Ganges River. The journey to Kholshi, almost ten years after her marriage, had been a difficult one.

Just under her chin, but plainly visible, is a scar that is nearly an inch long; it is a reminder of the time her husband beat her with a bicycle chain until she lost consciousness. That incident, and many others, had motivated her to take refuge with her grandfather; she hoped that her husband would go easy on her if she was surrounded by her relatives. (Her in-laws seemed to encourage the practice.) And indeed, the beatings had abated somewhat.

Amena, her husband, and their four children were squatters on her grandfather's land; on the day they arrived, they began clearing a small patch in an overgrown jungle where they were told they could build a house. After selling virtually everything they owned, they were able to build a small hut for 8,000 taka ($200). They had no furniture, and slept side by side on a blanket and some straw they laid on the ground. Her husband began working in the family's traditional business—selling aluminum cookware. It was not a lucrative enterprise, but it was the best they could do.

Amena had looked in on a center meeting being held near Shandha's hut. She had heard about Grameen, and was curious to see what it was. She thought *that* was the bank—a single hut, with one man and thirty women sitting inside of it. She had no idea there were other centers and employees, not to mention a concrete building in Zianpur. As the meeting broke up, Amena had hurried away, hoping that no one would see her. But Oloka Ghosh, her neighbor, had caught a glimpse of her, and now, more than a year later, brought her the news of the opening in group number seven.

Within days, Amena met Nobirun and Alow, who were determined to pass this second time, and two other new trainees—Fulzan Begum and Firoza Khatoon. They studied quickly, learning all the information from both Rohim and older members like Amodini and Shandha. Amena was forced to miss a few training sessions because of illness (she was pregnant with her fifth child), but everyone was relieved when they heard that Oloka was giving her supplementary training in her home. Having studied as far as third grade, Amena had an easier time learning the material than the other women, who had not gotten that far in school.

On the appointed day, the women were told to come to another center in Kholshi; they were one of six groups being tested that day. Amodini and Shandha went with the fivesome, and when the area manager came to them, he recognized Nobirun and quickly scanned the other faces. He was behind on his work that day—he had more group recognitions to perform at another branch—and decided to take a shortcut. He picked out the new member who looked the most timid and decided to ask her one question and one question only. If she got it right, they passed.

He pointed to Fulzan, and when she was able to recite decision number ten—"We shall build and use pit latrines"—the women were astonished to hear that they had received their recognition, pending the area manager's inspection of their homes (done to make sure new borrowers are in fact poor enough to be eligible to join). That was easy; none of the five women was in danger of being outside of Grameen Bank's target group—the landless and assetless, the "poorest of the poor."

When a new group becomes eligible for loans, two women, normally the poorest in the group, make a loan proposal, which will in most cases receive formal approval by the bank in several days. The first line of defense against bad business decisions is not the bank or its employees, but rather the other women in the group. If the first two borrowers to receive loans have any difficulty repaying, the remaining three will have their proposals delayed, reduced in amount, or, in extreme cases, denied altogether. Each member therefore has strong incentives to scrutinize her fellow borrowers' loan proposals and to apply a delicate combination of pressure and support to ensure that the money is invested properly and that the business succeeds. In practice, this means that poor families that would normally have no relationship, or perhaps an antagonistic relationship born of religious or caste differences or a generations-old feud, are almost forced to help each other. A group member might tip off a fellow borrower to the fact that she is about to buy a cow that is suffering from a disease likely to kill it—even if the seller is a relative. Another might help steer business, including her own, to a woman in her group. The impersonal forces of supply and demand are thus softened by a network of friends who want you to succeed for financial if not humanitarian reasons.

For a woman to get into such a network, husbands and village elders may need to be defied, and rules and regulations will need to be memorized, trust built up, and, finally, the group recognition test passed. For women like Amena and Fulzan, isolated from their society by illiteracy, poverty, and custom, these are considerable obstacles. A weeding-out process inevitably occurs; the loss of three women from group number seven after their humiliating failure to pass the test was not unusual. Sometimes, when dropouts occur, village elders complain about Grameen's policy of not forming men's centers. But by the mid-1980s, Grameen's senior management had concluded that women repaid their loans—and attended meetings—more regularly than men; furthermore, there was ample evidence to suggest that lending to a family's husband helped the husband, whereas lending to the wife helped the entire family. As a result, the percentage of women borrowers in Grameen had been steadily increasing, from 50 percent in the early 1980s to more than 90 percent a decade later.

On a hot spring day in 1993, group number seven and center chief Amodini headed off for the Zianpur bazaar. Fulzan and Alow were to receive their loans that day, having been notified at the meeting the previous Tuesday that their loan proposals had been approved. All the women got into their best saris, which in the case of the new borrowers were neither very new nor very attractive. Amodini wore a fresh-looking green sari with red trim, and when the clouds dispersed she opened up a black umbrella she had bought used for 70 taka. As center chief, she had to accompany any borrower who was going for a loan. As she walked down the dirt road that connects Kholshi to Zianpur with this spanking-new group—women who had never been to the area's central bazaar in their lives—Amodini recalled her own entry into the bank six years earlier.

Her group included three other net weavers and Rasheda. They, together with Nonibala's group, were trained by Ruhul Amin, a bank worker they remember as a strict disciplinarian. And then there was Aduree, poor Aduree. Everyone had been opposed to her joining the center. Hers was perhaps the poorest family in the entire village. One measure of her destitution was that of her thirty-four siblings (including many half sisters and brothers), only eight had lived past the age of five; twenty-six had succumbed before that age to hunger and disease. When she wanted to join one of the first two groups, everyone said no. "What if she dies, or her husband dies?" people asked. "She will default, and we will have to repay—those are the rules of the bank."

In desperation, Aduree, a Muslim, approached Nonibala, who had appeared to oppose her entry with less conviction than any of the others. Every day she came to her, begging her Hindu neighbor to stand up for her and let her into a group. Finally, Nonibala relented and told the other women that she alone would bear the risk of Aduree's default. That opened that door wide enough for Aduree to jump in. When Ruhul Amin and the manager suggested a 500-taka ($13) loan for Aduree, Nonibala supported her new friend in arguing for one three times as large. Again, they prevailed.

As the six women approached the northern tip of the Zianpur bazaar, Amodini smiled. Aduree had not only never missed a payment in six years, but had become something of a disciplinarian in the center, admonishing women who arrived even a few minutes late to their weekly meeting.

When the bazaar came into sight, Amodini noticed that the women's eyes had bulged as they took in sights they had never seen before—so many tin sheds so close together, the crush of people, men sitting in a tea shop, staring at them as they walked by. Amodini pointed to the Grameen Bank office. Again, she noticed the women stare with wonder at something they had never seen before—a concrete building.

As they entered the office, Amodini motioned the women to a bench against the wall while she walked up to Rohim's desk and informed him that they had arrived. He looked up from his paperwork and smiled at his center chief. "Is the group chairman here?"

"Yes, sir," Amodini answered.

"I'll call for you when the papers are ready."

Amodini walked over to where the women had huddled. Many of the people around them spoke in an animated and excited manner, but they were silent.

As Fulzan looked around the office, she studied each of the eight men who were sitting behind wooden tables arranged to form an inverted U. Five men sat facing the wall against which the women sat, and two were to their right, looking straight ahead at the desk where the manager sat alone on the other end of the office. They seemed so purposeful to her; she'd had no idea that there were so many bank employees like Rohim.

As she sat there, the enormity of what she was involving herself in overwhelmed her. Did they all know that she was a ditchdigger, one of that handful of women for whom poverty had become so extreme that she had been forced to compete for jobs that were normally reserved for men? Did they know that at that very moment her sister, who lived in a dilapidated thatch hut next to hers, was going around the village begging? Had some mistake been made?

"Fulzan Begum, come here," Rohim barked without looking up, interrupting her thoughts. "Alow Khatoon, you also come here." The two women, accompanied by their center chief, approached the table that their bank worker was sitting behind. Following Amodini's lead, they stopped just short of the desk and stood at attention. The two women's faces reflected the tension of the moment.

"The manager," Rohim began as he looked up from his papers, "will ask you some questions about the rules of the bank and your loan, as at a group recognition. Will you be ready?"

"Yes, sir," Amodini answered.

"You had better make sure they are prepared." Looking at Fulzan, he said, "Okay, you sign this," pointing as he spoke, "here and here." He made the same request of Alow, and after they had signed, he asked them to sit down and wait until the manager called them.

Fulzan began watching as the manager started handing out bunches of bills to groups of women who were gathering around his table. At the side of the table stood a man who was dressed similarly to Rohim; he must be their bank worker, she guessed. It was at this moment that she realized she had never in her life touched any bill larger than a 10-taka note. Often she was paid in wheat for her work as a ditchdigger, but on rare occasions she was paid in cash—3 taka for a full day's work when she started working twelve years ago, and more recently 26 taka (65 cents)—that would come in 10-taka, 5-taka, and 1-taka notes. Fulzan leaned over to Alow and asked, "Have you ever touched a twenty-taka note before?" With a blank look on her face, Alow replied, "I've never touched *any* taka before."

Rohim looked toward the benches, and his eyes met Amodini's. Not a word was spoken. They both knew it was time. The Hindu fishnet weaver tapped Fulzan on the leg and stood up. The other women followed her to the table.

These were to be the twenty-fourth and twenty-fifth loans that Jobbar Ali would give out today, though the first to new borrowers. He studied the group, his eyes fixing on each one briefly. All but Amodini averted their gaze when he looked at them. "Fulzan Begum?"

"Yes, sir," she replied in a whisper.

"What is the group fund?"

"It is . . . it is . . ." Beneath the table, Amodini gently grabbed Fulzan's left hand and squeezed. "It is an account," she finally blurted out.

"Who owns the group fund?"

"Uh, the five members of the group."

"Are you sure?"

"Yes, sir."

"How much did you ask for in your loan proposal?"

"Fifteen hundred taka, sir." She looked at a small pile of blue and white currency notes near the manager's right hand. Her heart raced, and she squeezed Amodini's hand harder.

"Your loan proposal passed. How much will you receive in your hands today?"

"Thirteen hundred seventy-five taka." Amodini had prepared her for that question, and she was proud to answer it in a loud voice that was beginning to suggest confidence.

"Where will the other taka be deposited?"

"In the group fund."

"And what will you use your loan for?"

"I will buy a cow and sell the milk."

Jobbar Ali looked down, counted the bills, handed them to Rohim for a recount, and then placed them and a slip of paper into a crisp brown passbook. As he held it over his desk with right hand,

Fulzan slowly reached forward. Her hand was shaking, and her lips began to tremble. Slowly, she wrapped her fingers around the passbook and, as the manager released his grip, brought it toward her. She stared at it at her side, but didn't open it at first.

"In the name of the Almighty Allah," Jobbar Ali offered, "use it well." Rohim looked on approvingly, and a broad smile broke out on Amodini's face. As attention turned to her new friend Alow, Fulzan finally let go of her center chief's hand and opened the passbook. There she saw notes larger than any she had ever seen before—100-taka bills. After staring at them for a brief moment, she closed her eyes and took a long, deep breath.

4

▲

Les Papillons

From 1976, the Ford Foundation's office in Bangladesh had been supporting Yunus's work with small grants, first to the Rural Economics Program and later to the Grameen Bank Project in Tangail. After Grameen became an independent bank in 1983, Yunus approached Ford with a request for funding to expand in the Dhaka, Patuakhali, Chittagong, and Rangpur districts. He worked out how much money he would need on his calculator, wrote a proposal in longhand, and presented it to Ford program officer Steve Biggs, who wanted to have some people with experience in banking to look at Grameen before he approved the grant.

After Biggs consulted with Foundation officials in New York, it was decided that Mary Houghton and Ron Grzywinski of the South Shore Bank in Chicago should come. Yunus agreed: their résumés suggested that they were asking the same sorts of questions about poverty, institution building, and community development that he was. As Houghton recalls, "We were chosen because we were the bankers who looked the least like bankers."

Houghton and Grzywinski had joined with two friends and raised the capital to buy the South Shore Bank, located in a struggling South Chicago neighborhood, which had been on the verge of failure. Under their leadership, South Shore Bank restored the community's confidence in it, won its depositors back, and began lending to people and businesses other banks would have avoided. They came to Bangladesh twice in 1983, and were intrigued by Yunus and what he was doing. After analyzing Yunus's five-year plan for Grameen, they recommended that Ford fund it, and went beyond their brief by suggesting that the Foundation pay for Yunus to come to Chicago to explore the possibility of replicating his program in the United States. Houghton, in particular, had been concerned about the plight of poor, inner-city women and low-income entrepreneurs and had been informally researching strategies that could address their problems. She was honest enough to admit to herself that her bank, for all its success, related to South Shore's poor mostly as depositors or as residents of the low-income housing that was renovated with its loans. She realized that others, of course, were benefiting from being employed by neighborhood businesses that were able to expand after receiving much-needed financing from South Shore. But she sensed that there was a pent-up demand for tiny amounts of credit among poor people in Chicago who wanted to start or expand small businesses, and believed that South Shore Bank was not meeting it. Grameen's group-based format struck her as a potential way to meet this demand.

Yunus came to Chicago in 1985, and a series of meetings was arranged with the staff of South Shore Bank and nonprofit organizations. People were skeptical about the idea of the Grameen model working in inner-city Chicago, but Yunus won over several of his critics. One University of Chicago scholar, for example, had had some disillusioning experiences working in India and was convinced Houghton had been bamboozled by Yunus. He felt certain that no program of any size on the Indian subcontinent could be free from corruption. But when he met Yunus in person, the sociologist became a convert.

Much of the discussion centered on Yunus's description of Grameen Bank's target group—"the poorest of the poor." In the United States, he was told, the poorest people need social services, not investment capital. But Yunus held firm, saying that his program was designed to work with the poorest and that he had no interest in working seriously with people if they didn't share his commitment. He recounted similar arguments that Bengali academics had confronted him with when he was getting started in Jobra, and reiterated his philosophy that every human being had the capacity to use credit to get out of poverty. Recalling those conversations, Houghton says, "While for most of us it was a leap of faith to believe what Yunus was saying, we *wanted* to believe it was true." So they kept listening.

At one meeting, Yunus asked a participant what he thought a poor person would need to start or expand a small business in the United States. He was shocked by the answer—$50,000. Yunus went on to say that if there weren't people who were willing to take loans under $5,000, and capable of making a go of it with that amount, then there were no poor people in Chicago that a Grameen-style program could help.

It would take several more trips between Dhaka and Chicago over the next few years for Houghton and several colleagues to establish the Women's Self-Employment Project (WSEP), one of the earliest attempts to replicate the Grameen methodology in the United States.

On his second Ford-sponsored trip to the States in February 1986, Yunus met Bill and Hillary Clinton in a restaurant in Washington, and both expressed enthusiasm about starting a Grameen spin-off in Arkansas, where Bill Clinton was governor. Hillary Clinton, Yunus remembers, was especially gung ho. "She wanted to start right away!" he recalls. Yunus had just returned from his first visit to Arkansas, where he was driven through rural areas to meet with "the poor" in order to judge the feasibility of adapting the Grameen approach there. He told the Clintons that he thought the program had a good chance of success in Arkansas.

The trip had got off on the wrong foot. His hosts—senior officials from the state government, South Shore, and the Rockefeller Foundation—thought Yunus appeared less and less interested in meeting with the local people at each successive stop. Later he would complain that he didn't think that any of the small-business owners he was supposed to meet were poor. Didn't they understand that Grameen was for poor people? Yunus remembers thinking. He thought his time was being wasted. On the second day,

Yunus persuaded the man from the foundation to bring him to meet some unemployed people and welfare recipients. It was at this point that Yunus began showing interest in the discussions.

Years later, Yunus recalled, "I asked the welfare recipients and unemployed people, 'Suppose that your bank lends you money to do something—what kind of thing would you decide to do?' Almost everybody said that a bank would not give them money, so why bother to talk about it. I said, 'Suppose they *would* lend you money.' I got more blank stares. 'Look, I run a bank in Bangladesh that lends money to the poor people there. I just had a meeting with Governor Clinton and he asked me to bring my bank to your community. I am thinking of starting a bank right here. Now I am trying to find out if somebody is interested in borrowing money from me. Because if there is no business, why should I come here?' I mentioned that my bank does not need any collateral, nothing.

"A woman who had listened very carefully said, 'Oh, I would like to borrow some money from your bank!' I said, 'Okay, now we are in business. How much money would you like?'

"She said, 'I would like three hundred seventy-five dollars.' I was surprised, because normally people don't say 'three hundred seventy-five dollars,' they make it a round figure, so I asked her what she wants to do with this sum. She said that she was a beautician, and that her business was limited because she did not have all the right supplies. If she could get a box of supplies costing three hundred seventy-five dollars, she was sure she could pay me back with the extra income. She also said she did not want to take a penny more than what the box actually costs."

Another woman, unemployed after the textile factory she'd been working at closed and moved its business to Taiwan, needed a few hundred dollars for a sewing machine. Still another woman wanted $600 to buy a pushcart from which to sell her hot tamales, which she informed the Bangladeshi professor were "famous" in her neighborhood. These interviews tickled Yunus, and he regretted that the trip was nearing its end.

One of the final interviews held during the trip was with a successful black Arkansas rice farmer. Yunus asked the farmer, "How many acres do you plant?"

"Oh, about two thousand."

"Do you have any problem marketing it?"

"No."

"Do you sell it locally?"

"No."

"Oh, you must export it to countries like my home country of Bangladesh, where there are food deficits."

"No."

"Then where *do* you sell it?"

"You see, there are these churches in New York City, and they feed the hungry and those without homes. We call them the homeless here in America. They are a good business for me. Always reliable buyers. The demand gets stronger every year. I just send it to these churches at such and such address, and they have plenty of use for it."

About a week later Yunus was in New York addressing the board of directors of CARE, the largest private relief organization in the world. They had asked him to address the issue of whether there was any reason for CARE to consider beginning operations in the United States. In his address, Yunus talked about Grameen's work in Bangladesh and his experience in Arkansas. One board member raised the issue of whether someone on welfare was actually poor, if you defined the poor as people who went hungry. In response, Yunus said that while he didn't know whether CARE should open a domestic program, he thought there *were* hungry people in the United States. He told the story of meeting the rice farmer in Arkansas, and how he supplied tons of rice to churches that were just a couple of miles north of CARE's office. "If you're not sure where these shelters are exactly, I can give you the phone number of this farmer, and he can tell you the addresses of all his customers up here. Then you can go see for yourselves if there is a hunger problem here in America or not."

Efforts to replicate Grameen's success in other countries got under way in the mid-1980s. Yunus helped a pilot project in Malaysia start up in 1986. The Malaysians discovered that the more they strayed from the Grameen system, the more problems their project experienced, and that conversely, the more closely they copied what they had seen in Bangladesh, the more success they had. A 1989 delegation recounted their experiences to Yunus and expressed their belief that the Grameen approach had near-universal applicability.

While the Malaysian experiment was progressing, Yunus was coming to the same conclusion on his own: cultures differ, but people are fundamentally the same. To Yunus, the culture of poverty transcended differences in language, climate, race, and custom. Pilot projects modeled after Grameen were springing up on five continents, and many were achieving success. Yunus firmly believed that a large proportion of the 200 million families living in absolute poverty in the world were a $50 or $100 loan away from escaping their predicament.

Many of the arguments he heard against the possibility of adapting Grameen in the United States had a familiar ring, since he had heard them in Bangladesh—that the poor can't invest, that they can't save, that they need training and social services before they can start a business, and so on. But the relative sophistication or general wealth of a society is irrelevant to Yunus. The fundamental point is always the same: the worst-off in any country are denied credit, the access to which, under the right conditions, can dramatically alleviate their poverty.

In August 1990 Yunus was sitting in his office in Dhaka, trying to write a speech that he would deliver several weeks later in Miami, Florida. He jotted down some notes concerning the ways banks don't recognize the intrinsic worth and capacity of human beings but simply look at the condition of their clothes and their collateral (or lack thereof). His bank didn't take any of these things into account, and he was searching for a way to illustrate the feasibility of his approach to an American audience.

Yunus always opens his own mail. On that day, he received a letter from a Tennessee woman named Tami White, who had read about Grameen and somehow located its address. "When I was a child trying to open up a simple savings account," she wrote, "I was put off by the bank's demand that I produce two pieces of photo identification. What would a child be doing with photo ID in the first place?"

White's experiences with banks since becoming an adult had not noticeably improved. "My mother recently received a $500 money order refund from the U.S. government," she continued, "to pay her back for a money order the post office had lost. She took it to the bank we were using, the day we went to close our accounts, and they refused to cash it for her because, as they said, 'You no longer have an account here.' She had to take it to one of the check cashing companies that have sprung up in the United States in recent years and we were shocked when they took 20 percent ($100) as a fee for cashing it.

"I started checking into these places and found that many people are forced to use them, mainly elderly people who live on Social Security checks and the working poor who cannot establish bank accounts because they cannot keep minimum balances, afford the per check charges or service charges, or show the bank they already have good credit. Some people have trouble providing ID to open accounts."

White went on to say that even cashing a paycheck can be difficult. "I always took my paycheck to the very bank it was drawn on and always to one of the same tellers. Every week they insisted on seeing my driver's license, and as if having a state-issued driver's license with my photograph was not enough, they demanded to see a credit card, too—presumably if I am in debt, I must be honest!"

She added, "So to discover you with your faith in people and your willingness to make money work for people in need has delighted me to the very core of my being."

Yunus read the entire letter near the end of his speech in Miami and concluded his remarks by saying, "The system we have built refuses to recognize people. Only credit cards are recognized. Driver's licenses are recognized. But not people.

"People haven't any use for faces anymore, it seems. They are busy looking at your credit card, your driver's license, your Social Security number. If a driver's license is more reliable than the face I wear, then why have a face? A voice? A smell? A touch?"

The title he gave to his speech was "Anything Wrong?"

By the time he delivered the speech, Grameen replication efforts were under way in Chicago, among impoverished rural people in Arkansas, and on an Indian reservation in South Dakota. The grand experiment—to discover whether a revolutionary idea hatched in the Third World could work in fighting First World poverty—had been launched.

On a hot summer afternoon in 1993, Gwen Burns sat at her desk, stared briefly at the bulletin board nestled in the deep recesses of her cubicle, and sighed. Looking at her watch, she saw that it was five-thirty and time to go. She delayed a few more minutes, tidying up a little and collecting what she needed for the meeting—a pad of receipts, pens, a sign-in sheet, and her appointment book. Placing them in her small briefcase, she stood up and walked out of her room, past the workstations of her colleagues Colete, Durga, and Jackie, and into a dark hallway. Before closing the outside door, she turned off the hall lights and flipped the knob that locked up their office.

She walked east on Washington Street in downtown Chicago, passing City Hall on her left. As she stood waiting for the southbound Clark Street bus, Gwen looked at City Hall and the Daley Center, two imposing monuments to those who control Chicago—the renowned "Daley Machine" that she, and many blacks in the Second City, have come to hate so much, without always knowing exactly why.

Gwen Burns was on her way to meet with nearly thirty women whose lives were far removed from the downtown scene. She pondered the fact that three of them had recently fallen behind on their loan payments. She was troubled—not so much because they were having problems in their business, which she understood, but rather because two of the women were becoming resigned to defaulting. Worse still, their "circle sisters" had barely lifted a finger to pressure them to make an effort to repay or to support them. Gwen had initiated a fund-raising campaign, to be organized by the members, to cover the missed payments. Had her prompting been enough, or too much? she wondered. There was a fine line between encouraging the women to come together and show unity and bullying them into it. If she stepped over the line, she knew the campaign would come to nothing.

Gwen caught her bus. As it passed under the train tracks over Van Buren Street, she clutched her bag, trying to recall whether she had brought her book of receipts. When she felt them, it reminded her that she would be leaving the meeting tonight with several hundred dollars in an unpredictable combination of cash, personal checks, and money orders. The morning after meetings with borrowers, Gwen always felt nervous as she went downtown to deposit the money. She had never been robbed with her repayments in hand, but in a city with so much senseless crime, one could never be too careful.

When the bus stopped at Cermak Avenue, Gwen stepped down and began trudging toward her car. Earlier that morning, she had parked it in a huge lot used by many South Siders who work downtown but can't afford to keep their cars in one of the pricey lots near their offices.

There was a pronounced lack of a spring in Gwen's step that Monday evening. The last three years had taken a toll on her. The long hours, the promotion she felt she deserved and didn't get, the fact that her leadership wasn't always recognized, and the bitter rivalry with a young, white, college-educated colleague all weighed her down. Yet as she said a prayer to herself, started her car, and began driving toward the Dan Ryan Expressway, she believed more than ever that the project's goals were righteous and its strategy sound. After all, a soft-spoken man from Bangladesh had told her so.

Of the many programs run by the Women's Self-Employment Project, the one that was the most difficult to launch, and has generated the most interest and controversy, is the Full Circle Fund (FCF). It has the distinction of being an effort to solve poverty in the industrialized world by using a strategy developed in the Third World. It encourages economic development in depressed communities by giving women access to investment capital of $300 to $1,500 if they agree to join a group of five peers and are able to persuade them of the soundness of their business proposal. Prospective borrowers' credit rating or access to collateral are not consulted as part of the process of approving loans.

The WSEP was started in 1986 by Mary Houghton, Elsbeth Revere, and Gail Christopher, with initial funding arranged by Sheila Leahy of the Joyce Foundation. It began by offering a training course for low-income entrepreneurs and setting up a loan fund for those who completed the course and wanted to start or expand a business. The FCF was formally launched in August 1988. The training programs were easier to secure funding for, and Connie Evans, WSEP's first director, was eager to hit the ground running. But after meeting Yunus, Connie committed herself to adapting the Grameen Bank approach as well. Her board debated the pros and cons of such a strategy, with Mary Houghton giving the most vocal support while admitting that South Shore Bank had experienced problems lending to low-income entrepreneurs. Connie and Mary plotted to raise the funds to begin a Grameen spin-off pilot project and send two WSEP staff members to Bangladesh.

When the funding was secured, Connie decided to bring Susan Matteucci, a recently hired MIT graduate, along with her. They wanted some practical experience before they went to Dhaka, so they used a Grameen handbook to set up two groups and dispersed four loans to borrowers before leaving for Bangladesh in November 1988. The two women had profoundly moving experiences in Bangladesh that provided the basis of a strong friendship. They met women like Amodini and Shandha who with the equivalent of $50 had transformed their lives. They spent long sessions with Grameen field staff, a zonal manager named Shamin Anwar, and Yunus. Susan continually had to explain that Connie was the boss, as nearly everyone assumed that the white woman was in charge. (This pattern would continue after they returned to the United States.) By the end of the trip, they jokingly called themselves "Grameen groupies" and vowed to make the program work in Chicago.

The meeting began late, but not without ceremony or some fun and games. Within the sterile confines of a recreation room in the Lindblom Park Field House on Sixty-first Street and South Damen Avenue in the depressed neighborhood of Englewood, Omiyale DuPart stood up and brought silence to the room with a wave of her hand. Omiyale—named Veronica Wilma Ramsey at birth, her adopted African name means "great, overflowing river"—then began the meeting.

"I would like to invite Ms. Pack to lead us in prayer." Twenty-six women, their skins different shades of brown but all of African descent, stood up and bowed their heads as Leverta Pack, an older woman wearing the kind of kinte cloth hat fashionable in South Chicago, delivered an inspirational prayer for the next ten minutes. She praised the Lord and gave thanks for the Full Circle Fund, family members, and much else. African Americans have a vibrant oral tradition, and many, like Leverta Pack, are able to extemporize with power and passion at a moment's notice.

Gwen took over. "We've been adding some women to the center," Gwen began. "Since we start our meetings with some kind of game, tonight we'll start with the name game.

"Each lady in the circle will say her first name and a word which begins with the first letter of her name and that describes her tonight." A low murmur ran through the room; there was a lot of shifting in chairs and at least one audible groan. "Then," Gwen continued, "the person to your left will repeat the name of each person who went before her and make up her own name."

After some general confusion, one woman volunteered, "Joanne, joy." All eyes moved to the woman to her left. "Leverta, loving," Leverta Pack blurted out with a laugh.

"But you need to say the name of the person who went before you," Gwen said quickly.

"Oh. Joanne, uh, joy; Leverta, loving." In quick succession there was an alert Andree and a likable Lynn. (Andree was the nine-year-old son of a woman sitting in the circle.) The game quickly got hard. Some women fumbled more than others. Two at first refused to play at all, saying they couldn't possibly remember so much; with gentle encouragement from Gwen, and poorly suppressed laughter from their peers, each did a respectable job. Finally it came to Glenda Harris, a heavyset woman sitting at the end of the circle. She recited all twenty-six names without a single error. The room erupted in applause.

When the commotion died down, Glenda said, "You know

what this goes to show you? Yeah, you *can't* say you *can't.*" A few women reflexively said "Uh-huh." "I looked at where I was sitting and I said, I can't remember all those names. It's im-*possible,*" Glenda continued, with a chorus of "That's right"'s and "Uh-huh"'s echoing in the background. "But when you concentrate your attention on something, and give it your best effort, nothing is impossible—nothing. You just *can't* say you *can't.*"

Omiyale stood up and brought the meeting back to order. The first item on the agenda was announcements. Several women stood up and talked about recent and upcoming sales events. The Black Expo, held two weeks earlier, had been a disappointment to some of them. The Ghana Fest, an outdoor festival celebrating African and African American culture that was scheduled for the following weekend, aroused strong interest. One woman described a seminar to be held for Full Circle Fund borrowers on the subject of repairing bad credit histories. "It costs five dollars to participate in the class, which isn't a bad deal if it ends up allowing you to get a credit card and a mortgage for a home," she said. From the number of nodding heads in the circle, it was clear that there was more than one person in the room with a spotty credit history.

Then came the subject of the three women who were behind on their loan payments. Omiyale reported that a decision had been made to hold a raffle to help them catch up, and urged everyone to help sell tickets. Lynn Hardy, one of the women who had fallen behind, reported that the first prize would be a television set and that raffle tickets would be available at the next meeting. From the looks on people's faces, the subject of impending loan default had been a matter of some controversy. A deadly silence fell.

Gwen surveyed the room, let the tension build for a few more seconds, and broke in, "You all *know* the good name that the Full Circle Fund has, and that Englewood is a model for the program. This center was formed with great enthusiasm, but I feel the spirit is dying out. Women are saying, 'I'm paying my loan, why do I have to worry about the *other* ladies?' Rest assured, y'all"—her voice became just a little sassy here—"just as easily as the Full Circle Fund came to Englewood, it can pack up and leave. So let's get this taken care of." The women immediately broke into applause, though it was not exactly clear what they were applauding. But the tension had been broken. Gwen, with a beautiful light brown face and hair braided in a checkerboard pattern, was clearly in command.

In short order, the center broke up into its constituent circles. Each circle has its own name, and the ones in the Lindblom center included "Kids First," "LIFE," and "Divine Principles." Chairs were rearranged so that groups of five women could meet in relative privacy to conduct their business. In one corner of the room, five women gathered; they had named their circle "Les Papillons" (the Butterflies).

The first point of business in the group meetings is for borrowers to pay their biweekly installments to the chairperson. Queenesta Harris, a slender young woman with oversized glasses, opened her purse, pulled out a checkbook, and wrote a check for $27. As she passed it to Omiyale, their eyes met briefly, and both smiled.

Queenesta lived on the western edge of Englewood. Like most of her neighbors, she feared the roving gangs of teenage boys who wreaked violence upon each other and the Englewood community. Sometimes it just seemed like too much for her—raising a precocious young girl, living in a violent and poverty-stricken neighborhood, relying on sporadic child support from her daughter's father, and meeting living expenses from the proceeds of a fledgling business subject to seasonal fluctuations.

It had been nearly a year since Queenesta first met Omiyale and Thelma Dean Ali, the charter members of Les Papillons. All three had been vendors at an annual sidewalk sale in South Shore, a predominantly black neighborhood somewhat more stable than Englewood. At the time, Queenesta had just recently begun selling black-oriented children's books to supplement her unemployment insurance stipend, which was due to expire. Her daughter, Shayna, then three, had come with her to the event and was, like Queenesta herself, drawn to these two women from the moment they met.

The three talked about many topics over the South Shore festival's four days: upcoming summer festivals, a rumored teachers strike in the fall, violence on the streets, and marketing strategies. At one point, Thelma mentioned her participation in the Full Circle Fund. As the event wore on, Queenesta was impressed by the business savvy the women demonstrated, and when the opportunity arose, she asked if it would be possible for her to join the program. The FCF particularly appealed to Queenesta because she considered any aid from the state—even unemployment insurance—to be a crutch, and to be avoided whenever possible. She attended a meeting ten days later, but the only space for a new borrower was in a circle whose members grated on her.

"That girl looked extremely uncomfortable the first night she came to our center meeting," Omiyale recalled, "but after seeing her work her business I thought she had a lot of promise." Queenesta had what Omiyale knew was most needed in a vendor—a willingness to actively engage potential customers, to entice them, without seeming pushy, to come for a look at your table. Success at outdoor events takes a kind of street charisma that not everyone is willing to cultivate in themselves. Omiyale knows; her children often cringe when they see her hawking jewelry and African artifacts on the street. One day, she hopes each of them—there are seven—knows the pleasures of owning his or her own business. It pains her to see succeeding generations of black people fall over themselves to get an ever-shrinking number of jobs provided by white companies while thousands of immigrant families slowly build a life for themselves by running stores that serve black consumers.

When a spot opened up two weeks later in Omiyale and Thelma's circle, Queenesta was the first person they called. She immediately agreed to begin training for the group recognition test. She passed the test in January 1993 and received a loan for $1,000, promptly investing it in cassette tapes and compact discs that she was selling from a counter she rented in a West Side bookstore.

Queenesta started selling music on the advice of Victor McClain, an irreverent entrepreneur and owner of West Side Books, who had acquainted her with Afrocentric literature and thought. Victor had once had a tenant who sold music, and he had done well. But since he didn't have the money to buy the cassettes wholesale, or the interest to learn about music, Victor was looking for someone else to invest in the venture.

Queenesta was an unlikely person to take him up on the proposal, but joining the Full Circle Fund gave her access to liquid investment capital. She figured she knew less about the rap, hip-hop, and house recordings that sell so well on the West Side than any other black person in Chicago. She didn't even own a radio, much less a stereo. And when she listened to the lyrics of the songs, she didn't like much of what she heard. But financial necessity gave Queenesta sufficient motivation to gain a working understanding of the market within three months; by July, she knew most of the popular artists and their bodies of work. A remaining challenge was to persuade her North Side wholesaler to reserve at least a few of the most popular cassettes for her when they came in.

At about the same time that she began selling music, she had taken to selling Afrocentric children's books to schools and day care centers that serve primarily black youngsters. Popular titles include Afro-Bets's *First Book About Africa: An Introduction to Young Readers* and versions of fairy tales such as *Cinderella* and *Beauty and the Beast* with black characters. As she sold more, she read more, and slowly she became convinced that black children like Shayna need from a young age to hear stories with black heroes. She would read the books to her daughter, carefully preserving each book so that she could sell it later on.

When the music and children's book businesses were slow, she would often sell general books, merchandise imported from Africa, and dollar earrings at street fairs and bazaars, on college campuses, and, during Black History Month, in the staff cafeteria of Allstate Insurance, which had laid her off in 1991. During her first year of operation, her businesses were shaky but growing, and little of her success, she believes, would have been possible without credit from the Full Circle Fund and the guidance of her circle members. "Being a single mother is very stressful. Sometimes you stop believing in yourself. But not these ladies," Queenesta once confided to her diary.

• • •

Back in the Lindblom Park Field House, Thelma handed her check to Omiyale. It was the largest payment made that night: $100. The loan, Thelma's third, had been for $3,500. She had used her loans to buy inexpensive merchandise that she sold at street fairs and bazaars in the Chicago area. The relative success of her business had made her something of a leader in her circle and center, but her strong opinions sometimes isolated her. Among the women in the center, Thelma is the least race-conscious. She was a vocal opponent of a proposal that the center join a protest against Arab and Korean merchants on Sixty-third Street. On occasion, she would clash with fellow Muslims in her center who belonged to the Nation of Islam. Their combination of racial separatism and Islam disturbed her; she couldn't understand why they would refuse to let a white Muslim into their mosque to worship (a courtesy commonly extended at hers). Sometimes relations would become so strained that Nation followers would fail to return Thelma's traditional Muslim greeting of *"As Salaam o Aleikum."*

As her center meeting drew to a close, Queenesta looked at her watch; it was almost nine o'clock. How long will Shayna hold out? she wondered to herself, looking at her daughter as she explored the bulletin board in the back of the room. So many of Queenesta's hopes and fears were tied up in Shayna, who at the tender age of four seemed to have inherited her mother's intelligence and her father's oversized body.

Omiyale got up from her chair and brought the checks to the table, where Gwen was collecting installments and issuing receipts. When she returned, Omiyale said, "How are we doing this week? Who's going to the Ghana Fest?"

"I'm *definitely* going there, sister. There's gonna be some heavy traffic at the Ghana Fest, I'll tell you that. There's gonna be some money to be made there, honey," Thelma answered quickly.

"Geri, how are you doing this week?" Omiyale asked a frail woman, perhaps fifty years old, who was sitting quietly in the group.

"Well . . . okay, I suppose . . ." Her voice trailed off. She looked up and swallowed hard. Her oversized glasses fell down her nose a bit, drawing attention to her pronounced cheekbones, slightly sunken cheeks, and freckled, light brown skin.

"What's the matter, Geri? You're among friends. If you can't bring it here, where *can* you bring it?" Omiyale said softly.

"It's just . . . I have this business selling, you know, aprons and gift baskets, but . . . but . . . it's hard. I feel so angry sometimes, having lost my job after seventeen years. It's hard . . . getting going in the morning, making my aprons—who's going to buy them anyway?" Her eyes began to moisten, and she suddenly buried her face in her hands.

"I hear you, Geri. I was laid off too, and sometimes I felt *so* angry," Queenesta said. "I felt worthless, another recipient of unemployment aid. Now I feel, I'm going to *show* the guy who laid me off by making my business succeed. That's how you can take out your anger, Geri. But as Victor says, self-employment has got to be your dream—it can't just be your hobby anymore."

"Listen, Geri, you have *got* to put the past in the past," Glenda added forcefully. "You've got to—"

"There's no problem with your merchandise, girl," Thelma interrupted. "You just gotta get into the habit of *selling* it." Thelma drew out the word "selling," and punctuated it with a right-handed karate chop into her outstretched left palm. "You know what happened to Glenda here. She said, 'No way I can sell.' Then we got her out selling her jewelry one day, and before she could say a word she made eight hundred dollars on her first time out."

"You make beautiful aprons, Geri," Omiyale added.

Thelma elicited a promise from Geri to complete two aprons per day, no matter how depressed she felt. In return, she and the others would work with her to find more buyers. "We're gonna be *calling* you," Thelma added, with a touch of humor in her voice.

The meeting broke up at 10:30. As the women slowly filed out of the room, halfway around the world thirty-five women would soon be gathering outside Shandha's hut in Kholshi. It was 8:30 A.M. in Bangladesh. By the time the repayment meeting there was over, Queenesta, Thelma, and Omiyale were in their beds, fast asleep.

• • •

Thousands of people coming to do business in Chicago arrive each day at O'Hare International, the world's busiest airport. Most who visit the city for business or pleasure never leave the downtown commercial district known as the Loop (so named because it is circled by elevated trains) and the yuppie areas north of the Loop and in the suburbs. The Chicago they see is a world-class city with stores, restaurants, museums, and all the amenities of modern life. But another Chicago exists, one considerably less inviting to the visitor.

Midway Airport, located in the far reaches of southwest Chicago, where the discount flights on airlines like Southwest and Kiwi land, is closer to this other Chicago. It borders on some of the more depressed communities on the South Side and the West Side. In January 1994, a new elevated train line, or el, was opened linking Midway Airport to the Loop, sparing tourists who had come on inexpensive flights the trauma of traversing this section of Chicago by bus or rental car.

Among the most violent and economically depressed neighborhoods on the South Side is Englewood, where the average family income is $15,615, half the city average. Gang-related violence is epidemic. Drive-by shootings have become so commonplace that many residents are too frightened to sit on their porch during hot summer afternoons. Shards of glass and garbage litter Englewood's streets, which are also full of abandoned cars. Men and women too high on drugs to move lie on its sidewalks, and conversations among its residents often center on the latest teenager to be shot or arrested.

Englewood began in the 1850s as a small settlement known as Junction Grove that grew up around a railroad station along the Southern and Northern Indiana line. Two decades later, one settler suggested that the village's name be changed because the dense oak forests that surrounded the local cottages reminded him of Englewood, New Jersey. The largely Irish, Scottish, and German residents had ideas of developing their village into a prestigious community. In 1889, Englewood was annexed by Chicago, and transportation links with the city's downtown were soon improved.

By 1920, the population had surpassed 85,000 and the corner of Halsted Avenue and Sixty-third Street was the largest shopping district in the country that was not in a downtown area. East of Halsted were upper-class families holding steady white-collar jobs, while west of the thoroughfare were working-class neighborhoods of more modest dwellings. As late as 1940, only 2 percent of Englewood's population was black—nearly all of them living along the western boundary of Racine Avenue and along Stewart Street to the east.

By 1950, the Black Belt of Chicago had expanded toward Englewood's boundaries, and ten years later 69 percent of Englewood's residents were African American. By 1968 the *Chicago Daily News* was moved to write, "The Englewood area, an urban badlands, has become the city's latest battleground for teen-age gangs. More than 10,000 youths there belong to fifty-nine gangs with descriptive names ranging from the Maniac Disciples to the Junior Loafers." Block by block, real estate speculators bilked home owners and home buyers for tens of thousands of dollars as the complexion of Englewood changed. By 1970, 98 percent of all residents were black and 35 percent were living below the poverty level. By 1990, Englewood's nonblack population fell to 1 percent, its unemployment rate was more than double the city average, and half of its families were living below the poverty line.

The mutually reinforcing processes of white flight and capital flight had turned Englewood from a thriving, working-class neighborhood to a depressed inner-city neighborhood. The same thing had occurred in many communities in the southern and western parts of Chicago. The rule of thumb was that once the black population in an area exceeded 8 percent, there would be a sudden drop in real estate prices, followed by panic selling. Few distinctions were made by whites about the specific black people who moved in. To white America during this period, a black white-collar worker and a black dope pusher were, at the end of the day, simply two black people who pushed down property values.

Today, a walk through Englewood will bring the visitor face-to-face with boarded-up factories where Germans and Irish once worked, crumbling and often charred houses, and overgrown vacant lots. Groups of young black men and boys parade aimlessly through the streets, while frightened schoolchildren wait for public transit to take them home before they fall victim to the dangers that lurk outdoors. Teens who regularly venture out of the house after dark are often in prison by age seventeen and dead by twenty-four.

Most people who had the opportunity to get out of Englewood have done so. The population is now less than 60,000. Many who remain are numbed to the violence, often holding out the faint hope that at least one of their children will avoid the temptations of gangs and, in the case of girls, early pregnancy.

Nineteen ninety-two was a record-breaking year for murders in Chicago, and Englewood's homicide rate was the third highest among nearly eighty communities in the Second City. The final slaying occurred on December 29 on Seventy-fifth Street, a short distance from the eastern border of Englewood. When paramedics came to the aid of the 647th victim of gun violence, they found the bullet-riddled body of a black high school student surrounded by some fifty young men milling in the street. One paramedic recalled the scene, saying, "All hell broke loose. There was shooting; the cops were outnumbered. Fifteen years on the job, and this was the worst scene that I have ever come across."

For Thelma, Queenesta, Omiyale, and other women in Englewood who borrow from the Full Circle Fund, the coming of spring and summer and the dozens of festivals and street fairs mean opportunities for making money. Small-scale vendors without a fixed storefront depend on people being out and about and in a mood to spend.

The biggest event at the beginning of the summer of 1993, the Black Expo held at McCormick Place, Chicago's preeminent convention center, was disappointing for those WSEP borrowers who were only able to make back their reduced booth fee. Queenesta, however, was one of those who did quite well. She had taken a $2,500 short-term loan from the Full Circle Fund to buy forty dozen T-shirts to sell there. Her landlord and mentor, Victor McClain, bought another forty dozen, and as a result they received a substantial volume discount, paying only $3.25 per shirt. They grossed $3,500, and with that retired Queenesta's debt and the cost of renting their booth. The plan was that as they sold the rest of the T-shirts, Victor would get back his investment of $2,500, and then the profit on the remaining four hundred T-shirts would either be split by Queenesta and Victor or plowed back into the venture to buy more inventory.

In July, to her surprise, Queenesta closed a deal in which she sold $1,900 worth of Afrocentric books to a teacher acting on behalf of her high school. It was her largest deal ever, and she made an $800 profit.

One afternoon in August, Queenesta was pleasantly surprised when Omiyale stopped by Victor's store, the first time any of her circle members had made the long trip from Englewood to the far West Side. Omiyale chatted with Queenesta for a while, dropped off some earrings she had made that Queenesta would display in her case, and talked business with a seamstress who worked in a room in back of the store. Before long, Omiyale was off, late, as always, for her next appointment.

As her chairperson left, Queenesta radiated a quiet pride. Having space in a store let her do something for Omiyale—display her merchandise every day in a good location. She would get a small percentage of the proceeds from whatever jewelry she sold, but that didn't matter as much as Omiyale's recognition of the progress she was making. It was also comforting to see a friendly face and a perky personality at a time when tensions were rising in the store between Victor and some of his own tenants who were behind on their rent.

Toward the end of August, reports of budget shortfalls that threatened to shut down the entire Chicago school system began to worry Queenesta. (Only twice during the past twenty years has August been without the prospect of such a crisis.) She was counting on selling a lot of books to schools in neighborhoods with predominantly black populations. A shutdown or strike would throw a wrench in her plans for a big breakthrough in book sales. And then there was her daughter to consider. If the schools closed, she would have to take Shayna with her as she did her business.

• • •

In the heart of downtown Chicago, on the seventh floor of a building on Washington Street, are the offices of the Women's Self-Employment Project and its founding director, Connie Evans. Some twenty-five women, two-thirds of them African American, work there in close quarters. The enterprise agents who collect the loan payments and form the borrowing groups, along with support staff, interns, and volunteers, work side by side in small cubicles with little privacy, while the professional staff members each have their own, albeit modest, offices. Connie's is the only office that has space for more than one guest.

Connie was one of four children raised by a mother who ran her own catering business in rural Tennessee, and at the age of thirty-six Connie was running an organization with an annual budget exceeding a million dollars. As a chief executive, she appreciates and rewards hard work and, like Yunus, sets high standards for herself and her colleagues—though she somehow lacks the soft touch of her mentor and fellow former resident of Tennessee.

When alone with her friends and close confidants, among them some of the most talented people working on social justice in Chicago, she enjoys the opportunity to open up about how insecure she occasionally feels running a large organization that is often scrutinized by foundations, the media, and academics. More than anything, Connie likes to laugh. It reminds her of when she was younger and wasn't responsible for running the WSEP. In recent years, the laughs have been less frequent. Sometimes she felt like leaving the organization she had founded, though—despite a series of lucrative offers—she could never quite make the break. Still, when times were tough, as they were in the summer of 1993, she certainly toyed with the idea. The prospect of working overseas appealed to her, and any number of international organizations would gladly have offered her a job.

During the summer, Connie was troubled by a spate of resignations within WSEP and the prospect of several more in the fall, and divisions within her inner circle about what was causing them. She suggested that hiring a chief operating officer to manage the staff and deal with minutiae would solve the problem and leave her free to do what she does best—communicating her vision of WSEP's role in the creation of self-employment for the inner-city poor so that foundations, media, and policy-makers take notice. But not all of her colleagues and trusted advisors agreed.

And then there was the issue of WSEP's expanding nationwide, with support provided by Subway sandwich tycoon Fred DeLuca. Connie presented the expansion idea to her board of directors in the fall. Their first question was whether she was committed to staying on as WSEP's director in order to see the process through. Connie said she could not guarantee that she would stay indefinitely; in fact, she went so far as to say that she might resign the following year. The board, disappointed in her response, nonetheless agreed to take several steps to evaluate the feasibility of the idea.

Meanwhile, Connie knew that she had some soul-searching to do. She decided to seek out the advice of her mentor, who at the time was having difficulties of his own. Muhammad Yunus was recovering from a severe ulcer that had been diagnosed only after he'd passed out during a meeting, while he was already preparing for cataract surgery. When she got the opportunity that spring to speak to him, she asked whether he thought she should leave WSEP and turn the job over to someone else. Connie, drained by all the long hours and stress that the work demanded, was hoping Yunus would give her the green light. Yunus, however, told her in no uncertain terms that she should not leave. He recognized how special Connie was, perhaps seeing some of himself in her. Losing her, he feared, would cripple WSEP's finances and, more important, its heart, for Connie, despite her youth, was an unusually gifted fundraiser and visionary. "Look at all the organizations that lost their leaders and within five years were in chaos," he said. It was not the answer Connie had been looking for.

Standing behind her small glass case of compact discs and cassettes in West Side Books, Queenesta Harris greeted her customers with a smile on a hot Wednesday in early August. Shayna sat on the floor beneath her, drawing on a piece of construction paper with crayons.

Business was slow. In the early afternoon, two black teenagers came in the door and said in loud voices, "Hey, Queen." They wore baggy jeans and turned-up baseball caps worn backwards, and they had a mission.

"Queen, you got the Briny mix yet?"

"Naw, but I should be getting it next week."

The two teenagers looked at each other, and then briefly toward the back of the store. There they saw African clothing and head-wear, and racks of books about black liberation, ranging from Carter Woodson's classic *The Miseducation of the Negro,* the Ko-ran, and a sympathetic treatment of the Nation of Islam to *Black Economics: Solutions for Economic and Community Empower-ment* and *Countering the Conspiracy to Destroy Black Boys.* The two young men had never read those books and, in all likelihood, never would. Queenesta often thought that the intensity and seri-ousness of Victor McClain and the store made the boys who bought her music uncomfortable. The location, she feared pri-vately, was "too black" for them.

After whispering something in his companion's ear, the larger of the two boys volunteered, "Catch you later, Queen." Both quickly headed out the door.

On days like this, Queenesta often wondered whether having her own business was enough to support herself. Several bills were already weeks overdue and she depended on the vagaries of an unpredictable market. When her doubts overwhelmed her, as they often did that summer of 1993, she pondered her past, wondering how she got into this vulnerable and uncertain position.

Despite living and attending Full Circle Fund meetings in the heart of South Chicago, Queenesta Harris is a West Sider. She grew up there, commuting to predominantly Jewish public grammar and high schools in the northwest of Chicago. While her education was first-class, and is reflected today in her speaking and writing skills, she never felt at ease with her white classmates, with whom she had little in common.

Queenesta's brother Delbert was killed in 1970 in a racially motivated highway attack by a white teenager who drove his pickup truck into Delbert's motorbike. Whatever stability had ex-isted in the family before that began to crumble. Her sister June fell into a depression from which she has never fully recovered; two of Delbert's brothers got involved in trouble and her father left the family for good. With only one meager income to rely on, the family often skimped on meals. Queenesta was outwardly stoic about it all, but the turmoil took its toll.

After graduation from high school, Queenesta took a job as a secretary with a large printing company that, at the time, had contracts with *Playboy, Jet,* and *Ebony* magazines. It was 1982, and her salary was $13,000 a year. When a black colleague urged her to get further education to improve herself, she pursued and earned an associate degree in industrial engineering. But by the time she completed the degree her company had lost the *Playboy* account. Anticipating her employer's failure, Queenesta took a job with the Allstate insurance company in 1986 as a claim associate.

At Allstate, Gary Williams, a black colleague, became Queenesta's mentor. He urged her to save and invest her salary rather than engage in the conspicuous consumption that he said was the curse of their race. A former professional football player, Gary showed Queenesta and other African American staff at Allstate his books—not literary, but financial: he had a quarter of a million dollars in the bank. Queenesta became pregnant in 1988, and Gary rebuked her for being on the verge of becoming another single black mother with no future. But he urged her to start investing so that when the money was added to some modest savings she already had, she would have $15,000 stashed away before her child reached her first birthday. Queenesta took up the challenge, and began sending $500 each month—about half of her take-home pay—to an investment advisor Gary had introduced her to.

Shayna was born in September 1988. Queenesta secured $200 a month in child support from Shayna's father and managed to meet the goal of saving $15,000. She was able to live off the interest and sporadic child support payments while she took a year off to be with her daughter, again following Gary's advice. To reduce expenses, she moved in with her mother, who still lived on the corner of Harding and Ferdinand streets on the West Side.

In January 1991, Shayna's father said he was a changed man. He urged Queenesta to move into her own apartment in the suburbs, and when she agreed, he paid for the move. At his urging, Queenesta adopted a different lifestyle—snappy clothes bought in the right downtown shops, nails and hair done just so, and a new car that came with hefty monthly payments and insurance. He arranged it so that the car was in his name and Queenesta made the payments. Gary Williams looked on all these developments disapprovingly.

In early June, Shayna's father moved into Queenesta's Oak Park apartment, and promises of marriage were in the air. The month quickly and without warning turned into a nightmare. Queenesta was involved in a car accident that left her car in the shop with $4,000 worth of repairs. By the end of the month, the arguments she and Shayna's father were having were heated enough to prompt Queenesta to abandon most of her belongings and move in with her childhood friend Doreen. Two days after moving out, Queenesta returned one final time to salvage what she could of her possessions—her and Shayna's clothes, some keep-sakes, and a sleeper sofa.

At the time, Queenesta was on medical leave from Allstate due to the car accident, and her supervisor was growing impatient. Just as she was due to return to work, Queenesta was forced to take some sick days when Shayna fell ill, and even after returning she was often late (owing to a two-hour commute and having to bring Shayna to day care). On one occasion when traffic had delayed her for nearly an hour more than usual, she drove into the parking garage and left Shayna sleeping in the car until she could show her face and do enough work so that she could sneak away to drop her daughter off at day care.

When Shayna fell ill again in early November and Queenesta was forced to take another few days off, her exasperated boss made her the victim of corporate retrenchment that would culminate a year later in Allstate's closing down most of its Chicago-area operations. She applied for and received unemployment insurance benefits that amounted to $233 per week for an initial period of six months. Suddenly, the reality of poverty and vulnerability had hit home.

Queenseta's friend Doreen was a single mother on welfare, a

prospect that, at the time, seemed an increasingly likely fate for Queenesta herself. The two resolved to get their lives going again. Doreen began going to college at night and doing secretarial work during the day. As she saw her friend struggle with her assignments, Queenesta realized that Doreen had never properly learned to read, write, or do simple arithmetic, and she decided to take it upon herself to tutor her.

As for Queenesta, the thought of getting another job was not an attractive one. As she had seen, the demands of taking care of Shayna, now three years old, were not always consistent with those of a nine-to-five job. Yet the prospect of welfare motherhood was even less appealing.

During her final days at Allstate, Queenesta had gotten into the habit of spending her lunch hours at Victor McClain's store, a ten-minute drive from her office. Surrounded by condemned storefronts, fast-food take-out joints, and a thrift store, West Side Books is an unlikely place to be a center of cultural and social ferment. Queenesta met Victor there one day when she was browsing among his bookshelves—he usually has only one copy of each book, and perhaps three hundred titles in stock. On repeated visits, she shared her troubles with him; in turn, he suggested that she read about black empowerment and get into business for herself.

"The Koreans, the Caucasians—they recirculate money and capital within their communities close to ten times before it leaves," he told her. "In the black community, we hardly recirculate it twice. We spend our money with white businesses, and we have a lower rate of entrepreneurship than virtually any ethnic group in America." One of the first books that Victor gave Queenesta, *Black Economics* by Jawanza Kunjufu, notes that the rate of business ownership in the white community is 64 per 1,000 adults, whereas in the black community it is one-seventh that rate. Besides discussing the obstacle of lack of access to capital, Kunjufu argues that status-conscious African Americans prefer the stability of working for white-owned firms in downtown Chicago, and using the regular income to pay off spiraling debts amassed while buying fashionable clothes and cars manufactured and sold by other ethnic groups, to opening businesses in the Black Belt that could serve their own race. Entrepreneurs from other ethnic groups fill the gap, the result being that 93 percent of the $200 billion to $300 billion African Americans spend annually goes to firms owned by other ethnic groups.

Lack of racial solidarity, African American scholars and activists such as Kunjufu contend, opens the door for immigrants from Korea, South Asia, and the Caribbean—the so-called model minorities—to start successful businesses in the inner city. Yet there is more at work here than meets the eye. It is rarely considered that many of today's immigrants were highly educated, middle-class people in their own country and are able to use their own money as investment capital or to tap into the support network of people who migrated here before them. Korean Americans, in particular, borrow from informal rotating credit and savings associations and can obtain merchandise manufactured in Asia at preferential rates.

While other immigrants came to America at a time and in a manner that *they* chose, and can access support networks both here and at home, African Americans were denied these opportunities. Even after slavery was abolished, its legacy left blacks economically disadvantaged.

While black people like Victor understand the historical reasons for their race's troubles, they try not to dwell on them. Instead, they work to motivate other African Americans to achieve new levels of racial solidarity and economic self-reliance.

One day, Queenesta was hurrying out the door of Victor's store to get back to work on time when she stopped to read a poster on the wall. It read, "Black Man, why do you spend 100 percent of your money with white society then turn around and blame them for 98 percent of your problems? Let us exchange our millions with ourselves. Let us establish an economic system among ourselves. We could change our conditions in 24 hours or less."

Queenesta mulled over her future and wondered if she would have the wherewithal to start her own business. At that moment, it seemed like an adventure in personal and communal uplift in which she was unlikely to ever take part. Little did she know that within several months, it would be her only realistic alternative to living off the dole.

• • •

With much of her head wrapped tightly in a scarf despite the
torrid heat, Thelma Dean Ali stood in front of a card table that
long ago had begun sagging in the middle, hoping to make a few
dollars selling her merchandise: socks, berets, earrings, Indian
scarves and purses, African oils and spices. Her table, just west of
Halsted Avenue, is in a prime location in the Maxwell Street
Market, the largest and best-known open-air market left in a
major North American city. Her place of business is less permanent and attractive-looking than Queenesta's, but it is often
more profitable.

Around noon, a beat-up white Cadillac cruised by slowly, and
the driver, a haggard-looking black man in a white undershirt,
leaned out the window and pointed at a pack of tube socks. "How
much?" he asked with a frown.

"Five bucks. Six in a packet. Most people charge six."

Deal.

Another man, apparently intoxicated, greeted Thelma a short
time later and asked for a body oil imported from Tunisia. When
he realized he had only 50 cents, Thelma measured out half of her
smallest vial, perhaps a few milliliters of fragrance.

Every weekday and Saturday, she arrives at Maxwell Street by
bus before 11 A.M., having spent the morning saying her prayers
toward the holy city of Mecca at 5:30, preparing her children for
school, and then doing some "shopping" in downtown Chicago,
searching for major bargains (going-out-of-business sales are the
best) where she can snatch up merchandise to resell in a few hours
at a profit and checking out the competition at five-and-dime
stores. (Normally, because she has so little overhead, Thelma can
undersell even the chain stores.) A few Korean wholesalers, her
Jewish friend Harry Zimmerman (now rather old but still selling
racy videos once a week), and auctions also supply her with goods
that move well here. By 11 A.M. she has set up her table, and she
stays open until dusk.

Sunday is special at Maxwell Street. Thelma leaves her house
at 5 A.M., arriving at the market by bus before 6:30, with the sun
barely peeking through the gaps in between the skyscrapers that
line Lake Michigan. If she were to arrive in "Jewtown"—as the

market is commonly called among black Chicagoans—any later than that, she would risk not having a four-by-ten-foot slot from which to sell. Some vendors are known to come as early as Saturday afternoon and to sleep in their cars overnight, even in the dead of winter, to ensure a choice spot for the Sunday bazaar. Fights are known to flare up when one seller begins to encroach on another's space by even a few inches.

Vendors and customers who come to Maxwell Street are looking for bargains and, as one Full Circle Fund borrower put it, "real people"—other poor folks who have not lost touch with their roots. Literally in the shadow of downtown Chicago, this is one place where blacks, Puerto Ricans, and Mexicans can let it all hang out. Geographically, the dominant Anglo-European culture is only a few blocks away; but for one day each week, it is thousands of miles away in spirit.

By seven o'clock the market is jammed with merchants and customers. There is hardly anything that you can't buy at a bargain—toys, spices, fresh produce, air conditioners, bicycles, adult magazines and videos, sports equipment, coffeepots, computers, books, shirts and sweaters, doorknobs, hardware, tires, diamonds, barber's chairs, vacuum cleaners, crutches, office supplies, bunk beds, pancake syrup, eight-track cassette tapes, jumper cables, perfume, sweatshirts, automobile and motorboat engines, typewriters, carpets. Most items are available in three states—new, used, and very used.

Cars edge through the market, with drivers and passengers looking in every direction for a good deal. Often they haggle over a price and make a purchase without ever leaving their vehicle; they are, as they say, "cruising." Near accidents between cars and other cars, cars and customers, and cars and vendors occur every few minutes. Several weeks back, a woman who'd bent over to pick up something was crushed beneath a car and pronounced dead at the scene.

Dense crowds—some 20,000 bargain-hunters come on a typical Sunday—push from one stall to the next. The sweet aromas of exotic cuisines mingle in the open air with the acrid smell of two-week-old garbage. Live blues is pumped out by two or more bands, as it has been for decades. (Some claim that the blues were born on Maxwell Street.) In these ways—and others that are less easily discerned at first glance—the Sunday market is strongly reminiscent of Bangladesh.

It's been that way for some time. In the late nineteenth century, the Maxwell Street area was an overpopulated, immigrant (mostly Jewish) slum with a bustling, Old World–style bazaar. Over time, the market became known as the Ellis Island of the Midwest, a place where an immigrant could get a toehold in an economy and culture he barely understood. Even today, one can hear more than a dozen languages being spoken by vendors and customers.

Many well-known personalities have roots here. Joseph Goldberg, father of the late Supreme Court justice Arthur Goldberg, was a fruit peddler on Maxwell Street. Ira Berkow, the *New York Times* columnist, sold nylon stockings. Samuel Paley, the father of William Paley, founder of the Columbia Broadcasting System, was a cigar vendor.

Despite the market's history and its role as a primary source of self-employment for low-income Chicagoans, there was serious talk of redeveloping the area in 1994 to make way for the expansion of the University of Illinois. In the waning months of 1993 and early 1994, a pitched battle for the very existence of the bazaar was being fought. It was a struggle of history versus modernity, of the economic needs of poor America against the establishment's thirst for expansion. (Indeed, where the university's campus now stands was once a tight-knit, lower-class Italian neighborhood that succumbed to Mayor Daley's pursuit of a new center of higher learning within the city limits.)

By the late afternoon of that hot July day, Thelma had $36 in her pocket and judged it a fair day, considering the heat. As she began to pack up her table, a black youth ran across Halsted Avenue with a hamburger in his hand and an old man in close pursuit, waving a spatula. Thelma chuckled at the scene, yet it reminded her of the challenges of raising black boys in this cruel city, a job made even more difficult when you are raising them to be Muslims.

On August 5, Thelma, Omiyale, and a woman from another group set off for Milwaukee's annual Afro-World Festival in Omiyale's van, a vehicle she recently inherited from her father. Three days later Thelma, selling T-shirts, sequined hats, hair accessories, and purses, had made $1,500, and Omiyale had grossed close to $2,000. Thelma, whose theory is that you only make consistent money on things that retail for between $1 and $3, was impressed at her chairlady's ability to talk people into buying merchandise that she sold for $80 to $100.

The festival ended at 11 P.M. Sunday, August 8, and the three women began their journey home at 1 A.M. in order to be sure to make it to their center meeting on time. The main item on the agenda that evening was how to get the women who'd lost money at the Black Expo up to speed on their loan payments. Thelma suggested that the newly constituted loan committee of herself, Omiyale, and Leverta Pack would take a more active role in scrutinizing future loan proposals and working with WSEP staff to negotiate solutions for cases of default. "This here center is about sisterhood, about us helping each other," Thelma said with her head tilted to the right and her arms gesturing wildly. "But let's have it be about *sisterhood* and not about *stupidhood*." She wanted to see future problems with loan utilization prevented. As it was, the entire center had to hold fund-raisers for the three women who were in trouble—one whose airbrushing business had slowed down, another whose merchandise was mysteriously stolen after being delivered by United Parcel Service, and a third who took the money and promptly used it to pay her son's tuition after telling her fellow borrowers she was buying a computer for a business venture she had given only the vaguest description of.

Omiyale led the discussion, but she felt uneasy about doing so, having herself fallen a few payments behind on a short-term loan. After taking a $3,000 loan from the Full Circle Fund to purchase inventory for the Black Expo, a loan that was to be repaid by the beginning of October, Omiyale had grossed a mere $1,300. She had taken more than half of the $1,300 to make a first installment on her loan, and used the remainder to catch up on business and personal bills that had been piling up. Thelma, Geri, Glenda, and Queenesta had no idea that Omiyale was courting disaster by carrying a debt of more than $2,300 ($2,200 principle and $112.50

interest) without any credible plan to repay it on time. In the Grameen system, the credit line of *each* circle member is dependent on
timely repayments by *all* of them. Unwarranted assumptions about
a peer's ability to repay has led to the ruination of some businesses
in Bangladesh. With the number of days of warm weather dwindling, Omiyale was flirting with just that disaster.

Throughout August, Thelma was hard at work selling her oils, hair
accessories, and toys (plastic water guns were especially popular).
August 14 was the traditional Bud Billiken Parade, for which no
fee was required to vend. She exceeded her goal of $1 in sales every
minute, bringing home $364 after five hot, sweaty hours.

August 15 was a rainy Sunday at Maxwell Street, so she grossed
only $50. Since she usually pays about 40 to 50 percent of the
retail price for her merchandise, that meant a $20 profit after car-
fare. On a hunch, she arrived early on Monday, anticipating that
some of the rained-out Sunday shoppers would come by. She was
right, and made $115. The next day she met the organizer of an
event called the Cocofest and reserved a booth for $11. On Friday,
August 20, she went to the Cocofest and made $120.

At a center meeting in the second half of August, two aldermen
were guest speakers. When several of the women asked about the
possibility of taking over one of the buildings the city had recently
seized so that they could start a "cooperative manufacturing venture," one alderman said, "I'll turn the deed over to you today for
free. But then you'll have to find about one million dollars to get
it up to fire and safety codes." When she heard that, Thelma, who
began participating in the Full Circle Fund with a $300 loan,
leaned over to Queenesta and said, "Why don't these women stop
their million-dollar dreams and just work their little businesses a
little harder?" She was, above all, an entrepreneur with both feet
firmly planted in reality.

In the middle of August, Gwen told Omiyale that she would be
announcing her resignation from WSEP in a few days, to be effective at the end of September. Omiyale, the first person to hear the
news, was crestfallen but tried to be supportive. She told Gwen

that she would organize a going-away party worthy of her service to the center—a center whose viability Omiyale doubted without the tenacity of the only enterprise agent she had ever known.

Around the same time, Queenesta was talking to Thelma about the Afro-World Festival in Milwaukee and mentioned her disappointment that Victor hadn't been able to sell more than $1,200 worth of the T-shirts they had bought together for the Black Expo. When she said that, there was a brief silence on the other end of the phone. After the pause, Thelma said, "Girl, Victor was selling them T-shirts so fast that Thelma Perkins and me had to leave our booths to help him. He sold more than twelve hundred dollars on the first day alone. We could hardly keep up with the demand."

As Queenesta put down the phone, she contemplated her mentor's deception and began mentally preparing herself for a decision that would profoundly affect her business, and his.

5

▲

Amena Begum's Dream

Squatting in a small thatch hut, Amena splashed some water onto the aluminum plate on which her husband had just taken his morning rice and began swishing around the contents with her index finger. As she did so, Amena snuck a glance at Absar Ali as he retied his longhi around his skinny waist and spat some phlegm from his mouth. Amena always kept her eyes on her husband when he was around the house, though she tried to do it inconspicuously, peeking up from her cooking or cleaning. Experience had taught her that when she had a few seconds to prepare herself for a beating, she was able to protect her face with her forearms.

Absar Ali pulled a *biri* (a type of cigarette popular on the Indian subcontinent) from behind his ear, lit it, and settled into a deep crouch. As he drew the smoke into his lungs, he looked absent-mindedly into the cloudy horizon. His wife could see beads of sweat forming on his back. The heat and humidity of the monsoon season were upon them, and in a short time traveling from village to village would become more difficult. He knew it was critical to make as much money as he could now that the canals were dry and his inventory was replenished. With one final puff, Amena's husband stood up, strode into their hut, crouched down, and maneuvered a four-foot-long piece of bamboo so that its midpoint rested on his right shoulder. Baskets full of aluminum pots and pans hung from rope tied to each end of the bamboo.

For the last two generations, the men in Absar Ali's family have made their living selling clay and, more recently, aluminum cookware door-to-door. They buy the pots in bulk at wholesale prices in Dhaka, mark them up about 25 percent, and spend their days as barefoot traveling salesmen. For many years, Absar, his older brother, and his father ran the business with little more than $100 in working capital. Family illness, bad customer credit, and other difficulties could deplete their inventory, but with three people working the business and sharing the capital, it was unlikely that all would run into difficulty simultaneously. If they did, there was always the village loan shark as a lender of last resort, but that carried a high price—interest of 10 percent per month, or more.

It was understood that when sacrifices had to be made to pay off debts, it was the women and children who made them. While nobody liked to see them go hungry, it was simply common sense that the men of the house needed their energy to go out and make the money necessary to pay off their loans.

Absar Ali adjusted the bamboo slightly, retied his longhi a second time, and began walking down a gentle slope toward a narrow path dividing an acre of maturing rice paddies. After snaking his way through the field, he lumbered up a slope leading to a dirt road that brought him into the heart of Kholshi. He neither said good-bye to his family nor looked back once he was on his way.

As she watched her husband, Amena splashed more water on the pots and plates and swished it around until everything began to look clean. Just then, a small flock of ducklings, perhaps a dozen in all, appeared from behind the tiny thatch hut where Amena cooked, waddling behind their mother. They were a noisy bunch, and they wanted to be fed. It was not quite far enough into the monsoon that Amena could trust that her ducks would find enough to eat in the shallow puddles that would become knee-deep swamps in the weeks ahead. She threw a handful of rice husk, and as the ducklings crowded around it, she deftly trapped them under an inverted bamboo basket. She stood and looked at them briefly;

her eyes and fingers gave the impression that she was counting the ducklings.

Barely four weeks before, Amena had given birth to her fifth child. While she still felt weak, Amena had no intention of spending forty days in bed, as is customary in Bangladesh. She was a busy woman now.

Two weeks after accompanying Fulzan and Alow to the Grameen Bank office to receive their loans, Amena had been due to receive hers along with Firoza. She had been determined to complete the transaction before she gave birth, though with each passing day it had seemed less likely that she would have time. Without the money actually in her hands, she'd feared there was some plan to eliminate her from the group at the last moment.

Already she'd had to overcome the doubts of her group and older members such as Shandha and persuade the Grameen staff to conduct the group training sessions in her home, as she was too weak in the last weeks of her pregnancy to go elsewhere. The worst obstacle had been having to defend her character while it was assaulted by other borrowers; in their eyes, she was a *nodi bhanga lok* (roughly translated as "a person of the broken river," meaning someone who repeatedly migrates due to changes in the course of the river).

Nodi bhanga lok are thought to lack the civilized qualities that come from living in one place all one's life. For membership in Grameen Bank, these people must overcome the suspicion that they are eternal migrants who will pick up and flee with their loans at the first sight of trouble. Even the poorest people in the area looked down on the disheveled refugees who were forced to set up a shantytown near the Zianpur bazaar after the river changed course in the aftermath of the 1988 flood. "Nobody has *ever* lived there before," one could hear people saying from the market as they pointed at the makeshift huts with barely suppressed disgust. Amena had a leg up on those people, as she was able to take refuge on her grandfather's land. Yet when she and her husband were clearing a small patch of land from a jungle on the edge of the house plot, Amena could feel the eyes of the entire village staring at them.

If it hadn't been for the determined support she received from her Hindu neighbor Oloka Ghosh and a Muslim woman named Zorina, she would never have been able to force her way into Nobirun's group after the original quintet failed their recognition test. Once she came in, however, her leadership skills and high educational attainment made her a natural selection as group secretary.

The evening before Amena was due to receive her loan, she went into labor. She called a cousin who was living with her grandfather to come and assist with the birth.

At 3:30 A.M., Amena gave birth to a baby boy, whom she and her husband would name Shahjahan. It was a difficult birth, but not the worst she had experienced. Still, after it was over she was unable to go to the bank, and the torrents of rain that had been thrashing the village since the previous evening showed no signs of letting up. As Amena lay on a thin blanket draped across the dirt floor of her hut that morning, she hoped that Nobirun and Firoza would walk the half mile to see her, but feared that instead they would go to the bank and get her in trouble for not showing up.

As it turned out, the women waited an hour for Amena before heading to the Zianpur bazaar with only banana leaves shielding them from the rain. When they told Rohim that Amena was late and might not arrive, he flew into a rage and tore up her loan documents. No one considered that she might have gone into labor; Rohim and the women guessed that she had been unwilling to walk the three miles to the bazaar during a rainstorm—a poor excuse as far as the bank was concerned.

When word about the birth of Amena's son reached Rohim the following day, it was suggested that a new date for disbursement be set for two weeks hence, but Amena got word out that she would be ready to pick up her loan in three days. All five women walked to the bank on the appointed day, as they had earlier that month for Fulzan and Alow, and Amena received her 3,000-taka loan.

Amena promptly turned over 1,900 taka to her husband, with which he was to restart his cookware business. She explained to him that of her 2,000-taka loan, 100 taka had been taken out for the "group tax" and what he was getting was the remainder. The next day, Absar Ali went to Dhaka and bought aluminum cook-ware. It was the first time since his and Amena's arrival in Kholshi that his merchandise had not been bought with a loan from a mon-eylender. There was a noticeable bounce in his step once he got working again, and longer intervals between what had once been nearly daily beatings he administered to his wife.

While her husband was in Dhaka, Amena was secretly negoti-ating the purchase of ducks, ducklings, and chickens with the 950 taka that she had kept back. Her plan was to build up a small livestock business without her husband's knowledge. Amena fig-ured that part of the profits she earned would be saved while the rest would go toward her children's education and food. She wanted to save to ensure herself against the thing she, and virtually all women in rural Bangladesh, fear most—abandonment by their husbands, either by divorce or death.

Until receiving the loan, Amena had felt powerless in the face of her husband's laziness—he would work for a few days and then rest until the money ran out. She had to contend with his fits of rage when he beat her and the children, and his desire to take a second wife as his brothers and father had done. For years she had tried to raise ducks and chickens on the side, stashing away what little she could save so she could purchase little gifts for her chil-dren—something their father would never think to do. She would sneak them a boiled egg to go with their vegetable curry, especially during the dry season. But with no capital, her activities were ex-tremely limited. If two chicks died, it might close her business for a year or more.

Now, with nearly a thousand taka in working capital, she had a chance to build up some savings. She still feared the beatings. A week after getting her loan, Amena was visited by Oloka Ghosh, who had heard her neighbor's cries during the frequent abuse of the last three years. Oloka told Amena to tell her husband that there was a Grameen Bank rule stating that if a borrower was regularly beaten by her husband she would be unable to get future loans. She did, and the frequency of the beatings went from every other day to once a month. Oloka then recommended that Amena tell her husband that borrowers whose husbands remarried were also at risk of being forced to resign from their group. For Amena, such trickery dredged up bitter memories of her fighting with her husband when he wanted to marry another woman during the time they lived in Rajshahi. It was during that conflict that she received the most frequent and severe beatings, including the time she was hit repeatedly with a bicycle chain.

"Aaki, come here," Amena called out to her eldest daughter as she wiped her face with the end of her sari. "It's time for school."

Aaki hurried out of the hut, poured some water in her hand from a clay pot, splashed it on her face, and, still avoiding her mother's gaze, said, "I'm going, Mother." She broke into a run as she crisscrossed a rice field on her way to the raised dirt road that her father had mounted a short time before.

Four months earlier, Amena had enrolled Aaki in a private school run by a nongovernmental organization called the Bangladesh Rural Advancement Committee (BRAC). It didn't cost anything except her and her daughter's time, and it was better run than any of the other schools around. The BRAC schools are something like privately run Head Start programs that aim to give poor children who have dropped out of the school system a way back in and those who are at risk of dropping out a boost in confidence. Yet in Kholshi, as in thousands of other villages in Bangladesh, local religious leaders were making threats against the BRAC school, saying it was set up to convert its students and their parents to Christianity. Many pointed to the fact that BRAC's female supervisor, who came each week from Ghior, rode a bicycle, an act of defiance against tradition that hardly any female Grameen Bank staff dared to replicate. There was talk that Islamic fundamentalists were plotting to burn down the school and perhaps the houses of some of the students, as had already happened in a few places in Bangladesh.

As always, Amena was frightened of being ostracized by the community, but she had a dream that she dared not tell anyone else yet—that her daughter would pass her matriculation examination and get a job, perhaps with the government or a private group like BRAC. At a parent-teacher meeting held soon after Amena was recognized as a Grameen Bank member, the BRAC instructor took Amena aside and congratulated her. Taken aback, Amena asked the woman how she knew. "I am a borrower in the center in the southern *para*," she said with a smile, "and I encouraged Nonibala to stick up for your right to join her center. With the help of the Almighty Allah, we will all come through this all right."

As Amena watched her daughter disappear into the horizon, she turned her gaze briefly to a small plot of land in front of her hut that she planned to turn into a vegetable garden. For years she had helped tend her mother-in-law's vegetables, though she hardly ever got to taste the fruits of her work. Now she planned to have a garden of her own, and if she could find a way to buy a hand-pumped tube well, she could tend it year-round, even in the dry season. It would also give her ready access to clean drinking water. Buying and setting up a hand pump would require close to 2,000 taka, but now that she was a member of Grameen Bank, even that seemed within reach.

In the distance, Amena heard her chickens squawking. In one motion she lifted the bamboo basket from over her ducklings and began calling her chickens—"*Ah-woo, ah-woo.*" As the ducklings and their mother began scuttling away, the chickens appeared from the underbrush in front of the house and scampered to Amena's feet. After they were fed, the secretary of group number seven began preparing lunch for her family. With the temperature approaching 95 degrees, and the humidity already quite oppressive, she had a long day ahead.

Muhammad Yunus exudes an uncommon degree of confidence, warmth, and, when necessary, firmness. He pushes his colleagues hard, but usually knows when to stop. He has a legendary memory that allows him, at any given time, to keep track of hundreds of projects carried out by thousands of people. To most, he appears at peace with himself and his work. But appearances are sometimes deceiving. In the spring of 1993, in a meeting with Grameen borrowers in Manikganj district, Yunus passed out from internal bleeding from his previously undiagnosed gastric ulcer.

Nothing angers Grameen's founder more than politics. On several occasions he was offered his choice of government ministries to run under President Ershad, and each time he refused without considering it seriously. "Ministers, even the president," he was known to say when people asked him why he turned down such prestigious and lucrative offers, "are hostages of the party they belong to. Theirs are largely ceremonial positions, with little scope to effect change."

When democracy returned to Bangladesh in 1991, Yunus and his colleagues were initially inspired by the discipline and restraint shown by the nation's 115 million citizens during parliamentary elections that were universally hailed as free and fair. But the optimism was short-lived. Newly elected parliamentarians spent most of their first session discussing their privileges rather than the nation's problems. A famine in the northern region of Rangpur, for instance, went ignored.

Two years after the elections, Yunus made a brief appearance on the nation's political scene. In August 1993, Dr. Kamal Hossain, one of the leaders of the center-left Awami League, announced that he was forming a breakaway party called the Gano (Democratic) Forum. Hossain had discussed the idea with Yunus before he made his move, and Yunus had reluctantly argued in favor of forming a new party. He admired Hossain's integrity and hoped that a new party would be free of the political hacks that filled the ranks of both major parties. "If you form a party," Yunus said, "don't let anyone join who has been part of any other party." Yunus's vision was a political force for those who felt alienated from politics.

Hossain scheduled the Gano Forum's inaugural convention for August 27 and asked Yunus to speak at it. Yunus had no interest in getting involved. Grameen already faced enough people— Islamic fundamentalists, leftist academics, and moneylenders— who wished the bank would go away; being seen as favoring one political party over the rest would only make things worse. Yunus searched for a way to say no to this friend who had gone to such lengths for him in the past.

Yunus declined at first, but Hossain worked on him. He sent M. A. Muhith, the onetime finance minister who had successfully pushed for the issuing of the Grameen Bank ordinance in 1983, to urge Yunus to accept the invitation to speak. Muhith had recently left a job at the United Nations and was working with Hossain to launch the Gano Forum. The meeting came and went, and still Yunus did not commit. Yet the phone calls, from Hossain and others, kept coming. Finally backed into a corner, Yunus agreed to give a speech, but only if he was part of a panel of speakers.

When Yunus arrived at the conference, he was struck by how many quotes from his earlier writings had been blown up and put on the walls. With more than a thousand activists assembled, Yunus delivered a speech that sent shock waves throughout Grameen Bank and the country's political circles. The title of the speech was "Some Political Thoughts from a Nonpolitical Citizen." The subtitle, in parenthesis: "If I Offend Anyone, Please Forgive Me."

Yunus fleshed out the problems plaguing the political scene in Bangladesh in stark terms. Heavily armed student wings of the nation's major political parties were making instruction at the universities all but impossible. The major economic issues facing the country, including an increasingly exploitative relationship with India, were being ignored. Senseless work stoppages called by the opposition groups, mudslinging and character assassination, and outright violence had replaced rational dialogue as the principal means of political discourse. Characteristically, Yunus resisted the temptation to merely criticize; he offered his own vision of a political party, and generically called it Amar Dol (My Party).

Amar Dol would be managed from the bottom up rather than from the top down. The village-level party committees, traditionally the lowest position on the totem pole, would have real power. They would be promoted to higher levels by virtue of their good works in their villages—improving education, raising agricultural output, bringing better health services. The local party leaders would be development workers first, political workers second. There would be no student front of his party, and any person who perpetrated violence in the name of Amar Dol would be punished, not promoted.

When in opposition, Yunus's party would cooperate with and, whenever appropriate, commend the government. All criticisms would be constructive, and no *hartals* (general strikes) would be called under any circumstances. While in power, his party would ensure that opposition parties have access to the media. An environment conducive to domestic and foreign investment would be created. Those who flouted the laws would be punished, no matter how influential they might be, and poor people who tried to help themselves would have more places to turn for support, though fewer places to turn for handouts.

The speech was a stinging, if indirect, indictment of both the ruling and opposition parties. Even though Yunus stopped well short of joining Gano Forum, with his speech he had made himself a major political player. With a network of 12,000 employees and 1.6 million families who claimed membership in Grameen Bank, many knew that he had a potentially formidable political machine—a machine he had the capacity to mobilize.

The media response was fast and furious, coming from the left and the right. *Jai Jai Din,* a popular weekly magazine, reprinted the speech in full, along with a positive editorial. Bodruddin Umar, a Marxist academic, wrote one of the first major responses in a daily newspaper. After castigating *Jai Jai Din* and others for being uncritical of Yunus's proposals, he accused Grameen's founder of being naïve and hiding his true intentions behind "foggy" ideas. But then came the clincher: Professor Yunus, who was widely known to have met Bill Clinton when he was governor of Arkansas, was, Umar said, an agent for U.S. imperialism who was about to launch his own party. The entire country, he warned, was in danger.

For weeks afterward, dozens of articles commenting on Yunus's speech from all across the political spectrum appeared in national periodicals. The managing director observed the fallout with bemused detachment, and never considered writing to correct some of the outlandish things his critics accused him of.

Six weeks after the Gano Forum event, Yunus's name was back in the news for a different reason. The *Doinik Janakantha,* the paper that published Bodruddin Umar's article, ran a story that began, "Yesterday, Professor Yunus met with President Clinton in the Oval Office of the White House." Suspicion of Yunus grew.

• • •

"What do you mean, you left it over there? That is my rice—taken from my land! You must bring it here," Fulzan Begum shouted at her husband, gesturing wildly with both arms as she spoke. Her undersized, ten-month-old daughter, sitting naked on the ground, started crying as her parents continued an argument that had begun earlier that morning.

Harun, Fulzan's husband, looked at the ground and said meekly, "I was going there after I cut the rice in the field. I just . . ." His voice trailed off, and for a moment he seemed lost in thought.

Fulzan picked up a shovel and took a threatening step toward her husband. "Go, now, and tell her you are bringing the rice here!"

"Okay, I'm going. I'll be back in a little while." He started walking down into the muddy culvert that separated Fulzan's tiny plot of land from those around it.

It was three and a half months since Fulzan had received her loan from Grameen Bank, and during that time she had taken the first steps down the bumpy road from destitution to subsistence.

Four years earlier, Fulzan and her two older sisters had suffered the last in a long series of abandonments. Their father, Hazrat Ali, a widower since his wife's death one month after Fulzan was born, succumbed to a mysterious disease. Hazrat Ali had long before lost his ability to care for his daughters, and for the ten years before his death he had survived by begging. Besides losing their parents, Fulzan and her sister Shundari had been abandoned by their husbands and were forced to spend many months on their own, a dangerous position for women in rural Bangladesh. Only their sister Golapi, who lived with her husband, had enjoyed any protection.

The three sisters had never been to school. At the age of ten, Fulzan joined her sister as a ditchdigger, a job of last resort for landless men and destitute women in rural Bangladesh. In exchange for a day's work, the girls received a small bag of wheat or three taka. (Grown men received nearly ten times that amount.) Between what they earned and what their father could manage, they missed only the occasional meal, though eating fish and meat were out of the question except during the Eid festivals. Over the years, Fulzan gained a reputation as the best female ditchdigger in Kholshi. By the time she was an adult, her skills were recognized in an unprecedented way—she was paid nearly as much as men.

During each dry season, thousands of rural Bangladeshis are employed to "move the earth." With a virtually inexhaustible supply of rich topsoil, fishing ponds can be excavated, roads built, rice fields lowered, or housing plots raised with only shovels and muscle. Proper preparation for the coming monsoon can mean the difference between a dry homestead full of rain-fed rice and fish that is connected to the bazaar by a dirt road, and a flooded, isolated hut whose owner's rice crop has perished in the swamp. Thus, the dry season means consistent demand for ditchdiggers like Fulzan, who can often find employment four or five days a week and earn 30 taka (75 cents) or a few pounds of wheat.

Whatever amount she could save was always spent during the rainy season, when work was slow. When it came time to arrange a marriage for Fulzan, there was no money for a dowry, so the best that could be arranged was a union with a young man from Faridpur district whose family was so poor that it was agreed that he would come to Kholshi to live with Fulzan and her father. (Normally, the new wife moves in with her husband's family.) It was only a matter of time before Fulzan joined the growing numbers of Bangladeshi women who are abandoned by their husbands.

In 1992, two years after Fulzan's father died, she began being visited by a man she had met digging ditches. He was married to a woman in the village and lived with his wife's family, but he was unhappy with her, primarily because she had been unable to bear him any sons. Harun said he wanted to take Fulzan as his second wife, but his mother-in-law told him she would never agree to such a union. To her, Fulzan was far beneath them on the social ladder—an earth-cutter, for God's sake! But Harun's wife told him that it was okay with her if he took a second wife, and shortly thereafter a small ceremony was held.

In the days immediately following the wedding, Fulzan lived with her *shoteen* (the word that describes the relation of one wife to another in a polygamous household). While the two wives got along, Harun's mother-in-law made Fulzan's life miserable. As the household's "little [second] wife," Fulzan was expected to do the lion's share of the housework while getting hardly any food to eat. When Harun was out working, Fulzan was forced to listen to repeated insults, delivered in vulgar language. After a month, Fulzan left. When Harun came to bring her back—she lived only a quarter mile away—Fulzan said that while she hoped he would spend time with her from time to time, she was going to stay put on her father's land. She believed that if she stayed with Harun's mother-in-law, she would become too weak to work and would slowly starve to death.

Settled back at home, Fulzan heard about an opening in the Kholshi center from Oloka and began taking steps to become a Grameen Bank member. When her group was recognized and she was allowed to make a loan proposal, Fulzan said she wanted to buy a calf. Up until then, she'd been able to raise cows only on a sharecropping basis, under which the owner would receive half of the increase in value of the cow. When the second recognition exam came and went successfully, she dreamed of finally being a cow owner. But as the day of the loan proposal drew closer, her husband began arguing for a different investment—leasing one-third of an acre of land with their $50-dollar loan. Just as Fulzan raised livestock on a sharecropping basis for lack of the investment capital needed to buy a calf or a goat, the little land Harun farmed was cultivated on a sharecropping basis. With half of the harvest going to the owner of the land, there was little reason for Harun to hope that he would ever realize the aspiration of all Bengali peasants—to eat rice grown on one's own land all year round.

The couple argued for many days about what to do with the loan. Harun, in an effort to soften Fulzan up, began spending more of his time, including nights, in his second wife's rotting thatch hut. Harun's mother-in-law was, naturally, not very amused. But even though the tin roof his first wife lived under shielded him from the elements, she could not provide that which would transform Harun from a sharecropper into a farmer.

It was ultimately agreed that Fulzan would give Harun the money to lease a *bigha* (one-third of an acre) of land, but that she had to be present when he finalized the deal with the landowner. The two would share the burden of paying the 40-taka ($1) weekly installment, and Fulzan would receive all of the crops when they were harvested. (Harun, as always, would be welcome to come and eat at her house after the harvest.) That way, Fulzan would be able, for the first time, to eat rice from her own land rather than buy it in the market—a major step up the social ladder. Furthermore, she would get to keep the rice husks, which she could use as feed for her livestock. It was also agreed that if and when she became eligible for a seasonal loan for buying fertilizer and insecticide, Fulzan would consider applying for the loan to improve the yield. Finally, Harun was made to agree that if, with the blessings of the Almighty Allah, they were able to repay the first general loan, Fulzan would be able to buy a cow with the second general loan.

Two days before, Harun had brought in the first rice crop harvested from the land. It was a good yield that would, after threshing, leave two *maunds* (164 pounds) of unhusked rice. Yet Harun had brought the fruits of his labor (and his wife's investment) to his mother-in-law's home—and that had provoked Fulzan's wrath. Her angry words had their desired effect. Later that afternoon, Harun delivered the paddy he had cut the day before. As Fulzan watched it being delivered, she tried to appear calm and relaxed, as though she had expected it all along. Nothing could have been farther from the truth—as the conflict subsided, Fulzan Begum picked through her harvest meticulously, her heart racing the entire time.

Before Indian independence, Kholshi was primarily a Hindu village. Perhaps one in five households was Muslim, and nearly all Muslims were daily laborers who worked in the homes and fields of the more prosperous Hindus. Relations between the two groups were peaceful, but distant.

Older people in Kholshi remember the famine of 1943 as the event that undermined this tranquillity. Several dozen people, mostly women and children, succumbed to starvation. It was during this time that widespread thievery, petty as it may have been, began. The social discipline that had reigned for so long in Kholshi had been shattered.

On independence in 1947, Kholshi became part of East Paki-stan. At the time, there was no fear of Muslim dominance over the Hindu majority. Only the wealthy Hindu landlords fled to India, their ornate estates left to crumble in the open air, their land in many cases confiscated by the highest or best-armed bidder, with the rest reverting to government ownership.

One significant improvement in the early years of Pakistani rule was that education became accessible, at least in theory, to low-caste Hindus and Muslims. A government school was built in Kholshi, and even though most of the teachers were high-caste Hindus—nobody else knew how to read or write—for the first time students included boys from all walks of life. While few children actually studied more than one or two years, it was nothing short of a social revolution that the son of a Muslim day laborer could be seen sitting next to the son of a Brahmin in primary school.

For centuries, the economy of Kholshi had been based on rice and fishing. As the Pakistani period progressed, irrigated agricul-ture was introduced. Low-lying land that had been virtually useless for monsoon agriculture (because it was submerged in as much as six feet of water) became prime soil for rice cultivation during the dry season, with the use of high-yielding seeds that required fertil-izer, irrigation, and constant weeding but produced yields almost three times greater than those of traditional varieties sown during the rainy season.

Kholshi was virtually untouched by the independence war in 1971, although terrified families from other villages sought refuge there from the fierce fighting between the Mukti Bahini and the Pakistani army. Often, the refugees would arrive with bamboo, thatch, and livestock in hand, ready, if necessary, to rebuild their huts on a generous stranger's homestead plot and prepared to stay for several weeks.

In December 1971, when independence was at hand, people of all social classes, castes, and religions looked forward to peacetime. Many thought that the future would bring about a society with all the social harmony and low crime of the British period, the widespread access to education and stable prices inaugurated under Pakistani rule, and the pride of living under a government run by ethnic Bengalis. Bangladesh would finally have its own industries, its own jute mills, and its own government. But those hopes crashed headlong into reality. Prices of essential goods skyrocketed, the law-and-order situation deteriorated precipitously, and the wheels of government ground to a halt. For the first time, virtually nothing happened without a bribe, and often it didn't even happen then. The only improvement people experienced was that for the first time, girls joined boys in primary school classrooms.

The 1974 famine hit Kholshi hard. Prices of essentials such as rice, salt, and cooking oil went through the roof. Those who had access to land, money, and productive resources made huge amounts of money buying and leasing land from poor families at rock-bottom prices. Moneylending thrived. During the years immediately following the famine, things returned to normal, except that the social landscape was littered with scores of families who were now deeply indebted to the wealthy families without any hope of getting out.

Beginning in the early 1980s, the Muslim community slowly became more assertive. But communal peace in Kholshi reigned until the destruction of the Babri mosque in India in December 1992, when young ruffians, emboldened by those among their elders who stood to gain from a Hindu exodus, went on a rampage that left all four major Hindu temples in Kholshi little more than rubble. In the months that followed, "Hindu flight," much like the "white flight" of South Chicago, took on the character of an inevitable and ever-accelerating process.

The early 1990s were a time of turmoil in Kholshi, not only among the two religious groups but also among the sexes and the generations. Grameen Bank, which by 1993 had more than a hundred members there, was well positioned to help shape that change, in subtle but profound ways.

6

▲

Omiyale DuPart

It was still well before dawn when Omiyale DuPart was dropped off at Newberry Street by her daughter, but Les Papillons' chairlady felt that she was late. Then again, Omiyale was always running late. Another ten minutes and that spot on the sidewalk would have vanished, she thought to herself as she set up her table. Omiyale never liked to miss Sunday at Maxwell Street. Loud, dirty, and smelly it might be, but she felt at home there. Only at Maxwell Street could she unload merchandise that wouldn't sell anywhere else, providing it was at the right price.

On this day, Omiyale was being helped out by Janet, her younger sister and fellow Full Circle Fund borrower, who had dreams of buying her first car with her profits. They often help each other out like this; Omiyale reasons that a relative is less likely to accept too low a price for one's merchandise. They transferred the stuff she wanted to sell from black garbage bags to a pair of fold-up picnic tables and a blanket spread out on the ground. They set out a used winter jacket, a winter hat, children's shoes, jewelry, oils, and spices. Some of the clothes were things that her children had outgrown and that had been lying around the house. Why not sell them? What's junk to me might be a treasure to someone else,

Omiyale figured, hoping that she might take in $100 between 6 A.M. and 2 P.M., perhaps $150 if it got a little warmer. Such thinking is the essence of Maxwell Street.

Omiyale is a mother of eight who was born as Veronica Wilma Ramsey and raised in a Chicago housing project. Ever since childhood she'd suffered from a stutter, and spoke as little as possible when she wasn't around family and friends. In the mid-sixties she met Paul DuPart, an aspiring artist, and they began dating. At the time, Veronica wore her hair "relaxed" (straightened), and often bleached it blond. Her wardrobe was full of name-brand miniskirts and she talked of becoming a model. To Paul DuPart, who was involved in the black consciousness movement and associated with the Nation of Islam, Veronica was a prime example of a black person who needed her awareness raised.

Paul explained to Veronica that she lacked understanding of who she was and who black people were. He told her that her hair and dress—her entire concept of beauty—was adopted from Europeans, that her values and ambitions had been shaped by an alien culture.

Even the stutter, he suggested, was a result of conscious and subconscious doubts she had about herself and her heritage. If you can simply learn to take pride in yourself and your people, he said, the stutter will melt away like a stick of butter in a hot frying pan.

Veronica listened closely to her suitor's arguments, and occasionally attended educational events with him. Among the speakers they heard together were Malcolm X and Elijah Muhammad. In time, they participated in marches and volunteered their time with black nationalist organizations. Omiyale changed her name, dress, hairstyle, and diet to conform to Muslim requirements, and to the surprise of everyone except Paul, her stutter vanished. Black consciousness, she concluded, had solved what a half dozen speech therapists had failed to.

The two were married in 1965, and within a year Omiyale was pregnant. They agreed that all of their offspring would be given African names and wear traditional dress. They would be brought up conscious of their culture and heritage. If possible, they would go to the Institute of Positive Education, an all-black private school on the South Side.

During the late sixties and early seventies, Paul worked in a succession of low-paying jobs while he took courses in the visual arts at Chicago State University, ultimately earning a bachelor of arts degree. Often, he studied during the day and worked at night. Though that meant financial hardship in the short term, they dreamed of a future in which Paul would find satisfaction and adequate remuneration as an artist.

Meanwhile, to try to develop a new source of income Omiyale began taking jewelry classes that were being offered by the Chicago Park District. Always the star of her classes, within a few years she was able to make a wide variety of earrings, necklaces, and pins out of silver and gold. She sold her handiwork to friends, often at house shows, and later at arts and crafts festivals. When Paul encouraged his wife to get a bachelor's degree at Chicago State University in the 1970s, she went part-time for a few years, but later dropped out. Instead, she learned to sew in another Park District class. Child-rearing was time-consuming, and she enjoyed making and selling jewelry and dresses more than sitting in classes with middle-class students half her age. For a time, she sold Tupperware after a successful Chicago-area saleslady recruited her to do so. That saleslady's name was Thelma Dean Ali.

By the mid-1980s, Paul was working as a mental-health aide at a psychiatric clinic, earning less than $20,000 per year to support a household that included five teenage children and two grandchildren. The family lived in Englewood. Omiyale had taken up selling at flea markets and rented a thrift shop in Hyde Park, the most affluent neighborhood on the South Side. On weekends, she often closed her store and brought merchandise that wasn't selling to Maxwell Street, where she frequently saw Thelma. The two women exchanged ideas and information, one suggesting a street festival the other hadn't heard of, the other leaking word of a going-out-of-business sale where they could pick up merchandise for next to nothing. They came to respect each other's business savvy and began to share booths at summer festivals and other events.

When the landlord from whom Omiyale rented her thrift store and with whom she had good relations died, the new landlord doubled her rent from $250 to $500. She tried to continue running the store for a few months, but the higher rent cut too far into her profit margin. In late 1988, she closed the store for good.

Omiyale worked the flea market–Maxwell Street–arts and crafts festival circuit during the spring and early summer, but when a lamp company advertised a position for an industrial polisher, she applied for and got the job. It paid $18,000 a year, and she was struck by the fact that she was the only black woman, and the only woman polisher, working there. Several colleagues remarked that she was chosen because of a new affirmative action policy, but that didn't bother Omiyale. By that time she was taking care of a grandchild and there was another one on the way. She supplemented her income by digging up worms in the parks after work and selling them to coworkers who liked to fish. She also sold them merchandise left over from the thrift store.

During the last six weeks of 1990, two events occurred that were to change Omiyale's life. The first was being laid off from her job; apparently, the lamp company didn't limit affirmative actions with minorities to hiring—it spilled over to firings as well. The second event occurred several weeks later—she heard about WSEP.

Omiyale heard about the Full Circle Fund by chance from a balloon seller outside the Seventy-fifth Street el station. Omiyale had never heard of anything like the Fund before, but it seemed like a good idea to her. After attending an orientation meeting, she told Gwen Burns she would have a group of five ready to meet with her in two days' time. Gwen was pleased and surprised by how eager Omiyale was; most women are somewhere between skeptical and afraid after they listen to her spiel, and many take months of coaxing before they are ready to commit. But Omiyale was just weeks removed from being laid off, and the ability to access credit without regard to her credit history was an opportunity she couldn't resist.

Omiyale called Thelma late at night after she returned from the orientation meeting to tell her about the Fund. Thelma agreed to help her friend pull together three other women by Wednesday night. After Thelma hung up, she said a prayer to Almighty Allah that this might be a genuine program. If it was, Thelma knew, it could only have come from the Creator himself.

Thelma, Omiyale, and three other women met that Wednesday at the home of Omiyale's mother on Garfield Avenue in Englewood.

To Thelma and Omiyale, joining the Fund meant more than simply access to a loan. In a pinch, both had usually been able to call in favors and borrow money from family members or other, more prosperous vendors. But the Full Circle Fund meant guaranteed access to increasing amounts of working capital as long as they repaid on schedule. There'd be no more begging, no more imposing on friends. Now they could concentrate on building up dignified businesses.

When Thelma took her first loan for $300, it nearly doubled the capitalization of her business. Omiyale was a bit more adventurous and took $1,500. In addition to credit, the program brought them in contact with other vendors, as well as with small, home-based manufacturers from whom they could buy wholesale. In the past, Omiyale and Thelma would hear of lucrative events only after they'd occurred, because fellow vendors were unwilling to share the information. Now, in a group with other women whose success was linked to theirs, they were more likely to get timely information, and the support and encouragement that they would need.

Shortly after three o'clock in the afternoon, Omiyale and Janet packed their merchandise into a taxi as they prepared to return home. They had grossed nearly $150 and heard about some upcoming events from other vendors. When everything was packed away, Omiyale jogged over to Thelma's table on Thirteenth Street to see how her friend was faring and to discuss the agenda for the center meeting to be held the following evening. A few minutes later, Omiyale was off on her way to Chicago's South Side.

For the most part, the Full Circle Fund operates in overwhelmingly poor, black neighborhoods. To understand the poverty of these areas, one has to consider Chicago's history. It is the nation's greatest blue-collar city, a product of the Midwest that lacks the sophistication of New York or the pretensions of Los Angeles. Chicago has been shaped by three distinct migrations—the first from Europe, the second from the Mississippi delta, and the third from Mexico. The result is a relatively young, very Catholic city, with neighborhoods that retain strong ethnic affiliations and a machine-dominated political system with plenty of graft to go around. It is also a profoundly racist city, though there have been periods in its history when the races coexisted relatively peacefully.

At the end of the eighteenth century, the land on which present-day Chicago sits was forest and prairie, uninhabited but for the occasional Pottawattomie Indian who passed through it. Somewhere around 1790, a French-speaking Haitian named Jean Baptiste Point du Sable established the first permanent settlement in an area the Indians had named Chickagou, their word for the wild garlic that grew along the shores of Lake Michigan and caused such a stench.

Six years later, du Sable, together with his Pottawattomie wife, Catherine, and their two children, moved on to Peoria. But in a short time he had left a lasting impression, for as late as 1835 Indians who by that time had been forcibly driven from the area were known to say, "The first white man to settle Chickagou was a Negro."

Between du Sable's departure and the 1840s, small numbers of blacks fleeing the depredations of the antebellum American South settled in Chicago. By 1850, Chicago had become an important terminal in the Underground Railroad, and while many blacks escaping slavery continued their journey east or north to Canada, others stayed in the Windy City. By the time of the Civil War, a thousand blacks were living there, mostly on the banks of the Chicago River. On the whole, they were accepted by white society, and on occasion they were held up as model citizens whom recently arrived immigrants from eastern and southern Europe would do well to emulate.

Still, black people were welcome only in small doses. When emancipation was declared in 1865, there was considerable fear of a large influx of freed slaves from the South. But no such migration occurred, and by 1870 a scant 1 percent of the city's population was black.

Despite blacks' small numbers, resentment began to build among the white working class against those who did arrive. Blacks were accused of depressing the general wage level and taking white-held blue-collar jobs. Riots broke out periodically, often involving the Irish, whose antagonism toward blacks was already the stuff of legend. But while blacks' treatment in the stockyards was often harsh, the freedmen were able to make their influence felt at City Hall. Within twenty years of abolition, most legal segregation outside the school system, including obstacles to securing the right to vote, was expunged from city and state statutes. The slow process of achieving equality under the law had begun.

Between the Civil War and the First World War, Chicago's population exploded from 100,000 to more than 2 million. After the Great Fire of 1871 (which destroyed some 17,000 buildings) and a smaller conflagration three years later, neighborhoods realigned, and the Black Belt south of the Loop was born, initially covering a stretch of land three blocks wide and fifteen blocks long.

As the black population continued to grow, it began establishing its own institutions, including newspapers, social clubs, and churches. A small but influential upper class and a growing middle class emerged and tried to exercise some control over those immigrants who failed to live by norms set by the church and the "respectable" black community in general.

On the eve of the First World War, Chicago's black population had expanded to 40,000. Chicago, however, was more concerned about absorbing a flood of poor immigrants from Europe than about relations with the Negro community. Blacks themselves were afraid that this massive influx of whites would threaten their foothold in the stockyards. New arrivals, often the despised and downtrodden in their own countries, were eager to avoid starting at the bottom in America; having a class of people below them from the outset, as blacks seemed to be, was doubtless reassuring. Despite this, ethnic communities of European origin and blacks lived peacefully side by side in many neighborhoods. Racially mixed marriages were uncommon but not unheard of.

During World War I, the European migration was reversed, with thousands of men returning home to take up arms. At the same time, the United States became the chief supplier for the Allied cause. This created a sudden need to boost industrial production in northern cities like Chicago even as the workforce shrank. The stage was set for a historic migration of some 60,000 blacks to Chicago between 1910 and 1920, a process facilitated in part by white recruiting agents (much hated by white southerners who needed their cotton picked) who crisscrossed Dixie in search of laborers, and later by the stories of riches that filtered back after the first waves of migrants secured good-paying blue-collar jobs that had been previously reserved for whites.

Recalling the extraordinary nature of that migration, Nicholas Lemann has written, "It was undeniable that the economic opportunity [in Chicago] was greater; that moment in the black rural South was one of the few in American history when virtually every member of a large class of people was guaranteed an immediate quadrupling of income, at least, simply by relocating to a place that was only a long day's journey away."

While the factory owners and politicians viewed the migration as a necessity, there was trouble in the streets. Newspaper headlines like "Negroes Incited by German Spies" and "2,000 Negroes Arrive in Last Two Days" did nothing to relieve the growing anxiety. One of the principal sources of animosity revolved around the question of where to house the new arrivals. The Black Belt, already overcrowded in 1910, needed to expand, and expand it did, at the expense of previously lily-white neighborhoods to the southeast. Real estate speculators of both races, eager to induce panic selling at rock-bottom prices by whites and then to make substantial profits by selling and renting those units to blacks, made out handsomely and came to be widely detested by whites and blacks alike. Homes of newly settled blacks, as well as those of the real estate men who brought them there, were being firebombed by angry whites by this time. There were fifty-eight bombings in the so-called transition neighborhoods in southeast Chicago between July 1917 and March 1921, one every twenty days.

In July 1919, the conflict boiled over in an event that would change race relations in Chicago forever. A six-day riot was ignited when a black boy swam into an area at the Twenty-ninth Street Beach that was reserved for whites, by custom if not by law. The boy was stoned by whites when he tried to swim ashore, and after swimming back out to sea, he drowned. Enraged blacks retaliated in force, and pitched battles were being fought in the streets within hours. During the next six days, the Irish who lived on the western edge of the Black Belt made repeated incursions into the Negro neighborhoods and burned buildings to the ground. Black youths, not to be outdone, responded in kind.

When the ashes had settled and the dead—thirty-eight of them—had been buried, the black and white establishments tried to make sense of the madness that had engulfed the city. A blue-ribbon commission was formed, and it laid blame for the riot largely on the housing shortage and the resulting real estate speculation. The commission also found fault with the police, the courts, and white society at large for failing to deal justly with the Negroes before the riot and for failing to protect them once it began. For black people, who had lived relatively peacefully in Chicago for decades, the riot marked the end of a positive period in race relations.

A customer was pushing at the door of West Side Books, to no effect. "It sticks—push hard," Queenesta Harris shouted from behind her counter. Her voice barely carried through the thick glass, but the man got the idea, pushed harder, and let himself in. It was perhaps the twentieth time that morning that someone had entered Victor's store that way.

As the customer walked toward the back of the store, he made eye contact with Queenesta but said nothing. "Hey, Ms. Johnson, where's Vic?" the man inquired. Dorothy Johnson, a seamstress who rented space from Victor, pointed toward a door leading to the conference room in the back.

In the front of the store, Queenesta strode up to the door and tried to fix it. She failed; the door had only two positions, open and stuck. Her attention drifted to a store across the street, on the corner of Mason Street and North Avenue, to a red neon signboard that had been placed in the window of a video rental shop three days earlier; it read, "JD's Records and CDs."

The establishment of JD's meant the end of Queenesta's reign as the only music retailer on her block. JD had most of the same titles she had, except that he carried a better selection of compact discs and charged about 50 cents more than she did. Though she didn't share with Victor her worries about being driven out of business, for the past several days she had been a nervous wreck. More than anything else, she hated that neon sign. Queenesta guessed it cost $300, and she feared that a flashy gimmick like that might lure her customers away.

This development came at an inauspicious time for Queenesta. She had been hoping to devote at least half of her time that fall to selling Afrocentric children's books to Chicago's public school system. She knew of only one other woman who was doing this in the city, and figured that this was the year to make a killing. Teacher consciousness had been raised, and by the following school year she was convinced another half dozen distributors would be competing against her. If she could get in good with a few teachers during the 1993–94 school year, she might receive a regular income for years with little additional effort. But the politicians didn't allow her plan to go forward. In September, the Chicago public schools had no budget and could not legally open. A bankrupt public school system meant no business for the foreseeable future. Thus, she was forced to concentrate her energies and investment capital in her music business.

As she returned to her counter and began nervously rearranging her cassettes, Queenesta's mind raced. Should I carry more compact discs? Do I have to drop my prices? How in the hell can I get a damned neon sign myself? Is this place too "black" for the sixteen-to-twenty-four age group? Will they feel more comfortable buying from a music retailer who is housed in a video shop? Just then, two teenagers appeared outside the door. "Push hard, it's stuck!" an exasperated Queenesta shouted out. After making eye contact with them, she made a pushing motion with her right arm. Seeing that, the boys got the message and let themselves in.

"Hey, Queen," the taller of the two boys called out.

"Hey, guys, what can I do for you?" They came directly over to her case and crouched down as they looked at the tapes. Queenesta followed their eyes, feeling a little embarrassed that she didn't have more in stock.

"Queen, you got that Digital Underground tape yet?" the taller boy said without looking up from the case.

"No, I'll try to pick it up tomorrow. That's the new one, right?" She pulled out a little pad of paper and made a note—"Digital Underground, NEW!"—and underlined it twice.

"Yeah. Queen, your competition across the street is fading you," the shorter teenager said, drawing out the word "fading" for effect. "He got the Digital Underground since last week."

Queenesta stared blankly, searching for a response. Seconds later, her customers completed their search of the tape case, fingered absentmindedly through the budget rack of compact discs, and made for the door. As they disappeared into the mass of cars and people on North Avenue, Queenesta put her elbows on the glass case and buried her face in her waiting hands.

When white soldiers returned to Chicago after the First World War they wanted their old jobs back, and by and large they got them. Black workers were either fired or demoted. Between this displacement and a brief recession in the early 1920s, most of black Chicago's economic gains during the war years were wiped out, and communal harmony continued to deteriorate as the Black Belt nudged into new territory and unemployed blacks were frequently employed as strikebreakers.

By 1925, however, a resurgent economy brought many unemployed blacks back into the workforce, and racial tensions temporarily subsided. The five years before the Depression were by all accounts the most prosperous ones the black community in Chicago ever enjoyed.

By the late 1920s, the Black Belt covered eight square miles. To anyone who was paying attention, it was apparent that black Chicago was evolving in a different pattern than other ethnic groups, which tended to band together in "colonies" or ghettos for one generation and then disperse throughout the city once their children had become Americanized. This option was not open to blacks, who, by virtue of their color and the legacy of slavery, could not move freely throughout the city without fear of reprisal by whites. There were certainly movements inside the Black Belt, but it was all contained within the same contiguous geographical unit. It would be a half century until even upper-class blacks could buy a house or apartment in most areas of the city.

Not all blacks disliked this apartheidlike arrangement. Many sensed that it held out the potential for unprecedented racial solidarity and uplift. Jesse Binga, a successful Negro banker of the pre-Depression era, reminded black Chicagoans that they had $40 million deposited in the city's banks and property with a yearly tax assessment of $2 million. Binga's vision was of a growing class of black businessmen who would serve and employ members of their own race. He pointed to seven black-owned insurance companies that each collected $100,000 in annual premiums and the phenomenal growth of the city's two black-owned banks (one of which was his).

This brief interlude of prosperity and optimism was rudely interrupted by the Depression, which by the mid-1930s had led to the dismissal of thousands of black employees, the bankruptcy of Jesse Binga's bank, and much more. In response, the call for black solidarity found new expression in a campaign known as "Spend Money Where You Can Work." The idea was that black consumers should boycott white businesses that refused to hire them. When the campaign met with some success, it immediately gained nationwide attention.

These victories were only a few drops in a sea of black unemployment and despair, but they were enough to entice more black migration from the Mississippi delta. Another 43,000 immigrants from the South poured in during the 1930s, including Thelma Ali's parents from Indianola, Mississippi.

After American entry into World War II the economy picked up, and for the second time in thirty years there were severe labor shortages in Chicago. Not surprisingly, between 1940 and 1944 another 60,000 black migrants arrived, aggravating the chronic problems of bad housing, overcrowded schools, and inadequate medical, sanitation, and recreation facilities in the Black Belt. The population density there reached 90,000 per square mile—as opposed to 20,000 per square mile in neighboring white communities—and tuberculosis death rates for blacks in the early 1940s were more than five times that of whites.

By the 1960s, Chicago mayor Richard J. Daley had perfected his political machine. As far as the Daley machine was concerned, incoming waves of black migrants meant more loyal Democratic voters. During his first several electoral triumphs in the late 1950s, support for Daley in black wards on the South and West sides was strong and, in at least one case, decisive. The housing crisis continued to grow, however, and with as many as 2,200 black migrants arriving every week during the late 1950s, Daley and his inner circle had to decide how to respond. Inevitably, they threw their lot in with those wishing to maintain the color line rather than break it down. Their strategy for solving the housing shortage was to build vertically inside the Black Belt rather than promoting the kind of scattered housing patterns that had achieved the integration of other ethnic groups in the Second City. The Robert Taylor Homes—"the largest public housing project in the world, twenty-eight identical . . . sixteen-story buildings," according to one writer—was opened in 1962, and blacks were herded into a place that would attain a notoriety virtually unparalleled in the industrialized world.

Social movements led by Saul Alinsky, Martin Luther King, Jr., the Black Panthers, the Nation of Islam, and others attempted to redress the growing poverty, anger, and isolation of the black ghettos as well as the often violent racism that characterized the neighboring white communities. But progress was halting, where it was made at all. Soon after coming north for a campaign, King was prompted to say after a particularly harrowing day of protests, "The people of Mississippi ought to come to Chicago to learn how to hate." Among the most controversial issues was that of overcrowded black schools. "Truth Squads" of black mothers were arrested when they attempted to document that nearby white schools were operating at well under full capacity. Yet for many years Daley was able to contain such protests while retaining an acceptable level of black support in elections.

This equilibrium broke down after the riots following King's assassination in 1968, during which large tracts of black neighborhoods on the West Side were burned to the ground (more than a quarter century later, they have yet to be rebuilt). Daley, incensed that things had been allowed to get so out of control, made his famous order for the police to "shoot to kill or maim" looters. From then on, many white politicians began to simply write off the black community, their strategy being to win election without their support and, consequently, without having any debts to black Chicago after being elected. With the dramatic exception of Mayor Harold Washington's historic election in 1983, the black community became more politically marginalized after 1968 than at any other time in the history of the city. At the same time, the social fabric of the black community began to break down.

Members of disadvantaged groups as diverse as Native Americans in the United States and Canada, Muslims in the southern Philippines, and low-caste Hindus in India can benefit from small loans delivered through organizations modeled after the Grameen Bank. Credit provided through peer groups allows poor people in these groups to capitalize on their survival skills and break the vicious cycle of discrimination in the labor market, low income, low savings, low self-esteem, and negative portrayals in the media. Needless to say, socioeconomic disadvantage often results from historical processes played out over hundreds of years and cannot, in most cases, be overcome quickly or easily. But the Grameen approach has manifest advantages over strategies that rely on the free market, private charity, government handouts, or hiring quotas. Low-income African Americans living in distressed inner-city neighborhoods are showing that they can benefit from small loans. This is particularly impressive and important when one considers the rapidly deteriorating socioeconomic conditions of inner-city blacks over the last three decades.

In 1965, Daniel Patrick Moynihan published his influential and controversial report *The Negro Family: The Case for National Action*. The Moynihan Report, as it came to be called, had many facets and subtleties, but critics focused on its treatment of the weaknesses of poor black families. The attacks were sufficiently vicious to virtually bring to a halt any serious sociological research on the black family. According to sociologist William Julius Wilson, "After 1970, for a period of several years, the deteriorating social and economic conditions of the ghetto underclass were not addressed by the liberal community as scholars backed away from research on the topic, policymakers were silent, and civil rights leaders were preoccupied with the affirmative action agenda of the black middle class." For close to two decades, the ghetto fell off the radar screen of the American consciousness.

Ignoring a problem does not, of course, ensure that it goes away. Much to the contrary, this one snowballed. While a quarter of all black births were out of wedlock the year Moynihan released his report, by 1980 that figure had ballooned to 57 percent. The percentage of female-headed households rose from 25 percent to 43 percent over the same time period. Though there were similar trends among other races, they were starting from much lower base figures and were well below the catastrophic proportions of the African American community. Nowhere were these trends being manifested more dramatically than in black Chicago, and in few places in black Chicago quite like Englewood.

The prevalence of single motherhood, caused in large part by widespread unemployment in the inner cities in the wake of jobs being moved overseas or to the suburbs, contributed to an unraveling of the social fabric of neighborhoods like Englewood, as did greater abuse of drugs and alcohol and the growing influence of gangs on young men.

With gangs inevitably come violence. Sociologists report that the leading cause of death for black men aged fifteen to thirty-four is homicide. A typical entry on the police register page of the *Chicago Defender,* on November 18, 1993, reads, "Wednesday found criminal activity on an upswing in the city. . . . A male in his 20s was reported dead on the scene by police in the 110 block of South

May Street. The victim had apparently expired from multiple gun-shot wounds to the body. . . . An African American male, age unknown, was in critical condition in Mount Sinai Hospital Wednesday. The victim was stabbed in the chest by an offender while watching a street fight in a parking lot on South Pulaski Avenue. The victim was allegedly stabbed for no reason. . . . A 16-year-old male was in good condition Wednesday after being shot in the right jaw. Police reports indicated that the teen was shot during an exchange of gunfire between rival gangs. . . . A citizen discovered the badly burned body of [a] man in an open garage in the 8100 block of South Racine Avenue Wednesday. The subject's age and identity could not be immediately determined." Nearly 5 percent of all black males will end their lives as a victim of homi-cide. Every four hours, a black child receives a gunshot wound. Yet these deaths often pass with barely a mention in the news media, and police rarely expend much energy trying to get to the bottom of black-on-black violence.

So, it is ironic that at just the moment when young black males are achieving predominance over American youth culture through rap music and hip-hop fashion, as a group they are suffering from massive, often self-inflicted wounds. Princeton scholar Cornel West, searching for the reason behind the carnage, writes, "[There is a] sense of worthlessness and self-loathing in black America. This angst resembles a kind of clinical depression in significant pockets of black America."

Marian Wright Edelman, founder and director of the Chil-dren's Defense Fund, wrote in a 1993 newspaper piece that a black girl had a 1-in-21,000 chance of receiving a PhD in mathematics, engineering, or the physical sciences but a 1-in-21 chance of being a victim of violent crime during her teen years and a 1-in-6 chance of having a child before she was twenty. Edelman noted that chil-dren who "should be dreaming of what they want to be when they grow up, what they'll wear at their wedding, how many children they want to have and what they'll name them" were instead "planning their own funerals."

The causes of the calamity have recently become the subject of intense debate between and among liberals and conservatives.

Some point to the isolation of the inner-city poor and their result-ing lack of connection with job networks and positive role models. Others blame generous welfare programs, a lenient criminal justice system, and genetic inferiority. Still others argue that in many re-spects, today's underclass exhibits behavior that is a predictable urban mutation of the social norms prevalent in the antebellum southern sharecropper society.

The Los Angeles riots of 1992 were a frightening reminder of the widespread anger within these tracts of our major cities where crime is rampant, economic activity moribund, gang warfare a daily fact of life, and single motherhood the rule rather than the exception. A man living in Harlem is less likely to reach age sixty-five years of age than a man living in Bangladesh.

The lack of any sustained program to revitalize the inner cities in the wake of the L.A. riots—or rebellion, as some prefer to call it—reflects the widely held belief among the public and lawmakers that there are no affordable solutions to these problems. So, with each passing month, the remnants of civil society vanish—corpo-rations leave, schools become battlegrounds, parks become drug bazaars, and buildings that once housed working people and local businesses fall into disrepair. Along the once majestic Garfield Boulevard in Englewood, boards replace windows by day and gun-fire resounds through the night. Yet white America seems stymied for solutions, and black America talks angrily of conspiracies against it. Why else, an increasing number of African Americans argue, are drugs, liquor, and guns (not to mention AIDS) made more accessible to them than basic amenities like supermarkets, police protection, regular garbage collection, and competent teach-ers? Nowhere are these feelings more strongly felt than in Chicago, one of the most segregated and racist cities in the world.

These social ills are, ultimately, the reflection of an economic reality. Black urban poverty is more concentrated and visible than the rural deprivation of the Adirondacks or the deep South. The Full Circle Fund is hard at work demonstrating that the Grameen approach can work with those on the edges of the worst American economic disaster areas, while other programs are making head-way in Arkansas and South Dakota, which, along with Englewood, make up a fair cross-section of economic disadvantage in the United States.

Thelma was perhaps the tenth woman to enter the room on October 3, 1993. Ever since Gwen had left, the Lindblom Park center meetings had been starting later and later, and they were not as well organized as they had been. On most occasions, no one took the time to arrange the chairs in a circle. The women sat theater style, a format that made the gatherings considerably less intimate.

Thelma greeted several women and took a chair next to Omiyale. The two began exchanging gossip and laughing as they watched a few more women straggle in. Thelma's head was covered in a scarf and she wore ragged blue jeans. Omiyale also came to the meeting dressed informally, though not quite as much so as her friend. Other women had come in their Sunday best, some with small children in tow. Colete Grant, Gwen's replacement and an entrepreneur herself, sat at a table in a corner of the room, busying herself with paperwork as the room slowly filled.

When Geri came into the room, Thelma stood up and walked over to her as she was signing in. The two women hugged, but in less than a minute the conversation turned serious. Thelma urged a reluctant Geri to announce that she was going to hold some house shows to sell her aprons and gift baskets later in the year. Thelma then hugged Geri again and the two walked over to where Omiyale sat. The center chief looked up at the women as they seated themselves, peering over her bifocals. She was thumbing through a gigantic, overstuffed three-ring file that contained all her Full Circle Fund papers.

Glenda Harris arrived and ambled over to near the window, joining Thelma, Omiyale, and Queenesta. The women exchanged greetings, and as was her wont Glenda touched each of them, plus Shayna, within a few minutes of arriving. But there was something restrained about her, and everybody sensed it. Finally Glenda blurted it out.

"Girl," she began as she looked at Omiyale, "I've made a decision."

Omiyale put her hand on Thelma's thigh and turned toward Glenda. "What's that?"

"You aren't going to be happy with this. I'm going to be dropping out of the circle."

"Oh, girl!" Omiyale couldn't contain her disappointment. "Why?"

"You all have given me so much inspiration and energy. You inspired me to get out there and sell my jewelry, but you know, my physical condition just doesn't allow me to run around to events like I've been doing, taking public transportation and all. It's hard just coming to the meeting." As Glenda spoke, her eyes moved from Omiyale to Thelma to Queenesta, and back again. "I'm gonna try to get into some kind of thing where I sell through a catalog; that's the vision I'm into now. I can't keep up with you. But how much I've learned from you . . . oh!"

Tears welled up in Omiyale's eyes, and Glenda began to cry as well. "Thank you, for crying, for being emotional about this," she said to Omiyale.

"There ain't no reason for you all to get wet over this," Omiyale said even as she began to cry. "Glenda, you have done fine, and if someone is going to leave, this is the way to do it. You have paid off your loan and settled up with us. We're happy for you, really. We'll just miss seein' you every two weeks, that's all. So don't go gettin' like that, ya hear!"

Omiyale grabbed hold of Glenda's hand and squeezed it hard. The two looked at each other, speechlessly, as tears gently rolled down their cheeks. "I'm going to be in touch with you all, that's for sure," Glenda said.

Glenda Harris lived, along with roughly a dozen other people, with the McFerrens, a husband-and-wife activist team that took in people who had lost or abandoned their families and needed a place to stay. The McFerrens called their home a "mission house where whoever loved God and desired to live there could." Hardly any action was taken there without being preceded by a prayer. Among the people who shared the house with Glenda and the McFerrens was Gwen Burns. Both she and Glenda were from broken homes and regarded their landlords as their parents.

Years earlier, while she was in the midst of her religious conversion and recovering from a drug habit that had turned her into a petty thief, Glenda had read an article about the Women's Self-Employment Project in a newspaper. But instead of following up her interest, she'd simply cut out the article and put it in her purse. It became a conversation piece, something she would unfold and show a friend. When she did so, she often expressed skepticism about whether such an organization would lend to low-income people without reference to their credit histories.

When Gwen told Glenda in 1989 that she had interviewed for a job at WSEP, then started working there and found that it actually did make loans to low-income women, Glenda wasted little time in joining. Gwen was pleased to be able to suggest Glenda to Omiyale as a replacement for an earlier borrower in Les Papillons who was leaving the circle. At their urging, Glenda began selling her jewelry at street festivals and indoor bazaars. On occasion, when she went to Springfield to lobby for more funding for Chicago public schools with Mrs. McFerren, she brought her jewelry case with her and sold while she protested, often earning several hundred dollars in the process. By the time she decided to resign from the group, she had enough regular customers to keep her business afloat and high hopes of persuading an upscale catalog like Spiegel to carry her jewelry.

As the others arrived, Thelma continued to reassure Glenda. Finally, Colete called the meeting to order and the women settled down. Colete asked one of the women to say a prayer to begin the meeting. Most of the women liked the ritual, but Thelma believed that it had no place in a business meeting attended by people of various religions.

Colete made some opening comments and then asked for announcements. One woman talked about a forthcoming event called Dance Africa, while another asked about having a senior WSEP staff member come to a future meeting to give a talk about accounting. By the third announcement, Thelma began whispering,

"Geri, it's your turn," in a soft voice. Yet Geri's hand remained by her side.

Finally, Thelma held up her hand and said, "Colete, Geri's got something to say."

"Geri," Colete said with a smile as she stood in the front of the room, "do you have an announcement?"

Geri bolted up from her chair and turned sideways so that she faced most of the women in the room. Her mouth opened for a brief instant, but nothing came out. Finally she said in a hurried voice, "You all know I'm making my gift baskets for Thanksgiving and Christmas, and I'm making . . . aprons, yeah, aprons; you've seen my aprons. I'm going to be having three shows in my home around the holidays, and I want all of you to . . . to bring your friends to my shows. I'll have the dates for you next week." As Geri sat down, she had a look of terror in her eyes. When Thelma patted her on the back, she looked back and smiled nervously.

Many budding entrepreneurs in the inner city can't afford a storefront to display and sell their merchandise. Instead, they hold shows in their own homes and in the homes of friends, where they can network and sell with little or no overhead and interference from government inspectors. For Geri, holding these events would be a milestone in her effort to expand her business. At Thelma's urging, she was going to invite several owners of retail establishments in Englewood to come to her home shows and consider carrying her merchandise on a consignment basis.

After announcements, groups of five women gathered in different corners of the room for "circle business." In the middle of the room, members of Lindblom's newest circle held hands and bowed their heads in prayer. Months before the Middle East peace agreement, five black women had joined together to ask God to bless their businesses and their circle, despite the fact that two of them were from the Nation of Islam and the remaining three considered themselves "Hebrew Israelites." After their prayer, they began discussing the first two loan proposals they would put before the center's loan committee. They had named their circle "Let Us Make Woman."

Les Papillons gathered in a corner of the room, and Omiyale

began collecting loan payments from each of the five women. There was discussion of Glenda's impending resignation, and what steps the others would take to replace her. Toward the end of the meeting, Omiyale noticed that Queenesta was being quieter than usual, and moved her chair closer to her youngest circle sister. "Queenesta, how is your business going?"

"Well, okay; a little slow, you know. It's just that this guy has opened up another record shop across the street from me, on North Avenue. And he has this red neon sign in his window. That sign, I don't have anything like it. I'm afraid people are attracted to stuff like that."

Omiyale closed her notebook and studied Queenesta, trying to gauge how discouraged she was. "You're gonna be all right."

Thelma, listening to the conversation, jumped in. "Are your prices competitive?" she began.

"Yeah, most tapes I sell for fifty cents less than he does."

"Well, I'll tell you what, business is business and people don't gonna be paying any extra fifty cent to look at a neon sign. Are your customers staying with you?"

"You know, they tease me, sometimes going back and forth, but most of them are still buying with me. I missed a couple of recent releases so I lost some sales, but I won't let that happen again. I'm going to a different distributor."

"I think Thelma's right—you'll do fine if you keep your prices low," Omiyale added.

As the group moved onto other subjects, a low murmur of voices from other circles poring over similar problems echoed in the background. Queenesta appeared to have had a weight lifted from her. Later she would admit that while she didn't feel she could be vulnerable around Victor, having the opportunity to let her guard down around the women in Les Papillons was a relief.

When the meeting ended at nine-thirty, Thelma walked over to Omiyale and said quietly, "I'm glad Queenesta has some competition. It will make her a better businesswoman. She'll have to work harder." Omiyale, listening to her old friend, pursed her lips and nodded. Several minutes later, the two women packed up their bags and began their long journeys home.

• • •

The day before the next meeting, Queenesta looked in her cash box and realized she had just enough to pay her installment. Weeks before she would have been too frightened by the prospect of missing a payment to invest that money and try to turn it over in a day, but in the latter stages of 1993 she was feeling more confident. That night, she went to the music distributor on the South Side, picked up a few popular titles she had run out of, and promptly sold all but one of them the next day. As she headed to the meeting, she congratulated herself for having taken a risk and then made $30 more than she needed for her payment.

During the meeting, Wanda X and Gheeliyah Rojas of Let Us Make Woman appeared before the loan committee of Omiyale, Thelma, and Leverta Pack to present their loan proposals. Both were requesting $1,500. Gheeliyah made a concise presentation about how she would use her loan money to buy supplies for her greeting-card business. She was an artist, and a fairly talented one at that; her cards were distinguishable by their trademark designs and messages written in shiny gold ink on black paper. When Thelma asked her how many retail outlets sold her cards, she conservatively estimated forty. Though she didn't mention it, and perhaps didn't even know it, they were sold in stores as far away as New York and Washington, D.C. After some brief discussion, the committee approved her loan for the full amount requested.

Wanda asked for $1,500 for a new business making decorative gift boxes out of used cigar boxes. Thelma and Omiyale asked how many she had sold to date. Wanda said she hadn't sold any. When they asked what events she was planning to sell them at, she said she wasn't sure. The discussion lasted more than half an hour, roughly double the time it had taken for Gheeliyah's proposal, and at the end of it the loan committee sanctioned $800. Wanda was disappointed, but her circle members who had watched the process unfold were relieved. They had asked her the same questions about her intentions in a special meeting they had convened a week earlier, without better response.

By the time the two women received their loans, JD's Records and CDs had closed up shop on North Avenue. The neon sign remained for several more weeks, but it was rarely turned on. By November, it was taken out of the shop's window for good.

The Haldar *Para*

From the days of the very first group training conducted by Ruhul Amin, the epicenter of Grameen Bank's work in Kholshi has been the Haldar (fisherman) *para*. Of the sixty Haldar families in Kholshi, most live in a narrow patch of land bordered on the south by a raised dirt road and a tiny marketplace, and on the north by a canal that remains filled with water from the early days of the monsoon until well into the dry season. During the months of rain, each homestead plot, on which up to five families might live, are islands separated from the others by water that is six or seven feet deep. People ferry back and forth by boat, if they have one, or by walking across wobbly bamboo bridges that are hardly four inches thick. Others, particularly the children, simply swim from place to place.

To one walking among the huts during the rainy season, the number and variety of fishing nets is striking. Some, fresh from being used, are tangled with water lilies, still dripping water, as they hang on a bamboo clothesline; others are in the process of being woven or repaired. The whole family joins in the work of net-weaving, but it is usually the woman of the house who directs the process. Nets are strung out, then rolled up along a post on the hut's veranda, where each new knot is carefully tied.

Over the last quarter century, the men of the Haldar *para* have had to travel ever farther to ply their trade as more and more of the rivers and canals flowing through Kholshi have died as a consequence of the whims of the Jamuna. Some of the fishermen have turned to farming and other professions, particularly during the dry season. The situation of the Haldar women has, however, changed very much for the better.

Before Grameen Bank arrived in the Haldar *para,* net-weavers like Devi, Shandha, and Amodini were in great demand for their services, but since they could not afford the working capital to buy the expensive thread they used, they were forced to work on a contract basis. A client would supply all the materials and pay the women 25 taka (60 cents) to weave them a net, a job that took as long as three days of full-time work. When they wove nets for their husbands, the women were often forced to borrow from the village moneylender. The loan was paid off by selling half or more of the family's catch over the first several weeks after the net was completed.

Access to capital from Grameen Bank changed all that. Now Amodini and Devi earn 100 taka or more from net-weaving over a two-to-three-day period; during the months just before and after the beginning of the monsoon, business is brisk, and their nets can be sold in the market just a short distance from their homes. Grameen Bank loans meant that on a given net, these women's profit quadrupled. In a world where a few pennies means the difference between eating and starving, this was a big step up.

During the 1993 monsoon, Devi made a bold investment of 30,000 taka to lease a large pond in a nearby village for seven years. She made a 10,000-taka down payment, half of it coming from her seventh Grameen loan and the rest from her savings. The final 20,000 would be due at the end of the coming dry season. If she couldn't bring her husband closer to the fishing, she would bring the fishing closer to her husband.

From the beginning, the superstitious Devi had invested her money wisely, diversifying from net-weaving into raising livestock and pigeons. Now she was trying to solidify her economic position. Devi enjoyed the honor of having the center house located on her small house plot, and felt that she wanted her home to be a demonstration to the newer borrowers of what was possible through Grameen Bank.

In a house plot next door, Shandha and her family were, like Devi's household, in a constant state of motion: feeding cows, weaving nets, fishing, cooking, stocking the birdhouse, which keeps a dozen pigeons. Sometimes the activity is frenetic, yet Shandha is firmly in control of all that goes on in her household. In a similar way, she is the matriarch of her center. No matter who is the elected center chief, Shandha retains a considerable amount of power. She counts the money and does most of the talking with the bank worker during the meeting; when there is a conflict, most of the women rely on her to speak up and resolve it. She has a motherly quality about her, and the women, a few of them ten or more years older than she, seem to like being mothered by her.

Yet there is a sadness about Shandha these days. Her five sisters, and many of her aunts and uncles, have emigrated to India. Sometimes she thinks she would like to go as well, but her husband is against it and Shandha is herself reluctant to give up her membership in Grameen Bank for the uncharted waters of India. But she is tempted nonetheless. Many of her friends seem to be planning to flee Kholshi in the post–Babri mosque era of Hindu-Muslim tension. Though Hindus like Shandha never speak about it in public, there are fears that after the next anti-Muslim incident in India, the Muslims in Kholshi will bypass the Hindu temples and come directly after the Hindu people. Harassment from Muslims who are eager to buy up land from Hindus leaving for India is a fact of life now. Yet her general anger at the Muslims is softened by her weekly contact with nearly thirty Muslim women at her center meetings.

As the 1993 monsoon wore on, Shandha became worried about Amodini, who lived in a nearby house plot, perhaps three minutes away by boat. Amodini had performed well in her year as the center chief, yet just as she'd turned over the reins things began going wrong for her. Her husband, Ramesh, got sick and couldn't go fishing more than once a month. Apparently, he suffered from a bleeding ulcer, caused perhaps by the same combination of tension and contaminated water that had afflicted Muhammad Yunus. To make up for his lost earnings, Manzu, their oldest unmarried daughter, took up fishing in the local canals with nets woven by her mother. Early in her father's illness, Manzu, along with her younger sister, snuck off one day in the family's boat without her mother's knowledge—believing, correctly, that Amodini wouldn't approve of their fishing alone—and made the case for allowing her to go regularly when she came back with nearly 150 taka worth of fish. Shocked and in tears when her daughters returned, Amodini reluctantly agreed that they could continue fishing until their father recovered. At the same time, Ramesh and his wife were being pressured by Amodini's older brothers to move to India. Only her youngest brother offered quiet encouragement for her to stay.

When she joined the bank, Amodini was the poorest woman in the entire Haldar *para,* living with her husband and children in a cardboard shack. Once she had run from her ramshackle hut during a heavy rainstorm to take refuge in a tin house where her mother and brothers were, and was horrified to see her mother standing in the doorway with a club, refusing to let her in. Thirteen years earlier, Amodini had had little choice when she'd returned home. The Dancing River had left her husband and his relatives with no choice but to scatter in a half dozen directions. Though she preferred to keep it a secret, there was no denying it—Amodini Rani Haldar was a *nodi bhanga lok,* a frequent migrator. To her mother and all but her youngest brother, that made Amodini less than welcome; at times, it made her feel something less than human.

Bending over, Amena swept her small courtyard with a *jharu,* a short broom of twigs. She swept expansively, leaving the dried dirt in neat circles. She put organic debris in her garden and dumped the rest behind her house. In Bangladesh, sweeping is as much for appearance as for waste removal, as there is hardly anything one actually throws away. An entire class of people make their living by going from house to house buying up *bhanga jinish* (broken things) from people in exchange for homemade sweets. These throwaways are sold to wholesalers and taken to Dhaka for recycling. Other things are reused locally; for instance, used paper is made into packaging that is sold to local grocery stores. Apart from the omnipresent animal droppings, Bangladeshi villages are remarkably clean—not because the Bengalis are compulsive about such things, but because there is always another use for something after it has served its primary purpose.

After completing her sweeping, Amena began gathering the grass that her daughter had collected the day before and putting it in a feeding bowl for the newest member of her family—her cow. In December, Amena had applied for a seasonal loan from Grameen Bank. She told her husband, Absar Ali, that the 4,000 taka she received was for buying a cow, and he promptly went to the weekly Ghior market, which was famous for cow-trading. Within several weeks, the cow started producing a liter and a half of milk every day. Amena would give a little to her children and sell the rest to a milk wholesaler who came to her house. Typically, Amena would tell her husband that she earned less than she actually did.

Another addition to Amena's house plot was a tube well for pumping up groundwater by hand. She took out a loan in November from Grameen to buy that, too. With access to a supply of fresh water, she was able to maintain and expand her vegetable garden during the dry season. By February her garden covered nearly one-sixth of an acre and included pumpkins, eggplant, beans, chilies, and spinach. She fed some of her harvest to her family and had her daughter sell the rest in the Zianpur bazaar, from which she often received 100 taka ($2.50) per week or more.

The year before, Grameen had embarked on a large-scale program to give loans to borrowers for purchasing and installing these hand-pumped tube wells. They give their owners sufficient water for drinking and irrigating half an acre of land. For several years, UNICEF had provided subsidies to Grameen borrowers interested in buying tube wells, and the success of the initiative convinced Grameen's management to adapt it commercially on a wide scale. Loans ranged from 1,500 to 5,000 taka, depending on the depth the pipes needed to be sunk to reach the water table.

As Amena finished feeding the cow, she took a short break,

sitting down on a *piri* (low stool) and preparing *paan* for herself. It was 11 A.M. and nearly 90 degrees. As she chewed on the *paan,* Amena looked around for her ducks and chickens. She now had twenty-five chicks and had given out another ten on a sharecrop basis to her neighbors, lest her husband realize how big her business had grown. Yet none were in sight at the moment. Her eyes drifted to her garden, to her cow, and finally to the manicured courtyard in front of her. Inside the hut, the infant Shahjahan was sleeping, and she peeked inside to see him before beginning to pump up twenty buckets of water, one after the other, to irrigate her vegetable garden. The tube well had been sunk thirty feet from the garden, and she always felt a little sore after doing this chore. Yet when it was done, she looked on proudly as the earth lapped up the water. Amena took one last stroll through the garden, deciding which vegetables to send her daughter to sell in the Zianpur *haat* (twice-weekly market) in the afternoon.

As she returned to the courtyard, Amena heard her infant begin to cry. He had woken up, and wanted to be fed. Amena cradled him in her arms and began breast-feeding him. When he had had enough, Amena laid him back down on the *kanta* blanket and began weaving a bamboo mat that she would either use or sell in the market. She had bought the bamboo with a few hundred taka she'd saved when she'd cut corners on sinking the tube well. Every few minutes, she would take a break, pick up a fan, and begin waving it above her son. After a short time, he fell asleep.

As Amena sat there, weaving a bamboo mat in her hut, her thoughts were turning to her brother. He had caused a lot of trouble for her, and she resented it. But what could she do?

Several months earlier, twenty-two-year-old Mozafer Hossain began spending time with a married woman in her forties who lived in the village. Over time, he began to call her his *dhormio ma,* which roughly translates as "adopted mother" or "godmother." There were a few raised eyebrows, but nobody made much of a fuss about it. One day, Mozafer and the woman—a mother of three—eloped to Dhaka and were married. He pulled a rickshaw to support them, and they were living in a slum near the Gabtoli bus station. On several occasions over the ensuing weeks, the woman's husband went to Dhaka to try to find his wife. Periodically, people who backed up the woman's husband came to Amena's house asking for information about her brother's whereabouts. When Amena told them she didn't know, they often insulted her brother and her family in vulgar language. Amena was forced to spend many humiliating hours listening to abuse.

The newlyweds had broken many taboos and crossed over a fine line separating two contradictory parts of the Bengali psyche— a modesty and conservatism dictated by Islam and an emotional, romantic, and even impulsive side. Since the bank's founding, stories have periodically circulated about borrowers who visited centers in other villages only to fall in love with someone else's husband. Occasionally, there are rumors of affairs between Grameen staff members, and there have been many cases of harassment of female workers by male employees eager to arrange their own marriages. Despite Bengal's reputation on the Indian subcontinent as "the land of poets and lovers," Bangladesh is hardly a permissive society. When things like the elopement of Amena's brother happen, villagers are both horrified and titillated; they condemn and at the same time are just a little jealous.

Amena enjoyed having a cow of her own. A cow (better yet, several cows) is both a tool for achieving economic progress and a status symbol in rural Bangladesh. A cow provides milk for consumption or to be sold in the market, pulls a traditional *langal* (plow) in the rice fields, and produces dung that is used as fertilizer or, more often, packed into cakes and used as cooking fuel after it hardens. With luck, a cow will yield a stream of calves that can be raised or sold. It can also be fattened and then sold for large sums of money at the time of the Eid festival. Misfortune, of course, can mean a cow's sudden death; it takes a discerning eye to know when to sell a cow, such as in the early stages of an outbreak of bovine disease.

For most of the poorest households, the best that can be hoped

172 ▲ ALEX COUNTS

for is to rent a cow from a wealthy family. But any increase in the value of the cow, and of any offspring, are shared with the owner, even though such costs as feeding, inoculation, and veterinary expenses are borne by the sharecropper. Grameen has allowed tens of thousands of sharecroppers to become owners; indeed, while walking around Grameen villages one often hears borrowers excitedly talking about how they have become a *teen gorur maleek* (owner of three cows).

One borrower who made good through cow-raising is Oloka Ghosh, the neighbor of Amena's who was so instrumental in getting her into the center. As Amena was repaying her first loan, Oloka was caring for eight cows. Five years earlier, before she'd entered Grameen, she'd had no livestock. In hard times her family had mortgaged their land and were forced to rely entirely on their caste profession—making sweets—for their meager income. But because they did not have milk of their own, they were forced to buy it in the marketplace. Sometimes, the prices were so high that they would have no alternative but to take a loss to fill their orders. Today, they have enough milk for both family consumption and their confectionery business, and sell the rest. Oloka's husband has even learned enough about the milk business that he now makes extra money by trading milk, buying cheaply in one market and selling dear in another. The working capital he needs to do this comes, of course, by way of seasonal loans from Grameen Bank.

When Amena visited her friend's large, tin-roofed hut, she often marveled at the idea of a poor person coming to own eight cows. Normally, a *nodi bhanga lok* squatting on a relative's land with virtually nothing to her name would feel ashamed walking into the home of someone who had so much. But Oloka had reached out her hand to Amena, and welcomed her into her home and center. Sometimes, when they were alone, Amena shared with Oloka her dream of owning eight cows herself one day.

No description of Bangladesh is complete without discussing the foreign aid it receives. Development assistance is the Third World equivalent of welfare, only it is provided to nations instead of people. Virtually no village is untouched by it, and thousands of people, foreign and Bangladeshi, rich and poor, have benefited from it. In a few cases, rich countries with progressive agendas, such as Sweden, Norway, Germany, and Canada, have made sure that a significant portion of their development assistance has been used to reduce poverty. Even donor countries and international organizations with less idealistic agendas can usually point to at least one Bangladeshi project they have supported that has improved the lives of the poor. Yet, despite all the good intentions, these success stories remain the exceptions.

One of the ways that Sheikh Mujib distinguished his administration from those that followed it was in his hostility to foreign aid donors. Charities faced major hurdles in establishing themselves in newly independent Bangladesh. On several occasions, even the mighty World Bank was put in the uncomfortable position of having meetings that it had traditionally run chaired by government officials. The hostility was in most cases more style than substance, as the country was in dire need of food, medical supplies, and other essentials after the war of independence. But Mujib and his political allies craved the appearance that they, not the aid agencies, were the senior partners in the effort to rebuild Bangladesh. This stance resonated with many Bengalis, who had long perceived themselves as servants in their own home.

After Mujib's assassination, the foreign community in Dhaka grew quickly, their expertise supposedly needed to manage a burgeoning portfolio of foreign-funded projects. By the late 1980s, the annual commitment of donations from the United Nations, the World Bank, and wealthy nations had ballooned to $2 billion—or $5.5 million every day. However, the primary beneficiaries of many projects were foreign and Bangladeshi bureaucrats. The community of contractors making their living off the aid business was doing quite well, but the people in whose name the aid was given often did not benefit. Bangladesh, virtually free of violence against foreigners, became a desirable posting for professionals from wealthy countries eager to earn hefty, tax-free salaries while being cared for by a coterie of servants. Few among those who came to help dispense aid attempted to learn the language, to mingle with Bangladeshis, or to find out about life in the rural areas.

In the late 1980s, a study conducted on the aid industry in Bangladesh published some remarkable findings. Among them was the fact that some three-quarters of all foreign assistance funds were being spent in the donor countries themselves, and that most of the rest paid for the services of a small cadre of Bangladeshi individuals and firms. To a considerable degree, aid had become a means for wealthy nations to employ their own people to dump outmoded goods and ideas on the poorer ones. One foreigner who took a real interest in the country wrote, "In the world of aid, almost no work is done by officials. Aid agencies contract with consulting firms to identify, cost out, and implement projects. . . . And consultants, who work for daily wages, albeit quite high ones, are not about to lose their friendliness with the aid agencies that hire them. One cannot imagine a Swedish aid agency, for example, recommending a project that did not use Swedish products. . . .

"And that, of course, is the problem. For the project often begins with the product, and the aid agency, responding to its political masters, [looks] for projects that sell the product. If Holland has excess capacity in its machine-tool industry or Britain wants to dispose of used telephone exchanges from Birmingham (two real examples), the aid agency will offer to give these items as aid." Meanwhile, many pressing needs in Bangladesh remain unmet because they do not require products that donors are eager to part with.

Among those who share the blame for this are citizens in industrialized countries. While they often respond generously with donations to relief and development organizations working in Bangladesh or other poor countries, they do little to ensure that these millions of dollars are used to empower the Third World poor. As a result, the money ends up supporting some surprising ventures. Some years ago, I was told a story by a U.S. government employee that illustrates the effects of private-sector lobbying on foreign aid. An American company that specialized in packaging lobbied for the passage of a piece of legislation to require that food aid sent to Bangladesh be bagged before it was shipped. The bill passed, and funds were spent to bag the goods, but when the shipments started arriving it was necessary to spend additional aid money to unbag them before the food could be distributed. In this way, resources are spent without any impact being made.

Even within the current system, a few talented Bangladeshis have resisted the temptation to enrich themselves by becoming highly paid consultants for the Western aid agencies. Instead, they have accepted funds, used them with integrity, and paid themselves local wages, even though they could have commanded hundreds of times more elsewhere. These people include Akhtar Hameed Khan and his Comilla Cooperatives in the 1960s, Dr. Zafrullah Chowdhury's Gonoshasthaya Kendra (People's Health Center), Khushi Kabir's Nijera Kori (We Do It Ourselves), and Fazle Abed's Bangladesh Rural Advancement Committee (BRAC). Yet these initiatives have faced enormous obstacles. When the government tried to replicate the Comilla Cooperatives nationwide, it succeeded only in destroying their good name. When Zafrullah Chowdhury took on the multinational drug companies and accepted help in doing so from the Ershad regime, he was ostracized from the political and medical establishments. In 1993, BRAC's nationwide network of highly acclaimed nonformal primary schools came under attack by Islamic fundamentalists, and dozens of the huts in which classes were being conducted were burned to the ground. Yet for the people these organizations served, they were often the difference between hope and despair, between life and death.

The misuse of most foreign aid is a double tragedy for Bangladesh. First, if used properly, it could do much more to improve living conditions in the rural areas and urban slums. If, for instance, $2 billion was simply transferred directly to the poorest ten million Bangladeshi families (representing half of the population), each family would each receive an annual grant of $200. This would represent a figure more than twice the size of a typical Grameen Bank *loan*. Even if they did not invest all the money, the recipients would mostly use it to buy goods produced by other poor people, thereby energizing the rural economy. (Consultants and bureaucrats often deposit their money in foreign savings accounts or buy imported goods.)

The reliance on external resources has a second pitfall. After occupying a proud place among the peoples of the world for hundreds of years, in the last half of the twentieth century Bangladesh has been reduced to being a beggar among nations. The cumulative effect on the Bengali psyche has been profound. Many of the best and the brightest have left the country, and most of those who remain do so with one foot in London, New York, or Washington. Even those of humble origins flock to embassies of Western and Middle Eastern countries, only to have their visa requests refused by ill-mannered officials after having waited in line for six or more hours. Middle-class families spend precious taka on imported goods despite the existence of less expensive, locally produced merchandise of equal or superior quality. Their assumption is that if it is Bengali, it is of low quality.

Perhaps the state of the nation's self-esteem, stung in 1974 by Kissinger's remark about Bangladesh's being "the world's basket case," was best expressed in a 1992 televised debate between two groups of Bengali university students from rival campuses. The subject was "the Bengali character." One young man approached the lectern and said that Bangladeshis were scoundrels, cheats, and liars, unwilling to work hard and too willing to take bribes. Foreigners, on the other hand, were hardworking, honest, and law-abiding; in short, the antithesis of Bangladeshis.

A member of the opposing debate team asked his opponent, "If everyone is so honest in other countries, why do they need jails? Why do they need police?"

The first debater had a ready reply. The reason other countries needed to build jails and hire police was to deal with Bangladeshis who had left home and broken the law abroad.

Yunus hated the fact that so much aid was misused and that it often further enriched the wealthy while demoralizing the nation. Even as Grameen itself accepted large amounts of foreign assistance between 1983 and 1993, Yunus rarely missed an opportunity to publicly criticize the donor community in Dhaka. Even the agencies that provided Grameen with grants and low-interest loans were not immune. Yet despite his frankness—or, some said, because of it—the financial support continued to pour in. But, much to Yunus's dismay, organizations in other developing countries that were replicating the Grameen model were not so lucky: rarely could they attract grants to expand their work.

Most donor organizations would only fund research, not the credit-providing bodies themselves. In one case, the International Fund for Agricultural Development (IFAD), a Rome-based U.N. agency created to assist the rural poor, had sent five "missions" to investigate the possibility of funding a promising program in Negros, an island in the southern Philippines. The project had been started after the precipitous fall in the world price of sugar, the crop upon which the entire island's economy was dependent. Within several months of sugar's plunge, more than half of the children there were victims of third-degree malnutrition. Each mission—essentially a team of European and American consultants—cost IFAD several hundred thousand dollars in airline tickets, per diems, and professional fees. Yet even after all that expense, more than a million dollars in all, they had been unable to make a decision about whether to fund the program. By mid-1993, the project was nearing collapse due to lack of money; had it simply received an amount equal to the cost of a single mission, it would have been able to reach several thousand more poor families and meet its monthly payroll. But that, unfortunately, is not how the aid business works.

In early 1993, Yunus decided that he would try to raise $100 million himself and then distribute the money to promising replication programs in Third World countries through the less rigid Grameen bureaucracy. In talking up this proposal, he cited the success stories from a pilot project he had initiated that provided small grants to these organizations. The initial response from international donor organizations was muted. But in the summer of 1993 the administrator of the U.S. Agency for International Development, newly appointed by President Clinton and eager to make his mark, made a grant of $2 million to the replication fund.

By the fall, the World Bank was interested in making a contribution. The World Bank and Grameen had had a long and sometimes difficult relationship. The World Bank was the preeminent development organization, created immediately after the Second World War and charged with rebuilding Europe. When that was accomplished, it turned to the undeveloped countries, a task that turned out to be considerably more difficult. But the complexity of the problem of Third World underdevelopment didn't prevent the Bank from extending $22 billion in development loans each year for projects designed by its staff. Every so often, a World Bank–funded project that failed received unfavorable media attention, and the project, or the World Bank itself, was compared unfavorably with Grameen. To many people at the World Bank, Grameen represented an increasingly well known success story in which the Bank had no role. That led to some tense moments between the two institutions over the years.

When the World Bank offered $200 million to Grameen in 1986, Yunus turned it down. His reasons—that he didn't need the money and wasn't eager to have arrogant World Bank consultants telling him how to do his job—were widely reported in the national and international press. What he didn't say was how much pressure Bank officials had put on the Bangladeshi government to urge him to accept the loan—pressure that the usually pliable bureaucracy admirably resisted. On another occasion, Yunus and World Bank president Barber Conable appeared on a forum that was being televised by satellite to dozens of countries. Out of the blue, Conable said that the World Bank was providing significant financial support to Grameen. Yunus replied that it was doing no such thing. Conable went on to repeat his assertion twice more, and both times Yunus denied it. Later in the program, Conable bragged that his economists were among the most talented and brightest people in the world. Yunus responded by saying that hiring smart economists doesn't automatically translate into policies and programs that are of any benefit to the poor.

At one point, the World Bank abandoned hope of direct involvement with Grameen and decided to make its own, super–Grameen Bank in Bangladesh, one which would combine features of Grameen with those of other well-known nonprofit organizations in Bangladesh. When the government asked for Yunus's opinion, he wrote a humorous memo mocking the idea, saying that if you took the head of a horse and the legs of a cow and the body of a goat, in theory you might have a good animal but in practice it would be of little use. When the World Bank abandoned that proposal, it expressed interest in providing substantial funding to the Bangladesh Rural Advancement Committee, the largest non-profit organization in Bangladesh. When those negotiations broke down, the Bank said it wanted to provide $75 million to a new, quasi-governmental foundation that Yunus had been instrumental in establishing that would provide low-interest loans to organizations willing to make credit available to the poor. After a lot of battles and some behind-the-scenes lobbying in Washington, the Bangladeshi government decided to take Yunus's advice and provide the equivalent of $13 million from its own resources to the foundation and refuse the additional World Bank funding. Finally, the World Bank took the project document for creating a super-Grameen and gave it to the Sri Lankan government, where it was dutifully accepted.

As these conflicts receded, a sympathetic official in the World Bank's headquarters talked to Yunus in 1990 about commissioning an evaluation of Grameen. After conducting such a study, the official pointed out, the World Bank could no longer argue with Yunus's work and might even come to respect it. It would also give the World Bank the role it wanted in Grameen's success, without giving it any operational power. Yunus discussed the proposal with his colleagues, and most of them recommended that he refuse it. They argued that such an evaluation would be hopelessly biased against Grameen, considering the tensions that had plagued the two institutions' relationship. Yunus was confident that the evaluation would be positive and decided to invite the Bank to do the research. His only condition was that it would have to include his response to the study in the final publication.

In the spring of 1993, Yunus received a draft copy of the part of the evaluation dealing with the "financial viability" of Grameen. By taking data primarily from 1991 and 1992, years in which Grameen suffered its first large losses due to increases in staff salaries, the World Bank researchers concluded that unless Grameen Bank raised its interest rate it would either be chronically dependent on donated funds or would have to fold up operations. Yunus protested, saying those two years were atypical of a general trend toward profitability, and asked the researchers to redo their calculations using data from the first six months of 1993. When they began using those numbers, the researchers were surprised to discover that they yielded results that were the opposite of the ones in their draft report. As the year wore on, Yunus began hoping that the process of recalibrating the findings would allow him to include the data from the second half of 1993, as they were even better than those from the first half. He knew the World Bank researchers would resist having to throw out their initial findings, but he believed there was a strong case for them to acknowledge Grameen's financial strength. In any case, if they refused he could rake them over the coals in his written response.

By 1993, the World Bank was eager to turn its relationship with Grameen around with a dramatic gesture, one that would conveniently be announced at a World Bank conference on world hunger that was scheduled for late November. The conference had been called in response to a twenty-six-day fast by a U.S. congressman, Tony Hall, over world hunger, and the media was sure to give it ample coverage.

Yunus left for a trip to the United States in which he was due to meet President Clinton on November 8. The meeting had been arranged by George Stephanopoulos, who had met Yunus in 1987 when, as a twenty-four-year-old aide to Congressman Ed Feighan, he had championed a bill that supported the Grameen approach to poverty alleviation. The initial meeting was postponed when a young White House aide wrote down the wrong date in the president's calendar. While his friends in Washington tried to reschedule the meeting, Yunus took a trip to Arkansas to attend a workshop on lending to the poor in North America.

Meanwhile, Yunus talked with a senior official at the World Bank. After some lengthy discussions, the two arrived at an agreement under which the World Bank would make an initial grant of $2 million to support international replication of the Grameen Bank model. (The World Bank had been interested in making a larger contribution as a loan.) In exchange, the professor agreed to allow the Bank to announce the grant with all the fanfare it wanted at the hunger conference, at which Yunus was to be a keynote speaker. Word of the agreement was leaked to nonprofit groups that were trying to pressure the World Bank into making its lending policies more sensitive to the needs of the poor and the environment. Yunus, a man never exactly embraced by the ideological left in his own country or abroad, was portrayed as having sold out by some of the activist groups. They feared that his speech at the hunger conference would be an endorsement of the Bank's approach to poverty alleviation, one that the activists felt was just a public relations ploy bought with a tiny sliver of the Bank's substantial resources.*

After returning from Arkansas, Yunus finally got an audience with President Clinton. Yunus presented Clinton with a letter that had been signed by officials of nearly a hundred prominent charities, such as CARE and Save the Children, urging that impending cuts in humanitarian foreign assistance be restored. The president promised to try to restore the cuts. The two men proceeded to talk about the developments that had taken place in Grameen and the progress of the Good Faith Fund, an Arkansas-based organization Yunus had just visited that had started a Grameen-type program at about the same time the Full Circle Fund had gotten rolling. Yunus also acknowledged the positive changes that Clinton had brought to the U.S. Agency for International Development. He told of coming from a meeting there, and how after years of feeling as if he were in enemy territory while at AID, he now felt that he was among friends when he visited. The conversation shifted to the World Bank, which Yunus wanted to see changed as well. Clinton invited Yunus to prepare a paper on how the World Bank should be changed.

By the time Yunus addressed the hunger conference, the $2 million grant for replication to Grameen had been announced, and the Bank's public relations machine was playing up the organization's leadership in taking this "unprecedented and historic" step toward alleviating poverty and hunger. Yunus, meanwhile, had shown the Bank a draft of his speech and was asked to tone down

*The Bank lends some $22 billion each year, or nearly $2 billion per month. The $2 million contribution to Grameen Trust was equivalent to less than the amount the Bank lends in an average hour.

his criticisms of the World Bank. Finally it was Yunus's turn to speak, and the activists and Bank officials nervously awaited his remarks.

Had the officials known Yunus better, they would have known that there was no point in asking him to moderate his remarks. On many occasions, he has forsaken diplomacy and formality for straight talk. At a 1988 conference convened by the Society for International Development, a professional organization for people working in Third World development, Yunus gave the opening and closing remarks. His first address was an inspiring vision of a world free of poverty, and the steps needed to achieve it. His second speech was rather different. Standing before hundreds of attendees, he said, "I am very disappointed in this conference. I came here thinking it was going to be about ending poverty in the world. Walking around the conference the last few days I have discovered that what it is about for most people is negotiating their contracts for the next year." After a brief pause, his candid observation was met with a standing ovation.

Yunus titled his speech at the World Bank conference "Hunger, Poverty, and the World Bank." After saying a few words linking the fight against poverty to the cause of human rights, Yunus went on the offensive. "The World Bank was not created to end hunger in the world" was his blunt assessment. "It was created to help development. To the World Bank, development means [economic] growth. Single-mindedly it pursues growth to the best of its ability until it is distracted by other issues like hunger, women, health, environment, and so on. . . . [The] people who work at the World Bank were not hired to eliminate poverty from the world. They were chosen for qualities which may not have immediate relevance for poverty reduction.

"In order for the World Bank to take poverty reduction seriously, these issues have to be resolved in favor of poverty reduction. This may require us to go back to the drawing board, to design the Bank from scratch." The latter sentence was widely quoted in the international press.

Toward the end of his speech, he described how he thought the Grameen Bank and the World Bank were different. "Stories that we hear about the enormous debt burden accumulated by a large number of countries around the world and the miseries caused by the structural adjustment programs imposed on them by the World Bank make us feel that our two banks work very differently.

"When we hear about how countries are made to pay these debts through their noses, surrendering the bulk of their export earning, leasing out valuable resources at throwaway prices to make extra income, sacrificing social and environmental considerations to earn enough to repay their huge debts, we find it difficult to accept that as banking. Causing misery to people, and to nations, cannot be banking." Not once in his remarks did he mention the World Bank's grant to support the international replication of Grameen Bank.

A chilly wind blew through the office, lifting up the edges of a few papers left over from a loan disbursement the day before. Jobbar Ali sat at his table and studied the form that told him about the loan disbursement he would orchestrate later that afternoon. All of his staff had left for their center meetings earlier that morning, and it would be another ninety minutes before any of them came back.

It was Monday, and the entire staff had headed to Bagutia together. Since it was the dry season, the workers had all taken their bikes with them. Meetings were scheduled so as to allow the staff to travel in groups for most of their journeys. This was a holdover from the branch's early days, when there were concerns about bank workers being assaulted and robbed on their way to and from meetings.

One of the names on Jobbar's list was Lutfa. He had met her several times during his twenty months as manager, and to him she was the kind of person Grameen was created to serve. Yet he knew she faced hurdles that no other borrower in his branch had confronted.

Lutfa Ali lived in Munshikandi, a village about a mile south of the Zianpur bazaar notable for a large cigarette factory owned by the hamlet's wealthiest man. It was also the village where the first Grameen Bank center under the Shaymganj branch was founded, its first two groups having been recognized a few hours before Shandha's and Nonibala's quintets were in December 1987.

Soon after Lutfa was born, her father died and her mother married a wealthy man in Munshikandi, though he already had several wives and could not adequately care for Lutfa or her brothers and sisters. Lutfa, by her own admission, was a mischievous young girl, always getting into trouble with her guardians and peers. One day, while she was studying in the second grade, her entire body swelled up and she was incapacitated. After she was confined to bed and lived in constant pain for more than four months, the swelling finally went down, only to reappear several months later. Her mother called on several traditional healers in Munshikandi to try to help, but nothing worked. By the time she was twelve years old, Lutfa was paralyzed from the waist down; her skinny legs would hang limply below her undersized body as she passed days sitting on her bed.

Third World countries, Bangladesh in particular, are not kind to paraplegics. Lutfa never had a chance to go to a hospital, or even to sit in a wheelchair, a device she had heard about but never seen. She sat on tables and mats and beds, and over time taught herself how to spin rope from raw jute, make bamboo mats and fans, sew blankets, and even raise ducks. But she and her mother had no money for raw materials—whatever she had went to buy food, as they had mortgaged all their land after Lutfa's father died. Lutfa busied herself with her crafts, but she made negligible amounts of money because all the work she did was done on a contract or sharecrop basis. The owner supplied the raw materials, she supplied the labor, and as a result she would get as little as 4 or 5 taka (10 to 13 cents) per day for her efforts. Still, it offered a distraction.

When Mannan Talukdar started working with the first Grameen Bank borrowers in Munshikandi, Lutfa always asked to be carried over to where the training was taking place. She was not alone among the villagers in being curious and watching the process, but all the jokes she cracked about the Grameen rituals—the saluting, the slogans, the Sixteen Decisions—made her stand out. As she later admitted, she was mocking the bank while at the same time desperately wanting in herself. One day when she didn't come to watch the training, Mannan asked what had happened to her, only to hear that her body had swollen up again. He canceled the session, hurried to Lutfa's house, and immediately cut off her blouse with a pair of rusty scissors. Her body had become so swollen that some of her clothes were constricting the flow of blood to her extremities.

A year after the disbursement of loans to the first groups in Munshikandi, Lutfa sent word to Mannan that she wanted to join Grameen Bank. He visited her hut and they talked about what she could do with a loan. Lutfa explained about how she could do an impressive variety of handicrafts and, with the help of her sisters, raise ducks and pigeons as well. Mannan was encouraged but not convinced. He went to Tepra to have a meeting with his area manager, the well-respected but sometimes bureaucratic Abdul Wahab. After hearing the pros and cons of letting Lutfa in, Wahab simply said, "Why not try it?" That was all Mannan needed to hear.

When Lutfa's group began to train for the recognition test, Mannan conducted the training himself, fearing that she would have difficulty learning the material. To his surprise, she learned faster than anyone else in her group. In spite of all the teasing, she had managed to memorize most of the information when she had observed the first center being formed, and could still recite it a year later. After receiving her loan, Lutfa became one of the most prosperous members of her center. Through raising pigeons and ducks, selling duck eggs, and selling her handicrafts she was able to pay a weekly installment of almost 300 taka ($7.50). She even used some of her profits to lease some land so that her younger brother could farm it and they could "eat rice from their own land." Now it was time for another loan, and Lutfa was putting on her finest clothes as she prepared to leave for the branch office.

Slowly the bank workers arrived back from the Bagutia center meetings. Most were drenched with sweat when they arrived. They began counting the money and entering the installments into the loan ledgers. (Every installment of every Grameen Bank loan is noted three times—in the borrower's passbook, on the collection sheet, and finally on the loan ledger. Each month, Jobbar spent hours reconciling all of them to make sure there was no funny business going on.)

Once a quorum was present, there was some spirited discussion about who among the bank workers would do the marketing later that afternoon. Rohim mentioned that he thought it was time they should break down and have chicken with their evening meal—the monotony of vegetable gruel and tiny fish was getting to him—but the others argued against it. They wanted to keep the daily per person cost of their communal mess at 24 taka.

At 12:15, Lutfa arrived on a rickshaw from Munshikandi. When she'd come for her first loan, she'd arrived via a broken-down wooden cart pushed by her sister. Today, she could afford the one-way rickshaw fare of 6 taka. Lutfa's group chairman and another borrower helped lift her off the rickshaw and onto a bench in the office. A bank worker came over after a short while and gave her the forms she needed to sign. Other borrowers had to go up to the bank worker's table to complete their paperwork and then to the manager's table to receive their loan, but in Lutfa's case the staff all came to her.

She enjoyed coming to the bank and all the attention she received; when Lutfa received her initial loan it was her first trip to Zianpur since she had become paralyzed. Women always asked her what she was able to do with her loan money, and she enjoyed telling about each of her income-generating activities. Often, she brought things that she made so that she could show the other women how skilled she was in handicrafts.

At 2:30 P.M., Jobbar and Ahlim went over to Lutfa and presented her with 7,000 taka and a brown passbook. It was her sixth general loan, and one of the largest the branch had on its books. As she received the loan, Lutfa smiled and said to her branch manager, "Sir, you should provide such good service to *all* your borrowers!" She drew out the word "all" for emphasis. When Jobbar laughed, the other borrowers—none of whom would have the courage to tease *boro saar* (big sir)—felt that it had been taken in jest, and began giggling among themselves.

8

The Maxwell Street Market

The low murmur of voices chatting at an elegant function could be heard from down the hall. A half dozen dapper security guards emerged from the mayor's chambers, and behind them walked Richard M. Daley. The son of Chicago's legendary chief executive began shaking hands with members of the assembled crowd; periodically, his conversations were interrupted by loud bursts of laughter punctuated by hand gestures and more hand-shakes.

The foyer on the fifth floor of City Hall is the venue for scores of receptions hosted by the mayor each year. On this evening in December 1993, the caterers had erected a long row of tables down the center of the marbled floor, on either side of which were offices and a large solarium. Elegantly dressed couples plucked hors d'oeuvres while men in full military regalia stood watch over the proceedings. In a few minutes, they would perform a changing of the guard. Above it all stood a cast-iron sculpture of George Washington.

As Geri Dinkins watched her city's mayor shaking hands and making the rounds, her own hands began shaking. What should I say to the mayor? Will I be tongue-tied up there on the podium? What if he doesn't like the apron? She held it out in front of her and frowned as she looked over the designs she had decorated it with—all having to do with the mayor's favorite sport, football.

Since 1990, Geri had been volunteering for the American Food Depository, a food bank for veterans' families that had fallen on hard times. Mayor Daley, like his father the mayor before him, supported the group, perhaps in recognition of the abilities of veterans and those who assist them to cast votes in tight election races. Soon after the Depository's annual reception for volunteers and donors in December 1992, the mayor's office contacted Cynthia Simmons, the organization's director, asking if he could host the following year's event at City Hall. She agreed.

When the mayor's office said that Daley planned to present Cynthia with a key to the city, Cynthia suggested that the Food Depository present him with one of Geri's aprons, as she owned several herself. When someone questioned whether the mayor would like the Afrocentric designs that normally appeared on her aprons, Geri replied that she could decorate it with any pattern the group thought appropriate. Cynthia suggested a football motif, since it was well known that Daley was a fan. That settled that.

At the reception, the mayor thanked the volunteers and presented Cynthia with a key to the city, and then a nervous Geri was called up to join him on the platform. As Geri pushed through the crowd, Cynthia explained that the mayor was being presented with a gift from the volunteers and veterans as an expression of their appreciation for his service to them. The mayor shook Geri's hand and invited her up to stand behind the microphone. As Geri looked out into the crowd, her face momentarily went blank. She couldn't remember ever being in front of so many people before. But after a brief moment of quiet, she regained her composure. A wide smile broke out on her face as she said, "Mayor Daley, on behalf of the volunteers and the veterans at Hynes Hospital, I'd like to present you . . ." She paused as she fumbled with the apron, displaying it from several angles so that both the mayor and the crowd could see the design. ". . . with a gift, a handmade apron with a design I think you'll like."

She handed it to the mayor, and after looking at it for an instant he held it out in front of him to see the entire design. Then, as he showed it to the group, he leaned over and whispered to Geri, "I *really* like it—thank you!" Geri felt his sentiments were sincere, and was relieved. The two stood and smiled as dozens of flashes went off in an orgy of photography. As Geri heard the applause from her fellow volunteers, her muscles relaxed and her knees buckled slightly. Her job was done.

The two stepped down onto the floor and posed for several more pictures, and as the mayor prepared to meet and greet some more voters, Geri leaned over to him and whispered, "I don't know if you remember him, but my brother Arnold Douglas went to school with you at De La Salle," a Catholic high school on the South Side.

"Oh, Doug—of course I remember him! Say hello to him for me!" And off he went, again—pumping hands, listening intently, laughing when the opportunity presented itself.

A short time after the mayor returned to his office, a large, middle-aged black man active in the Harold Washington Party— a rival to the Democratic party, which Daley headed—tapped Geri on the shoulder. "Hey, I really liked that apron you gave the mayor," he said in a deep voice. "Can I buy a dozen from you?" Geri was surprised by the request, the largest she had ever received. As she fished through her purse for some paper to write down her newest customer's name and phone number, her mind raced. How many new customers would the exposure from this event lead to? she thought to herself. Could she handle the demand? In the months ahead, she would have to find answers to those questions, but right then she was all smiles, trying to close the deal gracefully.

There were other important events for Geri over the holiday season. When she finally got around to holding the house shows Thelma had pushed her to announce at the fall meeting, they were well attended and she sold nearly $1,000 worth of aprons and gift baskets. The $350 loan from the emergency loan fund—the FCF's name for Grameen's group fund—helped her buy through mail order some towels and utensils that she used, alongside soap, spices, and occasionally aprons, to fill the baskets. Some were generic, while others were custom-made for repeat customers. She also purchased fabric for making aprons. It was easily her busiest holiday season since being laid off, and the income was used to pay the utility bill and the mortgage and to buy groceries. For the first time since she'd lost her job, Geri was spared the humiliation of having to wonder whether her heat would be turned off at some point during the winter. Over the 1993–94 winter, she made enough to pay all her utility bills on time.

During the planning of her final show, which was to be held shortly after the City Hall event, Geri called Fort Smith, a man she knew from church, to do some networking. Fort had taken early retirement from the local phone company when, in the wake of the Bell breakup, his job was being phased out.

Fort was an entrepreneur who had started by selling jewelry at street fairs in order to make ends meet after losing his job with the telephone company. After learning the retail trade, Fort tried his hand at making jewelry from scratch, and was surprised at how easily it came to him. Sometimes, customers gently told him that he was selling his work for considerably less than its true value. They encouraged him to try marketing his work to North Side boutiques serving primarily upscale white clients. When he did, he succeeded. He persuaded swanky mail-order catalogs like Spiegel to carry some of his pieces, and soon he was wholesaling his handmade earrings for $25 to $50 a pair. This was a major breakthrough, as it often takes WSEP borrowers like Glenda, many of whom are as talented as Fort, years before they are confident enough to charge that much.

But though his jewelry-manufacturing business thrived, Fort continued, from time to time, to feel the bite of racism. On one occasion, the perpetrator was not white but black. At a high-society function, he was making small talk with an African American celebrity with national name recognition. The woman, noticing that Fort was admiring her earrings, said casually, "These are made by the famous jewelry designer Fort Smith—I bought them for one hundred and ten dollars."

"Madam," he replied after overcoming the shock of hearing that his earrings were selling at twice the suggested retail price, "I *am* Fort Smith."

"Oh, yes you are, dear," the woman said condescendingly. She could barely contemplate the idea that the "famous designer" the saleslady at the jewelry store had talked about was the black man she was talking to. Only later that evening, when the master of ceremonies introduced Fort to the crowd, did she realize her error. Fort tells stories like this one with a self-deprecating wit that makes him a genuinely likable character, but feelings of humiliation lie just below the surface.

In the fall, Geri had heard that Fort was opening a retail store in South Shore along Seventy-first Street. With her last show approaching, she telephoned him in early December to ask if he would be willing to give her some of his jewelry on consignment to sell at her home show; she figured it would go well with her aprons and gift baskets, and be sufficient reason to invite people who had already attended one of her earlier shows. Fort made a counteroffer: recounting to her some bad experiences giving out his merchandise, he invited Geri to have the show at his store.

Close to twenty people came to the show, and Fort liked what he saw of Geri's line of goods. Sales were okay, but somewhat less than what Geri had hoped for. At the end of the event, Fort asked if she could leave some of her aprons and gift baskets at the store so that he could sell them for her. At first, he would give her the entire retail price, and if they sold well they would arrange a wholesale price that she would get and a retail price he would charge. The arrangement worked well for both parties. In February, as Fort's retail business grew, he offered Geri part-time work at his store, which he called The Glitz. She would help keep accounts, clean up, assist him in making jewelry—"If I could learn to make earrings, so can you," he would tell her with a laugh—and deal with customers. In the spring, the job became full-time. By then, Fort had persuaded Geri to raise the retail price of her full aprons— which continued to sell well—from $15 to $30. They agreed that the wholesale price should be somewhere between $15 and $18. That was the first, but not the last, business tip Geri would pick up from her employer.

After two years, Geri's nightmare of unemployment, bankruptcy, and depression was over. The days of lying in bed, cursing her predicament, and wondering where the grocery money was coming from were past. Later that spring, after she had collected a month's worth of full-time wages (at $5 per hour), she would confide to a friend, "If it wasn't for the support of the women in the WSEP program, I would not have made it through these two years, financially or emotionally. The meetings gave me a reason to get out of bed and get on with my business. Left alone, I really think I might have died. Now, through working my business, through something I used to only do as a hobby, I have found employment again, stability again, certainty again."

The Maxwell Street Market has often been under threat of closure. In the 1960s it was truncated to make room for the Dan Ryan Expressway. Thirty years later, the University of Illinois at Chicago (UIC) was after the land the market stood on.

Opposition to UIC's efforts to close the bazaar came from two separate pressure groups that feuded with each other as much as with the university. The Maxwell Street Market Coalition was organized under the direction of Art Vasquez, a Hispanic community leader. It proved to be more vibrant than a group called Friends of the Market. The Coalition helped place pro–Maxwell Street op-ed pieces in the *Chicago Sun-Times* and were influential in persuading the city and the university to look into moving, rather than closing, the market.

One of the objectives of the Coalition was to overcome the resignation that most vendors felt and instead create a sense of possibility and urgency. Thelma Ali, for one, had responded to their entreaties, attending several meetings during the fall and winter to discuss strategy or organize protests. Among the events she attended was a November 30 meeting held at the Harold Washington Library where activists appealed to the city's Commission on Community Development to block the sale of the city-owned land the university wanted to buy. Lew Krineberg, a longtime political activist who was well connected to prominent Chicago progressives, arranged for Congressman Bobby Rush, Alderman Madeline Haithcock, and State Senator Jesus Garcia to attend the hearing. After the university made a lavish presentation (including a slide show), Rush, a former Black Panther, took center stage to blast the city and the university for not consulting with the communities involved, and called the plan to move the market "unwise and foolhardy." The mostly pro-market crowd broke into delirious applause at the end of his remarks. But as the meeting closed, the commission voted—without any debate—to go ahead and sell the 500,000 square feet of city-owned land that fell within the jurisdiction of the current market. Despite the official rebuff, many activists were heartened by the display of solidarity from three prominent politicians. As a result, Krineberg—who had joined the effort to save the market at the urging of Art Vasquez—assumed increasing importance within the Coalition.

After the November 30 meeting, Thelma confided in her diary, "They be saying so much about helping the poor help theyselves, creating enterprise and markets and so forth—and here they's destroying the best marketplace the city's got. This just doesn't make no *sense*. And it's not fair to the small people who come here to make a few bucks." Several days later, after attending another meeting, she added, "This is like a comedy. The city spends all its time crying about economics, about lost jobs—and they ain't doing nothing to let people make a few dollars in this market. And then you hear the city talk about how much it's trying to encourage all these communities to get along with each other—the Palestinians, the Koreans, the Chinese—yet they closing the only market where all these ethnic groups come together in a harmonious situation. And then they's complaining about welfare, but there's lots of people who have been laid off who are staying off welfare because they's able to work their business in Jewtown. People's just greedy—greedy university and a greedy city."

The city was certainly hoping to profit from its policy. Clearing the neighborhoods immediately circling the Loop of eyesores like the market and housing projects, and replacing them with upscale housing for professionals, meant big money for developers and construction firms who were vital to the mayor's candidacy, fewer traffic jams on the expressways, and an expanding municipal tax base.

But the opponents of Maxwell Street often tried to frame the debate in different terms. They described the bazaar as dangerous and as a venue for criminals to sell stolen goods. Many of these accusations were based on myths, half-truths, and, perhaps, the unbridgeable cultural divide between the uptight establishment who would reap the windfalls of gentrification and the colorful, multilingual patchwork of minorities and bohemians who bought and sold at the market. While people in the redeveloped communities nearby were often afraid to go to the bazaar, on a typical Sunday morning, when twenty thousand or more customers crowded into the market, there were rarely any violent incidents, despite the fact that only two policemen were assigned to the area. (And when one does see those officers, it is most likely that they will be shopping, not patrolling.) Indeed, in an article published several months later, a veteran police officer from the area told a reporter, "We do get people coming down, saying they've found their stolen property in the market, but it's not common, and the merchants are quick to give things back. They don't want trouble."* Yet perception often bests reality. The selling of X-rated videocassettes with explicit covers, often sharing space on a peddler's table with diapers and back-to-school supplies, gives the market a seedy reputation.

The Coalition decided to propose that the university share the area with the market. But it was often sidetracked by Krineberg's desire to broaden the Coalition's mandate, to discuss city-side issues beyond the predicament of the market. Krineberg was joined in the Coalition spotlight by a modest, impressive professor from Roosevelt University, Steve Balkin, who worked placing opinion pieces in influential newspapers, contacting journalists, networking with University of Illinois students and professors who opposed the market closing, contacting sympathetic city officials, and more.

For years, Balkin had worked in a small economics department that was overshadowed by the more influential and conservative faculty at the University of Chicago in Hyde Park. Balkin concentrated his efforts on the theoretical and practical implications of encouraging entrepreneurship as a strategy for assisting low-

---

*Quoted in the *London Economist*, April 23, 1994. The officer, not surprisingly, "asked not to be identified for fear of angering the mayor."

income people. Among his hands-on experience has been training prisoners in the fundamentals of entrepreneurship so that they can start businesses upon being released.

His most comprehensive—if not particularly well-read—book, *Self-Employment for Low-Income People,* made a strong case for programs like WSEP while acknowledging their limitations. He described successful schemes in Britain and France to get the unemployed started in business while making a case for the adaptation of programs like Grameen Bank in the United States. But he made the point that for such initiatives to succeed, the "overregulated" U.S. economy would have to be tinkered with to be made more user-friendly to low-income entrepreneurs. Above all, places like Maxwell Street, he argued, should be defended, expanded, and improved.

To Balkin, adapting the Grameen Bank to poor urban areas of industrialized countries and maintaining markets like Maxwell Street are inextricably linked concepts. Welfare reform, health care reform, community reinvestment laws (meant to discourage the practice of redlining), and striking down municipal ordinances that make home-based businesses illegal also play a part. But increasing access to markets that have low overhead and high traffic is perhaps the most basic need. It struck Balkin as ironic that at a time when the president of the United States and leaders from both parties were talking about creating federally supported "enterprise zones," and while Chicago was itself competing fiercely for funds to set one or more of them up, that same city was moving to eliminate an indigenous cauldron of entrepreneurship with a history of success spanning more than a century. Giving large, white-owned firms tax breaks to set up in low-income areas was one thing, but allowing the poor a place to set up their own businesses was apparently quite another.

When it became clear in 1989 that the University of Illinois planned to expand into the area where the Maxwell Street Market was held, Balkin saw it as a threat to a rare success story in the type of microcapitalist economics he had spent his life studying. In a report written with Alfonso Morales and Joseph Persky, he calculated that $3.2 million would be lost to the local economy in the first year the market was closed. But financial losses, he added, would not be the only impact. The market, he said, is a source of entertainment and activity for low-income youth and young adults, a diversion from crime, and a place where young entrepreneurs outside the corporate culture can exchange information on new products, sources of supply, stores for rent, people to do business with, and wage employment. Balkin's paper quotes one young vendor saying, "It keep [sic] you away from the street. I used to go hang around with my friends. Now, when I come home from the market, I'm tired and I stay home."

Perhaps the most persuasive argument for continuation of the market, though, comes from the university itself. A 1993 memo from its Great Cities Advisory Committee—created to define the role the university should play in the community—said, "Since the university is not the sole repository of knowledge, the pursuit of knowledge requires increased interaction with the off-campus public.

"Specific types of programmatic activities are recommended: assist in economic development of the UIC neighborhoods without displacing current residents, engage in technology transfer activities to increase business success [and] assist minority and female-owned businesses and new ventures . . ." Yet the only technology the university was willing to bring to bear on Maxwell Street was a bulldozer, and whenever the concept of "shared space" was brought up, the university rejected it, saying it was unwilling to become a "landlord" for a "flea market." The fact that the market operated on the day the university was closed, or that Stanford University coexisted peacefully with a Sunday market on its campus, failed to move the UIC bureaucrats.

In the spring, the Coalition, like the Friends of the Market group before it, disintegrated into warring factions. An elderly Italian woman came up to Thelma Ali's table on Maxwell Street one Sunday and, seeing her reading a flyer about an upcoming protest in front of City Hall to save the market, felt compelled to share something. "You know," she told Thelma, "they did the same thing to us thirty years ago. They said they wanted to take over the land, they said they were going to do all sorts of things to help us relocate and readjust, and once they tore down our neighbor-hood, we got nothing. Now this is happening to you, too. I feel so bad for you."

Such is the price of progress in America's second city.

In the third week of January 1994, WSEP held a dinner for Full Circle Fund members in the Prince Mustafa cultural center on Eighty-second Street and South Ashland Avenue, owned by Belvia Muhammad, a borrower in the Let Us Make Woman circle. The event was arranged by Colete Grant, who hoped it would smooth over some of the hurt feelings created by the sudden departures of Gwen and Jackie the preceding fall. Talk about circle business or WSEP business would be forbidden; the invitation announced, "No loan payments, no circle business, no talking shop." This was a time to break bread together and create warmer relationships.

Queenesta had been unsure whether she would be able to go to the dinner until the last minute. She had been working her counter at Victor's store all day, and it wasn't until five-thirty that she found a free minute to call Omiyale and ask if one of her daughters could baby-sit for Shayna while they attended the func-tion. Queenesta prepared to leave the store before closing—something she knew Victor would give her a hard time about. But what did Victor know about being a single mother? And anyway, Victor was feeling somewhat contrite since Queenesta had con-fronted him about all the money he'd made on the T-shirts they had bought at last year's Black Expo, and as a result her $150 rent was being waived for the first three months of the year.

As Queenesta walked eastbound on North Avenue toward her car, she looked across the street, trying to discern if any stores might be going out of business—ones that she might be able to move into once the weather broke. The sidewalk on the north side of the avenue was covered with a foul combination of snow, ice, and uncollected garbage; the stores were primarily seedy-looking fast-food joints with bulletproof glass separating customers from employees, and liquor stores owned by Koreans. City Sports, a successful white-owned sporting goods and clothing store, had the most attractive window; several vacant stores, however, created a more depressing picture. So intent was Queenesta on looking for a future home for her business that she walked past her car and needed to double back to it. If Omiyale could only repay her short-term loan, Queenesta thought, I'll have a clear path to opening my own store this spring. Until Omiyale cleared her account, nobody in her circle could take out any new loans.

Queenesta had never been to the Prince Mustafa cultural center before, and as she searched for a place to put her coat her eyes wandered around the place, taking in the decorations. Drapes with African designs covered the drab blue walls that Belvia had inherited when she took over the storefront. A picture of Elijah Muhammad, the onetime leader of the Nation of Islam, was hung below a Chinese flag. On an adjacent wall, a large map of Africa hung to the right of a newspaper article about Muhammad that included a picture. Next to that there was a sign that read, "To Lengthen Thy Life, Lessen Thy Meals."

Belvia Muhammad wanted to create a vegetarian restaurant and cultural center with Islamic and African decor. It was to get moral and financial support for this vision that she had entered WSEP. At the time of the dinner, she was concentrating her efforts on getting the license to open a legal restaurant. On several occasions she had been tempted to start without the licenses, but Thelma Ali had helped persuade her to "do it legal." By year's end, all her coursework would be completed. Until then, renting her storefront out for events like the WSEP dinner would pay the bills.

On this night, the middle of the main dining room was filled with a half dozen long tables covered with white cloth and colorful ethnic centerpieces. The assembled staff and borrowers of the Full Circle Fund, a few coming from as far away as Rogers Park on the North Side, engaged in animated dialogue as they waited for the buffet to begin. Staff tended to congregate with staff, and members tended to gravitate to other borrowers they recognized. Queenesta, dressed in a stylish gray sports coat she wore over a red turtleneck, went straight to Omiyale and Thelma, who were already sitting at a table in the front, discussing circle business despite the official restrictions on doing so. Omiyale had dressed up for the occasion, wearing a gold and black jacket and a black scarf around her head, while Thelma was characteristically underdressed. As the three began talking, Leverta Pack and Thelma Perkins of their center settled into chairs at the table and joined in.

After the meal, Colete called for people's attention and gave some brief introductory remarks. Clad in an elegant two-piece traditional African dress with a matching kufi and earrings (all made by Full Circle Fund borrowers), she stood behind a menorah with seven burning red candles (Colete, like some borrowers in the Lindblom center, is a Hebrew-Israelite) as she spoke. Colete had never appeared so relaxed while speaking in front of a group; on this night, she finally seemed to shake free of the shadow of her popular predecessor Gwen. She began calling circles up to the front of the room, where she handed them carnations and certificates of appreciation, drawing attention to their latest accomplishments as they stood beside her. Periodically, she invited other enterprise agents—two had been hired just a few weeks before—to do the same.

Toward the end of the program, Colete said, "And now I'd like to call up Les Papillons, a group that embodies persistence. These sisters have hung together and been unified under very difficult conditions. They are some bonded sisters." She paused, and the room fell silent as she cleared her throat. Colete seemed to be momentarily overcome with emotion. Then she continued, "At a meeting just a few weeks ago, they . . . I don't want to go into it, but for me they define the idea of sisterhood that this program is about." Colete was referring to a meeting in mid-October when Omiyale, faced with the prospect of falling behind on her payments on her short-term loan, broke down sobbing when she learned that doing so would prevent Geri from borrowing from WSEP for the Christmas season. The four women responded by urging Omiyale not to be so hard on herself and agreeing to loan Geri $350 out of their emergency loan fund. For Colete, it was a defining moment for the circle and for herself as a WSEP employee. She saw a group of borrowers solve their own problem rather than giving up or depending on her for a solution.

"Now I'd like to call up all the women in Les Papillons!" Loud applause broke out. Omiyale and Queenesta took their certificates and flowers and got big hugs from Colete, but Thelma stayed in her seat. "Pick one up for me, Omiyatta," she called out, revealing one of several ways she mispronounced her friend's name. Colete asked Thelma to come up, but again she refused. Perhaps she didn't want the attention, or maybe she just felt she was underdressed. When Colete asked a second time, all eyes turned to Thelma, but she sat, smiling and defiant, unwilling to go through with the ritual. Finally, Colete said she'd give the certificate to her later.

Queenesta spotted a tall WSEP staff member sitting by the wall. As far as Queenesta could tell, she had a look of disgust on her face as she watched; her disdain seemed focused squarely on Thelma Ali. How dare she look that way, Queenesta thought. That woman doesn't know anything about Thelma Ali. Rage boiled up inside her. They're just looking at how someone dresses, and how they act in public, not what's inside, not how successful their business is! If they only knew about how Thelma really is, they would realize, Queenesta said to herself. She looked at Thelma, her head wrapped in a ski hat and a silk scarf, her face bereft of makeup, her legs covered only in black denim pants. That, she thought, is a real entrepreneur—down at Maxwell Street every day during the spring and summer, taking a sewing class this winter to learn how to make African children's clothing that her customers had been asking for.

In the background, Connie was giving her speech to conclude the program. But for the rest of the evening Queenesta reflected on the cultural divide separating the black middle and upper class from the black lower class. The differences had led to occasional misunderstandings between WSEP staff and clients and among the staff itself, as "field workers" like Colete tended to come from more humble backgrounds than the highly educated professional staff. Victor, always ready with an opinion, likened the tension to that between the "field nigger" and the "house nigger" during the days of slavery. All the same, despite occasional flare-ups and misunderstandings, WSEP was quietly proving that the educated black professional class *did* have something useful to say and do for their economically distressed brothers and sisters. Even if some of the staff might look down on Thelma's fractured grammar and humble dress, in WSEP Connie had created a mechanism that allowed black women professionals to administer a program that gave their low-income sisters access to loan capital and a forum for giving, receiving, and exchanging valuable business advice. Indeed, it was such a rare service and so well provided that the clients accepted the organization's few white staff members, such as Susan Matteucci and Tiziana Dearing (the public relations director), with a remarkable degree of openness. Sometimes, in the hustle and bustle of putting out a "product" and working through the internal politics that all organizations wrestle with, the significance of that achievement was lost. It took a person like Thelma Ali, who was so clearly benefiting from the program and considered it a work of divine inspiration, to remind everyone of how special it was.

A winter characterized by heavy snowfall and below-normal temperatures had at least one desirable effect—it kept potential perpetrators and victims of violence off the streets—but it also brought the economic life of the city to a standstill and caused hundreds of thousands of dollars' worth of damage to Chicago's infrastructure. In January, peddlers and small-scale manufacturers like Queenesta, Omiyale, Thelma, Glenda, and Geri assessed their profits from the Christmas-Kwanzaa season and prepared to cash in on Black History Month (BHM) in February. Those weeks before BHM were a time for hunkering down and trying to resist the temptation to use working capital to meet family expenses. Queenesta was busy lining up bookselling events for the following month while Thelma was learning how to sew at a city-sponsored program. Thelma was also looking into taking advantage of volume discounts by buying fabric in bulk and then selling some on a retail basis and using the rest to manufacture her children's clothing. She was determined to learn how to make the kufis that Omiyale had required her children to wear in the 1970s, long before they had become fashionable.

Black Chicago had been through a rough few years, but there was some good news. It was revealed in January that violent crime was down 4 percent in 1993, and in districts such as Englewood and Morgan Park where community policing was being tried, it had been reduced by as much as 19 percent. During the first two months of 1994, Englewood in particular continued the progress it had made the previous year. The neighborhood's first homicide of 1994 did not occur until March; during the previous three years, there had been a murder there, on average, every four days. A senior police commander in Englewood credited his community policing initiative as well as work focusing on prevention and carried out by nonprofit groups such as People Educated Against Crime in Englewood (PEACE) and the Christ United Methodist Church.* Others thought the gang summit in the fall, during which a tenuous truce had been declared among black gangs, was having an effect. Whatever the cause, for the time being, prayers that the carnage that had come to characterize life in Englewood would abate were being answered.

The red digital display read 8:10 when Queenesta's alarm went off, but it was actually earlier than that. Queenesta set her clock thirty-five minutes ahead to give her a little push to get moving in the morning.

It was January 28, and snow had been falling gently in Englewood since the night before; the temperature was hovering at around 15 degrees. It was turning out to be a bitter winter, even by Chicago standards.

Queenesta rubbed the sleep from her eyes as she sat up. It was scarcely three hours since she had gone back to bed after Shayna had woken her up, suffering from chicken pox. As Queenesta showered, she considered the day ahead. First there was the issue of getting books on consignment from the wholesaler. The management of the store had changed hands, so they might not let her take as many books as she needed. Then there was the business of tracking down her sister's friend, whom she would try to hire to work the month of February; going to West Side Books (more than likely to receive a tongue-lashing from Victor for not being in the store that morning); finding someone to take care of Shayna in the afternoon; getting some cassettes from the music distributor; and attending a WSEP meeting downtown at five-thirty. Queenesta

---

*PEACE, formed in 1991 when Englewood led the city in homicides during a bloody turf war among the gangs, created after-school drop-in centers for students and brought in motivational speakers such as businesspeople and reformed gang members to speak to students in school.

peered into her bathroom mirror to see if another night of interrupted sleep showed on her face.

Queenesta is an attractive woman in her early thirties. As a
statement of principle, she wears her hair natural rather than relaxing it with chemicals. She had done that a couple of times in
her youth, but now, as a self-aware black person trying to turn her
brothers and sisters on to their culture and heritage, she has no
time—not to mention money—for such things.

As she brushed her teeth, she thought about what she should
be doing in order to realize the most challenging of her New Year's
resolutions—opening her own store. Queenesta's successes at the
end of the year had given her the courage to begin planning to go
out on her own. Kwanzaa, a postharvest celebration held in Africa
during December that many African Americans observe, had been
profitable. Most of her income had come from selling books. The
rest came from renting African clothing for customers to wear at
special events such as weddings and cultural gatherings. She had
come up with this idea in November during a week when she
wasn't sure how she was going to make her loan payment. Within
a few weeks she'd made more profit in renting the clothes than if
she had sold them. Dorothy Johnson, the seamstress who also
rented space from Victor, was impressed with the way Queenseta
created a thriving rental business from nothing; months later, she
would ask for Queenesta's advice on how to begin a rental venture
herself.

During December, selling at Kwanzaa events was a good way
to keep away from Victor's store, which for nearly two weeks had
no heat. The staff was forced to spend those days wearing over-
coats and mittens as they helped a dwindling number of customers.
Victor blamed this on his Korean landlord, and was in a foul mood
the entire month.

January was a time to rest up between Kwanzaa and Black
History Month, observed in February, and the Black Women's
Expo, held in mid-March. Queenesta was behind in her preparations for Black History Month, and dealing with Shayna's chicken
pox, which necessitated taking her out of school for a week, complicated things further. Queenesta had planned to spend some time
during the month looking for a new storefront, but she had little

time to do so. Still, she continued to think about the move and to discuss it with close confidants. The main question in her mind was whether she would try to locate it near Victor's store (in order to keep her regular customers) or move to another section of Austin.

At 7:45, it was time to rustle Shayna up and get her moving for the long day ahead. As Queenesta passed the front door, she inspected the plastic sheeting she had taped over the cracks in the door to keep the frigid air out and the heating bill down. Upon entering Shayna's room, she gently sat down on the edge of her daughter's bed. As soon as she woke up, Shayna began reaching for her scabs. "Pat it, don't scratch it, Shayna!" As she got up and began walking to the bathroom, Shayna slapped her arms and her head.

While she cooked a breakfast that Shayna would eat in the car, Queenesta phoned the home office of her book distributor in New York. She was concerned that the local wholesaler would not have all the books she wanted. That would be catastrophic during February, when there were thousands of dollars to be made selling black-oriented books. During Kwanzaa, she had been forced to go to events with titles she knew didn't sell very well because the selection had been so poor at the wholesaler's. She wanted the New York office to send her a shipment directly. That, of course, would mean paying for them up front at 60 percent of the cover price. But she had events lined up, and more important, had working capital with which to pay for a COD shipment. She was able to persuade Luther, her main contact at the head office, to send her two boxes of books she knew were in demand. He also tried to reassure her that the new management of the Chicago distributorship was in place and that she could count on them supplying her in the future. (Months before, some employees had stolen thousands of dollars' worth of books and almost driven the operation out of business.)

After getting off the phone with Luther, she called her contact at the McDonald's Corporation to confirm an event in its corporate cafeteria in mid-February. "Hi, this is Queenesta Harris of Kids Are People Too," she began. "May I speak to Ms. Carter? Hi, yes, ma'am, I'm calling about the event on February eighteenth. Yeah,

okay, right, similar to that, uh, can you hold for a minute? . . .
Hello, hi, hold on, Sheila. . . . Yes, Ms. Carter, I just need the address. Uh-huh, okay. Are there going to be other vendors? Ah. Can
I bring African artifacts and oils to sell? Yes? Good. I'll see what
happens. . . . You want a variety of books, fiction and nonfiction?
Okay. How about *Waiting to Exhale*? Yes. What? Oh, yes, I'll be
sure to bring the Black Heritage Bible! People been asking about
that? Yes, definitely. Okay . . . Thank you, Ms. Carter. . . ." The
relatively new Black Heritage Bible was popular. In addition to the
King James text, it carried footnotes and supplementary essays explaining African and African American contributions to the Bible
and Christianity. It was a big seller in black Chicago, and since it
retailed for nearly $50, each sale meant a profit of about $18 for
vendors.

Queenesta talked for a minute with Sheila, Victor's twenty-one-
year-old daughter, who looked to her for womanly advice. Sheila
wanted to come and live with Queenesta, but Victor didn't want
her living anywhere but with him or her mother until she got a
full-time job. Victor resented his tenant for not giving her the same
advice, but Queenesta thought the best thing she could do was to
help Sheila think it through herself. That mess was just one more
reason she wanted to leave West Side Books.

She made another call, to her Chicago distributor, to try to get
hold of some more Black Heritage Bibles. She was told that there
were forty in stock, and that they were going fast. Hearing that,
Queenesta canceled her plans to go get some compact discs and
cassettes. Getting as many Bibles as possible was the first priority.
Perhaps she could persuade the new manager in Chicago to let her
have eight or ten on consignment. After making a few more phone
calls to confirm events for February, she packed up Shayna's breakfast and finished her ironing. In this frenzy of activity she spotted
Shayna scratching her scalp again. "Pat, don't scratch! Pat it,
Shayna!" she said with a combination of humor and exasperation.

"But, Ma! It itches. And my stomach hurts."

Queenesta drove Shayna to the school where Queenesta's older
sister Venita worked as an aide. Venita was a rock in Queenesta's
life—stable, dependable, even when her own life was chaotic. It

was Venita who was able to get Shayna into school a year early, it was Venita who would often sell Queenesta's T-shirts and other merchandise to her students, and it was Venita who looked after Shayna when her mother needed to be minding her business.

"Hey, Neeta," Queenesta called out as she walked in the door. "Hey, Pommy," Venita replied, using a nickname that her younger sister had been known by since childhood.

Shayna's classroom was dreary, its walls built with cinder blocks, furnished with tiny plastic chairs for tiny people, decorated with construction paper that had lost its luster between September and January. As the two sisters talked, Shayna began playing with classmates she had not seen since she had gotten chicken pox. Queenesta disapproved of the youngsters' influence on her daughter; they were rowdy and making little progress on their ABCs. She had noticed some bad habits that Shayna had picked up since she'd started school here in September. She hoped to transfer Shayna to the elite Von Steuben High School on the North Side, where Queenesta herself had studied.

"Neeta, can Shayna come over today around two?" It was a question Queenesta had asked many times, and one to which she virtually always received a positive answer.

"Sure, Pommy."

"And that guy who works here as a janitor that I met, I want to call to see if he can help me sell books during Black History Month. But I lost his number. You got it, Neeta?" Queenesta had three events on a single day in February, and even if she could get Omiyale to cover for her at one of them, she would have to hire someone to look after the other. Finding reliable employees willing to accept pay of only $5 an hour was one of many challenges she was coming to face in her business.

Queenesta left the school with Shayna and drove to her book wholesaler. She had established her creditworthiness there and could usually take as many books as she wanted, though there were limits on titles that were in short supply. Within a week, she had to return all unsold books and pay 60 percent of the retail price for everything that she had sold. The wholesaler bought the books for half the retail price, making his margin 10 percent of the final selling price.

Queenesta found a new clerk at the desk inside the warehouse. She reminded him that she had a good record of paying for and returning books, and asked if she could load up a cart of books to take for Black History Month. The employee looked Queenesta and Shayna over and reluctantly agreed. Queenesta began walking up and down the aisles, picking up copies of books that had sold well during Black History Month the previous year. She was relieved to see that the store was better stocked than it had been during December. She flipped through new titles, especially works of fiction with which she was less familiar and new titles claiming to explain to black men how to understand black women, and vice versa. Those had sold very well during Kwanzaa. She took some time choosing a selection of Toni Morrison books; Victor had told Queenesta that demand for her novels had grown since Morrison had been awarded the Nobel Prize in Literature in the fall.

The narrow aisles were arranged like those of a college bookstore, with several copies of popular titles stacked on wooden shelves. Shayna alternately followed her mother and found her own way. Occasionally, she would pick up books with attractive pictures on the covers and try to sneak them onto the cart.

After spending nearly two hours in the adult section and piling more than two hundred books onto her cart, Queenesta headed over to the children's book section. As she passed some well-known stories, she recalled an encounter with an older African American woman customer last February. The woman had been delighted to see a black Cinderella. Even though all her children were grown, she couldn't resist buying that book for her bookshelf. The look of wonder in the woman's eyes as she made the purchase was one of the fondest memories Queenesta had from her short time as a book retailer.

The man behind the counter got on the phone and called his boss in New York. After a few minutes of talking in a hushed voice, he put down the phone and yelled, "Hey, Miss Harris, Luther from New York wants to talk to you." Queenesta picked up one extension as the clerk listened on the other. Within a few minutes he was convinced that Queenesta was reliable enough to give a large consignment of books.

A short time later, after making her selections of children's books, Queenesta approached the counter and began unloading. The manager piled the books according to price to make it easier to calculate how much Queenesta would owe next week. After some animated discussion, she persuaded the man to let her take eight Black Heritage Bibles and give her ten days to settle up with him. After calculating the retail value of the consignment at $2,600, they loaded the books into cardboard boxes and Queenesta began lugging them out to her car. By that point the snow was falling harder than at any time since the previous night, and Queenesta nearly slipped several times on the sidewalk.

That completed, Queenesta dropped Shayna off at school and headed toward Venita's house a few blocks away; she would have to leave the books there until she picked her daughter up later that night. Queenesta mounted the stairs with her first box of books, and as she searched for a place to store them, she looked at more than a half dozen of her sister's children and grandchildren, many sitting on a musty floor as a black-and-white television droned on in the background. An infant was lying on a ratty couch. There was a commotion in a back room.

Venita, Queenesta knew, had a hard life, though she took it all in stride and tried to be both loving and firm with all her little ones. Since the previous year, she had been studying at a nearby junior college in hopes of earning a teaching certificate; the qualification would double the money she was earning as a teacher's aide. To do so, on many days she worked from eight to four, raced home to change her clothes, cook dinner, and set up her oldest daughter for baby-sitting duties, then left to get to class by six o'clock. Her classes usually ended at ten o'clock, after which there was homework to do. It was draining, but Venita, like her sister, had ambitions of improving herself. In a family that had known more than its fair share of tragedies and setbacks, they shared a common dream and did what they could to support each other. Their mother, living a half mile away in the house they grew up in, pitched in as much as she could.

It took twelve trips to bring all the boxes up, and when she was done Queenesta's body was covered in sweat. She had only enough time to grab a quick meal, her first food of the day, before the meeting. Queenesta arrived at 116 West Washington Street at 5:30. She walked through the narrow hallway toward the elevator, rode it up to the seventh floor, and went directly to the conference room. There were already a half dozen women there, among them Pam Bozeman, an attractive, newly hired WSEP staff member who would run the meeting. Queenesta sat down and greeted a woman sitting to her left. She was not a borrower from the Full Circle Fund, but was involved in another WSEP program for self-employed women. Her business was selling gifts—stuffed animals, flowers, and toys—that were packaged inside of inflated balloons. She had some samples scattered around her chair. "I can't tell you how I get them in there, but I can sure sell you one!" she said to a woman sitting next to Queenesta. There were a lot of smiles in the room, and more than a few business cards were being exchanged.

Some twenty years before, Jesse Jackson's Operation PUSH had begun holding a Black Expo in Chicago to showcase the products and services of the finest black-owned businesses. This would give black consumers a chance to sample goods produced by their own race. Over time, Black Expos began being held in other cities across the country, even though for many years they were not held in Chicago for lack of interest and revenue. But in 1990, the Chicago Black Expo had started up again.

They were usually held in July. In 1993, a spin-off event was inaugurated—the Expo for Today's Black Woman, popularly known as the Black Women's Expo. The purpose was to showcase products used by black women, and the idea was that it would be less profit-oriented than the revitalized Black Expo had become. The collaboration of V-103, a black radio station, was sought, and it responded by giving the event cheap advertising.

In 1992, WSEP leaders were able to persuade the organizers of the Black Expo to allow them to buy a block of booths at a reduced cost. Their argument was that the Black Expo should not be only for large, already successful black-owned firms but also for small businesses run by low-income people. Twenty women involved in the Full Circle Fund were able to rent booths during the 1992 and 1993 Expos, though with mixed results. The Black Women's Expo offered another opportunity for Full Circle Fund borrowers to sell, and the meeting Pam had called was to let them know about the deal they had struck with the organizers.

At 5:45, Pam called for order, just as Thelma Ali and Omiyale rushed in and sat down. Clearly there was more interest in the Black Women's Expo than had been expected. As Pam started to talk, Omiyale began piling see-through plastic containers of her cookies on the table in front of her.

Over the next two and a half hours, Pam went into detail about the offer WSEP had gotten from the Expo organizers and led the women through the forms they needed to fill out. "The Expo organizers expect there to be fifty thousand customers over the three days, and we can get you booths for $450 each. That's $400 for the booth and $50 for a sixty-second advertising spot on V-103." It was a bargain deal, so good that nearly a hundred people not involved in WSEP had already called Pam to try to get in on it. This was WSEP at its best, negotiating the same kind of cut-rate package deals for its low-income entrepreneurs that larger firms can get for themselves by virtue of their size. Pam radiated justified pride at her achievement, and stayed late into the evening to help the women take advantage of it. Her presentation was sprinkled with humor; the women, many of whom had never met her in person before, appeared to be taking to her well. For her part, Pam thought that the process of minority women overcoming poverty and dependency by starting microbusinesses was nothing short of "magical." As a black woman from Chicago's South Side who had made it into the middle class, she respected the skill and faith needed for a low-income, single mother to find her market niche and exploit it sufficiently to guarantee a reasonable income.

As a further concession, the Expo organizers had given WSEP women the option of sharing booths. Pam asked for a show of hands to see who planned to buy individual booths. Along with eleven others, Omiyale raised her hand. Thelma, sitting to her right, was aghast. She had thought she and Omiyale had a tacit understanding to go in together. Thelma had gone as far as to borrow the money from another vendor at Maxwell Street to put down the $150 deposit that night. As she sat in a silent rage, Thelma considered her alternatives. Since Queenesta was also going in alone, that meant she would have to either forgo being a vendor at the Expo or go in with someone she trusted less than the members of her own circle.

As the meeting broke up at close to nine o'clock, women gathered in small groups to discuss what it all meant. People who had agreed to share a booth exchanged telephone numbers, their hopes and fears, and plain old gossip. Queenesta went over to the table where Thelma and Omiyale were sitting and, sensing the tension between the two women, said a few words before excusing herself and beginning her long trek home. As she walked toward the elevator, several women pushed by her, hoping to grab a package of Omiyale's cookies before she sold out.

Queenesta trudged from 116 West Washington to the underground el stop at the corner of Washington and Dearborn, and then to the stop where she had parked her car. Finally she drove to Venita's, picked up a sleeping Shayna and her books, and began her journey back to the South Side. After finding a parking space, she put Shayna to bed and then lugged the books one final time, from her car into her living room. It was a few minutes past eleven o'clock by the time she finished.

She would begin a similar routine tomorrow. Queenesta had a lot to do; it was only a few days before her busiest month of the year would get under way.

9

▲

Krishna Das Bala

Khashem studied the board, his clenched fist separating his chin from his knee as he sat on the bed, clothed only in a longhi. A lighted candle flickered, illuminating Rohim's face. He too was pensive and staring at the pieces on a chessboard. On a bed a few feet away, Krishna Das Bala, a new staff member, was playing the tabla, a percussion instrument popular on the Indian subcontinent. In a dark corner of the hut Mustafiz gossiped with Shahjahan.

Khashem picked up his rook and held it aloft for a moment before taking Rohim's bishop. While he did so, Anis, the peon, walked into the hut with Ahlim. "Anis, sweep it up," Khashem ordered without looking up from the game. Anis inspected the ground, where hundreds of flies lay dead or dying. Throughout the Bengali summer, which begins at the end of February and continues until May, the men mixed insecticide and molasses twice each day and left the concoction on a leaf from a banana tree in the middle of their hut. This brought the men temporary respite from their torment, but in several hours another swarm would replace the one that had perished.

Anis picked up the banana leaf, dragged it outside, and began sweeping up the flies with a *jharu*. By the time he was done, Rohim had conceded the game to Khashem, and they decided it was time for dinner. They rolled out the bamboo mats, squatted down, splashed some water on their plates, and uncovered the aluminum pots filled with rice, vegetable curry, and lentils.

"Mustafiz, Shahjahan, come and eat," Khashem said. It was an awkward moment; all six men were in the hut, but there was room for only three in the dining area. Ahlim was the most junior bank worker, so he would wait, as would Anis, who, as the peon, would eat after everyone else was done. Khashem liked the idea of eating while listening to Krishna playing the tabla, so he would also eat later.

Khashem was the senior assistant, a post usually given to the most experienced bank worker at a branch and one that entails considerable accounting responsibilities in addition to the servicing of three or four centers. It is a position halfway between bank worker and manager, and it confers upon its holder additional unwritten authority and responsibilities. The men consulted Khashem, whom they called *boro bhai* (big brother), before making all but the most mundane decisions concerning their communal living arrangement. Khashem, in turn, was responsible for resolving personality conflicts, arranging going-away parties for departing staff members, and giving pep talks to colleagues who were falling behind in their work.

Krishna Das Bala had been transferred to Shaymganj in January 1994, and upon arriving was assigned to ten centers. Among them were centers number two and forty-two, the ones in Kholshi's Haldar *para*. The manager, Jobbar Ali, thought it was a good idea to assign a new Hindu staff member to run centers whose leadership shared his religious beliefs. Though he liked and trusted Rohim, he was obliged to rotate responsibilities for particular centers at least once a year.

When Rohim turned over his responsibilities for center number two to Krishna, he felt satisfied by what he had accomplished. After four years of holding steady at six groups, he had shepherded the members of the seventh group through the processes of formation, training, recognition, and taking their first loans. As the women moved steadily toward completing repayment of those loans, and applying for new ones, he was pleased with Amena and Firoza's steady progress, as well as Fulzan's, though hers was more halting. Nobirun, the group chairman, was struggling, and Alow had dropped out in December. Rohim's greatest satisfaction had come from ensuring that all five women, with the possible exception of Firoza, had been extremely poor when they joined.

In the wake of 1991 salary raises for Bangladesh civil servants, which Grameen had felt compelled to match, the bank had decided to increase worker productivity by expanding centers from six to eight groups. Since then, there had been cases where the leadership of established centers had been reluctant to admit women from very poor families into newly forming groups. Older borrowers, who had once been destitute themselves, often preferred women who were *already* at the economic level they themselves had progressed to since joining. There were cases of destitute women being actively discouraged from joining old centers. Rohim believed that one of the most challenging parts of his job was to maintain the focus on the "poorest of the poor," and he took pride in Amena's group having been established in the true Grameen spirit, but he was quick to credit Shandha—the most important leader in a center of a half dozen influential women—with encouraging the inclusion of four desperately poor Muslim women in the seventh group.

As Krishna bicycled toward the Haldar *para* on a Tuesday morning several weeks later, he saw farmers cutting stalks of rice with iron sickles and tying them into bundles that their children then carried on their heads back to their compounds. The light greens and yellows of the matured paddy that remained to be cut shimmered amid the deep greens of the bamboo jungles that surrounded the homestead plots. Landowners and sharecroppers alike wore the smiles of a successful harvest, one that allowed them to settle debts, barter for other goods, and enjoy home-cooked *pitha* (pastries made from rice flour and molasses). Many foreign visitors, expecting the barren landscapes and emaciated children of the

Horn of Africa, have been surprised by the lushness of Bangladeshi villages.

Only two-thirds of the women were at the center hut when he arrived, and that annoyed Krishna. Yet he realized that many of the women had rice to thresh before the monsoon came, and decided not to make a big fuss about it. Most of the remaining members arrived within ten minutes.

"Listen, I'm not going to delay very long today," he barked out as he took his seat. "Two of our staff are on vacation and I have to collect installments from four centers today." The women took that as a cue to forgo the ritual opening and closing of the meeting. Shandha handed Krishna her passbooks, and he began marking them up in his distinctive handwriting, with all the flourishes one would expect from someone who had been dreaming since childhood of being a professional artist. When he finished, he put them aside and took another handful of passbooks from Nonibala as he worked his way backward toward Amena's group, which was sitting in the rear.

The women initially responded to Krishna's seriousness by talking in hushed voices, but within fifteen minutes the usual animated dialogues—punctuated by laughter, gossip, and an occasional flaring temper—resumed. At one point, Krishna, without looking up, asked, "How has your rice harvest turned out?"

"Very good, sir," several women blurted out. "Ask Shandha how she did, sir," another said excitedly.

"Shandha?" Krishna said, looking at her as she counted her group's installments.

Shandha flashed an embarrassed smile, but upon prompting by Amodini said, "Sir, I have received forty *maunds* [more than one and a half tons] of rice this time!" Shandha looked at Amodini as she said it, and both smiled.

"My goodness," Krishna exclaimed, his raised eyebrows and dropped jaw revealing his surprise.

"Sir," Aduree called out from the second row, "I have made a big leap forward, too. Just last week I got back a half acre of land that I had mortgaged twelve years ago." Since the time when she'd persuaded Nonibala to allow her to join the bank, Aduree had been saving so she could get her land back. Money from her vegetable gardening and from her husband's rickshaw-pulling, cow-fattening, and chicken-raising had been put aside. Slowly it had grown to 5,000 taka, two-thirds of the sum needed to get the land back. They'd mobilized the final 2,500 taka by selling goats. Finally, they had saved enough to reclaim the land they had mortgaged to avoid starvation more than a decade before.

In rural Bangladesh, agricultural land is much more than just a place where you farm. There is something spiritual about the relationship between a family and its land. It is status and power and, above all, food security. Other assets can be lost; a cow can be stolen or die, a house can burn down, a handloom can be ruined in a flood. But land is always there; indeed, natural disasters are as likely to improve its fertility as ruin it. Bangladesh, one of the earth's largest flood plains, is home to some of the world's deepest and most fertile topsoil, which receives annual replenishment during the monsoon. Furthermore, it sits atop readily accessible groundwater that can be inexpensively pumped up for irrigated agriculture. Despite growing problems related to the overuse of chemical fertilizers and unwise irrigation methods, land remains the center of all dreams, hopes, and fears among the rural people. It is hardly an exaggeration to say that people have killed their next of kin in disputes over one-hundredth of an acre of land; in the nearby village of Ruha, such things were commonplace.

Grameen's impact can be measured by the fact that many of its borrowers are slowly reclaiming land mortgaged to wealthy villagers. Others lease in new parcels and, on rare occasions, buy a small tract on the open market. The overall trend in the countryside is just the opposite—indebted small farmers are forced to sell off or mortgage their land until they have nothing left and become day laborers in the rural areas or migrate to the big cities. Rarely does one meet a rickshaw driver in Dhaka who was not a victim of this process, and who doesn't dream of one day reclaiming his ancestors' land.

"How much did it cost?" Krishna asked Aduree.

"Seven thousand five hundred taka [$190], sir. We repaid the money before the village *matbars* [elders], and everything is final. We will be planting *aus* and *aman* rice crops on it this year." Aduree enjoyed bragging about her accomplishments, and none more so than this one. She still felt she had something to prove to the other women, even six years after elbowing her way into the center. Though she didn't realize it, gaining access to a half acre of land had increased her assets to the point where if she were trying to gain entry to Grameen, she would be denied because she was too wealthy.

There was a lot of good news in the center. Nonibala, her five-year-old son Dalim Kumar nestled in her lap, told of her income from making cottage cheese, ghee, and sweets. The price of milk in the market was low, which meant big profits for her family—often as much as 1,000 taka ($25) per day. (By comparison, Krishna made about 110 taka [$2.75] per working day after having received two promotions.) With the coming monsoon, fishing nets were in high demand, keeping Devi, Shandha, and Bedana busy. Firoza from the seventh group told of her plans to reclaim one-third of an acre of mortgaged land.

But not every story was a happy one. Amodini's husband was still sick, and getting sicker; she asked Krishna for a group fund loan to pay for medical treatment. A relative of Shandha's in the third group had migrated to India two weeks earlier, and Alow's spot in the seventh group remained vacant. Over the past three months, a member of the second group had been abandoned by her husband, watched as three of her cows died, and seen her eldest daughter run away from home.

Krishna finished with the passbooks and his collection sheet and began taking wads of bills from the group chairmen. The first two groups gave him around 1,300 taka ($33) each, while the next four owed about 200 taka less. Amena's group had the smallest installments, totaling slightly more than 600 taka.

Toward the end of the meeting, a woman from Devi's group snuck into the center. She handed her chairman some bills, reimbursing her for having laid out installment money a few minutes earlier. Aduree upbraided the woman for being late, but she ignored the admonishment. Unsatisfied, Aduree stood up and began speaking angrily. "What excuse do you have for being late? I live farther away than any of you. We all have work to do with the harvest, but this is only one hour a week. What excuse could you have for being late, tell me. I'm never late to these meetings, ever!" The women listened as Aduree went on. Some laughed, others guffawed, and a few cheered. The offending borrower took it in stride, staring straight ahead with a blank expression during the outburst. Finally, Krishna told Aduree that her point was well taken, Aduree returned to her squatting position, and the meeting closed.

Before Krishna headed off to his other centers, he walked with Amodini to her hut and visited her husband. He greeted her family with the traditional *"nomoskar"* that Hindus exchange upon meeting, and inquired about what was probably a bleeding ulcer that needed prompt medical attention. Krishna didn't have time for the visit, but since he was new to the center he felt he had to prove his willingness to do the little extra things that endear bank workers to their members. Amodini raised the issue of the group fund loan. Her fellow group members agreed to sanction it, but Krishna's approval was necessary. He said he would raise it with the manager, and told Amodini to come with her group on the following Saturday. The loan would be for 2,000 taka ($50), but it would be given on the condition that she use it for modern medical treatment rather than the traditional healing that was the norm in remote villages, where many people had never seen as much as a bus or a paved road, much less a qualified doctor. Amodini agreed, and received the money in due course.

"Hello, Mannan! I had *heard* you came back. Come here," Muhammad Samsuddin called out. The Kholshi union chairman had come to an annual festival held in the village of Baze Taluk just after the harvest. There he had run into his old adversary Mannan Talukdar, the founder of the Grameen branch in Shaymganj. Scores of vendors filled a half acre of land, selling clay pottery, bangles, necklaces, sweets, fruit, toys, and other merchandise, most of it for less than 5 taka. While most of the vendors and customers were men, a surprisingly large number of women had come. They were decked out in their best saris, holding their children's hands and pushing from stall to stall, bargaining over items laying on vendors' blankets. Thelma Ali would have fit right in here, and Omiyale would have done a brisk business selling butter cookies.

Mannan, by that time working in Grameen's head office, had returned to the branch he had established on a weeklong assignment. He recognized Samsuddin and greeted him with a warm handshake. As is customary in Bangladesh, the men continued holding hands for the first few minutes of their conversation.

"Where are you posted now, Mannan?" the chairman asked.

"In Dhaka. I was transferred there from Manikganj, and joined the monitoring and evaluation department."

"So you are some big important official now, Mannan," he said with a laugh. "Why don't you come join me for some coconut juice out on the field here." The two men walked toward an open spot on the grass, removed their sandals, and sat on them. Samsuddin called a young man over and ordered him to bring two coconuts. He looked the part of a union *porishod* chairman—slightly overweight, wearing a *panjabi* that covered his longhi as far down as his knees, and speaking in a deep, self-assured voice that comes from years of being in charge.

As they began talking, the chairman studied Mannan. He was twenty pounds heavier than when they'd last met. The accumulated tensions of more than half a decade of managing Grameen branches showed on his face. At forty-two, he finally looked his age after years of hiding it successfully.

Mannan had not particularly liked Samsuddin when he had been the local manager. The chairman had stirred up rumors about Grameen and discouraged people from joining. He knew that people feared Samsuddin, whereas they respected Munaf, the former chairman. Mannan understood the difference, and acted accordingly.

Samsuddin wasted no time in reviving their old argument. "I'll tell you, Mannan, I still don't like this Grameen Bank you work for," he declared. "And I'll tell you why. People are taking these loans and they cannot use the money well. Many people are creating debts for themselves and getting into more trouble than they were in before. Sometimes I am called upon to help these people out." Mannan raised his eyebrows to register disbelief. He had spent the past several days visiting borrowers he had trained and given their first loans six years earlier, and while there were a few cases where he was disappointed by a member's lack of progress, in many more instances he was shocked and humbled by what he saw. In every center he visited, women grabbed him by the hand and begged him to come see their new house, their cows, their chickens, their vegetable gardens, or their rice harvest. Whenever he tried to leave, there was always another woman who became agitated, refusing to let him go until he saw the assets *she* had accumulated. It made for long days, but ones that were among the most satisfying of Mannan's life.

"But I will admit," Samsuddin said after a long pause, "that *some* of your borrowers are doing pretty well. One widow who used to be a servant in my household is now living in the southern *para*. She owns five cows! I think she has taken out loans worth sixty thousand taka from you, and is a rich woman now. But how am I supposed to find servants now that everyone can buy cows for themselves?" Samsuddin laughed at that one, and Mannan chuckled too.

The conversation shifted to the business of running the union. Samsuddin mentioned that it had been a bad year for him, as he had only been able to skim 600 taka off of the wheat that he had been given by the government to pay for rural maintenance projects. The year before, he had pocketed many times that amount. "Being a chairman is not so easy," he reminded Mannan at one point.

As the conversation drew to a close, Samsuddin couldn't resist one final jab at the man who had brought Grameen Bank to his union. "Mannan, Grameen is okay and all that, though it causes me headaches. But tell me one thing—why is Grameen acting like a new East India Company? Can you tell me that?" Mannan frowned when he heard that.

For the previous few months, Islamic fundamentalists who opposed Grameen and the Bangladesh Rural Advancement Committee (BRAC) had been circulating wild stories in the press, claiming that the two organizations were part of a Western conspiracy to recolonize Bangladesh as the British East India Company had done three centuries earlier. Other stories claimed that Grameen and BRAC staff had admitted that they'd taken a secret pledge to convert the rural poor to Christianity. On occasion, one could hear politicians in the rural areas telling stories of people digging up the corpses of Grameen borrowers to prove that they had been branded with a cross after joining.

Mannan didn't take the bait, but simply reminded his companion that Grameen was a Bengali-run program founded by a Bangladeshi economics professor who was being mentioned as a Nobel Prize candidate. When the conversation ended a few minutes later, Mannan clasped hands with the chairman one final time and promised to try to visit him before he returned to Dhaka. Then he mounted a bicycle and headed toward the Zianpur bazaar.

It had been an emotional week for Mannan, as he had been able to do what few founder branch managers have done—inspect their handiwork years after being reassigned. He spent several hours each evening talking with the bank workers, impressing them with his ability to recite the names of virtually all 1,500 borrowers who'd joined during his tenure. He, in turn, was impressed with the way several of the staff members, including Mustafiz and Rohim, had done their homework on the project area. He thought their blunt assessments of who were troublemakers and corrupt— judgments that influence decisions upon which a branch's success can depend—were largely accurate. They were grade A bank workers, in his opinion, while Ahlim was below average and all the rest were one or another shade of mediocre. He included Krishna in this third group.

One morning he found Mustafiz lying on his bed, moaning and writhing as if in pain. But Mustafiz's anguish was from mental rather than physical anguish. Mustafiz recounted the story of a borrower in the village of Baze Taluk who was selling her house, which had been bought with a Grameen housing loan, and could not be talked out of it. The house had been dismantled early that morning and was being moved to the buyer's plot.

The staff considered this a serious matter. Perhaps the ultimate slap in the face a bank worker can receive is to have one of his borrowers sell her Grameen-financed house. In most cases it is a response to a woman's inability to meet her weekly installment, a sign that Grameen has not helped her very much and that she is ready to wave the white flag in her struggle for progress toward a dignified, poverty-free life. For Ahlim, the bank worker responsible for this center, it was a disappointment; for his colleague Mustafiz, it was an outrage. Yet neither had made any progress.

Mannan went to the scene and convened a meeting of all the interested parties. He described to the prospective house buyer the difficulties the sale presented to Grameen. He played to the man's ego, calling him a gentleman who could afford to buy a house anywhere. Why, Mannan asked, did he want to buy it from a poor woman who didn't have anything else? The man agreed to return all the building materials and to reconstruct the house. But he was unwilling to accept Mannan's offer to pay for the cost of rebuilding it; he promised to bear the expense himself, because he respected what Mannan had done for the community.

Next Mannan turned to the woman who had sold her house. Now that she could have it back, would she take it back? The crowd fell silent as it waited for her answer. She explained that she had sold it to buy a used rickshaw for her son, the family's only prospect for a steady income in the months ahead. Mannan proposed that she take a loan from the group fund to buy the rickshaw. The woman began to complain that her group members had not wanted to sanction the loan, but before she could get very far Assia Begum, the center chief, waved her hand and said to Mannan, "I'll handle it." That ended that. Two hours after Mannan arrived in Baze Taluk, the agreement that had eluded four bank employees and a center chief was completed, and the meeting broke up.

On his last night before returning to Dhaka, Mannan spent several hours telling stories to the staff. One was about the 1988 flood, when Mannan and his staff lived in an abandoned school classroom. One morning the staff awoke to find that a foot of water was flowing through their makeshift dormitory and that a live cobra had snuck into bed with a bank worker. After killing the snake and securing their belongings, the men rented boats and spent the next four days visiting Grameen members. They had received no instructions to do so from their superiors; it was simply understood that in times of disaster, the staff was expected to maintain close contact with their borrowers. Mannan described how he demoted his senior assistant to a bank worker when he hesitated for several hours before deciding to join in the disaster-response effort.

At one point during the flood, Mannan discovered a Kholshi borrower who had taken refuge on her roof and was in the middle of giving birth. He assisted with the delivery, brought her to a village midwife who lived on higher ground, and named the newborn Bonna (Flood). Since arriving at the branch, Rohim had heard stories of how the staff had responded to the flood, and the loyalty among the borrowers that their actions created.

A second story was more humorous, reflecting the presence of mind and character needed to be an outstanding manager—a post Rohim dreamed of occupying one day. Mannan told of being posted to Shaymganj along with Ruhul Amin and Rofiq ul Islam. One evening, after the three men had spent several days together, the bank workers admitted that they had been branded troublemakers at the branches from which they'd been transferred. Both assumed that they had been sent to such a remote location as punishment for their transgressions. Mannan gave them a long lecture about how he would not hold past actions against them, and told them that if they worked hard he would ensure that they received promotions. At the end of the conversation, the two bank workers looked at each other, both apparently wanting to ask a question but too shy to do so. Mannan encouraged them to say what was on their minds.

"Sir," Ruhul Amin began sheepishly, "what did *you* do to get posted here?"

Without missing a beat, Mannan thought of the perfect white lie. "Well, you see, I am being punished because of my temper. On several occasions, I assaulted bank workers working under me."

During the ensuing months, Ruhul Amin—the founder of Shandha's center—and Rofiq performed as well as any bank workers Mannan had ever known. They, and Mannan, received their promotions in record time.

• • •

One afternoon, shortly before the monsoon, Krishna cycled to Amena's house. *"As Salaam o Aleikum,"* Krishna called out as he dismounted his bicycle after entering her courtyard.

"*Salaam,* sir," Amena replied as she walked out of her vegetable garden to greet him.

"So this is your garden, Amena," Krishna said as he walked over and touched some of the maturing eggplant, pumpkins, and chilies. "You sell these to wholesalers who come here?"

"No, sir, my daughter Aaki sells our vegetables at the Zianpur *haat,* and in the Kholshi bazaar, after school. Sometimes she goes to the Ghior *haat.* We get a better price that way. Lately I've been making a hundred fifty taka per week." Amena called her son to roll out a bamboo mat on her veranda so that Krishna could sit down.

"Very impressive," Krishna said. "She's studying in the BRAC school, right?"

"Yes, sir."

"And your chickens and ducks?" he asked as he took a seat on the mat.

"They're in the jungle, sir. Jackals have eaten a couple of the chicks. I . . ." She looked around and said in a hushed voice, "I have given out a dozen on a sharecrop basis, sir, so that my husband, you know . . ." Krishna nodded. He had heard about the situation from Oloka, and approved of Amena's strategy of keeping some of her assets concealed. He had been told that it was several months since she had received her last beating, and that slowly the abuse of the children was declining as well.

He asked Amena if she thought Rukia Begum should be allowed to join her group. Rukia had been part of the group that had failed its recognition test fourteen months before and had not reapplied.

"I think it is a good thing, sir. She will pass the recognition test this time. She has seen how well we've done and is eager for a second chance."

"She's not getting any pressure from relatives to join, is she?"

"I don't think so, sir. She wants to raise a cow. I think she'll fit in very well." Amena heard a faint noise, and it reminded her of something. "Sir, I think there's been some tragedy in Fulzan's compound. Perhaps you should have a look. I don't get along with the people who live near her, the families that squat along the side of the pond. But maybe you should go."

"What's happened?"

"Somebody said a child has died. I'm not sure."

Krishna looked at his watch. He wanted to inspect the loan utilization of two members in center forty-two, and the afternoon was slipping away. Yet duty called. "Can your son show me the way?" he asked.

Long before Amena's son and Krishna walked up the steep slope separating Fulzan's house plot from the footpath ten feet below, they had heard the cries. Fulzan's niece Zorina, the daughter of her older sister Shundari, who lived in a tiny thatch hut next to hers, was rolling in the dirt, screaming gibberish. Next to her, lying on a blanket, was the lifeless, emaciated body of her son. Incense was burning a few inches away from his head. The tiny corpse's shriveled skin, sunken face, and brittle arms reminded Krishna of pictures of famine-stricken Somalia he had seen in the newspaper.

Krishna looked at the body and gasped. He had not seen anything quite like this since the famine of 1974. Fulzan, Shundari, and group chairman Nobirun paced around the small courtyard, their pallid faces reflecting the seriousness of the moment. Each had seen the boy spend the last six weeks coughing and wheezing his way closer and closer to death's door, losing a little more body weight each day. Traditional healers weren't able to do anything, though one took 200 taka for trying.

"Fulzan," Krishna called out as he walked toward her. "Is that your sister?"

"That's my niece. Her only son has died, just now." As Fulzan said that, the wailing resumed again. By now the boy's mother was covered in dirt and her sari was in tatters.

In the year since she'd joined the bank, Fulzan had made some progress. She now ate rice from land farmed by her husband more than ten months of the year, and had bought two sheets of tin for her roof with money she made from selling jute and duck eggs. For the first time in years, she would not be exposed to the elements during the monsoon. But all was not well. Two months earlier her cow had died, forcing her to replace it with a sharecropped calf from a wealthy family. When she received her second general loan, she decided to invest most of it in leasing some more land for her husband to farm instead of trying her luck with another cow. With the few hundred taka left over she bought some chicks and ducklings to raise. She was also pregnant, though it hardly showed, despite the fact that she was ending her second trimester. Fulzan was praying that this time she would have a boy.

For someone as poor as Fulzan, the path out of poverty would most likely be slower than that of her peers. It might take five years, or even ten, for her to stabilize. In between, there would be setbacks—cows that died, crops damaged by pests, medical emergencies. It was possible that one of those crises could ruin her, but with the ditchdigging to fall back on, and the support of people like Amena and Shandha, it was more likely that she would continue on her unsteady but generally upward course. When asked, she said that Grameen was her savior, but it took a discerning eye to distinguish the changes that had occurred in her life over the fourteen months since she'd joined the bank. One measure of that change, however, lay in what she was *not*—the mother of a child who had succumbed to slow starvation.

"Listen, listen—listen!" Krishna yelled, trying to gain the attention of Fulzan's niece. "There's nothing to be gained by crying. Allah has taken your son, and that is final. No amount of drama will bring him back. Here, here's fifty taka to arrange for a proper burial." He handed the pink bill to Fulzan, and, turning back to the niece, added, "Put your attention toward that, would you?"

In a softer voice he said, "Fulzan, I'm sorry to hear about your cow dying. I've heard you've sharecropped another cow."

"Yes, sir."

"Okay, I'm going over to the Haldar *para*. I'm late. See that the burial is taken care of quickly—don't let her be like this for long. It'll make her sick."

"Yes, sir."

Krishna descended to the footpath, grimacing as the wailing

started over again. He knew that Fulzan's family had just lost its first son in two generations, and understood what a blow that was to their social, economic, and psychological well-being. Over the next few days, Krishna continued to be haunted by the image of that lifeless boy.

At the head of the parade were Yunus and Shah Nawaz, the Dhaka zonal manager, talking casually as they walked through the village. Yunus was asking questions about what he had just seen at the Shekherchar Narsingdi office, a window on the future of Grameen. For the first time, a branch had been fully computerized, an experiment that had cut the bank workers' time spent doing paperwork by 70 percent. In an era of eight groups per center and three loans per borrower, it was the only realistic way to go. This personal visit had reinforced Yunus's commitment to computerize at least one branch in each zone by the first quarter of 1995. Bank workers had told him of the extra time they were able to spend with borrowers in the field, something that Yunus knew was necessary in order for Grameen to thrive.

Yunus and his entourage moved to the center hut, where the center chief greeted him. "Sir," she asked Yunus after he sat down on a bench, "may I have permission to start this special meeting?"

"Yes, go ahead." The center chief shouted out orders, and the other women responded—arms forward, arms crossed, arms forward, arms crossed, arms forward, and then standing and crouching three times before resuming a relaxed crouching position. Yunus gave the center chief permission to sit down and then turned the meeting over to Shah Nawaz, who introduced the managing director. As he did so, Yunus surveyed the women and the men standing outside the hut. He liked going to the field, even though he did it less frequently now than he used to. It always seemed to teach him something that he could bring back and integrate into his work, and this day would be no exception.

"As Salaam o Aleikum," Yunus began after he was introduced. The women returned the greeting. "I have come here as a guest of your staff, and I would like to know a little bit about the progress you are making in your businesses. Many of you, I know, are involved with weaving. Is this a profitable profession? Have the loans helped you? Is it getting better every year, or worse?"

The center chief stood up and saluted Yunus. "Sir, most of us are involved with handlooms, though some are raising cows and doing other things. I have three handlooms myself. When I first thought of joining the bank, the idea terrified me. Learning the rules and the decisions, signing my name, defying the things people said against the bank, taking money—it all seemed impossible. But I built up my courage, joined with some friends, and tried. After recognition, I received a loan of one thousand taka, and it felt like so much. I had never seen so much money before, and I was frightened that I would not be able to invest it well and make the twenty-one taka I needed to meet my weekly installment." As she spoke, the woman stared at Yunus, swinging her arms to emphasize particular words and phrases. The constant state of motion her hands were in disguised the fact that they were trembling.

"But now, I have made a lot of progress. Today, my weekly installment is more than one thousand taka—more than the amount of my first loan. And I have no problem paying it. So from being unable to dream of taking one thousand taka for an entire year I am now paying that to the bank every seven days!" She smiled broadly as she said that, then opened her right hand, which had been clenched into a fist, as if to say, "I could give you one thousand taka right now, if you wanted it."

"Is this really true?" Yunus asked. He had never heard of a borrower having such a high weekly installment. It was not clear if he was asking Shah Nawaz or the center chief, but the borrower answered herself.

"Yes, sir, my installment is one thousand and sixty-one taka." Another woman, sitting two rows behind the center chief, stood up.

"Sir, I am the deputy center chief, and while my installment is not one thousand, it is more than eight hundred."

A woman from the fourth row rose to her feet and added, "My installment is seven hundred fifty-one, and I have lots of money now. Here, look—I always have money just to carry around with me." She untied the end of her sari, revealing a handful of crumpled bills. She carefully unfolded and handed each of them to Yunus, one by one. There were three 100-taka notes, then a 50, then two more 100s, then a 20, then three more 100s. When she had taken them out of her sari, it hadn't looked like there were more than three or four notes of small denominations. (In Bangladesh, the larger the note, the more it is worth, with 2-taka notes being bigger than 1-taka notes, and so on.)

Yunus inspected the bills, counted them, and returned the wad to its proud owner. He asked the women to sit down and said, "Is this just a few of you, or are there many with such large installments?"

"Oh, many, sir," one woman called out.

"Let me ask this. How many of you have installments of more than one thousand taka?" Three women raised their hands. Yunus looked at Shah Nawaz, and then back at the women. "What about between eight hundred and one thousand taka as an installment?" Five more women raised their hands. He continued asking until he got down to 500 taka, and by then nearly twenty arms were erect.

"Well, when I started with Grameen Bank, I was giving out loans that were sometimes smaller than the one thousand taka your center chief started with. I gave out loans for five hundred taka, for three hundred taka, for one hundred taka, even for thirty taka. These loans were no joke—they were serious business, and repaying was not always easy. So I am used to talking about small sums. But not until today had I ever heard of Grameen Bank members paying more in a weekly installment than they had borrowed when they joined. That is no small thing, something I could have never imagined. Until today."

The meeting drew to a close, and Yunus began his visits to the borrowers' homes to see their handlooms, their employees, their livestock, and their houses. As striking as the scale of their operations was the docility of many of the women's husbands. A few just stood beside their wives, tending a cow or a goat while their spouse explained the family business to the professor.

When he returned to the branch in the late afternoon, Yunus wanted to look at the books. He asked if other centers had so many borrowers whose installment was more than 500 taka. The staff claimed that it was typical of more than half of the centers in the branch, and produced ledgers and collection sheets to prove it.

On his drive back to Dhaka with Shah Nawaz, Yunus spent a long time in silent contemplation, and finally said, "It really had never occurred to me that a woman's installment could be more than one thousand taka. I have seen the aggregate numbers coming into the head office, but I couldn't quite grasp what they meant at the level of a single borrower. So many people say we are just lending to people and they are struggling along with small-scale operations, not growing, not breaking through to higher levels of productivity, not leaving poverty. But it is impossible to say that about a woman who is paying one thousand taka every single week. These are not struggling poor people—these are authentic rural entrepreneurs. I had never imagined."

Yunus drifted back into thought, and all Shah Nawaz could think to say was "Yes, sir."

The van sped toward Dhaka, where Yunus would resume his daily routine the following morning. For many weeks, his thoughts would return to the 1,000-taka installments and crumpled 100-taka notes of the Shekherchar Narsingdi branch. He thought it signified the dawning of a new era at Grameen, and he wondered what the achievements, challenges, and risks of that era would be.

On May 24, Rukia Begum traveled to a center in Bilpara with Amena and Shandha and took the group recognition test for the second time. The program officer asked Rukia three questions, one about the group fund, another about the responsibilities of membership, and a third about the Sixteen Decisions. She answered them all without so much as a pause to collect her thoughts, and in so doing gained recognition and entry into the seventh group, more than a year after her failure. Five days later, she walked to the bazaar and took a loan of 2,000 taka.

10

▲

The Hip Hop Shop

Omiyale stood on her porch on South Dante Street, waiting for her son Hkeem at 5:15 on a cool morning in early April. She was surrounded by black plastic garbage bags containing one hundred packets of warm butter cookies and another hundred plastic bags of fruit. Omiyale had spent the entire night baking cookies, sorting fruit, and packaging. Since 3:30 she had been feeling light-headed, but she had no choice but to finish up and get ready for the morning rush hour.

February and March 1994 had been bitter months for Omiyale DuPart. Her troubles stemmed from having been unable to repay her short-term loan of $3,300 (taken to buy inventory for the Black Expo in July 1993) by the due date of Friday, October 1. Though she made a $105 payment on that day, nearly $2,300 remained unpaid.

At the time, her circle members were supportive despite the large amount that was overdue. Even Geri, who had been forced to take a smaller loan as a consequence of her chairlady's difficulty, told Omiyale to take whatever time she needed to repay. Queenesta asked if she could help sell some of Omiyale's merchandise from her counter at Victor's store. Thelma, though she gently questioned

Omiyale on all the time she'd been putting into solving the problems of *other* circles (instead of getting herself back on track), let her friend know she was available for support. On several occasions, Thelma tried to arrange transportation for Omiyale so that she would not be late to events at which she was selling.

November and December 1993 were not good for her business, and some of Omiyale's modest profits had to be diverted into solving family crises. She made only two payments totaling $120 on her short-term loan in December, though she managed to keep current on her payments on her long-term loan. The final month of 1993 was hard on other borrowers, too; Thelma, perhaps the long-term FCF member with the fewest missed payments, bounced two checks to WSEP (but then made a triple payment during the first week of January to get up to date). In January and February 1994, Omiyale's business—trading African imports, selling handmade jewelry and home-baked butter cookies—continued to struggle, her profits too small to do anything more than make twice-monthly payments of $112 on her long-term loan, buy some merchandise for Black History Month, and put down a deposit for the Black Women's Expo, scheduled for the second week of March.

By February, Thelma and Queenesta were headed into the final stages of repaying their loans and were hoping to take larger ones to buy inventory for the spring and summer. Both began to wonder when, or whether, their chairlady was planning on repaying her short-term loan. Peer support was being slowly transformed into a combination of peer *pressure* and peer support. While Queenesta gave and received help from Omiyale as they coordinated a series of vending events during Black History Month at Chicago State University, she was not above gossiping on the phone with Thelma about how many times Omiyale had missed deadlines she had set for herself for clearing the debt. With each passing week, the tension grew.

The following dialogue from a meeting in early March, just before the Black Women's Expo, gives a flavor of the prevailing mood in the group.

THELMA: The first thing we need to talk about is the short-term loan. Why isn't it paid off? This is March seventh.

GERI [to Thelma, embarrassed and trying to change the subject]: I saw you at Maxwell Street yesterday, and I wanted to show this to you. You can get fabrics, pieces, at Crate and Barrel, like scraps.

THELMA: The question is, why is the short-term loan at two thousand two hundred and fifty-two dollars as of February eleventh?

OMIYALE: It is still at that amount because I have not been making that money, I've been making payments on my long-term loan.

THELMA: We thought you were also making payments on this one. It's the eleventh month of this loan. We are hoping it will be paid off before April.

OMIYALE: I'll be generating money from the Black [Women's] Expo.

THELMA: Say you don't do well at the Black Expo. What is the backup?

OMIYALE [irritation in her voice]: I've made arrangements to get money. If I don't make all the money, I've made arrangements to come up with it.

THELMA: What?

OMIYALE: I'll take a loan from someone, okay.

THELMA: What date will it be paid off?

OMIYALE: Tuesday, March fifteenth or sixteenth, which is it?

THELMA: Geri, please make a notation that Omiyale has made a commitment to pay it off by Tuesday. The season is beginnin', and we need to figure out how to get some money [for our businesses].

Omiyale believed that Thelma's pressure was overly vindictive—retribution for deciding not to share a booth with her at the Black Women's Expo. But however much she disliked the pressure, she recognized that the Full Circle Fund (and Grameen Bank before it) was set up to encourage such interactions, however uncomfortable, when borrowers fall behind. It's what differentiates Grameen and the Fund from nonprofit organizations and government initiatives that are unable to get their beneficiaries to put anything back into the program. That may have seemed fine to Omiyale in theory, but it was painful in practice. After all, she had *created* her group, and her center. Many women, including Thelma, owed their participation to her.

Queenesta, Thelma, and Omiyale all did reasonably well at the Expo. Even Geri, who took Thelma up on an offer to sell her aprons at Thelma's booth, made out fine, selling more than a half dozen aprons and taking orders for more. In fact, for the first time since WSEP had started putting together packages for its clients to participate in Expos, not a single woman failed to make at least enough profit to pay off her booth space. Several made substantial sums of money. This was a triumph for Pam, who was rewarded with a promotion. Thelma grossed $950, mainly selling clothing she had made at her sewing class, hair accessories, and dollar jewelry. For a woman who hadn't known how to sew six months earlier, it was encouraging. Just before the Expo, Thelma celebrated the ending of the month of Ramadan, in which Muslims fast from dawn until dusk every day until the Eid festival. The day before the Expo began, she got dressed up in an Indian sari and went to her mosque. Thelma enjoyed praying with Muslims of different nationalities, and was always amused by the Pakistani women, who told her that they had never been able to go to the mosque before they came to America. Ending the fast gave her the strength she needed to endure the rigors of running her booth over the three days.

Omiyale made $1,300 at the Expo, though after paying for her booth space and inventory she had only $405 profit left to make a payment on her short-term loan. When she explained that at the next meeting, the women did not press her to borrow the money to repay the rest of the loan, but instead encouraged her to keep earning a little at a time. Thelma recommended that Omiyale concentrate her efforts on baking and selling her butter cookies. She believed it was the best product her friend had. (Thelma once remarked, "Some people have a million-dollar idea and some don't.

I don't. But Omiyale's cookies, if she markets them right, could make her a millionaire. They's so good—mmmm—you just eat one and you can't stop, you want to eat five or ten.") As far as Thelma could tell, butter cookies were Omiyale's ticket out of debt. Omiyale, as much as she resented the harassment, knew that the advice was good, and after the Expo she began devoting her energies to her cookie business. With only a single oven, it took her close to eight hours and $33 in raw materials to make $100 worth of butter cookies. She knew it would only be by paying off her short-term loan that she'd be able to borrow enough to buy an industrial oven that would cut her production time by 70 percent.

At 5:25, Hkeem pulled up in front of his mother's house. He jumped out of the car, apologized for being late, and started helping his mother load her bags into the backseat. Twenty-five years old, Hkeem DuPart was a dashing ex-marine who had served in Asia and Central America. While he often cringed at his mother's being a street vendor, he, more than anyone else in the family, helped her out. Once, when she was selling a thousand T-shirts outside of Chicago Stadium during the Bulls' push toward their first championship, he offered to be his mother's bodyguard because the stadium was located in a rough neighborhood. When his mother asked him to help sell, Hkeem feared the embarrassment of having one of his friends see him hawking T-shirts. Yet, after watching his mother make steady progress, he decided to swallow his pride, and in a short span of time he'd sold more than one hundred shirts. Even after that, it still shocked him when he saw Omiyale selling at Maxwell Street during the winter months, warming her hands over a burning garbage can alongside fellow vendors who looked like hoboes. If other ethnic groups accuse blacks of being overly status-conscious and not industrious enough, Hkeem sometimes thought, they certainly hadn't met his mom.

Hkeem dropped his mother off by the corner of State and Eighty-seventh. Omiyale grabbed a packet of cookies in her right hand and a bag of fruit—a banana, an apple, a pear, and a few grapes—in her left and waited for cars headed for the expressway. One, a beat-up white Cadillac, refused to even slow down as Omiyale waved the cookies and fruit at the driver. A woman in a gray Honda decelerated, took a look, and smiled at Omiyale as she shook her head. Probably didn't have exact change, or access to her wallet, Omiyale thought. It's nice that she slowed down to make eye contact, though.

Finally, she got the attention of a middle-aged black man in an Oldsmobile. He stopped, rolled down his window, and said, "Is those one dollar?"

"Yes, sir, one dollar for the cookies and one dollar for the fruit!" Omiyale replied excitedly.

"Uh, give me some cookies." As he reached for his wallet he added, "And give me some fruit, too."

"Sure will." Omiyale smiled, handed him the two bags, and made change for a $5 bill. As the car pulled away, she felt that sense of relief a peddler always gets from making her first sale of the day. She headed back to her bags and grabbed some more.

At 7:45, she was down to ten bags of fruit; the cookies, as usual, were gone. She would have liked to stay, but there was a grandchild to send to school and appointments to keep. She stuffed the empty garbage bags into the one containing the leftover fruit and ran across the street ahead of an eastbound number 87 bus. As Omiyale boarded and parted with her fare, she greeted the driver with a smile and headed to the back.

By 8:05, Omiyale was home, preparing Atukwe, the five-year-old son of Bayyinah, her second-eldest daughter, to go to kindergarten. Atukwe's mother had already left for her part-time job, so it was left to Omiyale to get him on his way.

At 8:23, Omiyale splashed some water on her face, laid her money out on the table, and counted it. It was mostly 1s, a few 5s, one 10, and one 20—$189 in all. Since she had a little left over from last week to buy the sugar, butter, and flour, she crammed it all in her pocket as she ran out the door—she was late! Alternately jogging and walking along Ninetieth Street, she progressed steadily toward Stoney Island Avenue. At 8:45, she arrived, sweaty and racked by a headache. Five minutes later, Colete pulled up in her car at the corner of Ninety-fifth and Stoney Island, from where they would drive to the WSEP office. They had agreed the night before to meet there.

"Hey, girl," Colete said. "You been up all night, huh?"

"Yeah," Omiyale replied with a sigh. "Just like last week. But I gotta get this paid off, ya know."

"You got the money?"

"Yeah, here's a hundred and eighty-nine. I might have more next week, but I wanted to give you this right now, before I have any time to spend it on anything."

"All right. Let me write you a receipt." With her car still running, Colete filled in and signed the receipt, took the money, and counted it. "Great job, girl. I'll see you Monday night."

"Yeah, I guess you will. I'll try to have another payment then, a big one." As she began walking back to her house, Omiyale pondered the day ahead: catching a little nap, picking up Atukwe in the early afternoon, cooking him lunch, picking up her granddaughter from day care, buying fruit, flour, sugar, and butter from wholesalers, and getting the entire production process going again. There were rides to arrange and telephone calls to make.

At the Lindblom center meeting the following Monday, Omiyale informed her circle members that along with her payment on her long-term loan, she was making a payment of $826 on her short-term loan and had given Colete $185 the previous week. Most of that money had been earned from selling cookies and fruit on the Eighty-seventh Street on-ramp.

Those payments brought the balance on her short-term loan down to $857. Two weeks later, it would drop to $586. Three weeks later, she went downtown to present Colete with a $400 money order that completely cleared her account. Principal and interest were repaid, and as she clutched the receipt, Omiyale DuPart burst into tears. With the rest of the FCF staff looking on, Colete embraced her center chief until the last tear was spent.

By then, Queenesta and Thelma were in the final stages of preparing their loan applications, for $5,000 and $4,400, respectively. It was not a moment too soon, as both were on the verge of seeing investment opportunities for the summer slip away.

• • •

In 1992, Omiyale's second year in the program, she began having success selling African imports. She initially became interested in African products from a cultural standpoint; though her activist days were over, she still thought it was good for African Americans to be in touch with their rich native culture. If she hadn't made much of a profit, it wouldn't have particularly bothered her. But to her surprise, she grossed more than $2,000 selling African imports at each of several events during the summer of 1992, and in the fall investigated the possibility of buying direct from Africa. Incautiously, she invested $2,000 in a joint venture with two Africans she had met at a festival—all of which she lost without seeing any merchandise. Yet it is testimony to how far her business had come since she'd joined the program that she was able to withstand the loss without missing a payment on her loan.

In the spring of 1992, two of Omiyale's relatives passed away. She and her sisters stood to inherit substantial sums from the estate, but a protracted legal battle ended up consuming the bulk of the wealth. The entire episode made Omiyale bitter—couldn't she just have ended up with a small amount of money, something like $5,000 that would give her a little cushion in her checking account, ensuring that she didn't always have to be at risk of bouncing checks?

Repaying her short-term loan through cookie sales was a defining experience for her. Until then, baking butter cookies was a diversion, something she enjoyed pursuing less than her African import and jewelry ventures. Indeed, she had been looking to phase it out. But the marketplace was becoming flooded with African goods, and she had a growing number of regular customers for her cookies. As she completed repaying her short-term loan and contemplated her next loan from the Full Circle Fund, Omiyale thought seriously about buying an industrial oven and getting a baker's license.

Her vision was to open a bakery from which she could wholesale what would be called Mama Omiyale's Lunchroom Butter Cookies. As far as Omiyale could tell, since time immemorial kids had been eating butter cookies in public school cafeterias in Chicago. Her idea was to re-create the taste that the students had grown up with; only her cookies would be larger and sold in packets of four. The wholesale price would be $1 per package, the retail price double that. Even if she didn't match Mrs. Fields's success, it might at least get her to the point of having some spare cash in her bank account. Others suspected it could do more than that; as Thelma often reminded Omiyale, she rarely if ever failed to sell out, whether she was selling to poor folks or rich, white, black, or Hispanic. Now it was time to test it on a larger scale, to see if this was a "million-dollar idea."

In the middle of April, while Omiyale was in the throes of paying off her short-term loan and Queenesta was enjoying her first few weeks in her new store, the curtain opened on the final chapter of the Maxwell Street saga. Several weeks earlier, Isabel Wilkerson of *The New York Times* had run a tribute to the bazaar, writing, "For 120 years, the Maxwell Street Market has been the mall of the dispossessed. . . . Now Maxwell Street faces extinction."

And face extinction it did on Wednesday, April 13, when the Chicago City Council voted on whether to sell the city-owned land that fell within the jurisdiction of the bazaar to the University of Illinois. Up in the observers' gallery, some eight hundred promarket activists watched, cheering those who supported their cause and booing those who didn't. Thelma Ali was there, as were Steve Balkin and Lew Krineberg. They had all come to see the end; or, perhaps, they faintly hoped, to bear witness to a miracle.

What they saw was two aldermen nearly coming to blows over the issue; only police intervention prevented a fight. When the vote was taken, the motion to sell the land to the university passed 33 to 10. The *Chicago Tribune* reported the deliberations in the following day's paper in an article entitled, "Ready to Rumble? Step into Council Chambers." While the *Tribune* had hardly adopted a pro–Maxwell Street stand, columnist John Kass did not shirk from describing how the city had shafted the vendors by selling a market in which an estimated $20 million in sales are made each year for a measly $4.25 million—money that UIC would receive from Illinois taxpayers. "The agreement," the article noted, "will evict more than 800 vendors by Labor Day, and only about half of them will be relocated in a sanitized version of the market to be established on Canal Street between Roosevelt and 15th Streets." Kass added that the planned Canal Street market area was itself already threatened, targeted by the city as a parking-lot-to-be for a proposed riverboat gambling complex. If there was one thing Mayor Daley had his heart set on more than the growth of UIC and the gentrification of the area around the Loop, it was gaining approval for Chicago-based riverboat gambling. The market was to be moved out of the way of one speeding train only to be put in the path of another, larger one.

The council, unfortunately, was not satisfied dealing only one blow to Chicago's low-income entrepreneurs. On the same day it sealed Maxwell Street's fate it passed another motion that significantly curtailed the right of peddlers to operate in the downtown area and around the stadium where the World Cup soccer games would be held in June and July. Poor peddlers, the city council declared, would be shut out of the bonanza in the name of presenting a sanitized Chicago to the world. Low-income vendors would also be shut out of the market for selling merchandise at other events the city had scheduled at taxpayer expense, including the 1996 Democratic convention. Alderman Ted Mazola, the chief opponent of Maxwell Street (and one of the pair who almost came to blows over the issue), led the way on the peddler ban as well.

In the weeks after the vote, periodicals ranging from *The Washington Post* to London's *The Economist* commented on the passing of the market. Reporters tended to wax nostalgic about the bazaar, but many were sympathetic to the desires of the city and the university. Most had more in common with the UIC and City Hall public relations people than with black hubcap vendors and Mexican tamale makers. And, to be fair, there were strong arguments for the university's expansion. But they weren't so strong as to preclude it from finding some kind of accommodation with the market. The compromise that many wanted was to let the university expand but to require UIC to share the space with the market on Sundays, keep the number and cost of vendor slots the same, and work with the vendors to clean the place up and improve it.

Chicago Tribune columnist John McCarron wrote about the failure to compromise. "Nobody ever went to jail for a lack of imagination," he said, "so there's no sense calling it criminal that the University of Illinois at Chicago is about to snuff out the Maxwell Street Market.

"The school is acting a bit paranoid. Arrogant, to be sure. Even a touch racist, though one hesitates to drag out that overused brickbat. But it's not criminal . . ." McCarron went on to describe a compromise the city had proposed some years earlier. Though it was a pro-UIC plan that reduced the size of (but stopped short of eliminating) the market, the university responded by fiercely lobbying against the proposal, which by the time the city council took its vote in April 1994 was long since forgotten.

McCarron closed his piece by reprimanding UIC for its refusal to assist the area's ethnic enterpreneurs and criticizing the university's lack of foresight, purpose, and imagination.

For lack of that imagination, Thelma and Omiyale were forced to begin considering how they would adapt their businesses to the loss of the greatest poor people's market in North America.

Occasionally, people visiting the Full Circle Fund ask about the borrowers who have left the program. Through 1993, all who had done so had settled their accounts, leaving the program with an enviable 100 percent repayment rate, even if many of the payments were late. If Glenda Harris is typical of those who have stopped participating in the program, the impact of FCF has been substantial.

Soon after Glenda left Omiyale's circle in the fall, she began working full-time for Westcorp, a community development organization located in one of the most depressed areas on Chicago's West Side. Westcorp was founded and directed by Corretta McFerren, a fiery and charismatic woman who had effectively become the godparent to dozens of people like Glenda who took refuge in her South Side home. Westcorp was involved in a campaign to reform the Chicago public school system, and also ran classes for young black men and young black mothers. In all its programs, the philosophy was to be straight with the kids while giving them the tools to improve themselves.

Getting a full-time job did not, however, mean that Glenda's Ethnic Treasures went out of business. Far from it. To supplement her modest paycheck, she continued to manufacture jewelry. She sold it during protest marches, at picnics in the park, from her home, and, mostly, from Westcorp's office in the basement of Malcolm X College. Janitors were among her best customers; they, like many others, discerned that Glenda's small velvet board was filled with quality jewelry at reasonable prices. Often, young people who were hanging around the office, or the McFerrens' home, became part of the production team.

Glenda often earned $300 to $500 a month from her business. She frequently had no choice but to stay up until the wee hours of the morning to replenish her stock because her regular customers had received their paychecks and cleaned her out. That, combined with her salary, enabled her to buy more exotic "parts" to make more expensive jewelry while having a surplus to save or to use to pay for communal expenses at the McFerrens'. Her business income also made it possible for her to buy the medicine her doctors prescribed for her arthritis.

By the spring, Glenda was back teaching jewelry design at several public schools; her favorite was one in which all the students were teenage mothers. She enjoyed the times when she was able to take an interest in a disruptive young mother and focus her energy on a project. Teachers often marveled at how she could transform chronic disciplinary cases into purposeful jewelers. With Glenda's encouragement, teachers at two schools where she taught set up tables to sell student-made jewelry on days when parents were required to come in and pick up report cards.

The quality of the students' work gave Glenda an idea. In Chicago, black teenagers and Korean shopkeepers are often at each other's throats. Glenda would ask the shopkeepers, who were often accused of not putting anything back into the community, to agree to display and sell student-manufactured jewelry. In exchange for doing so, they would get a percentage of the retail prices—which Glenda imagined would be $6 to $10 per piece—and would be able to post signs announcing that they were in a joint venture with a local school. That would be good for business, as the students would naturally urge friends and relatives to go to the stores selling their jewelry. Preliminary discussions she had before the school year closed with students, public school administrators, and Korean store owners were positive.

Due to a funding crisis at Westcorp, Glenda and her colleagues received their last paychecks on March 15, and were not paid again until the MacArthur Foundation gave the organization a grant in the fall. For the intervening months, Glenda continued to work full-time at Westcorp but turned increasing energy toward her business. Modest living and steady sales kept her from financial hardship; indeed, she was often able to lend her colleagues small sums of money to get through the lean times.

As she pursued Coretta McFerren's dream of educational reform and her own vision of linking wayward black teens with ostracized Korean merchants, Glenda's Ethnic Treasures continued to grow. The business advice and encouragement of her peers, as much as the infusion of $1,500 in loan capital from the Full Circle Fund, had gotten her going. She stayed in close contact with Omiyale and Thelma, often inviting them to events at Malcolm X College where they could sell their wares. Sometimes, she would have customers sent her way by women from the Lindblom center. As a result, Glenda felt a strong sense of loyalty to her circle sisters and the Full Circle Fund, and continued to reap the benefits of her participation long after she had left.

During the first week of June, Thelma and Queenesta received their new loans. They were among the largest ever given out by the Full Circle Fund. Before getting final approval, their applications had been pored over by their circle members, the center's loan committee, Colete, and, finally, a panel of senior WSEP staff.

Thelma presented a detailed analysis of her cash flow during the previous year and her plans for the coming one. She listed a series of events at which she would participate—the Black Expo, the Ghana Fest, the Haile Selassie Fest, Rock Around the Block, the Summer Kwanzaa Fest, the Evanston Garage Sale, the Afro-

World Festival in Milwaukee, and the Taste of Oak Park. In addition, she planned to be at Maxwell Street every Sunday and occasionally during the week. Her daughter Shashona would help out when there were two events scheduled on the same day.

Thelma listed the wares she planned to purchase with the $4,400 she would receive. Prominent among them were dollar earrings, toys, Tunisian body oils (on which the markup was more than 300 percent), hair accessories, plastic rings, snappers,* sunglasses, and T-shirts. She also wrote down some of the items in her fall back-to-school line, such as tube socks and sweatshirts. In all, it was an impressive presentation with which nobody argued.

On April 1, Queenesta had opened a store one block away from Victor's on Austin Boulevard. Now she was applying for $5,000. In the last three weeks of March, following the Black Women's Expo, Queenesta had turned her energies away from Victor's store and toward her own place. She bought glass display cases from stores going out of business, hooked up a phone and an alarm system, and decorated. She brought her cassettes and other goods over from Victor's at the end of March, but it was not enough to make her store look full. She asked Duwondes Nixon, her on-again off-again boyfriend who had encouraged her to leave Victor's store, to become her partner. Nixon, a plumber who had some money stashed away, agreed and invested close to $2,000. Queenesta put every last cent of her own into the store, ignoring her bills and living on a bare minimum.

Before the opening, Queenesta was nervous. Victor was planning to sell tapes and CDs himself and she had no idea how much business she might do. She didn't have to wait long to find out. On the first day she did more business than in her best *week* ever at Victor's store. Omiyale and Colete came, and saw for themselves the brisk business Queenesta was doing. During the last week of April she made more than she had during her best *month* at Victor's. When she announced these results at a center meeting on April 18, Queenesta received a rousing ovation. Several borrowers

---

*Tiny, legal explosives that children play with, so many times less powerful than a firecracker that you are able to actually set them off in your hand.

expressed their interest in putting their merchandise in her store, which she had named the Hip Hop Shop and was gearing toward young people aged sixteen to twenty-four.

In May, sales remained strong, often exceeding $200 per day. She also continued to sell at outdoor festivals, and planned to do so more in the summer. And when a man who had agreed to sell beepers out of the store decided not to follow through, Queenesta learned the basics of the beeper business in a week. By mid-June she had twenty-five beeper customers (who brought her $150 in profit per month) and a toehold in a lucrative side business.

At the end of May she hired Nixon's teenage nephew Anton to work at the shop so that she would be free to pick up merchandise and attend events. Anton related well to her customers. On one occasion he filled the store with people to hear a series of rap artists perform. Sales approached $500 that day. For his part, Nixon—whom she described to her circle members as a "silent part-ner"—was doing plumbing work for some people to whom the Hip Hop Shop owed money and, in so doing, was getting the bills reduced. In late April, Queenesta and Shayna left their West Englewood apartment and moved in with Nixon, who lived in Austin, not far from the store.

Yet Queenesta still felt her business was undercapitalized. Upon receiving the $5,000 from the Full Circle Fund, she immediately bought multiple copies of the most popular cassettes and compact discs, and other merchandise as well. She also put deposits down to reserve booths at several summer events.

The loan was deposited in her account in the second week of June. By that time, she had an increasing number of regular customers buying at the store, and the future looked bright for Queenesta Harris and her daughter Shayna.

In June 1994, President Clinton outlined his plan to reform the welfare system. The welfare debate has rumbled on for years, with little effect. Opponents attack the whole idea of welfare, dredge up examples of so-called welfare queens, and contend that there is no incentive for many people to even try to find work. Of course, there is a substantial underclass, most noticeable among minorities in the inner cities, that is dependent upon government assistance. A job is often seen as the answer to their problems. Clinton himself instituted programs in Arkansas to encourage people to get "from welfare to work" and claimed in his '92 campaign that 18,000 people had come off welfare in his state because they had found work. Now he wanted to institute national "workfare" programs to force people off welfare, and to limit benefits to two years for younger recipients in an attempt to make them find a job. But often an individual, especially a single mother, is worse off in a job than on welfare, and this is where organizations like WSEP can come in.

The kind of low-paying jobs that welfare recipients find usually do not provide the health care that they would receive under a government plan like Aid to Families with Dependent Children (AFDC). Out of a check hardly larger than the government's, they would have to find money for child care and transport costs, in addition to being subject to any doctor's or hospital bills. Jason DeParle described the predicament of welfare mothers in *The New York Times*. While many found work, they often had to return to welfare because they couldn't afford to stay off it. Up to 40 percent of all welfare mothers were "cyclers," he wrote, trapped in a series of low-paying jobs punctuated by stints on welfare. While the addition of incentives like subsidized health insurance and child care for those who return to the workforce might improve their situation, there is another avenue that can be explored.

In *The Grameen Reader,* Muhammad Yunus wrote, "[The] removal or reduction of poverty must be a continuous process of creation of assets . . . by the poor person, enabling him to earn more and more. Self-employment, supported by credit, has much more potential for improving the asset base of the poor than wage employment has." Yet the obstacles to self-employment for the poor in the United States are immense. Despite attempts to strengthen the Community Reinvestment Act, a law that encourages banks to lend in deprived neighborhoods where they traditionally accept deposits but do not make loans, it is difficult for even established small businesses to get credit. An article in the

Chicago Sun-Times in July 1993 noted that 41 percent of small-business owners nationwide used personal credit cards to finance investments because they couldn't get bank loans. Welfare recipients are in a worse predicament. Asset limitations discourage them from legally accumulating money to start up a business. If they do manage to get going, any income, whether it is profit or not, will likely disqualify them from receiving benefits. Zoning regulations often make home-based business—one of the most practical options for a poor, single mother—illegal. And many cities—New York, Chicago, and Los Angeles among them—have recently enacted legislation restricting the kind of street vending that is often the first step for a budding self-employed entrepreneur.

Despite the hurdles, a surprising number of the unemployed do try to escape from poverty and welfare by starting a business. One study found that 9 percent of unemployed male workers started up some kind of enterprise in 1980, and were three times as likely as someone with a job to do so. "This research," concluded Steve Balkin, "refutes the conventional wisdom that low-income people are unlikely to become small-business owners because they lack skills," an argument that Muhammad Yunus was making 11,000 miles away. Slowly, a few policy-makers and activists are beginning to recognize the untapped potential of the unemployed as entrepreneurs. Donna Wertenbach, the director of programs for Women Interested in Self-Employment, an organization in Hartford, Connecticut, has said, "Show me a welfare mother alone with two kids who manages a family on $600 a month, and I'll show you a financial wizard. The women who come to us are highly motivated, brilliant scramblers and they all know they have no other place to go."

Self-employment holds a number of advantages over the workplace for many of the unemployed. The hours are flexible—they can adapt a work schedule to fit any family situation. It allows people with street smarts and traditional skills, rather than book smarts and technical skills, to exploit their strengths rather than be held back by their weaknesses. As we have seen, many WSEP members have turned hobbies into jobs. Self-employment also allows individuals who do not work well in a rigid hierarchy of authority figures a chance to run the show.

In some countries, programs have been tried that pay unemployment benefits in a lump sum for those who want to start a business. In the United Kingdom, the Enterprise Allowance Scheme was extended to 88,000 unemployed people in its first three years, and 86 percent of them were still operating their businesses three years later. The cost of each job created was £650, or about $1,000. (By way of comparison, the average cost of creating employment through the Job Corps program in the United States, which focuses on wage employment for unemployed youths, is more than $15,000.) In France in 1984, one-third of all businesses started in the country were the result of a similar initiative.

Whether publicly or privately funded, programs that encourage self-employment offer both a way out of welfare dependency for enterprising individuals and a way to alleviate the poverty that can continue to afflict people in dead-end jobs. WSEP offers a shining example of the profound effect such ventures can have on people's lives. In some cases WSEP enables a welfare mother to take a loan and open a store or start a manufacturing or service enterprise. In others, the impact is more subtle, but no less important. Geri, Omiyale, and Queenesta, for example, joined the Full Circle Fund soon after becoming unemployed. Had they not been able to get loans and moral support to start a business—or in Omiyale's case, to recapitalize an old venture—any or all of them might have fallen into a cycle leading to welfare dependency, social isolation, and depression. Omiyale is in no doubt of that. "Everyone should, at least once in their life, be self-employed," she often says. "It builds character. I have said to my children, you have to try it once. After you have created your own job, you can decide whether you want to work for someone else again."

WSEP demonstrates that access to credit, networking, and appropriate training for self-employment can, and must, play complementary roles to creating incentives for the unemployed and people on public aid to get jobs. Indeed, instead of merely pushing people to "cycle" between welfare and dead-end jobs, an additional set of policies and programs that open doors for self-employment can allow people to cycle in between running a business full-time, operating it part-time and working part-time, operating it part-time and working full-time, and working full-time with their business on hold. It creates more options for low-income people and allows them to explore their potential more fully; the current paradigm, in contrast, narrows options and limits potential.

Low-income African Americans face an additional obstacle to starting a business—racism. One of WSEP's most important accomplishments has been to show that poor black women from distressed neighborhoods can benefit from its approach. One of the reasons it has succeeded where so many initiatives have failed is that black women have, not surprisingly, proven more willing to take a chance and join an organization run by other black women. In addition, several foundations have, to their credit, been eager to fund a black-run organization doing effective work in the inner city. Being trusted by beneficiaries, philanthropic organizations, and some government agencies has created a fertile ground for social change.

Yet, despite its success, WSEP employees, no less than the women they serve, feel the effects of racism all the same. Black professional women who work there often have difficulty hailing cabs in downtown Chicago. Connie Evans, who can remember the Ku Klux Klan marching in Franklin, Tennessee, when she was a child, is occasionally mistaken for a housekeeper by other guests when she stays at expensive hotels. When low-income white women come to WSEP orientations and find out that the organization's senior positions are all filled by blacks, most never attend another meeting. White foundation representatives or journalists who are shown products manufactured by black women who borrow from the Full Circle Fund often express an impolite degree of astonishment at their quality.

A Caucasian WSEP staff member remembers having lunch with a white foundation official some years ago. Both agreed that helping black women pull themselves up by their bootstraps was a noble objective. When the employee mentioned how appropriate it was that such work was being done by an organization headed by a black woman, the foundation official became dismayed. Clearly embarrassed, she explained that it had never occurred to her that Connie Evans was black. Before long she was saying, "Oh, and I had heard such *good* things about WSEP. I had no idea . . ." After the meal was over, the employee burst into Connie's office, told her the story, and began cursing white people in a manner that would have sounded militant coming from a black person.

Despite the reality of racism, there is a largely unknown legacy of black entrepreneurship in the United States—a legacy that WSEP and organizations like it are trying to revive. Even in the days of slavery, some blacks were not only free but prosperous farmers and merchants. Several thousand of them actually owned slaves themselves. As early as 1853, northern blacks began holding conventions on the subject of black economic development. Their objective was to spur entrepreneurship while at the same time persuading black consumers to buy goods produced by black companies and sold by black retail outlets. Leaders such as Booker T. Washington, Marcus Garvey, and Elijah Muhammad urged African Americans to secure their economic base even as more traditional figures were arguing the nascent civil rights agenda. Yet the shadow of slavery loomed large.

"Free blacks in antebellum America," writes one scholar, "exhibited many of the same characteristics as European immigrants: self-selection, an enterprising orientation, small [business] size, self-help institutions, and occupational niches. . . . If slavery had not existed, there would have been no large number of blacks entering the U.S. economy, ignorant and penniless. If that [had been] the case, blacks would have started in America on a firmer economic foundation and . . . there might be no underclass today . . ."

In a poorly conceived attempt to empower former slaves, the federal government created the Freedman's Bureau and the Freedman's Bank during Reconstruction. Neither made much headway, and the latter institution was forced to close in 1874, at which time the federal government refused to reimburse depositors fully. Only after several years did they receive 61 cents on the dollar. This fiasco prompted W.E.B. DuBois to write, "Not even ten additional years of slavery could have done so much to throttle the thrift of the freedmen."

In recent years, however, black establishment figures, including influential political leaders, have begun to place increasing emphasis on entrepreneurship. In many cases, they have adopted the rhetoric of Booker T. Washington, whose focus on vocational education, self-improvement, and accommodation with whites earned him a reputation as an Uncle Tom among many of his contemporaries. Present-day African American leaders are attempting to find a more sensible balance between entitlements and responsibilities, and between economic and political empowerment. And despite its caustic rhetoric, some attention is finally being paid to the constructive efforts of the Nation of Islam to inculcate self-respect, self-reliance, discipline, thrift, and entrepreneurship among its adherents.

Yet, at the close of the twentieth century, the rate of black entrepreneurship remains relatively low. According to the Census Bureau, in 1990 there were only 425,000 black-owned firms in America, an amount that accounts for 2.4 percent of all corporations, partnerships, and sole proprietorships. The bureau also estimates that 3 percent of black men are self-employed while the rate is 7.4 percent for whites, 9 percent for Chinese Americans, and 16.5 percent for Koreans. Perhaps more important, the percentage of the nation's *assets* that African Americans own is minuscule. Sixty percent of all black households have a net worth of less than $10,000, and the median net worth of black households is less than 10 percent of that of white households.* Lack of assets means lack of access to investment capital for potential entrepreneurs, which is compounded by the practice of redlining. Most blacks see their future as employees and consumers, rather than as business owners and investors.

Yet it is precisely the steady progress blacks have made as employees and consumers that holds promise for black entrepreneur-

---

*According to the Census Bureau, the median net worth of black households in 1988 was $4,169, while that of white households was $43,279.

ship, even among the poor. In 1991, African American consumers spent an estimated $216 billion—or close to $600 million every twenty-four hours. In Chicago alone, blacks spend $9.6 billion annually—a figure greater than the gross national product of all but three sub-Saharan African countries. Certain products that blacks spend proportionately more on than whites are dependent on African American patronage for their survival. According to a 1991 article in the *Chicago Tribune,* "African American consumers purchase 18 percent of the [nation's] orange juice, 20 percent of the rice and Scotch whisky,[†] 26 percent of the Cadillacs, 31 percent of the cosmetics, 35 percent of soft drinks, 38 percent of the cigarettes . . . and 40 percent of the records and movie tickets." African American males aged thirteen to twenty-four, who make up 3 percent of the U.S. population, buy one in five Nike athletic shoes and more than half the Starter jackets.

To the extent that black manufacturers and retailers can tap into this market, they will thrive. By one estimate, only 7 percent of black spending ($15 billion) now goes toward black manufacturers and retailers. To raise this percentage, African American business owners will need to continue to educate black consumers about the advantages of "buying black" while at the same time doing their homework and investing wisely. Studies indicate that more than one-quarter of black consumers take into account whether a product is being produced and sold by someone from their ethnic group, and anecdotal evidence suggests that this consciousness is growing. Thelma, Queenesta, Geri, Glenda, and Omiyale are all examples of women who have done their research, invested accordingly, appealed to racial solidarity (to varying degrees), and experienced success. With assistance from programs like the Full Circle Fund—and there are now thirty-eight organizations in the United States that run "peer lending" programs serving primarily low-income, minority entrepreneurs—thousands of African Americans (and other low-income groups) will be able to

---

[†]But, according to the U.S. Department of Labor, blacks spend 20 percent *less* per household on alcohol than whites.

turn their undercapitalized "hustles" and hobbies into legitimate businesses capable of lifting them out of poverty.

Of course, this approach to poverty reduction in the United States has many critics, some with valid points. There have certainly been boondoggles in which taxpayers' money has been wasted in ill-begotten efforts to encourage self-employment. There will surely be more. But Omiyale, Thelma, Geri, Queenesta, and Glenda didn't really care about such matters. For them, the objectives were to borrow, invest, earn, meet family expenses, borrow again, invest again, and earn more. That they often enjoy what they do, or that they have met close friends through the program, or that they are periodically interviewed by journalists curious about their progress, is secondary. The main thing is money—how to invest it and how to make it.

11

Dry Money in a Monsoon

By early July, the 1994 monsoon was in full swing. Meltwater from the Himalayas carried by swollen rivers to the Bay of Bengal was augmented by the torrents of rain. Footpaths became canals, and farmland was transformed into swamps in which traditional strains of rice, jute, water lilies, and fish flourished. Dips in the dirt road leading from Zianpur to Kholshi filled with as much as four feet of water, making it impassable by bicycle or rickshaw. This tripled the length of the time it took for Krishna to travel to the Haldar *para*.

On July 12, Krishna made his way to the Haldar *para* the hard way. Avoiding the waist-deep canals along the main road, he weaved his way through rice fields in which the water came up to his ankles. Still new to the area, he had to stop several times and ask farmers the most direct path to his destination. By the time he arrived at the Kholshi bazaar, he was fifteen minutes late. The only way to the center hut from there was by boat, and he found someone to row over.

As he sat down and began marking up the passbooks, women continued to arrive and fill out the groups. Many of those who were coming from other *paras* were soaked, having swum part of the way. Doing so required dexterity, as borrowers were obliged to present dry bills and passbooks to their group chairmen. Each Tuesday morning, one could sit in Amodini's veranda and watch the women swimming with one hand and holding their installments aloft with the other. Periodically, there was grumbling by Muslims who wanted the center hut moved, but it never amounted to anything. Shandha was extremely well liked and respected, and had lent virtually everyone money for their installments on one occasion or another, so nobody was willing to push the issue.

During the previous month, Amodini had frittered her group fund loan away on traditional healers while her husband's bleeding ulcer continued to deteriorate. She had applied for an 8,000-taka loan, but Shandha and Krishna had agreed only to 5,000. It was on her return from collecting that loan that she found her husband dead. She ran to Shandha's house and cried for hours. Shandha promised to take up a collection after the next meeting to defray the funeral expenses, thereby keeping most of Amodini's loan money intact.

The demise of Amodini's husband was a reminder of the difficulty Grameen has faced in trying to break down rural superstition and reliance on faith healers. This is particularly true in isolated villages like Kholshi. On numerous occasions during the 1994 rainy season, Krishna was confronted with practices that ranged from comic to tragic. At one meeting, he noticed that most of the women had taken off their bracelets. A woman in a village some miles away was said to have dreamt that her son would die if she did not remove her bracelets. And, according to the story, when she woke up and kept them on, her child died. Afterward, Krishna was dismayed by how many unadorned arms he saw. Still, he was pleased that at least one dissenter said, "Allah gave me my son, and Allah will take him when the time is right. I'm not removing anything."

If that had been the end of it, Krishna would not have been concerned. But Amodini's husband's death, and the prolonged illnesses of two women in the center, would likely have been avoided with modern medical attention, he felt. Despite Krishna's warnings, precious taka was spent on traditional healers instead. While a few borrowers did seek out professional medical help, at times he felt dejected about how many continued to rely on quacks. When he heard that Supi, the current center chief, was considering spending several thousand taka on an unreliable doctor to help overcome infertility in order to save her marriage, Krishna was enraged (though he could take solace in the fact that even in the case of divorce she would not be ruined, since she had registered a sizable amount of her family's land in her name since joining the bank). He didn't even get involved in actively trying to discourage the practice of giving dowry, which was widespread in Kholshi and most villages in Bangladesh, Grameen or no Grameen.

Of course, there were reasons for the reliance on healers. Sometimes their treatment appeared to work, particularly when the only thing afflicting a patient was fear. More important, government hospitals were located considerable distances from many villages, were often left unstaffed, and usually offered low-quality care. Though free in theory, treatment by government doctors often came with a hefty price tag. A terrified patient would be wheeled into an operating room only to have the doctor inform him that he had no confidence in the abilities of the nursing staff or the cleanliness of the surgical instruments with which he had been provided. The doctor would propose that the surgery be performed in his private clinic on the other side of town, at a cost that would likely send the patient's family into debt. As if that wasn't enough, poor people, unable to afford hotel fees, often had no place to stay when their loved ones went into the hospital. (A bribe, however, would sometimes get them permission to sleep on the floor, alongside their relative's bed.) With the alternatives so uncertain, it was little wonder that promises from quacks to come to your home and provide a cure for a few hundred taka were often accepted.

Several days after her husband died, Amodini told Shandha about her fear that her brothers would start pressuring her to move to India—which was exactly what occurred. Shandha, already reeling from the loss of four of her five sisters, strongly encouraged her to stay.

Three weeks later Amodini was still in mourning and did not make it to the meeting (though she had given Shandha her installment). Krishna looked up from his paperwork, made sure that all the group chairmen were present, and said, "Listen. You know that it is time to elect a new center chief, don't you?"

"Yes, sir," a few women offered as they passed money back and forth.

"Well, you can begin deciding who you want to support." For the next twenty minutes, while Krishna and Shandha counted and recounted the taka, there was a more animated discussion than usual. A few conversations were clearly confidential, while others were audible from Devi's hut fifteen yards away. Women reached across rows and touched their group chairmen, urging them to declare themselves candidates and pledging their support. Some of the chairmen shook their heads, while others were coy.

Over a four-week period during the early part of the monsoon, more than 50,000 Grameen centers in Bangladesh rotate their leadership. While it is often a smooth process, it can occasionally be wrought with intrigue, deception, and double crosses at crucial moments. And the center chiefs hold the purse strings, having the power to reduce or deny loan proposals. They are the chief liaison between the bank and borrowers.

"Okay," Krishna said as he put a rubber band around the thick wad of bills he had collected. "It's time. Who do you think should be the next center chief?"

"Let it be Supi for another year," one woman in the sixth row shouted out.

"Yes, yes," two more added.

"But you know," Krishna said with a touch of exasperation, "that Supi cannot be center chief, because she is not a group chairman this year. You know the rules, don't you?" Supi had been the fifth group's chairman for the past two years, and Grameen's by-laws had forced her to stand down a few weeks earlier.

"Sir, I don't want to stand for election," Nobirun said from the back row.

"Me neither," Zomella added from the second row, winnowing the list of candidates to five. "I think we should choose Shandha," she added, reaching forward and touching her nominee as she said the words. Before that could get very far, group one's chairman took herself out of contention. Shandha talked about how she was still depressed about her relatives' moving to India, and hinted that her husband was planning an August trip there to see if they might follow. The eligible candidates dropped to four.

Krishna had refereed dozens of elections over the years, and each was different. Some went by consensus, while in others actual votes were taken. Often, the decision had been made before he brought it up, though occasionally the process played out in front of him. "What I think would be a good idea is if the four chairmen who are left speak up for themselves, saying why they would make a good center chief," he advised.

His proposal was greeted with silence. Finally, Zomella said, "Let it be Shandha. She can change her mind." Shandha declined again. As she did so, Krishna noticed that the normally talkative Zorina, the chairman of the third group, had hardly said a word all morning. Failing to take herself out of the running, Krishna thought to himself, was probably Zorina's way of declaring her candidacy.

Perhaps recognizing this herself, Shandha said, "I think Zorina would make a good center chief. Why don't we consider her?" Shandha's nominee smiled broadly, and within five minutes the decision was made. Zorina, after all, was a safe choice. She had been center chief once before, the first Muslim to hold the position. Recently she had purchased a one-quarter share in a shallow tube well, and was receiving more than 2,000 taka in profit each winter from her investment. In short order the chairman of the fourth group was chosen to be deputy center chief.

From the beginning of the Grameen experiment, Yunus had wanted to empower his borrowers politically as well as economically, though his early attempt to federate the centers at the village level had ended in frustration. But that had hardly dampened his determination to make democracy real for his membership. Starting in 1983, when Grameen became an independent bank, borrowers were given the right to elect, from among themselves, a number of members to Grameen's board of directors, reflecting the percentage of the bank's shares that they owned. By 1994, borrowers had bought more than 90 percent of the shares of Grameen, leaving the government's ownership at less than 10 percent and its representation on the board of directors limited. Though some accused Yunus of creating a governing body that would rubber-stamp his decisions, he felt it was an integral part of his democratic ideal. Later he made rotation of center chiefs mandatory, after he had heard that some centers were being run by the same person since their inception and that elections had become a formality or, in some cases, had been discontinued.

But for Yunus, borrowers' taking an active role in the governance of their center and the bank was only the beginning. Recognizing the potential power the vast numbers of landless, poor Bangladeshis could wield if they mobilized themselves, he urged Grameen borrowers to involve themselves in local politics. During the second half of the 1980s, his efforts began to pay off. Borrowers and their husbands began to win election to their union councils. To Yunus, this signaled that financial success was slowly translating into political influence. When Ershad fell from power in 1990 and democratic elections for Parliament were called for February 1991, Yunus thought it was time for Grameen's members to flex their muscles. Centers were encouraged to decide upon one candidate during their meetings, to agree to vote as a bloc, and to parade to the polling stations together, complete with banners identifying themselves as Grameen Bank members. Grameen families responded in thousands of villages across the country, including Kholshi. Above all, borrowers were encouraged to vote, even if it meant "choosing between two devils." Yunus told them that it was their civic responsibility to decide which candidate was the least devilish.

The following year, during local elections, borrowers and their family members were urged to interview candidates in their center huts, to vote as a bloc again, and to run for office themselves. As a result, more than four hundred members of Grameen families won seats on union councils, and two were elected to the powerful post of union council chairman. Many others lost by small margins. Afterward, some politicians who lost their seats visited Yunus in Dhaka and blamed him personally for their defeat. The managing director reminded politicians who made this accusation that the bank had not given instructions to borrowers about *whom* they should support, only that they *participate*. He strongly urged the politicians to spend their time talking to their constituents and not to him.

The auditorium on the third floor of the main building in the Grameen complex was alive with warm greetings among old friends. They were the bank's zonal managers, twelve men under whose control were hundreds of bank workers, tens of thousands of borrowers, and millions of taka in outstanding loans. They had gathered for the 1994 zonal managers' conference, an important forum for debate at Grameen in which participants are encouraged to criticize the head office and each other, in the belief that if peer pressure is good enough for the borrowers, it is good enough for the zonal managers.

After a ceremony identical to those that open every center meeting, Yunus addressed the conference. "Welcome to another family reunion. Together, we can look at where we are and where we are going." He paused and smiled, trying to put everyone at ease. "The most significant thing I can say as we look at the last year is how much more powerful Grameen has become because of our increased self-reliance and economic viability. We have been virtually free of foreign aid funds since the middle of last year. Now, as you know, we are getting our funds from the money market and from Bangladesh Bank. Bangladesh Bank is a very clever bank run by clever people, and they have loaned us one billion taka [$25 million] during the last year—more than they have ever given to a single venture. Other banks are eager to lend to us on even more attractive terms.

"Our borrowers have increased their capability to absorb larger loans, and we have been able to meet their demand and become more financially secure in the process. Through the end of 1992, we had lent a total of $311 million. Through May 1994, our cumulative disbursement has risen to $1 billion." Yunus paused to let the figures sink in, and the zonal managers, noting the gap, looked up from their writing tablets and tried to make eye contact with the managing director.

"Another way to measure our progress is that it took us seventeen years to lend our first billion dollars and yet we are on course to lend $1 billion between January 1994 and December 1995. We can now use half a billion dollars every year. One can also look at branch profitability. In 1993, one-third of all branches were profitable, and even fewer the year before that. In the first two quarters of 1994, half of the branches and half of the zones made a profit. Conservative projections indicate that 65 percent of the branches will make a profit in calendar year 1994. Now, Bangladesh Bank has promised to make a decision within twenty-four hours on any request for funds we submit to them, which befits our being the largest bank in Bangladesh. So please, tell your staff that what we dreamed about three years ago during our darkest hours has come true—even better than we dreamed." Many of the men smiled knowingly, recalling the time when a trade union that was affiliated with the ruling Bangladesh Nationalist Party and run by disgruntled employees had brought banking operations to a virtual standstill for several weeks in 1991.

It had, indeed, been a successful year for the bank. But there were indications that as the scale of lending increased, there had been some drop-off in the quality of staff-borrower relations. Fewer staff members, some said, had time to visit sick children, inspect loan utilization, and stick up for their members in village disputes. While few doubted that many of the borrowers could, after eight or more years of borrowing, handle the large sums they were receiving, there were fears that bank workers, under pressure to increase their loan portfolios, were failing to distinguish between formerly destitute entrepreneurs who could easily invest 60,000 taka ($1,500) and women for whom a loan of 4,000 taka ($100) was plenty. In the head office, there were two schools of thought— one arguing that the increase in lending had been long overdue, the other charging that it was foolhardy. Yunus tended to fall somewhere in between the two extremes.

"There are also things in the last year that have not been positive, some of which we know about, and some of which we may not yet know about. How often, for instance, are borrowers simply taking their seasonal loans and using the money to repay their general loans? A borrower may do this occasionally, but if it is too widespread it signals future repayment problems for us.

"Some people have asked me about expanding the number of branches, the number of borrowers, and the number of zones. What we need to concentrate on right now is taking full responsibility for the two million poor families who have *already* joined Grameen Bank. We need to renew our sacred pledge to work with them to eliminate all signs of poverty from their lives. When the last family of those two million crosses the poverty line, our job will be complete—not before. So, one of the things I would like to do at this conference is inaugurate the concept of the poverty-free center. I am going to ask that you return to your zones and give me proposals for how we are going to measure this and make it an integral part of our planning, monitoring, evaluation, and auditing. I will also want estimates from all of you about where your zone stands now with respect to poverty-free centers and branches." Faces were lighting up around the table, despite a heat and humidity that was already building and would only get worse.

"I will also be interested in tracking how many centers there are where every family has, and is using, a sanitary latrine. In how many centers is every school-age child in school? There are other matters we will take up in these three days—the drought in Dinajpur and Rajshahi districts, proposals to change how the group fund is operated, attacks on us by Islamic fundamentalists, and corruption within Grameen. We will hear about charges that the nonpoor are joining our old centers, and about the fundamentalists in Sylhet and Bogra, but also about the rebirth of Rangpur zone, which we considered closing down three years ago.

"But the main thing we need to consider is whether we are getting away from our main objectives. Are we still showing respect to all of our members, or do we treat them poorly in the rush to get all these loans out? Are we putting too much pressure on them to repay when they are in hardship, thereby creating more hardship? We need to recognize that there will be losses in this business, there will be loans that will have to be written off.

"Some of you have asked about our interest rates. As you

know, the government continues to reduce its rates and forgive loans, even though the beneficiaries of these loans are the wealthy people, the clever people. Yet to keep our institution strong we have not been able to do this. First we should remind ourselves that when we raised our interest rate [on general and seasonal loans] from 16 to 20 percent in 1991, we promised ourselves that it was a temporary measure, not a permanent one.* Now, since we have made solid progress toward financial viability, we should think about reducing it. But the way I'm thinking about it, rather than actually reduce the rate we will keep it the same but divert one-fifth of interest payments to other uses. For instance, we could create a scholarship fund that would ensure that no student in a Grameen family would be prevented from becoming a doctor or an engineer because of financial reasons. Or a health insurance fund for all of our members. The goal of this would be to ensure 100 percent guaranteed health and education for all Grameen families. This is another thing we can talk about.

"You may know about the spread of the Grameen approach internationally. We have had 3,500 visitors from 85 countries visit Grameen in recent years, and now there are Grameen replications in more than 30 countries. And here in Bangladesh, there are 4.5 million people involved in poverty-focused lending programs. That means there are some 20 million poor Bangladeshis benefiting from Grameen or a similar program."†

After Yunus completed his opening address, the twelve zonal managers detailed the state of their zones. A few were frank about their failures and frustrations, while others painted unabashedly rosy pictures of the branches and areas they were supervising. Other officials also spoke. One was running a project to gain a foothold in the national and international textile market for Bang-

---

*The manner in which this was done left the amount borrowers paid at the end of their loan cycle virtually unchanged. Before July 1991, borrowers paid 16 percent simple interest charged on a declining balance (thus amounting to about 8 percent of the principal) *and* a contribution into a life insurance fund that equaled one-quarter of the interest payment. When the interest rate was raised to 20 percent, the contribution into the life insurance fund was reduced to virtually zero, even though the amount paid out to deceased borrowers' families remained unchanged.
†Assuming that the average family size is five.

ladeshi weavers, including some 50,000 Grameen borrowers who had taken loans for spinning and weaving. He said that in October 1993, the cumulative production by weavers who were cooperating with Grameen (many of whom were not Grameen borrowers) was 250,000 yards. By August 1994, that was their *monthly production,* and it was hardly keeping up with the demand. Others described experimental projects to develop fisheries, agriculture, health care, and natural gas. One of the two women in the room talked about her UNICEF-funded program of training Grameen borrowers to be village midwives, and how it had cut maternal death rates in half.

The conference continued for nearly seventy-two hours. At times it was deadly boring, while at others it alternated among invigorating, tense, and comic. Yunus was present virtually the entire time, and approved nearly every zonal manager's request to innovate and experiment. He appeared engaged but permissive. When one zonal manager gave a speech about the need to combat the fundamentalist threat by "going to the mosque more often to prove that we are good Muslims," Yunus nodded without noticeable emotion. On a few matters, though, he put his foot down. An aide suggested expanding the number of job classifications for which shoes were provided, and Yunus immediately dismissed the proposal.

With the conference nearing its end on the third day, Yunus made his closing address. He tried to capture all the elements of the conference, and the state of Grameen, through use of the English phrase "critical mass." He proposed to his colleagues that over the past twelve months, the bank had made a quantum leap in its capacity to cause socioeconomic change and respond to institutional challenges. "We have met the fundamentalists, who have raised protests, burned our documents, incited people, and so forth, by organizing at the local level. Rather than overreact, we told the borrowers to stick up for what was theirs, and in the process many people who had never supported us before have come to our side. This is not a threat anymore, but an annoyance. Certain zones have invented new slogans in which borrowers chant how they will support people who support them and organize against people who organize against them. We will copy and distribute these slogans, and the lessons learned from local organizing. I would almost say that the disturbances of the last year have been a blessing for us, not a curse. This is critical mass.

"Furthermore, we have unprecedented political strength. If we can ensure 100 percent voting among the 2 million Grameen families in the next elections by ensuring 100 percent registration now, the impact will be enormous. This is critical mass. We have $50 million in group fund savings, and millions more in other savings accounts. There is not a single company in Bangladesh that we could not buy with our borrowers' collective savings. That is critical mass. We are now the biggest bank in the country, and we loan more money in rural Bangladesh than all the other banks combined. That is also critical mass. Our borrowers have achieved this, and we have simply played the role of facilitator. Things that used to take us years, like the time it takes for a branch to be profitable, are being cut in half. Now we must take advantage of this critical mass and accelerate the process of eliminating poverty from the lives of each and every member of Grameen Bank."

The courtyard was alive with activity. On a veranda, Nonibala Ghosh was cutting a tin pan full of *sandesh* (white sweets that look like small Christmas cookies) into bite-size pieces to be sold at a village festival later that afternoon. Inside the hut in which Nonibala and her husband slept, her twelve-year-old son cranked the handle of a rusty machine that skimmed the cream off the milk he poured into it. The cream would be used to make ghee. Another son stoked the flames underneath an industrial-size tin in which the milk would be cooked until it was ready to be transformed into cottage cheese.

Flies hovered over the tins of milk outside the hut that had yet to go through the creamer. A few feet from the oven, four cows were tied up, their heads buried in bowls of feed. Later, they would receive the special treatment that comes as a result of being owned by a Ghosh household—they would be fed whey, a by-product of cottage cheese production. People in the village said that that was what kept Noni's cows healthier than anyone else's.

Nonibala's eldest son walked his bike into the compound, having traversed a two-foot-deep canal that divided the household from Kholshi's main road during the rainy season. Strapped on the bicycle were two plastic containers that each contained about ten gallons of milk he had procured from Bagutia. Earlier, Noni's youngest son had brought ten gallons from the Zianpur bazaar, and Gopal, her husband, thirty from the Kholshi market.

"How much?" Noni called out to her son.

"Twelve, got it for twelve today." Buying milk for 12 taka per kilogram* meant big profits for the household. The day before, Noni's eldest son had traveled to Dhaka to deliver a large order of cottage cheese, and he'd be making another delivery today. The family had a contract with a confectionery shop in the Kalabagan neighborhood to deliver whatever quantity of *chhana* (cottage cheese) it requested within twenty-four hours. That meant that each day, two of the men in the family packed up the *chhana*, laid it across the bicycles' crossbars, and began a twelve-mile trip to Aricha, where one of the two would board a bus going to Dhaka to make the delivery and take the following day's order. When there were transport strikes, the men would bicycle the sixty miles from Aricha to Dhaka and return the next morning.

Because of the low price of milk that day, Noni's family would likely see a profit of 400 taka ($10) from the cottage cheese and be able to make another 300 taka worth of ghee. But when the price of milk exceeds 15 taka per kilogram, as it does several times each year for a total of six to ten weeks, they are forced to absorb short-term losses to fulfill their contract.

For Gopal and Nonibala Ghosh and their five sons and three daughters, such risk-taking and profits are fairly recent phenomena. In 1987, the family was landless and owned very few assets. They earned money making ghee and *doi* (yogurt), but didn't have enough working capital to buy even one *maund* (ten gallons) of milk and had no cows of their own, so all their dairy products had to be bought in the market. They often had to take loans from

---

*In Bangladesh, milk and other liquids are measured by weight, not volume. One kilogram is roughly equal to one quart or one liter. Thus, the price of milk in the example above is 48 taka ($1.20) per gallon.

village moneylenders at 10 percent interest per month, and when they did, at least half of their profits went to the loan sharks. There was never enough food to go around, especially when the price of milk was high.

Nonibala was born in 1950 in the village of Munshikandi, in a Ghosh *para* a short distance from where the paralyzed Lutfa lived. Despite the size of her family, she doesn't remember living in poverty—at least not the kind she came to know after her marriage. Her parents made ghee, *doi, chhana,* and sweets and sold them locally and in Dhaka. The family was not free from tragedy, however; her youngest brother died in childhood from typhoid fever, and her youngest sister succumbed to diarrhea as an infant.

Nonibala, who never attended a day of school, remembered spending her childhood bringing food to her male siblings and relatives when they worked in the fields. She recalls that it was when she was about thirteen that the marriage proposals began coming in. The first four were turned down when someone in Noni's extended family found something objectionable in the boy or his family. The fifth came from a well-known Ghosh family in Kholshi, and a union was arranged. A traditional Hindu wedding was held, but Noni thought it strange that the role usually played by her mother-in-law was taken by her husband's aunt instead.

After moving in with Gopal Ghosh's family, she learned that her mother-in-law was actually her stepmother-in-law. She learned that Gopal's mother had died soon after giving birth to her only son, and that Noni's husband stood to gain as many as ten acres in inheritance from his deceased mother. Arguments over who had the right to farm the land broke out soon after the wedding, and Gopal promptly filed a lawsuit against his father. Over the years, legal bills accumulated, and both father and son were forced to sell off land in order to pay them off. The two rarely talked to each other, though to save money they often traveled together by rickshaw to the Manikganj courthouse. By the time Noni's father came to Kholshi and resolved the dispute by calling a *salish* (village court), the family had been ruined.

When Noni heard about Grameen Bank in 1987, she attended a meeting at which Mannan Talukdar spoke. What he said interested her enough to cause her to go to the Kholshi bazaar for a meeting that was attended by six thousand people. Then she let it be known that she was eager to join the very first group. In a short time two groups were set—Shandha would chair one, Noni the other. It took them more than a month to undergo group training, during which several women learned to sign their names. After recognition and the submission of loan proposals, the ten women went to the Zianpur bazaar to get their first loans. Though Noni was eager to receive her 2,500 taka and expand her business, she respected the Grameen practice of giving the first two loans to the neediest women in the group. In her case they were Aduree and Zomella. In due course she received hers.

Suddenly, the family went from being unable to afford one *maund* of milk to being able to purchase six. For the first time in years, there was no need to rely on the village moneylender. Production, and profits, soared. After joining the bank she sent her son to work in another Ghosh household to learn how to make cottage cheese, as she had a dream of resurrecting her father's business. Her son spent eighteen months there and learned the trade. But on one of his last trips to deliver *chhana* to Dhaka, he was involved in a bus accident. The medical treatment cost Noni 16,000 taka, throwing their business for a temporary loss. The 1988 flood hurt, too. But they were always able to make their weekly installment, and each new loan meant a replenishment of (if not an increase in) their working capital.

By early 1993, with Noni in possession of four cows of her own, the family, through her son, was ready to try to get a *chhana* contract in Dhaka. When the family her son had worked for learned of his plans to secure a contract, they threatened to kill him. Ultimately, an agreement was reached with one store owner, but to avoid suspicion Noni's husband signed it on behalf of the family instead of her son. They told the store owner they were from another district, which helped ensure that no one would discover that Nonibala's son was involved.

Chhana production was profitable for nine or ten months of the year, and with a line of credit from Grameen Bank the family could bear the losses when the price of milk went up. If the need arose, Noni could take a loan from her group fund. By mid-1993 the family had four cows and the contract. They were able to eat better than ever, buy new clothes for everyone, and marry off the eldest daughter—no small feat, considering that wedding expenses and dowry totaled 45,000 taka ($1,125).

Noni has been the center chief once, though if the women had their way she would have been elected two or three times. She enjoyed the authority that came with the position, but it took up too much of her time. After she began *chhana* production in 1993, she had hardly an hour of spare time between dawn and 10 P.M. In any case, she often thought, people came to her anyway for advice, whether she was center chief or not. Her center was unique in that its two most powerful women—Noni and Shandha—were rather shy and unassuming, rarely speaking up during meetings unless the situation called for it. Supi, the most influential Muslim, was also rather reserved. Other women were full of bluster but never earned the respect of their peers.

"Cutting" *chhana* was no simple task. After heating the milk slowly toward the boiling point, all the while stirring it to prevent it from turning, Noni would have her sons quickly transfer the hot milk into a metal canister. After letting it cool a few degrees they'd measure out the whey, mix it in, and then carry the canister to a small pond, where it would cool and yield a mix of cottage cheese and whey that they later separated using thin towels that served as sieves. It was a process that looked easy enough, but errors of only a few degrees or seconds could ruin a batch. This day, with an order of fifty kilograms of cottage cheese, required four separate batches.

A short time later, the *chhana* was loaded onto the two bicycles and the boys cycled off with their loads. It was four o'clock in the afternoon, and with luck they would arrive at the shop in Dhaka by seven-thirty. They would collect 3,500 taka and head to Aricha, where they would stay overnight with relatives. While they all slept, the *chhana* was turned into a dozen or more varieties of sweets.

Wiping her forehead with her sari, Nonibala further smudged the dot of vermilion on her forehead. She lifted up the first canister of whey and carried it over to the trough where the cows were feeding. As she poured it in, one of the cows let out a loud belch while the other dug in. When she was done, there was cow dung to be packed into fuel cakes, though she was likely to give that task to her eldest son's wife. Then came bathing, cooking the evening meal, and preparing the ghee.

On a brief break from work, Nonibala reflected on the difference in life since she'd joined Grameen. "We have made ourselves a proud Ghosh family again. Just like people used to come to my father's place to congregate, gossip, and buy ghee, *doi,* and sweets, they are coming to our house now. I can help out my neighbors when they fall into difficulty, like my father did when he was alive. We may have more flies than most households, but I'm not sure you could find one that is more hardworking or more happy." That was as close as Nonibala Ghosh was ever likely to get to bragging.

12

▲

The Black on Black
Love Festival

Two young black men in their early twenties entered the store.
"Hey, Queen," one said as he approached the counter.

"Hey, how you doing?" Queenesta replied, talking loudly over
"Level of a Gangster," a song by the rap group Top Authority
being pumped out of a pair of speakers on opposite ends of the
Hip Hop Shop.

"Oh, all right. Listen, you got that MC Eiht cassette in yet?"

"Naw, that's not gonna be released until the first week in July.
I'll have it here the day it's released." MC Eiht was the hottest new
rap artist, and Queenesta had been getting requests for his new
release for at least a week. Among the songs the tape would contain
were "Niggaz That Kill," "Compton Cyco," and "Nuthin but the
Gangsta." That's how they do it, she often thought; they begin
building up demand for a product and then delay putting it on the
market until people can't bear waiting any longer. Young people,
she and recording company executives knew, love to have what
they can't get.

The second young man stood silently alongside his friend. His
eyes wandered around the Hip Hop Shop, from an eclectic collection of posters hanging behind the main counter to a second,

smaller case holding compact discs, sunglasses, and a few pieces of hematite jewelry imported from Nigeria. He turned around and looked at a mural painted on the middle of the wall, depicting black men and women dancing. The figures were somewhere between realistic and caricature; their positions and state of dress were risqué, even lewd, but not obscene. One of the characters wore a T-shirt with the words "Hip Hop Shop" written on it.

On either side of the mural were racks of T-shirts and baseball caps. The shirts were printed with black-pride messages, abstract art, and pictures of rap artists. Most of the baseball caps were blank with adjustable leather straps in the back; that, as Queenesta was discovering, was the style that summer. In the back of the store was a black wooden cabinet filled with jars of penny candy, incense, and Snickers bars that went for 50 cents. Next to that was a metal rack filled with potato chips made by a black-owned company that put Afrocentric antiviolence messages on the backs of the bags.

"You sell beepers?" the second customer asked Queenesta as his friend squatted down and looked through the cassettes at the bottom of the case. (The rap tapes were displayed there, while the "dusties" and gospel titles were kept on top to attract the older crowd. Her more mature customers might get offended when they saw the rap titles and leave the store in a huff. Queenesta knew that the teenagers, on the other hand, would look until they found what they wanted.)

"Yeah, a Bravo Plus will run you eighty bucks. If you have a beeper, I can turn it on for twenty-five."

"What's the monthly charge?"

"Ten bucks, and another five if you want voice mail. Here, let me show you a Bravo Plus. And we sell cases, too." Initially, Queenesta's agreement with the beeper wholesaler Chicago Pagers earned her $5 in commission for each $10 she brought in. Later, she successfully negotiated a 20 percent increase in her commission.

The first man stood up. "Let me see that one," he said, pointing to a cassette titled "Straight Up Gangsta Shit: Volume 2." The case had an illustration of three menacing-looking black men holding smoking handguns. It was one of several "mixed" tapes Queenesta carried that contained copies of popular rap and hip-hop tunes, and was one of her most consistent sellers. In the beginning, she bought the so-called hot mixes from the wholesaler, but over time she began meeting the mixers and buying direct from them. By June she had met DJ D-Man, a black teenager who had produced a series of bootleg hot mixes, and in July the creator of "Gangsta Shit," a man in his twenties of black and Latino ancestry, walked into the store to do business.

Queenesta opened the case from the back and plucked out a copy of the cassette. Under it were two more. "Here," she said as she handed it to him, "do you want to see a playlist?"

"Yeah," he replied as he studied the cassette's cover. It glorified defiant black men who made fortunes through illegal and violent means. Images like that were stirring up controversy around the country—in op-ed columns, town hall meetings, and living rooms of the poor and the wealthy; among black, brown, and white. They made Queenesta uncomfortable, but they sold. So they stayed, at least for now. The best she tried to do was to push positive, non-violent rap artists like Arrested Development to customers she thought would be open to it.

Queenesta grabbed a black, three-ring notebook from behind the counter, opened it, and fingered through various mimeographed papers held in plastic covers. When she found the list of songs on "Gangsta Shit," she handed it to her customer. He read it over, his feet tapping to the beat of a new song that was playing.

"How much is this?" he asked, showing Queenesta the cover of the tape.

"Nine forty-nine, plus tax."

He reached into the pocket of his baggy shorts, pulled out a $20 bill, and handed it to Queenesta. "Here."

She clutched it, and as she headed to the back where she kept her cash register, she said, "That's ten twenty-two. Do you want a bag?"

"Naw."

The other young man was looking at the beepers through the store's third glass display case. There was a look of wonder on his face. As Queenesta gave his friend change, he said, "I'm gonna come back next week and pick up one of those. How many months do I need to pay in advance?"

"Just one."

"Thanks," he said as the two began moving to the door. "I'll see you next week." Queenesta did her best business right after payday.

As the two walked out the door, a person inside the store could hear the new customer saying, "That's cool."

Queenesta looked at her watch. It was almost time to pick up Shayna from day camp. This meant closing the store for a few minutes at just the time business usually picked up, but such were the realities of being an entrepreneur and single mother. As she locked the door and pulled the gate shut, she taped a handwritten note on the glass door. It read, "Be back in five minutes."

After they returned, Queenesta talked to Shayna about her day in between helping customers. She was training her daughter to sell the candy, as she had visions of Shayna going into business for herself one day, perhaps running a Hip Hop Shop after it became a franchise. It kept her occupied and purposeful, and out of trouble.

Queenesta always worried when Shayna played out on the street with the kids who lived in the apartment above the Hip Hop Shop. Those children spent most of their time unsupervised and had already lost one of their siblings to social workers from the Department of Child and Family Services. She was afraid that Shayna would develop a hard, street-smart edge. When Queenesta saw her daughter carrying the youngest child on her hip one day, she rebuked her. Babies, she told Shayna later, do not take care of babies.

Some of the teenagers who visited the Hip Hop Shop on that sweltering afternoon in late June seemed to know Queenesta; they tended to linger for a while after they had made their purchases. A few were allowed to come back behind the counter and switch the tape that was playing on the stereo, while others who were less bold just asked Queenesta to change the cassette or radio station. The ones who didn't know her tended to come and go quicker, though they sometimes fell into conversation with her or other customers. Queenesta was eager to get to know the young people who came in her store.

Some of the people who came in that night bought cassettes and candy, while two purchased baseball caps and another gave her a beeper to turn on. The store was loud, lively, and frequented almost exclusively by blacks, most of them young, many arriving in groups of two or more. The phone rang frequently, though sometimes Queenesta let it go through to her answering machine. On one occasion, a call came for a young man looking through the cassette case. It was sticky and hot, the humidity relieved only by two fans that pointed toward the area where customers stood.

At eight-thirty, Duwondes Nixon arrived. Shayna gave him a big hug when he walked through the door, and he was soon bantering with customers and telling Queenesta about his day. Whenever someone left the store, he invariably yelled, "I'll holler at you later, guy."

Though the hours written on the front door indicated that the Hip Hop Shop closed at eight, Queenesta kept it open until five past nine. When the three of them locked it up, pulling iron gates behind the glass windows and the door, chaining them to cement pillars, and activating the alarm system, Queenesta and Shayna got in her Honda while Nixon headed to his beat-up van and drove to his apartment. Shayna would be in bed by ten.

As Queenesta was pulling out of her parking space, she looked at a storefront around the corner. Painted on its blue awning were the words "Moonlight Records—Tapes and CDs." Work was going on inside; preparations, she imagined, for a July 1 opening. She frowned as she stared, but tried to put what she saw out of her mind for the moment. She thought she knew why this store had come to her block, but instead of simply ruing her bad luck she was devising a plan to confront her new competition. It was a good plan; but was it good enough?

Thelma arrived first. Then Leverta Pack knocked on the front door of Geri's house on West Fifty-ninth Street, in the heart of Englewood. A few minutes later, Queenesta's car drove up. As they waited for Omiyale, the four women exchanged small talk and tried to entertain Shayna.

"How much you do today, Queenesta?" Thelma asked.

"Uh, about two-fifty. And I got three new beeper customers. I think in a few months I'll be able to pay my rent through the income from beepers."

"That's good."

Queenesta was dressed in a plain white shirt with three-quarter sleeves, shorts, and sandals. Her hair was still closely shorn from when she had it cut at the end of the Black Expo at McCormick Place, in a booth a few stalls down from her own. She and Duwondes had grossed nearly $1,000 at the event, in addition to $200 they made at the store on Saturday. They sold sunglasses, T-shirts they had printed from drawings made by local artists, and African artifacts they were selling for a former tenant of Victor's (on which Queenesta's commission was 30 percent of the retail price). Thelma, vending from a stall in the next room, made $1,100 on dollar earrings, rings ranging from 25 cents to a buck apiece, necklaces that ran as much as $3, toys, snappers, whoopee cushions, and oils. Her best customers were children and teens. Parents seemed happy to bring their youngsters to her table—they could get something for each of their kids and still spend less than $10. Her daughter Shashona helped out on Friday and ran her table at Maxwell Street on Sunday. When she made good money, as she did that weekend, Thelma paid her daughter $20 or $30.

As the women waited for Omiyale, Leverta Pack asked Geri about the gift baskets she had sold for Mother's Day. Thelma let Geri know that she had found a new wholesaler for fabric and proposed that they make a bulk purchase together. A knock on the door interrupted the discussion. It was Omiyale. She walked in, greeted everyone, and settled into an empty chair.

It was July 12, time for the Lindblom center's loan committee and Les Papillons to hold a joint meeting to discuss Omiyale's loan proposal. If they approved, the women would sign off on it that night and Omiyale could submit it to Colete for final approval. At the center meeting the night before, Thelma and Geri had studied the paperwork, but time had run out. They had scheduled this meeting to go over the proposal in depth.

"Well, here it is," Omiyale began. "How do you want to go over this?" She held up a document consisting of about fifteen pages—a filled-in Full Circle Fund loan application.

"Omiyatta, I didn't see your cash flow for 1993 when I looked over your loan packet last night," Thelma said. Her voice, with its subtle edge so early in the evening, suggested rough waters ahead.

"I have, you know, cash flow for the last twelve months and the next twelve months, projections." Thelma thought Omiyale should have information from January 1993 onward. After some back-and-forth, the two agreed, with the concurrence of Leverta Pack, that what she had was sufficient. Then they turned to other issues.

"What parts should I go over?" Omiyale asked.

"Omiyatta, you need to go over *all* of it," Thelma said, drawing out the word "all" for effect. After the trouble the group had gone through during the last year, Thelma wasn't going to leave any stones unturned as they scrutinized Omiyale's current proposal.

"Okay. Name, Veronica DuPart." She read her address, phone number, and Social Security number. "Gross income from business in June, $1,257. Other members of the household earning money in June: Jahlillah, $300; Paul DuPart, $2,100; Oloo, $200. My products: African imports and general merchandise. How long have you been operating your business? Since 1991." As Omiyale read off sections detailing other aspects of her business, Thelma wrote furiously on a piece of paper.

"Current savings, $160. Inventory from warehouse, $400. Amount of loan requested, $5,375. Term, eighteen months. Payment, $144 . . . Now here's the section where I break down what I'm going to spend it on. A used commercial oven, $1,250. Ladies' dresses, fifty pieces at $25 each. Novelty toys, 842 pieces at 50 cents each. Hats, 117 at $5 each. Glow lights, twelve tubes at $39 each. Twelve dozen bangles, and they cost $1 each. Do you want to hear all of these?"

"Yes," Thelma and Queenesta said in unison. Leverta nodded, while Geri sat still, expressionless.

"Two hundred eighty-eight pieces of earrings, which will cost me $288. Twelve dozen anklets at $1.50 each and twelve dozen necklaces at $2 each. And then $250 goes in the emergency loan fund."

"Are you going to use the oven in your home?" Thelma asked.

"Yes."

"Why aren't you including the flour and butter and sugar you need for your cookies in your proposal?"

"No, I already . . . I have them already, and I will finance any more I need out of my profit."

There was a brief silence in the room. Thelma was weighing whether to pry further. She suspected that some of the loan money would be diverted to buy the raw materials Omiyale needed to make the cookies, and thought the proposal should reflect that. Was her friend overextending herself? Was she planning on using the money to buy a plane ticket for her planned trip to Africa? Upon reflection, Thelma decided to let it go, for the moment.

"And here are the places where I will be selling," Omiyale began, breaking the silence. "Out of my home, at the Georgia Fest, the Cocofest, the Ghana Fest . . ."

"Do you have deposits put down on these events, or are these just projections? I want to know if you're locked in or just thinking about it, Omiyatta."

"I don't have deposits on all of them. Just some of them." Thelma scrunched up her face; she clearly did not approve. "But *you* weren't locked into the festivals you were doing when you did your loan pa—"

"When I put together my loan packet," Thelma shot back, "I was locked into *every* festival except Windows to Africa in September. I had put deposits down on all of them."

The meeting was tense, but Omiyale had expected as much. The preceding months had reduced her from founder and leader of the Lindblom center to a borrower whose judgment was open to question. After all the strokes she had received from people associated with WSEP, her fall from grace had left her bitter.

The previous Saturday, Omiyale had confronted her pain in an unlikely place. She had been invited to make a presentation about WSEP at a conference held in Washington, D.C., by a grassroots, nonprofit hunger advocacy group called RESULTS. Connie had been asked to recommend one of her borrowers to go and speak, and she'd suggested Omiyale. The conference organizers had agreed that she would be able to sell handmade jewelry to the three hundred conference-goers from a table in the back of the room after she gave her speech.

RESULTS (which I served for three years as legislative director) is a unique organization in modern American politics. Founded in 1980 by Sam Harris, a high school music teacher, it combines new-age philosophy and sixties idealism with a rare willingness and capacity to play political hardball. Overwhelmingly white and middle-class, it has made significant contributions to the fight against world hunger by arm-twisting legislators into rerouting foreign aid funds toward new, innovative antipoverty initiatives and refocusing existing programs for the poor. Muhammad Yunus is a board member and a fan. In fact, it was partly at his urging that the organization had begun focusing more on domestic poverty in the late 1980s. The invitation to Omiyale was a step in that direction.

Early in the conference, RESULTS staff reviewed the year's accomplishments. Among those mentioned were millions of dollars in foreign assistance funds being shifted to health and education projects and a successful campaign to have the U.S. government make a $2 million grant to Grameen. Omiyale was impressed. Here were people coming from all over the world, at their own expense, who had developed close relationships with their legislators and who were using those contacts to improve the plight of poor people. That such things went on had never occurred to her. Years had passed since she had participated in marches with Paul, and she felt politically impotent. Only once had she called her congressman, when Hkeem was having some difficulty in the marines. She never heard back. Yet these middle-class white folks were volunteering hundreds of hours a year to ensure that legislation be passed to enable poor people in the Third World, and the United States, to borrow money as she was doing from WSEP.

When Omiyale appeared before the group at six o'clock that evening, she haltingly told the story of how she had been laid off, found out about the Full Circle Fund, joined, and began borrowing, investing, and earning. She talked about other circle members, how they hustled and peddled and earned enough to stay afloat. The audience was spellbound, and after a short time many eyes in the crowd were moist. Though they had been provided reading material on efforts to replicate the Grameen Bank in the United States, most of them had never been able to visualize it working. Yet in a presentation that lasted no more than twenty minutes, Omiyale DuPart broke down the unspoken fear that the inner city was too far gone for Grameen-style projects to help. When she finished, Les Papillons' chairlady was given a rousing ovation. Later that evening and the following day, she sold nearly $500 worth of her jewelry and engaged in scores of animated conversations. Never had Omiyale been around so many white people and felt so comfortable with them. To them, she was not just a vendor but an inspiration and a source of hope. After so many months of struggle, it was an energizing experience.

Back in Geri's house, Omiyale ran off a list of events at which she planned to vend from July through January, carefully noting which she had put deposits on and which she had not. She went on to describe the profit margin on all of her goods. She planned to sell the imports she brought back from Africa for quadruple what she'd paid for them, whereas for merchandise bought in the States the markup might be half that. If she could pick up goods at a going-out-of-business sale or auction, her margin would be higher.

She told the group of her plan to build up her production capacity to 2,000 packages of cookies per month, on which, if she sold them all, her profit would be more than $1,300. With the new oven, she reported, she could make a hundred packages in three hours, rather than the eight or nine it had taken her in the spring.

Thelma pressed Omiyale on her plans to market the cookies until she was satisfied, while Queenesta questioned her projections for selling merchandise at fall and winter events, when business is usually slower. After more than two hours, the four women agreed to sign off on the proposal. Relieved, Omiyale passed around a form on which all the women present put their signature.

Over the next two weeks, Omiyale prepared for her trip to Africa to buy merchandise. On July 27, she departed Chicago en route to Senegal and Gambia, money in hand and hopes high. The worst was over for Omiyale DuPart; it was time to get her business back on track.

In July, Queenesta's store began its fourth month of operation. A few days before Moonlight Records opened, she dropped her cassette prices and commissioned a struggling black artist to make up a sign that read "Sale—All Cassettes $8.99." She paid him $20 for his efforts. Sales increased, but her profit margin, already razor-thin, grew even smaller.* By then, Queenesta had confirmed her theory about why Moonlight had chosen a location so close to hers. It was being run by the brother of the man who ran the distributorship from which she bought most of her compact discs and cassettes wholesale. When they had seen Queenesta's sales increase substantially during the spring, they realized that she had a good location—one that they now planned to run her out of. Belatedly, Queenesta started buying from another wholesaler as well so that neither of them could get a clear picture of how sales were going. But by then, the wholesaler's brother had committed himself to the location on North Avenue.

The impact of her competition, however, was not as severe as she'd feared. When her copies of MC Eiht arrived, she sold out. A few customers told her they had put off buying it until she got it in. Another popular title, Big Mike's "Something Serious," was also going fast. By the middle of July, she was holding her own

---

*Queenesta would get current cassettes for roughly $6.50. The wholesaler or distributor is able to buy them in bulk from the record companies for about $1 less than that.

against Moonlight. Many Hip Hop Shop customers stayed loyal, and the beeper business continued to grow. Baseball caps, T-shirts, sunglasses, and candy were a steady source of profits.

One day, a black teenager came into the Hip Hop Shop and told Queenesta that he didn't feel comfortable in Moonlight. It was a revealing comment. Perhaps without her full understanding, she had created one of the few places in the neighborhood where black teenage boys could come in and not evoke fear and suspicion. Korean and white store owners were considered the worst, glaring at black teens through bulletproof glass and often asking them to make a purchase or move on. Even stores owned by black adults, such as Moonlight, did little to make teenagers of their own race feel welcome. It was as if every seventeen-year-old kid was a gang member who was scheming to rip them off, and it made the young men feel angry.

Queenesta tried to create a different environment. No bulletproof windows, no partitions, no glaring. She said hello to all her customers, even the few she had heard were involved with the two local gangs, the Four Corner Hustlers and the Gangster Insanes. If someone wanted to hear a tape, she played it. If the kids wanted to stick around for a while and talk with their friends, she let them. The teenagers, in turn, realized when they were getting in the way of other customers, and moved to the sidewalk when it got crowded. They brought their friends to her store, and never went to Moonlight. They felt comfortable enough to approach her on the street and ask her when she was getting a particular tape in. It was not that she was oblivious to what was going on; on two occasions, she caught kids trying to steal CDs from her case. But she was unwilling to run another place that indiscriminately treated black young men in an inhuman way. Her attitude was generous, but more important, it was good business.

Her approach was paying off handsomely. Sales often totaled more than $200 per day, and were growing. Queenesta talked hopefully about opening another store in late August that would concentrate on beepers. A black Muslim friend who worked for Motorola had promised to help her set up a state-of-the-art system so that she could turn beepers on herself.

For reasons that escaped many people at the time, Thelma Ali had nagging doubts about what Queenesta was doing. To her, it all seemed too much, too soon. She didn't care for Nixon, and had reservations about mixing romance and business. The idea of opening up a second store so soon was too much for her rather conservative tastes. Thelma wanted to talk to Queenesta about her business at center meetings, possibly to allay some of her fears, but Queenesta often arrived late. She explained that she hadn't been able to close her store early because Nixon was working a plumbing job. The other women accepted her excuses, but Thelma's misgivings persisted.

Thelma got there at 9:45, fifteen minutes before the event was supposed to start. Shashona and her friend Luanda were with her to help out, and it appeared that they were the first to arrive. Confused, they spent their first few minutes wandering around the grounds of 4300 South Federal Street, one of the high-rises of the Robert Taylor Homes. Thelma was looking for the organizer of the Black on Black Love Festival, but she was nowhere to be found.

As Thelma glanced around, she grimaced. The concrete and dirt was covered with broken glass, and everything was rusted and covered with grass and shrubs. The buildings looked innocent enough at ten in the morning, but she knew better. Many of the women living here were drug users. Kids had little or no adult supervision, and gangs ran the entire operation. As she watched a few young men walk lazily from one building to another, Thelma said, to no one in particular, "Role models need to be people, not just things you read about in books."

Around her were black garbage bags full of merchandise she planned to sell. On this day, her inventory was limited to goods that retailed for $1 or less. She had sold at housing projects before, and knew that the people who lived there didn't have much money. The event probably wouldn't bring her more than $60 or $70, but she felt a responsibility to go. Most vendors were too scared to go to festivals held at the projects. Another woman in the Lindblom center had canceled at the last minute, forcing Thelma to go it alone.

Just then, a car pulled up along South Federal, and a teenager and a dark-skinned woman in a clown outfit got out. Thelma recognized Carol Simms—known to everyone by her nickname "Impy"—and her son Ian, and went over to help them unload. She had heard that Impy was going to perform at the festival, but figured that she would be a no-show.

Impy was a survivor. She was one of the cleverest entrepreneurs in the Full Circle Fund, but a string of family crises had prevented her from making much progress since she'd joined the program. Because one of her circle members had fallen into default in 1993, she could not take any additional loans from the Fund until her center raised the money to retire the debt. Impy, who had paid off two loans without missing an installment, was leading the effort to clear the arrears.

"Hey, Impy, when did they tell you they's gonna start this thing?" Thelma asked.

"Oh, they told me eleven."

"Eleven? They told me ten. Let's go inside and see what's going on."

The two women walked to the front of one of the buildings, leaving their children to stand guard over the merchandise. They saw benches filled with people, mostly men in their twenties and thirties. Others stood in small groups, and nearly everyone looked disheveled. Many were smoking cigarettes. A few younger people cracked up when they saw Impy's clown suit, but most didn't seem to notice.

Thelma and Impy walked through a doorway and into a hallway that was being mopped. Everything had a hard edge to it—the steel grates over the windows, the cinder blocks that had become dislodged from the walls, the expressions on people's faces. "Hey, we're looking for Ms. Issachar," Impy said as she peeked in an open door.

"She's right in here," a teenager replied.

Thelma and Impy met Esther Issachar, and soon learned of the disorganized state the event was in. The festival was to start at eleven, they were told, but it was clear that an eleven-thirty launch was more likely. Though the two women had been promised tables when they had signed up to do the event—Thelma had paid $20 to vend, whereas Impy was to receive $60, plus her table, for doing her clown routine—there was only one table, and that was reserved for selling artwork by local kids. Thelma tried to convince the organizer that she was due a table. "I would've brought one from home if you hadn't put that on the form," she said. But her pleas fell on deaf ears.

Thelma and Impy returned to the basketball court. They would try to make do with milk crates and some bits of wood. A half dozen teens wearing blue hard hats were sweeping glass off the concrete without noticeable enthusiasm or effect. Looking at the desultory manner in which the work was being done, Thelma said to Impy, "There's just too many people here stacked up on top of each other. It's just *too much!*"

Impy knew the Robert Taylor Homes better than Thelma did. She had been raised in one of its buildings, located a few blocks north of 4300 South Federal, by her mother, Dorothy Carter, another Full Circle Fund borrower. When they had arrived in the 1960s, it was a relatively attractive place to live. New residents were screened and routine maintenance was done. By the time they moved out in the mid-1970s, the entire complex was in an advanced state of decay. Nearly two decades later, it was an urban badlands with few redeeming qualities. Vincent Lane, chairman of the Chicago Housing Authority, had proposed to begin tearing down the high-rises and moving the people who lived there into low-rises scattered around the city. Alderman Dorothy Tillmon, an acerbic critic of the Daley administration not eager to have the voters who'd elected her dispersed, objected vociferously to the plan and called for Lane to resign. A combination of her opposition and bureaucratic inertia continued to stall the plan.

When Impy left the projects, she wanted to explore the country. She had met too many young people who had never even seen Lake Michigan, much less other cities and states. At sixteen she ran away from home, settling for some time in Oklahoma City. There she was raped; nine months later she gave birth to her son, Ian. Soon after, she moved again, this time to San Diego. Ian was an attractive baby with soft, light brown skin, and she was able to get him into television commercials for diapers. The income supplemented the money she made doing odd jobs; by then, she was becoming a consummate hustler.

By the time she and Ian moved back to Chicago, Ian was making the transition from cute infant to handsome preteen. She got him some work modeling children's clothing at fashion shows. Ian was not only attractive but also strong and athletic. By age twelve there was already talk of his becoming an Olympic boxer. Some promoters were so eager to get him fighting that they bribed Impy to let Ian enter amateur tournaments, a fairly common practice for promising young pugilists. She, meanwhile, earned money printing business cards and jewelry, performing as Dready the Clown at birthday parties and special events, singing in nightclubs, teaching jewelry design at classes sponsored by the Park District, and vending at festivals and arts and crafts shows.

In 1991, Impy joined the Full Circle Fund with her mother and began borrowing to increase the capitalization of her businesses. Her financing needs exceeded what first-time borrowers were allowed to take, so she persuaded her mother to turn over most of the money she borrowed to her. Within a year she was becoming known as one of the program's success stories. Then disaster struck.

During the riots following the Chicago Bulls' second NBA championship, Ian snuck out a back door of their ramshackle house in Englewood. All the commotion excited him, and he wanted to see what it was all about. Within minutes, he was knocked unconscious when a blunt object crushed the right side of his face while he was standing in front of a liquor store on the corner of Damen Avenue and Seventy-first Street. Ten months later, he was released from the hospital with a reconstructed face, a glass eye, and permanent neurological damage. His careers in modeling and boxing were over, and he was placed in a special school for slow learners.

Impy, with financial and moral support from WSEP staff and beneficiaries, pulled through. But by the time Ian was released from the hospital, her long-standing asthma had worsened. Then, the

Full Circle Fund staff discovered that she and Dorothy Carter were related and forced Impy to leave her circle and form a new one.* Impy joined a new group, one of whose members was a woman who drifted in and out of homelessness and began missing payments on a $1,500 loan. Impy was then pressed into service to help repay that loan, and organized a twice-monthly vending event at a local community college for all the women in her center, from which 15 percent of everyone's gross sales was given to WSEP to help retire the debt. At the rate they were going, it would take more than a year to finish the job.

In May 1994, local gang members began to recruit Ian. He was confused by the process, but knew enough to resist their overtures. He became angry when the young men called his mother a "black African bitch" when they saw her on the street, and there were scuffles and fistfights. One evening, gang members called Ian out to the alley and tried to douse him with gasoline and set him on fire. He was lucky to receive only minor burns. But as they fled, the teens set Impy's garage on fire, destroying it, her neighbor's garage, a van Impy had bought for $700, and nearly $2,000 worth of merchandise. A few days later, a bullet passed through her upstairs window and lodged in her wall, shattering a mirror along the way. With her insurance money, she was able to restart her business, but there was nothing left to rebuild the garage or buy another van.

Vending and performing were ways for Impy to get her mind off her troubles while making some money. As she and Ian unpacked her bags, Luanda and Shashona erected two makeshift tables. A short time later, children began to arrive. They gravitated to Impy, who asked for nickels and quarters from kids who wanted to play some of the games she had devised. Others came to Thelma's table, looking longingly at her merchandise.

"Is this free?" one seven-year-old asked.

"No, these here's a quarter," Thelma replied, pointing to sev-

---

*One of the rules the FCF had adopted from Grameen restricted membership in groups to people who were not blood relatives.

eral boxes of rings she had bought for $6 a gross. "You go wake your mommy up and ask her for twenty-five cent." It was 11:25 on a Thursday morning.

Others crowded around the table, sampling the toys and frequently buying the snappers. During the entire festival, the crackling of snappers going off resounded in the background. The children's clothes were dirty and their behavior was often unruly. More than anything, they longed for attention. Thelma gave it to them while keeping a watchful eye over her merchandise. At one point she said to Shashona, "Where is these kids' adult supervision?"

Twenty yards away, a cookout was under way and rap music was playing loudly. Ian, increasingly oblivious to his mother's efforts to keep the children entertained, swayed to the beat of the music. He smiled as he watched adults and teens at the barbecue pit drink their stashes of alcohol.

"Come over here," Impy shouted. She led the children to a coatrack she had found on the street and converted into a basketball hoop. "It's a quarter to play, and whoever gets the most shots in wins a stuffed animal." The kids crowded into a ragged line, pushing each other in the process. A fight nearly broke out, but Impy distracted the boys and began collecting quarters. Toward the end of the game, she saw one boy who had lost making a G with his fingers, a gesture Impy recognized as a gang sign. "I hope that G is for God, little man," she said tartly before turning her attention back to the game. She gave the eventual winner a small stuffed bear—one of a batch she'd bought mail order for $2.75 a dozen—and began another game, in which the kids competed to get a steel ball to the bottom of a plastic maze.

Thelma was doing a steady business. Sometimes she let Shashona and Luanda run the table while she fell into conversation with Impy's mother, who had arrived at 12:15. She asked about what the Robert Taylor Homes were like in the 1960s.

"Oh, lovely. And look what's happened!" She pointed to all the broken glass on the concrete.

"I was vending once at Cabrini-Green," Thelma explained to Mrs. Carter, referring to one of Chicago's most notorious housing projects, "and those kids started lighting everything on fire. I's never going back there. Can you imagine that? All day I was there and I didn't see one adult the whole time."

Dorothy Carter nodded in agreement, her gaze wandering over to the table selling arts and crafts for $5 and up. They had yet to make a sale. Thelma looked over there too, and when her eyes met Mrs. Carter's she said, "Can't really sell anything for more than fifty cent here."

"Yeah," Dorothy responded with a sigh.

"Hey, Mrs. Carter, could you please give me a stuffed animal? We have a winner here!" Impy called out. Her enthusiasm was beginning to wane, but she pressed on.

By 2 P.M., many of the youngest children had scattered, though some kept coming to buy things from Thelma and to play with Dready the Clown. Impy pushed on with the games, even when some older boys began mocking her. The cookout was progressing slowly, as most of the cooks were drunk by then. The event's organizer was nowhere to be found.

Impy Simms walked away from the Second Annual Black on Black Love Festival with $65 in small change and her $60 appearance fee. Thelma grossed $80. It was a small amount of money earned under trying conditions, but both hoped they had made a small contribution to the children who passed their days in the Robert Taylor Homes.

Thelma Ali's mother, Mary Junkim Dean, lives in a rent-subsidized apartment on the North Side and supplements her pension by cleaning house for white families several times a week. "I don't have nothing against white folks," she says. "They work, save money, buy whatever they want, even a building. If poor people or black people could save money and build something for themselves, imagine!" Among her heroes is the legendary Mayor Richard J. Daley, though she has doubts about his son, Chicago's current chief executive.

Mary Junkim was born and raised on a cotton farm near Indianola, Mississippi. Her father was a fairly successful cultivator, though not so prosperous that his children didn't have to sew most of their own clothes and the blankets they slept under. Mary remembers baling cotton from a young age and going to school only four months out of the year.

Mary's paternal grandmother was a slave who was freed as a child and later married a Native American. All his children and grandchildren loved Mary's grandfather; they were crazy about his straight hair and exotic facial features. Even though the marriage didn't work out, he kept in touch with Mary's grandmother and all the children and grandchildren until his death. Sometimes he would come with his new wife and spend holidays with them. Both he and Mary's grandmother lived into their nineties.

In 1937, Mary was seventeen years old and recently married to Jesse Dean. He convinced her that their future was in Chicago. He went up first, secured a job, and sent for her a month later. For several decades, the couple moved around the city, often living in or near a housing project until just before it began going downhill. Both Mary and Jesse worked in factories, though after some years Mary concentrated primarily on domestic work.

Mary and Jesse Dean had eleven children, including three sets of twins, Thelma being one of the first pair. Four of her children have died: two passed away in their twenties, and the other two in their early forties. The youngest to die was killed by police, who had mistaken him for a suspect in an investigation. While the children were growing up, the couple separated because of Jesse's constant drinking. But husband or no husband, Mary Dean had high standards for parenting. She stayed up late at night hand-washing clothes and then woke up early the next morning to iron them. "Oh, no, my kids didn't go to school with rough-dried clothes," she says. "And I used to get up and fix them breakfast, though nowadays people just tell their kids to pour some cereal or they give 'em a quarter to buy a candy bar on the way to school."

Mary remembers Thelma as a teenager who partied hard and wore miniskirts. She gave Thelma and her other children the freedom to attend parties, but she always picked them up herself when it was time to come home. They appreciated the freedom but respected its limits.

When Thelma was eighteen, she was invited to a party where

most of the guests were Muslims. There was no drinking, no flirting, and no groping. All of the alcohol-induced sexual tension she
was accustomed to was replaced by polite conversation. Everyone
stayed until five o'clock in the morning, when the Muslims began
to pray. "I watched them praying," she remembered, "and I said,
'What kind of mess is this?' But then I began thinking about it, and
I realized that this had been the first time I'd been to a party and
been able to be myself."

Several days later, a friend called Thelma to tell her that one of
the Muslim men wanted to see her again. She resisted at first, but
finally agreed to get together for Friday prayer at his mosque. Religion had never appealed to her, and she was afraid she'd get
bored. But she liked what she saw: women sitting on one side, men
on the other, everyone engaged in serious talk about families and
responsibility. After that, Thelma became a regular at the mosque
and stopped wearing miniskirts. She had several encounters with
a man named Edward Ali; soon, he proposed marriage. Thelma
agreed, and the two were wed.

Mary Dean wasn't sure about her daughter's marrying a Muslim, but she didn't interfere. When she saw him hurrying home
from work in the middle of the day to change his babies' diapers
and bottle-feed them while Thelma was out selling Tupperware,
she accepted him as one of her own.

The most Thelma's husband, a self-employed builder, made in
a single year was $21,000. With five children to clothe and feed,
that pushed their finances to the limit. They were never able to buy
a house, and as renters with children they faced discrimination.
Landlords, whether black, white, or Asian, either refuse to rent to
families (especially if the children are black teenage boys) or charge
25 to 50 percent more than they would otherwise. It's one of those
iron laws in south Chicago that everyone knows and nobody questions.

To ease the strain on the family, Thelma got involved in selling
Tupperware. Before long she was invited to a sales conference in
Atlanta, recruited into a supervisory role, and given a company
car. That forced her to learn how to drive. Among the people she
recruited to work under her was Omiyale DuPart. But after six

months she gave it up because several of her sales agents were failing to pay for merchandise the company had sent them.

Thelma decided that she liked selling, and began vending at flea markets, Maxwell Street, and other events where the entry fee was under $20. The capitalization of her business was extremely low, perhaps a few hundred dollars, but she was able to make extra money for family expenses and to involve her daughters in the enterprise. It was not until she joined the FCF that she would have the working capital to enter more lucrative events like the Black Expo or the Afro-World Festival in Milwaukee where vendors are charged as much as $500.

Once, at an auction where she was trying to obtain cheap merchandise, she met a Jewish man in his early seventies named Harry Zimmerman. Both wanted shoes, and rather than engage in a bidding war they decided that Thelma would let Harry get all the adult sizes while he would not contest the children's shoes. That deal began a long friendship between them, and later between Thelma and Harry's son Marshall. The Zimmermans owned a men's clothing store on the corner of Halsted and Maxwell, and Harry had been a vendor at the bazaar in his youth. The Zimmermans were among the few merchants in the area who sold to blacks on credit.

Over the years, Harry and Marshall let Thelma purchase merchandise through contacts they had, at lower cost than she could get it elsewhere. She appreciated that, and in turn sold their tube socks from her table on the south side of Maxwell, since many people would not do back-to-school shopping at Harry's shack, which specialized in videos. Overall, Thelma thought most Jewish people were tolerant, generous, and industrious, and when she called the bazaar "Jewtown" it was meant as a tribute to Jewish ingenuity rather than an ethnic slur. She looked down on Muslims and other blacks who thought all of their race's problems were caused by Jews.

When Thelma and her husband were married, they attended a mosque associated with the Nation of Islam. They tried to screen out the teachings they disliked, but over time they switched to an orthodox mosque. To Thelma, who came to take her faith more seriously than her husband did, it was not right to mix Islam and racial separatism. She enjoyed worshiping with different races. The imam in the orthodox mosque seemed to her to emphasize the right things, such as fasting during the month of Ramadan.

By 1993, Thelma was forty-two years old, had been married for twenty-four years, and had five children aged fourteen to twenty-three. Her two sons worked in her husband's business when they weren't in school, something that kept them busy and, for the most part, out of trouble. Only Akbar, the younger of her two sons, had been tempted by gangs, but his parents and older brother talked him out of joining. Thelma's oldest daughter, Colleta, married a young Pakistani in the fall of 1993, and by the summer of 1994 there was talk of the tall, slender, and beautiful Shashona's marrying a boyfriend who had gotten a job with the postal service. He wasn't a Muslim, but Thelma was willing to bless the union if it made her daughter happy. Both Shashona and Hyiatt (Thelma's youngest daughter) worked in their mother's business.

On some social issues, Thelma is fairly conservative. She opposes giving out condoms and information about homosexuality to schoolchildren, and has little patience for people who believe that they are entitled to anything. She says, "America has gold in it; you just have to go out and work for it." She also has no tolerance for people who are unwilling to put the time into making their marriage and families work. She, like her mother, is a realistic disciplinarian. Her kids can swear and listen to loud music, but not in the house. She knows they drink at parties, but they know never to come in late or with liquor on their breath. Thelma and Mary also share the view that the things that matter in life are hard work, thrift, simple living, and keeping one's family together.

The commotion started at 8:30 A.M. Sunday morning. Queenesta and Duwondes were setting up their booth at the annual Haile Selassie Festival in Washington Park; thirty yards away, Thelma and Victor were setting up their booths. They had arrived nearly an hour before in an effort to secure booth space and get ready for the festival's second day. Thelma had already sent her daughter to Maxwell Street.

Business had been good for everybody on Saturday, and Sunday was traditionally better. A pair of West Africans who had driven in from Los Angeles to sell imported jewelry and wood carvings had taken over space that Dorothy Johnson, Victor's seamstress tenant, had used the day before. When she arrived, she spent twenty minutes trying to get her spot back.

Seeing her predicament, Nixon and Victor got involved.

"Hey, man," Victor said to one of the Africans, "why you being so disrespectful to Ms. Johnson and taking over her spot?"

"Those the rules—first come, first served. You got to get here early," the newcomer replied.

His companion jumped from behind his table. "You don't say anything! We got this space fairly, man. I do all the talking."

"The rules is," Victor began, "that you get the space you had on Saturday. Anyway, this is a matter of respect." Nixon, standing next to him, nodded in agreement.

The event organizer called on two off-duty cops who were acting as security to mediate. Both were black and wore T-shirts that read, "Homicide, Chicago Police Department: Our Day Starts Where Yours Ends." Thelma wandered over and asked what was going on. After getting the story, she said to Nixon, "I'm afraid those *are* the rules. I've been coming here for three years. You gotta get here early on Sunday or you lose your spot."

After nearly thirty minutes of negotiations, the Africans agreed to share the booth, but there wasn't enough room. Angered but resigned, Dorothy found another space. After she was set, Victor came over to Queenesta's table, where she had laid out her merchandise: sunglasses, T-shirts, and cassettes. "Why'd you do that? Any other time you would have just kicked Ms. Johnson to the curb." Queenesta said it in a humorous way, and Victor laughed.

"I said I was with her, didn't I?" he responded absentmindedly as he fell into conversation with Nixon. As they talked, the first customers were beginning to arrive, and other vendors were setting up on the lawn, behind the tables that lined the footpath. They were the less serious vendors—many were just combining a day in the park and a little business, or were trying to avoid paying the entrance fee.

It was another hot, cloudless day that held out the promise of good sales. Anticipation was high, and black Chicago came out in force for the festival. Omiyale was vending, as was her older sister Taile. So was Janet Johnson, Omiyale's younger sister who had saved enough of her business profits to buy her first car in June. Her next goal was to buy a house.

Colete was there. She had joined with other Hebrew Israelites to sell vegetarian tacos. Wanda X and Belvia Muhammad, the Nation of Islam believers in the Let Us Make Woman circle, came by to see what was going on, as did former enterprise agent Jackie Taffee. Glenda showed up in the early afternoon and talked with her former circle sisters. Shayna sold cold juice from a cooler for a quarter, while Nixon and Queenesta concentrated on sunglasses. Both engaged passersby in conversation, helped them select the right glasses, and then closed the deals. They sold for $5, four times the price Queenesta had paid through mail order. Over the course of two days, she and Nixon would go through close to two hundred pairs, outselling all the other sunglass vendors at the festival. When Nixon persuaded Queenesta to drop the prices of T-shirts from $10 to $8, they began to move too.

Thelma did a steady business selling T-shirts—the most popular had a large picture of Nelson Mandela—toys, sunglasses, and dollar jewelry. She stood there with her trusty purse slung around her torso, ritualistically reshuffling her merchandise every few minutes to make her table orderly. Between her sales at the festival and Maxwell Street, she grossed $550 over the weekend. Yet she was more disturbed than ever by Nixon.

She was bothered by the incident with the West Africans. Thelma knew that the Africans were technically right, and she thought that Nixon knew it as well. Yet being right didn't seem to mean anything to Nixon; might meant right, and he had been intent on putting the Africans in their place. He and Victor made an imposing pair, and had been confident that the cops would side with them. But what will happen, Thelma thought, when Nixon and Queenesta run into difficulties? Will he be any more willing to negotiate in good faith with her than he was with the Africans? Thelma didn't believe he would be.

Earlier that month, Queenesta told Thelma that Nixon had proposed to her and that she had said no, at least for a year. Hearing that made Thelma even more worried. She feared that the relationship was headed for disaster, but when she tried to bring it up, Queenesta didn't want to listen.

As the sun set behind the festival, huge speakers pumped out live and recorded reggae tunes. "We don't know our history," one song declared, "we're killing ourselves. Black people—we don't know ourselves."

Darkness meant selling glow lights, those green, glow-in-the-dark necklaces so popular at night festivals. They retailed for $2, and selling a tube of forty meant about $45 in profit. Omiyale, Thelma, Queenesta, and Victor were selling them. Queenesta outsold the others, sneaking behind the stage where all the reggae performers were relaxing and quickly selling out. Victor, not so lucky, was forced to let his last ten go for next to nothing. But he had done well selling kufis, and had made several contacts with potential retailers. His dream was to manufacture hundreds of kufis per month and wholesale them for $3 each. Among those who agreed to try selling them was Thelma Ali.

The Lindblom center meeting was nearly an hour old, and Colete announced that Joanne Sandler and Karen Doyle, two women from Washington, D.C., who had been observing the meeting, would spend the second hour asking the borrowers about their businesses as part of an evaluation of seven programs supporting self-employment for the poor. Karen Doyle worked for the Aspen Institute's Self-Employment Learning Project (SELP), which was being funded by foundations that had been providing support to WSEP and other programs. Joanne Sandler was a consultant for the evaluation project. Colete and Mary Morten, WSEP's director of policy, said that they would leave the room so as to allow the women to speak freely.

There were some uneasy moments in the beginning of the discussion. Joanne Sandler said they were trying to learn what worked and what didn't about peer lending programs. One circle member who had never gotten her business started said, "You mean, you're trying to figure out how to support us, the participants—you're not talking about the women downtown, are you?" Thelma and Omiyale cringed at that one. Thelma especially resented the way a few of the women bad-mouthed the "downtown" staff. Some WSEP employees, she realized, were better than others, but why couldn't her circle sisters just appreciate what this program gave them, without complaining about what it didn't?

"*And* the women downtown," one of the guests weakly answered.

Embarrassed laughter and guffaws filled the room, and above it all Thelma could be heard saying, "We're all in this together. We're all in this together, everybody."

One borrower started talking about the difficulty she and a male partner were having in getting all the licenses they needed to set up a bazaar and restaurant in Englewood. "There are people out there, who make the laws, who do not want to see black people succeed. And you can write that in your report and tell everyone in Washington." Thelma sighed audibly and raised her hand.

"See, in order to operate a business . . ." She paused, looking directly at the woman who had spoken. "No matter how this society is set up, whether you feel the rules are wrong or whatever . . . They might have been set up by the wrong people, but that is the law. You have to learn how to work around it."

"Ladies," Omiyale broke in, "we're going to move right along—"

"If you're going to do something," Thelma said over a lot of chatter, "you got to do it right. You can't help someone if they want to do it, if they want to operate it wrong." Omiyale, with some effort, finally restored order. The two visitors asked why the women had become self-employed.

There was a brief silence, which Thelma broke by saying, "I got into business to give my children more choices in life. When I grew up, all there was was to go to school, be educated, and work for someone. I had only had one choice in life. I wanted to give my children five choices in life. The choices are to go to school and become educated and to come in their father's business, to go to school and become educated and to come into your mother's business, to go to school and become educated and to work for someone else, to be educated and work your own business, or to go to school and be educated and decide not to do anything." Women began to laugh, but over them Thelma added, "But those five choices, that's why I started my business." Some began to clap.

Queenesta, with a sleepy Shayna in her lap, went next. "My reasons was similar to hers. Because there's a trend, with, um, black people, that they teach their children that they *have* to get *a job.*"

"Right," one borrower concurred.

"And in order to break the psychological chains, I thought that it was up to me. I thought it was better to show her than to tell her. Now, I've been self-employed since soon after she was born, so that's the only thing that she knows. And that's the only thing I want her to see. So that this is what her goal would be, to be self-employed."

Karen Doyle asked about whether the prospects for wage employment in their community had gotten better, worse, or stayed the same over the last few years. The unanimous opinion was that the situation was worse. The women discussed the reality that most of the stores in their communities were run by immigrants who were inclined to hire their own people as they expanded.

B. J. Slay, who sold beauty-care products and employed four people, spoke up. "Every other ethnic group supports each other, except for us. And until we do that, we can sit and talk all day long and nothing will change. Yet for most people, ignorance is bliss. When I worked, I didn't feel all this, but when you're out here hustling for your bills, you think about it. 'Cause you gotta make ends meet."

A short time later, the meeting broke up. Thelma went over to Omiyale and wished her well on her trip to Africa. Though neither woman would admit it, the frost that had settled over their relationship during the first part of the year was lifting. It was none too soon, as the circle was about to be thrown into an unexpected crisis.

• • •

A customer came to the gate, peered into the darkened store, and paused briefly before pushing on the steel gate. To his surprise, it was locked. "Hey, man, we're not open today," Duwondes Nixon called out. "We're gonna be closed through about Tuesday." The customer looked to his left, at a large wooden board that had been taped over a gaping hole in a shattered window. It was Sunday, July 31, at 3:30 P.M., still a half hour before the normal closing time for the Hip Hop Shop. But this was no normal day.

Nixon looked down into the main display case. It was empty. The sunglasses and baseball caps in the other cases remained, but the compact discs were gone. He reached into the case and took out a black baseball cap. No, I've never taken stuff from the store, he thought; even when I've taken candy I've put money in the register later. But in the process of putting the cap back he stopped. What the fuck, he thought as he pulled it out a second time and put it on. Nixon activated the alarm system, chained the bars behind the windows, and walked out.

Several weeks earlier, Nixon's van had broken down, making it considerably more difficult for him to take on plumbing work. That allowed him to spend more time at the Hip Hop Shop, which was fine with him since he was trying to get out of the plumbing business anyway. At first, Queenesta liked it, too; she was having to spend more time managing the beeper business and was making plans for opening the new store. But in a short time it became an irritation. Nixon had ideas about remodeling the store and dropping the prices of the merchandise—ideas that Queenesta didn't agree with. And he had no money to finance his ideas. When Queenesta, always worried about keeping as much money as possible invested in cassettes (since she still did not have the selection that Moonlight Records did), said she wanted to keep things the way they were, Nixon began subtly challenging his partner's accounting methods. Before long he was suggesting that she was socking away money without his knowledge. By then, he had become much more than the "silent partner" Queenesta had told her circle sisters about in May. Looming over the growing dispute was Nixon's unsuccessful marriage proposal.

On Friday, July 29, they were awakened in the middle of the night by a call from the police. Someone had smashed a hole in one of the Hip Hop Shop's front windows and set off the alarm system that automatically notified the police. Nixon, Queenesta, and Shayna rushed to the store and arranged to have the window temporarily secured for $80. Queenesta and Nixon suspected that the attack might have been the work of a local wino whom Nixon had cursed out the day before when he had tried to beg inside the store. Nixon didn't deny that that was conceivable, but he resented the way Queenesta tried to blame him for it. Pretty soon, tempers got short, and old issues, like dropping prices, got brought up. At one point Queenesta asked angrily, "Why don't you let me buy you out of the business?"

"You want to *what*?"

"I want to buy you out."

"No way; we got to talk this thing out, but no way I'm getting out." Hearing that, Queenesta stormed out of the store. Nixon discovered the next day that Queenesta was moving her things out of his apartment, and he took the advice of a friend and removed the cassettes and compact discs from the store as a bargaining chip. That way, Queenesta would have to negotiate with him. Yet when she saw the empty cases, she screamed, "Why are you tryin' to gangsta the store, Nixon? Why?" and left. Gary Williams, Queenesta's mentor from her Allstate days, who also knew Nixon, came by that same weekend to try to mediate the dispute, but when he saw the merchandise gone, he became disgusted with Nixon and backed away. Victor tried his hand at resolving things, but also gave up. By then, Queenesta was living with her sister June, and her belongings were being stored in three different locations. Nixon had changed the locks on the store and was sleeping there (lest Queenesta sneak in during the night).

Successive plans to recover the store from Nixon failed, principally because both of their names (rather than Queenesta's alone) were on the business license.

During the weeks immediately after the takeover, it became difficult for Queenesta to do anything without falling into hysterics. She contacted her beeper customers to tell them that she was temporarily relocating that part of her business to Victor's store. She went into the Hip Hop Shop one final time to pick up her cash register and several other things that were indisputably hers. But when she tried to take a display case she had bought with loan money from WSEP, Nixon said no.

When she called Thelma to tell her about what had happened, she didn't hear "I told you so" but received a commitment to sanction a loan from the emergency loan fund after Omiyale returned from Africa. Somehow, Queenesta managed to make a $144 payment on her loan on August 8, and another one two weeks later. But Thelma recognized that Queenesta was in a precarious and dangerous situation—living in a tiny apartment with her sister and on the brink of homelessness. More than anything, Thelma told her not to go back to the store.

In late August, Victor left for his own trip to Africa, and Queenesta agreed to look after the store. The beeper business had recovered, but it was barely enough to pay grocery bills and buy gas, much less make her monthly car payment and meet her obligation to the Full Circle Fund. On September 5, she missed her first installment. At about that time, two more holes were smashed in Hip Hop Shop windows. Nixon continued to operate the store, though he often couldn't open until the evening, when his plumbing jobs were completed and he could get back to Austin on public transit. He dropped the prices of most of the merchandise.

Queenesta had no store, virtually no merchandise, and an outstanding loan. She moved back in with her mother for the month of September, and began planning to restart her business.

13

▲

The Sixteen Decisions

Krishna was holding a center meeting in the Haldar *para* at the end of the monsoon season. Sitting on a mat, he began silently marking up his collection sheet and the passbooks. Krishna wasn't a big talker. Unless there was some reason to speak up, he busied himself with his paperwork and let the women run the meeting the way they saw fit. Sometimes Shandha thought he should take a more active role in maintaining discipline; for her, his lecture on timeliness the previous week had been long overdue. No matter how well respected Shandha was, she knew a bank worker could have a more immediate impact on the goings-on in her center than she was able to. Shandha was, after all, a realist—bank workers were educated men, and she was an illiterate woman. In few societies do a person's education and gender assume more importance in how much respect they are accorded than in Bangladesh.

Krishna called for the passbooks from each group and deducted the week's installment from the running balance. For general and seasonal loans he subtracted 2 percent of the principal, for tubewell loans 1 percent, and for housing loans 40 taka. As he did so, he reflected on how much more difficult it was being a bank worker in 1994 than it had been five years before. Then, there was one passbook per borrower for general loans and perhaps two or three housing loans per center. Servicing a center meant filling in roughly forty passbooks. On this day, Krishna would be handed more than one hundred. The volume of money that was collected each morning, and lent out each afternoon, had grown proportionately.

One striking thing about Grameen center meetings is the manner in which financial transactions are conducted. Before Krishna collected the money, he wrote in each borrower's passbook that she had paid her installment in full. Only later was the money collected, and even then it was handed over by the group chairman, not the individual. When Krishna was ready for it, he collected 1,265 taka from Shandha's group. He compared the amount with what they gave him last week, and if there was any difference he checked to make sure it was because they had received a new loan or paid one off. He would assume that there were no missed payments unless he was told otherwise. Collecting the money from the group chairman is meant to reinforce the idea that the primary problem-solving unit in the Grameen system is the group, not the bank worker. In Grameen branches where irregular payments are common, bank workers are often forced to collect the money first and to do so from each individual directly.

Another striking thing about center meetings in Bangladesh is how cramped they are. Shandha's center house is no more than twenty feet long and eight feet wide. Every Tuesday morning, thirty-five women, as many as ten children, and one bank worker squeeze into it. The meetings in Chicago, by contrast, are attended by fewer people in spaces more than six times larger. Chairs are spread out there, reflecting the zone of privacy that Westerners respect and Asians have difficulty comprehending; for the women in the Lindblom center, a group of twenty to thirty is unwieldy. In many respects, though, the actual content of the meetings is the same in Chicago and Bangladesh: the money changing hands, the problem-solving, the gossiping, the exchanging of business tips. In both places, the pleasure the women take in being with other women in an environment where their economic (rather than domestic) responsibilities are the center of attention is palpable.

As the meeting wore on, notes began piling up in front of Shandha. Amodini, wearing the white sari of Hindu widowhood, sat next to her friend and tried to straighten the stacks out. It was a small gesture, but it signified that she was feeling like herself again; the period of mourning for her husband was over. On Shandha's advice Amodini was husking rice to earn extra money, since the market for fishing nets was shrinking with the ending of the monsoon. It took Amodini some days before she found the wherewithal to follow Shandha's advice, but once she did it gave her a sense of purpose. It also supplemented the income her daughter brought in from fishing, since Amodini had virtually no livestock in the months after her husband's death. (She had been forced to sell whatever she had to meet her weekly installments, arrange the funeral, and pay off the quacks.)

"Will you have five women for me next week?" Krishna asked Shandha as he looked up from counting some bills.

"Yes, you can give them their first training next Tuesday, if you want." Pressure had come from the area manager to increase the number of groups in each center to eight. Shandha had said in the spring that she didn't think there was anyone else who wanted to join, but now, in September, she was singing a different tune. Among those who were expressing interest in joining was Amodini's sister-in-law.

"Tell them to come here then," Krishna replied. "Are there any loan proposals today?"

Four women stood up. Krishna took down the first three proposals. They generated little controversy and were completed in a short time. Then came Rasheda from the fifth group, who had recovered from typhoid in July and wanted a loan for a tube well.

"Sir," Rasheda said, "I need a tube well. Please sanction a three-thousand-taka loan."

Krishna looked up from the form on which he had noted the three loan proposals that he had accepted. He studied Rasheda, and surveyed the women sitting in her row. "Rasheda, how can we trust you?" Two years earlier, Rasheda had sold the house she built with a Grameen Bank housing loan. Even though she had never missed a payment on the loan, the bank saw it as a major breach of discipline. Now she had to face the consequences.

"Sir, I need a tube well. We have to go a great distance to fetch water now."

"You said you needed a house three years ago, but then you sold it. Why will this be any different? Maybe it will be safest to give you no tube-well loan, after what you've done."

"Sir, I will use it well."

"Sit down," Krishna said. He returned to the other three loan proposals and let Rasheda stew. She pulled her sari over her face and began to cry. Krishna said suddenly, "Group number five chairman, stand up."

A woman sitting on the far left of the group stood. "Do you support this loan proposal?" Krishna asked impatiently.

"Yes, sir."

"Will it be utilized correctly, or will she sell it?"

"She will use it correctly, sir," the woman replied firmly but respectfully.

"Supi, stand up." The former center chief rose. "What about you—do you support it? Will you take personal responsibility with your group chairman, to make sure the loan is used properly?"

"Yes, sir," she said, looking Krishna in the eye as she spoke the words.

"Zorina, stand up." The dark-skinned center chief joined the other two women. "What about you?"

"I support the proposal, sir. She needs a tube well for drinking water and to irrigate her vegetable garden. She will use it right. She came and spoke to me about it yesterday."

Krishna surveyed the three women. Finally, and inevitably, his gaze shifted to Shandha. "What about you?"

Though she was sitting no more than a foot apart from the others, Shandha stood up too. She looked back at Rasheda, made eye contact, and looked down at Krishna. "I am behind it too, sir," she said softly.

"Okay, sit down, all of you," he said. "Rasheda, stand up." He went through the formalities of asking her all the information he needed for the draft loan proposal—her husband's name, the amount, and the use. Then he called the four women applying for loans, and the center chief, to come up and sign the proposal. When that was complete, he asked the women to practice a ritual that they hadn't done for some time—chanting slogans at the end of their meeting. The manager was likely to come to the first group training session, and he liked to see things done by the book.

Shandha was the only one who remembered how to lead them in the slogans. With everyone standing, she called out, "Unity, hard work, and discipline."

"Unity, hard work, and discipline," the other women echoed.

"That is our creed," Shandha yelled.

"That is our creed," they repeated three times.

They went on to recite other slogans about their children's education, building dignified housing, and drinking clean water. They ended with a chant that has a distinctive sound to it in Bengali, though it loses something in translation. "The light of Grameen Bank," Shandha intoned. The women repeated the words. "May it burn in every household."

Understanding Grameen ultimately requires some familiarity with Muhammad Yunus's core beliefs. A careful reading of his lectures and correspondence in 1993 and 1994 highlights the four ideas that underpin his life and work—simplicity, sacrifice, gradualism, and faith.

Pervading all of his work is the notion "Keep it simple." It is undeniable that the influence of Nicholas Georgescu-Roegen, his mentor from Vanderbilt, is still felt. Yunus believes that virtually all technical jargon can be eliminated, opening up specialized knowledge to common people, even if it takes a little longer to explain an economic or scientific concept using layman's language. To his thinking, the shallow intellectual stays mired in complexity, while the true intellectual strives for simplicity. Georgescu was a true intellectual, and Yunus tries to be another. His arena, however, is an organization rather than a classroom.

As Yunus created Grameen, he resisted all attempts to make the bank's policies more complex. He instructed his staff that business was to be conducted openly, explained thoroughly, and expressed in simple mathematics that a determined illiterate person could grasp. Repayment is made in fifty equal installments of exactly 2 percent of the loan amount. Savings is 1 taka. Interest is paid in the two weeks after the payment of the last installment, making the repayment period exactly one calendar year. The group tax is 5 percent of the loan amount. It is hardly an exaggeration to say that Grameen borrowers with no schooling understand more about the bank they borrow from and save at than most college-educated Westerners understand about the financial institutions they do business with.

But simplicity is more than an operational strategy. It is also a philosophy. Yunus has tried, often with a touch of humor, to convince people that problems, and their solutions, are not inherently complex, but rather that people make them that way. In a seminar on the malaise of the Bangladeshi economy, Yunus is likely to interrupt a jargon-riddled academic debate and say something like "I think the problem is that people aren't working hard enough" or "If people in government became sincere about serving the country, these problems would clear up." Occasionally colleagues take such assertions seriously, but more often Yunus's comments are met with blank stares before the discussion returns to the ethereal planes.

If simplicity is one pillar in the foundation of Yunus's philosophy, sacrifice is another. To him, it is essential: putting in long hours, finishing a job properly, encouraging fierce competition among colleagues (in order to bring out the best in all of them), and making do with a modest salary. If his staff is unwilling to make sacrifices for the good of the bank, he wonders, how can they ask the borrowers to do so for the good of their centers? When it is argued that Yunus should raise wages of his senior staff because their abilities and work ethic would be worth many times that on the open market, he shrugs. When a senior staff member with ten years of outstanding service to Grameen leaves to take a cushy job abroad, Yunus says all the right things while privately fuming about how people use successful poverty-alleviation programs to land high-paying jobs. Part of sacrifice, he believes, is keeping one's word, whatever the cost. In 1993, on the evening that Yunus collapsed at a center meeting and spent the afternoon undergoing tests that revealed he had a severe ulcer, he snuck away to a function in his honor he had promised to attend at the Belgian embassy.

His third core belief is gradualism. Yunus has concluded that lasting social change most often—and perhaps always—comes slowly rather than in a burst of revolutionary fervor. This belief has shaped his work, and as a result, throughout his career his methods and achievements have been belittled. The left has blamed him for not going further in attempting to redistribute assets; many so-called radicals have scoffed at the idea of giving credit while stopping short of advocating their preferred solution, land reform. The right has called him a welfare advocate disguised in capitalist clothing. In both cases, his program does not match up to their ideals. In reality, of course, Grameen doesn't match up with some of his own ideals, either. But it passes the test that guides all the major decisions in his life—is doing it an improvement over doing nothing? Time and again, when people find fault with Grameen, Yunus admits its theoretical and programmatic deficiencies while defending it as superior to the status quo. A man who was more of a perfectionist, or more impatient about bringing about sweeping social change, would have either abandoned the Grameen experiment or run it into the ground. Instead, he has let it evolve in a way that has allowed two million people to benefit.

But the belief that stands apart from all others, and sets Yunus apart from virtually all of his peers, is his faith—not in religion, but in people, especially poor people. In late 1994, I was talking to an American who had returned to Bangladesh after an absence of several years. His understanding—and love—of the country was still obvious. When pushed, he spoke disparagingly of the aid agencies in Bangladesh and even about leaders of well-respected nonprofit organizations in the country. Intrigued, I asked him about what he thought of Yunus. His answer was revealing.

"Yunus is a mensch. All the other organizations, whether donor or nonprofit, share the belief that these poor Bangladeshis can't really do anything for themselves—they need handouts, subsidies, something. From the early 1970s Yunus was the only one saying, 'Hey, these people can do something for themselves, they have abilities. There is nothing inferior about Bangladeshis.' That's what sets Yunus apart."

That faith in the ability of poor people is what makes Yunus, after all the dust has cleared, a capitalist, though a unique one. Many people who share his commitment to the poor reject capitalism. Often they want to soften capitalism's hard edges for the poor by instituting subsidies, welfare programs, and protectionism. Sometimes they embrace socialism. But Yunus is unapologetic about his championing of capitalism and his belief that the poor will be able to compete effectively if the obstacles preventing them from doing so are removed. He yearns for a more humanistic, but no less competitive, economic system. In an expansive speech given in June 1994 to a Rotary convention in Taipei, he spelled out his views.

"The essence of capitalism is expressed in two of its basic features: profit maximization and market competition. In their abstract formulations these were not supposed to be conspiratorial against the poor. But in real life they turn out to be the killers of the poor. . . .

"The profit maximization principle is recognized as the best principle to ensure the optimal use of resources. Free market competition ensures that you are pushed out of any uncomfortable position when your competitor finds a better product or a better way of doing business. It is the driving force for all innovations, technology changes, and better management." The bases of capitalism were sound, he was saying, but when they are put into practice they often create unacceptable outcomes.

"In the conceptualization of the capitalist world we have installed a greedy, almost bloodthirsty, person to play the role of profit maximizer. Not only have we deprived him of all human qualities, but we have empowered him by giving him all the institutional support he can use while depriving that support to everyone else (e.g., banks will give him all the money he wants, but not recognize other people). On top of it, we conceptualize that the entrepreneurs are a very rare and special breed of people. We are lucky to have them with us. We must give them all the privileges they ask for." Yunus believes that everyone has marketable skills, and he wants the capitalist world to reflect that.

"If we imagine a world where every human being is a potential entrepreneur, we'll build a system to give everybody a chance to materialize his or her potential. The heavy wall between the 'entrepreneur' and 'labor' will be meaningless. If labor had access to capital, this world would be very different from what we have now. We build what we imagine. In the past we have imagined the wrong way, [and] as a result we got a wrong world. By formulating our axioms the right way, we can create the right world.

"In the 'right' world, we'll have to forget that people should wait around to be hired by somebody. We must instill in everybody's mind that each person *creates* his or her own job. We'll build institutions in such a way that each person is supported and empowered to create his or her own job: self-employment. Wage employment will come into the picture only as an alternative to self-employment. The more self-employment becomes attractive, wide-ranging, and self-fulfilling, the more difficult it will be to attract people for wage jobs. Women, minority groups, the physically handicapped, and the socially handicapped will benefit from self-employment becoming more rewarding and convenient.

"Mass production of a product," he admitted, "leads to economies of scale under any production system. But there is nothing that makes it obligatory to organize this mass production under one roof. Home-based production based on self-employment can be as mass-scale as in a single-roof, wage-based factory system. The more we can move toward home-based production by the self-employed masses, the more we can come close to avoiding the horrors of capitalism.

"In this alternative vision of the capitalist world, instead of one motivating factor—'greed'—to keep it in motion, we can introduce social consciousness or social dreams as another motivating factor. Both types of people can be in the same marketplace, using the same tools and concepts of capitalism but pursuing completely different goals. In addition, there will be middle-of-the-roaders, who will mix both greed and social objectives, according to their tastes and abilities.

"This alternative vision of the world will not be as black as it turned out under the greed-alone scenario. This capitalist world can accommodate all shades: white, gray, and black. I think this is the most realistic vision of the world under any framework, capitalist or noncapitalist.

"I am inclined to believe that the role of social-consciousness-driven entrepreneurs will become more important than the role of greed-driven entrepreneurs in the newly configured capitalist world. The role I am assigning to social-consciousness-driven entrepreneurs in the new configuration of the capitalist world is assigned to the State in a socialist framework. The State did not do a good job in this role.

"Can capitalist concepts, tools, and frameworks allow, support, and promote economic activities leading to achievements of social objectives in parallel with narrow personal objectives? My answer is an emphatic yes. Yes, it can be done, provided we can create, strengthen, and widen the role of social-consciousness-driven entrepreneurs through building supportive institutions, state policies, educational systems, and social rewards mechanisms and creating international support systems and solidarity networks. . . .

"By joining the ranks of social-consciousness-driven entrepreneurs," he urged the Rotarians, "you'll gain more in social respectability than you'll lose in dollars and cents of personal income. Above all, you'll be a happier person. If you become social-consciousness-driven entrepreneurs with your total commitment, I can assure you you'll build an entirely different world than what we have now. The world that we can build will be free from poverty and human indignity. . . ."

This unveiled optimism has many sides. Yunus argues against provision of free health and education for the poor. He suggests that the important thing is that people be given the means to earn an income so that they can pay for health, education, and other essentials. Until such time as they can pay with money, education and health should be provided in exchange for a "social payment," such as a poor person agreeing to organize a sanitation program in his or her village. He also argues against protectionism, arguing that the poor can compete in the international marketplace and that the beneficiaries of protectionism are most often the "rich and clever" people (even though tariffs and quotas are often erected in the name of workers and the poor). These arguments are heresy among many progressives, but they are consistent with Yunus's faith in people to find their niche in the marketplace if given access to the same tools as wealthy entrepreneurs. To Yunus, capitalism under conditions of equal access to investment capital is ultimately a progressive socioeconomic system. Above all he dislikes the idea of special rights for certain classes of people; "entrepreneurs" no more deserve special access to credit than "the poor" do to free health care. In an ideal world, the wealthy would not have privileged access to money for investment, and the poor do not have privileged access to money for consumption.

Yunus's brand of humanism leads to a dim view of formal religion. He occasionally comments that the unattainably high standards of conduct to which the leaders of the great religions hold people make them ashamed to participate actively in their places of worship. Religion, in his mind, should take into account the reality of people's lives; moreover, religious leaders should strive harder to improve people's lives here on earth. While he is a proud if not especially devout Muslim, he occasionally laments that Islamic leaders oppose Grameen while Christian priests in places like the Philippines are among its most enthusiastic supporters. Once, when asked about whether he worshiped any God, he responded by saying that he worshiped "the God in each human being."

Amena walked gingerly next to a row of plants in her vegetable garden, picking off a few green chilies and eggplants to be sold later in the afternoon. She placed them in a basket she had woven some years before. Amena was agitated. Her husband had returned from Dhaka the night before, where he had been pulling a rickshaw to earn money. His absence had given Amena a chance to reshuffle her livestock, since he had found out about some of the chicks and ducklings she had sharecropped out before the monsoon. It was a constant game they played, and while she was unable to conceal all of her assets and earnings, she did hide some. She had even bought a small share of an irrigation pump for the coming winter rice crop without her husband's knowledge.

"Come here," Absar Ali shouted to his wife. "We're going to talk now." Amena's parents had already huddled with her husband under the shade of a tree. Amena pulled up a low stool to join the family meeting.

Four weeks earlier, word had reached Amena's compound that her younger brother, the one who had eloped to Dhaka with the older, married woman, had been killed by a truck one night while pulling a rickshaw. The following day his body was delivered in a coffin and he was buried on Amena's father's homestead plot. Ever since, people had been coming to the house and passing judgment, saying that Allah had judged Amena's brother's actions by taking his life. It was a dark time for the family.

"What do you think we should do?" Absar Ali asked his father-in-law. Amena's father had a haggard look about him. Amena and her parents had each lost at least five pounds since the death; none of them were eating regularly as they dealt with their grief.

"I think we should move to Munshikandi. This place is a bad place for us, with bad memories. We have relatives there; we can stay with them. There are others there from our home village."

"I don't like this place anymore," Amena's mother said in a whisper.

Absar Ali looked at his wife. "What do you think?"

"It is your decision, of course, but I think that we should stay here," Amena began. "We should approach our uncle and see if he will sell us this land. I think he will agree to it. Perhaps we could pay in installments, over several years. Then we could finally settle down somewhere."

"Amena," her father began, "we are people of the broken river. Wherever we go, the river will follow us. That is our destiny. We will never settle down."

Absar Ali interjected, "But I think Amena is right. At the moment we are squatters. If we go to Munshikandi, we will be squatters. But here we have the possibility of purchasing some land. We may get a loan from this bank to help buy some land to live on.

Then we can stop being people of the broken river. I think we should stay."

"Father," Amena began, "many people have accused us of many things, but have you noticed that no families from my borrowing group have said anything? They have remained supportive. If we move, we lose the ability to borrow, we lose this garden, we go back to living off the moneylender." Amena had a more purposeful look about her than she'd had in several weeks.

"I think we have a good thing here," Absar Ali said as he took out a cigarette and began twirling it in his fingers. "Amena has gotten involved in a good thing. We can buy aluminum cookware, we can buy our own rickshaws, someday we can take a house loan. I think we should stay."

Amena's father looked at his son-in-law and began to cry softly. "He is gone, my son is gone, nothing will bring him back," he said haltingly. "But if it is Allah's will that we stay here, and if it is your will, then perhaps we will remain here."

Finally, Amena seemed to have the commitment she had sought for so long. Immediately after her brother had died, Amena's husband and parents had begun talking about moving out of Kholshi. Amena wanted to find a way for them to stay. The first person she talked to was the uncle who had inherited her grandfather's land. Amena won an oral commitment from him to sell her family the quarter acre of land they now lived on for about 15,000 taka ($375). Then she sent her husband to talk to her uncle. She didn't tell him how far she had gotten in the negotiations, but suggested that the uncle would be willing to sell for a reasonable price. That would ensure that Absar Ali believed that the deal was his, not Amena's. After her husband returned from that meeting, Amena began to discuss the benefits of staying in Kholshi with him. She emphasized the BRAC school, the hand-pumped tube well they had bought and sunk, the vegetable garden, and, most important, the membership in Grameen. Amena painted a picture of a future in which her loans for investment would grow to 10,000 taka per year, they would receive a housing loan of 25,000 taka, and they would perhaps one day come to own a shallow tube well. She also talked of his owning a small fleet of rickshaws, of leasing in several acres of land, of buying expensive fishing nets at a discount from her friends in the Haldar *para*. On one occasion she suggested that they visit some of the older borrowers in her center to see what a Grameen-financed house looked like.

Absar Ali didn't commit himself to settling in Kholshi until the family meeting. Amena's parents were in no condition to move on their own, which virtually ensured that they would remain in place for the time being. If she could arrange for the family to put a down payment on the housing plot, their roots would be firmly planted in a village where they would be likely to spend the rest of their lives.

Despite the tragedy and uncertainty that characterized the fall, Amena and her husband's businesses were growing. During the second week of September they sold a cow for 5,000 taka that they had bought a year earlier for 2,500. They used half of the money to buy a new calf and the rest to repair their house, invest in the cookware business, and buy some ducklings. The vegetable garden continued to be productive. That kept expenses on groceries down and yielded a steady stream of income from sales that daughter Aaki made at village markets. Amena continued to do a good business raising chickens and ducks, selling some of the eggs and giving others out on a sharecrop basis. By the fall, twenty months after she had received her first loan, Amena had 3,000 taka stashed away, money she hoped to use to put a down payment on her land and pay school fees for Aaki. Absar Ali was doing well in his cookware business and pulling a rickshaw in Dhaka when business was slow. He was so busy, and so dependent on his wife for investment capital, that his beatings of her had virtually ceased for the first time since they were married.

After the meeting broke up, Absar Ali hoisted his inventory of aluminum cookware on his shoulder and headed off to work, Amena returned to her vegetable garden, and Aaki fed the chickens before going off to school. Amena spent more than an hour weeding and pruning the plants, and as she did so she tried to imagine what this small plot of land would look like in ten years' time— what kind of house they would live in, how many cows they would have, how much rice they would receive after each harvest, what sort of job Aaki would have. They were dreams that people of the broken river rarely indulge in, and though they were new to Amena, they were not daunting.

In 1994, the Shaymganj Daulatpur branch disbursed 35 million taka ($875,000), received 24 million taka ($600,000) in installments, and earned a profit of approximately 600,000 taka ($15,000). As in previous years, not one payment was missed by any of the 2,400 female borrowers. In January 1995, the branch had 519 groups spread throughout 71 centers, and a cumulative disbursement of 73 million taka ($1.8 million). These milestones were achieved despite being situated in an area where the poverty and malnutrition are severe even by Bangladeshi standards and entire villages periodically disappear into the advancing river.

Were the Shaymganj Daulatpur branch the only thing Muhammad Yunus had created, it would be an impressive accomplishment. But as 1994 closed, there were 1,045 Grameen Bank branches that reached into more than half of all the villages in Bangladesh. Collectively, they lent nearly $400 million during 1994. Many of those branches outperformed Shaymganj, either because they were older, were run by better staff, or were situated in a more favorable agroclimatic region of the country. Siraj-ul Islam, the area manager responsible for Shaymganj and eight other branches, is often teased by colleagues who say that he runs a "half area." Due to the poverty and uncertainty created by the river, his disbursements and profits are 40 percent lower than those of his colleagues in Dhaka zone. He expects his promotion to be delayed as a result.

The genius of Muhammad Yunus's work is not that he figured out how to empower poor people with loans, but that he was able to develop a model that he could replicate more than a thousand times while maintaining control over the quality of the enterprise. The difference is critical to understanding the implications of what he has accomplished. One branch can serve 2,000 people, whereas a thousand branches can serve 2 million. It takes an entirely different set of skills to start a pilot project than it does to successfully "franchise" it. Pilot projects reach hundreds of poor people; franchises touch millions.

In circles where poverty and environmental issues are discussed, one often hears the comment "Small is beautiful." Tiny programs tailored to local needs are romanticized, while anything big—governments, corporations, even large nonprofit organizations—is distrusted. Rarely is it considered that while small may often be beautiful, small is, after all, still small. A world in which thousands of successful pilot projects reach a tiny percentage of the world's poor, and leave the vast majority untouched, is a world where mass poverty is destined to persist and deepen.

It is hardly an exaggeration to say that nearly every major problem facing the world has several solutions that have been proven effective on a small scale. But only if the best of those projects can be replicated or franchised, and expanded while maintaining reasonably high quality, will there be hope for resolving the interconnected mesh of social, environmental, and economic injustices that are tearing at the insides of humanity.

Muhammad Yunus has demonstrated that large-scale replication of an effective antipoverty strategy can be both successful and profitable. He resisted the temptation to keep Grameen small (and easily controlled by him), and in the process reached 2 million borrowers, created a highly decentralized management structure, and trained a workforce of 11,000. Doing so has not always been easy. Striking the right balance between keeping all Grameen branches similar while allowing for innovation and experimentation came after years of trial and error. The conditions that gave rise to widespread employee discontent in 1991 was a result of bigness, and so was the gradual decline in the zealousness with which some employees carried out their duties.

Fueling the aggressive expansion program was the managing director's faith in the ability of people to use credit well *even when they were not directly supervised by him*. Many Grameen critics predicted disaster when Yunus was not there to monitor everything, but their fears have proven largely unfounded. Bangladeshis, long portrayed as lacking the skills for middle management and business ownership, have demonstrated those abilities as Grameen staff and borrowers.

Other poverty-focused credit programs in Bangladesh, many of them Grameen imitators, now reach 2.5 million *additional* families. Furthermore, Grameen replication programs in other Third World countries now reach tens of thousands of people, and many projects are growing rapidly. Each month, dozens of people from other Third World countries come to Bangladesh to learn how Grameen works so that they can start similar projects after returning home.

For many years, one of the most serious criticisms of Grameen was that credit was not the "magic bullet" Yunus believed it to be. The problem of poverty, critics argued, was complex, and needed a solution that took into account not only its financial dimensions, but also things like ignorance, political powerlessness, and ill health. Other programs that provided credit, for example, required that borrowers undergo a six-month course on literacy and political organizing before they were allowed to take a loan. Experts scoffed at Grameen's requiring as little as seven hours of training before releasing loans to borrowers. The conventional wisdom questioned whether poor, uneducated people knew what to do with small loans without more guidance from above.

Yunus rejected these ideas. He admitted that poverty was a multifaceted problem, but he did not believe it necessarily needed a multifaceted solution. The poor, he argued, already had skills, were already politically conscious, and were already aware of the need for schooling and taking care of their health. It was first and foremost their lack of income that made using their skills impossible. Providing investment capital for additional income generation, he asserted, would unlock the capacity of poor people to solve many, if not all, of the manifestations of poverty that affected their lives.

The success of the Sixteen Decisions tends to support Yunus's thesis. Ten years after they were framed, research has confirmed that there had been significant progress in most areas. A high percentage of borrowers tended vegetable gardens and planted saplings, sent their children to school, and had improved the condition of their housing. While motivation and training from Grameen employees certainly played a role in some cases, many of the borrowers would have taken most of these steps regardless of the bank's urgings. They are simply the widely accepted actions one takes to escape poverty when there is additional family income. Most poor Bangladeshi families, for example, don't keep their children from school because they don't value education. Far from it—they accord it high importance. But lack of income—due to unemployment and indebtedness—makes sending children to school unaffordable. Some Grameen borrowers in Kholshi were at one time squatters on government land that was effectively ruled by one wealthy family. Before joining the bank, they were not growing vegetables near their huts because the fruits of their labor had in the past been seized. When they received loans from Grameen to buy their own homestead land, they became avid cultivators. In many cases, the poor lack only the financial resources—and not the motivation—to break through social backwardness.

For the bank workers on the ground like Krishna, the spirit of the Sixteen Decisions showed itself in the solidarity it engendered. In center number two, generous group fund loans were sanctioned for sick members. Borrowers who were unable to pull together enough money to make their payment at a center meeting received interest-free loans. When the husband of a group member became ill during the summer of 1993, she was given a group fund loan and 400 taka from a special, onetime collection. After her husband died, borrowers contributed the food the woman needed to put on a modest funeral reception that allowed her to begin life as a widow with a modicum of social dignity.

The fourteenth decision states, "We shall always be ready to help one another. If anyone is in difficulty, we shall help him or her." Members of Grameen's 58,000 centers do help one another, even if stories about mutual support are sometimes exaggerated for the benefit of journalists and other visitors. This support is a shock absorber for the bank and its members, enabling them to weather tough times. If Shandha's center implemented this decision more faithfully than most, it was still a powerful stabilizing force in the lives of tens of thousands of poor families whose social support network had been virtually nonexistent before they joined the bank.

Yunus's approach, then, is simple, hands-off, and franchisable. But that does not guarantee success for everyone who tries it. Hundreds of frank discussions with Grameen staff and borrowers has left this author with the impression that roughly 60 percent of the members who take loans are able to make rapid and sustained improvements in their life after joining. Another one-quarter or so may spend years making small, halting improvement in their standard of living. Much of their progress, however, can easily be erased by a natural disaster or major family illness. For the final 10 to 15 percent of borrowers, participating leads to no impact or a negative one. While these figures may vary slightly across different regions of the country, there is a surprising degree of agreement among staff about their accuracy in describing a typical branch. And some initial research by social scientists has tended to confirm these estimates.

While one could argue that a more intensive, hands-on approach would be helpful to those borrowers who are unable to achieve more progress, Yunus responds by saying that failure by borrowers can almost always be traced back to mistakes made by the staff in administering the credit program. His faith in poor people's ability to get out of the rut is unshakable. But more to the point, if Grameen tried to solve every problem of every borrower, it would lose money and be unable to operate on the scale it does now.

In 1980, all the programs in Bangladesh providing credit to the poor (including Grameen) reached fewer than 100,000 families. Fourteen years later, that figure had grown to 4.5 million, or an increase of more than 4,500 percent. By 1994, close to half of all families living in poverty in the country were borrowing from poverty-focused programs. Instead of paying 120 percent annual interest to moneylenders, these families were paying 15 to 30 percent interest to development organizations. The difference represented a massive transfer of capital from loan sharks to poor people. The impact on poverty, landlessness, the oppression of women, and political powerlessness at the village level has been profound. Early studies have indicated that many poor people in Grameen villages who have never taken a loan benefit as well, because as more people become involved in self-employment, the pool of agricultural wage laborers goes down and, as a result, their wages go up.

With determined leadership by governments and donor organizations, the Bangladesh experience can be studied and adapted in other Third World countries on a massive scale. While there are genuine differences among countries and cultures, there are striking similarities among the life circumstances of landless day laborers (and their families) living in the rural areas of Asia, Africa, and Latin America. And while changes will be necessary to adapt the Grameen approach—just as changes were necessary to make McDonald's thrive in Europe and Asia—those doing so will have the advantage of knowing all the experiments that were tried in Bangladesh and failed.

If only five countries—India, Pakistan, Indonesia, Nigeria, and Brazil—could, over the next fifteen years, achieve what Bangladesh has in the last fifteen years (reaching one-half of its extremely poor families with credit), one-quarter of all families living in absolute poverty in the world would have access to credit and a chance to escape poverty. Of those five countries, two (India and Pakistan) share much with Bangladesh in terms of culture and economic conditions. Indonesia, and to a lesser extent Brazil, already have several successful Grameen-style programs in operation. Nigeria has a longer way to go. Countries as diverse as El Salvador, Vietnam, Malaysia, and Bolivia have experienced an explosion of micro-credit programs in recent years.

The funding and technology to achieve this growth during the next decade or two is already in place. The ingredient in the shortest supply is the one that, in theory, could most easily be created—faith. Until the people who make decisions about national and international priorities share, to some degree, Muhammad Yunus's belief in the ability of poor people to use credit to create self-employment and escape poverty, the Grameen experience will be regarded as a freak of nature instead of a call to reorganize anti-poverty strategies at the local, national, and global levels. Those who explain the bank's success as a function of its founder's charisma fail to recognize the "charisma" of thousands of employees and hundreds of thousands of borrowers, and ultimately do a great disservice to Yunus's lifework. Ironically, the more people focus attention on the founder, the more it reduces the importance of what he has done and makes it unlikely that a serious effort will be made to make it available outside of Bangladesh on a wide scale.

In the years ahead, Yunus sees the purpose of his work being to convince decision-makers that the genius behind Grameen's success is not *his* genius, but that of the bank's borrowers. Because only if they come to share his faith in people and untangle themselves from the paternalism that shapes poverty programs of both the left and the right will his dream of a world free from poverty be realized in his lifetime. Changing that mentality may prove a greater challenge than making Grameen work in the first place. More likely than not he will fail. But that, of course, is what people said when he started making loans in Jobra in 1977.

Toward the end of the monsoon, Fulzan gave birth to a premature, underweight infant. To her and her husband's despair, it was a girl. Had it been a boy, Fulzan's relationship with her husband would have improved dramatically. As it was, he became distant, and spent more time with his first wife. It seemed that whichever of his two wives bore him a son first would become the favorite.

The second half of 1994 was remarkably unkind to Fulzan. The pregnancy took its toll on her. Her cow died, and when the owner of her sharecropped calf asked for Fulzan to return it, she received only 300 taka though she was due 500. Fulzan took in a calf from another family. The fragile state of her health and that of her infant precluded the possibility of ditchdigging for many months. Raising cows, ducks, chickens, and vegetables was her only source of income besides the crops her husband cultivated on land she had rented.

In October she took all the profits she'd accrued since she'd begun to borrow and invested them in improving her small hut. She bought two sheets of corrugated tin, and with them was able to secure her entire roof. She replaced the rotting thatch that had constituted her walls, thereby plugging the gaping holes that had denied her any real privacy during her adult life. She also bought some wood and had her husband build her a door with a latch that allowed her to lock it from the inside. All of this cost her 2,000 taka. While her renovated hut was barely twenty square feet and five feet high, far smaller than those of the older borrowers in her center, it provided the best living conditions she'd ever enjoyed. Shelter for her two children was a priority for her, as it was for her group chairman, Nobirun, who made similar improvements in her hut after the 1994 monsoon.

At about the time that Fulzan was working on her house, the eighth group completed its group training and attempted to gain recognition. But on the appointed day, the women were not equal to the challenge. The group chairman was unable to begin the meeting correctly, and, rather unexpectedly, one woman couldn't stop giggling. As the day for the retest neared, two members of the original quintet dropped out. When Shandha spread the word that the group was looking for two new women in a hurry, Fulzan sent her niece Zorina, who had returned to the area with her husband in August. She had only two days to learn all the rules, but Zorina knew some already from the time when Fulzan was training, and she did so well that Shandha decided that she would be group chairman.

The reconstituted group passed. When it came time to make loan proposals, Zorina asked for 2,500 taka while the other four, all Hindus, asked for 5,000. Zorina used the money to buy some chickens and goats. Amodini's sister-in-law, who was the group secretary, invested her money in a convenience store that she ran out of her hut. Within two weeks she was grossing 300 taka per day, as it was easier for the women in the Haldar *para* to buy from her than from the shopkeepers in the male-dominated Kholshi bazaar. Soon her weekly profit soared to 400 taka, more than enough to make her weekly loan installment of 100 taka. Zorina didn't have such immediate success, but it was hard to tell from talking with her. She radiated optimism, and was proud of being group chairman.

In the end, Fulzan Begum seemed destined to struggle harder for her progress than other women. If Amena falls into the category of borrowers who make rapid and permanent progress out of poverty, Fulzan and Zorina would fall into the second category of women who make halting progress that is constantly in danger of being reversed. After nearly two years as a borrower, she still had a hard life. But no one who had seen her hut both before she joined Grameen and after she made the repairs in October 1994 could deny that, despite all the setbacks, the ability to borrow had brought a few important improvements to her life in a relatively short period of time.

In early October, rumors swept through the Grameen head office that Yunus was going to win the Nobel Prize for Economics. A few days later, it was announced that three American economists were sharing the award for their work on game theory. Many concluded that Yunus's work was not theoretical enough to pass muster with his fellow economists. Nobody ever receives the Nobel Prize in Economics for something practical, they said. Tradition was not about to change, at least not in 1994.

On October 16, Yunus traveled to Des Moines to receive the World Food Prize, a lesser award but one that still carried a $200,000 cash prize. Grameen's managing director announced that the money would be used to endow prizes for bank workers and borrowers who performed exceptionally well. In a story about Yunus's receiving the award, *USA Today* columnist Mark Memmott wrote, "The three winners of the Nobel Prize in Economic Science got a lot of attention last week. Reporters called from around the world. Their pictures were in newspapers everywhere. Meanwhile, another economist who won a major award last week received his $200,000 in relative obscurity. But Muhammad Yunus," Memmott concluded, "didn't seem to care. . . ."

14

"We're Here for You"

Thelma couldn't wait any longer. "Okay, let's go over my receipts," she said to the three other women of Les Papillons and a prospective new member named Margaret Roberts, a friend of Queenesta's who was going through the orientation process. It was just before 8 P.M. on October 17, and they were in the Lindblom Park Field House for their twice-monthly center meeting. Fifteen minutes earlier, the women had divided into small groups according to which circle they belonged to, and there was a lot to do.

Thelma pulled a crumpled, weathered plastic bag from her purse, reached inside, and grabbed its contents—nearly one hundred receipts she had been given by wholesalers from whom she had bought merchandise in June and July. She believed in doing things by the book, even if Colete didn't always pressure her or the others to do so.

Over the next twenty minutes, Thelma went through her ratty pile of receipts, some for as little as five dollars. She read them out—"Hair accessories, twenty-seven dollars and fifty cents"—one by one and passed them around. The other women inspected each of them in turn and then handed them to Geri, who was keeping a running total to make sure it was roughly the same as Thelma's loan amount.

Borrowers are required to go over receipts before their circle sisters and show them to a senior WSEP staff member to ensure that merchandise they promise to buy with their loans is, in fact, bought. Thelma's demeanor during the process was solemn, her voice strictly monotone. She believed there was something sacred about receiving credit and handling it with integrity, and it showed. Les Papillons would not be treated to any of her usual humorous outbursts on this night.

"Geri, what's the total at now?" she said at one point.

"Uh, wait a minute . . . it's at four thousand five hundred and twenty-two dollars."

"Well, I really don't have to do any more, because that's more than my loan amount. The rest of these receipts are for things I bought after I started rolling my money over." After a brief pause, she said, "Queenesta, are you going to be able to do your amortization?"

"Uh, you know, all of my merchandise was stolen, and so were my receipts," she said weakly.

Time was running short, as there was a guest speaker there that night. Omiyale, Thelma, and Geri began paying their installments. Omiyale wrote a check for $144, while Thelma counted out $100 in 5s, 10s, and 1s and Geri produced a check for $11. As the women gave Colete their payments, Thelma suggested that Omiyale go through her amortization for the loan she received in July at the next meeting. Les Papillons' chairlady had returned from Africa in August with two suitcases full of merchandise on which she had spent $1,500, and by mid-October was well on her way to selling it all for $6,000. Omiyale was considering another trip to Africa in February, to be financed out of her profits. She was eager to do business with a Gambian wholesaler she had met on the last day of her trip who was willing to offer her extremely good prices. In September she had bought a used commercial oven and set it up in her house and was now producing a hundred cases of cookies in under three hours—roughly one-third the time it had taken her in the past.

"So, Queenesta, you aren't making a payment tonight, right?" Thelma asked matter-of-factly as she began putting her receipts back in the plastic bag.

"No." It was her fourth straight missed payment, dating back to September 5. On October 1, Queenesta had opened a new store, called Q's, that was eight blocks east of her old location, and she was specializing in beepers. She hated the fact that she was behind, and felt angry with Thelma for bringing it out in the open. "Kathleen [Robbins, WSEP's loan fund manager] told me that she will be coming out to my store and working out a new payment plan for me. My installment will be based on what my actual revenue is from my store. Once we work that out, I will not technically be in default, as long as I continue paying my new installment."

Thelma and Omiyale were dismayed. Even though it meant that the circle's borrowing privileges would not be suspended, it was an unprecedented arrangement. Thelma and Omiyale resented that Queenesta had gone over their heads, and were disturbed that Kathleen Robbins had apparently gone along with her. Thelma had agreed to sanction a $1,000 loan from the group's emergency loan fund a month earlier, even though she had doubts about the way Queenesta was going to use it. She felt she and the others deserved more than this fait accompli.

"Queenesta, are you *sure* that is what Kathleen is sayin'?" Thelma asked. "They ain't never done nothing like this before," she added, looking at Omiyale.

"Kathleen said this is what they are going to do to help us out."

"But you done already missed four payments," Thelma responded. Her voice was calm, but she was on the verge of losing her cool. "How are they going to get you out of default without you making those four payments up?"

"It doesn't sound right to me," Omiyale added. Queenesta bowed her head and covered her eyes with her hands. She began to weep softly, and for a moment the group sat without a word being spoken.

Then Margaret jumped in. "You know, when I heard what this group was about, about people coming together and supporting one another and being sisters, I was so inspired and I thought I just had to join. But how you're being with Queenesta, this isn't sisterhood. It's mean. Queenesta didn't lose her merchandise through any fault of her own. It was stolen. She isn't responsible for this." As she spoke, Margaret looked at no one in particular, but it was obvious that her displeasure was focused on Thelma. She was hoping to get Omiyale on her, and Queenesta's, side.

"Look," Thelma said in response, her hand karate-chopping the table for emphasis, "it's not about who's responsible or *whatever*—it's about doing things right, by the rules. The rules this organization set up are good rules, and we agreed to go by them. I don't want to get into the issue of why Queenesta lost her merchandise, because ever since the Haile Selassie Fest, and even before, I've been saying that this man is *no good*. If Queenesta had asked my advice, I would have said don't move in with him, don't get involved with him, break off the partnership, whatever."

"I'll tell you why I did what I did," Queenesta said as she fought back more tears, "because Kathleen seemed like the only person who was able and willing to help me through this whole thing."

"You never asked—" Thelma began.

"Let me say something," Omiyale interrupted. "I want to say something." Thelma leaned back in her chair, and despite her frown she was eager to turn over the floor to her chairlady. "I have not said very much about it, but I went through some hard times earlier this year with my short-term loan, and I still have scars. And I have to say that you never really seemed to want any help or advice from me with all that's happened. And I just think that if you're going to do something with Kathleen, we should be involved."

Thelma, looking Queenesta directly in the eye, added, "Listen, if it takes you months to clear this loan, that's okay. We're here for you. If all you can pay is ten or fifteen dollars every two weeks until the end of the year, do that. We all want a solution; we all want you back on your feet. Just don't stop coming to the meetings, don't drop out of communications with us. As long as you're here, we can work out a solution."

Geri and Omiyale concurred. Then Colete was drawn into the conversation, and after hearing about Queenesta's discussions with

Kathleen Robbins, she agreed that no decision could be made without involving her and everyone in the circle, if not the entire center. That decision, and Colete's serene demeanor, seemed to put everyone at ease. The women completed the short orientation session, which consisted of reading some of the Fund's rules out loud and asking if Margaret had questions, and began moving back to join the larger group. As they stood up, Thelma said, "Queenesta, just don't stop coming. We can work this out, whatever it takes. Just don't stop coming."

Q's was larger and airier than the Hip Hop Shop. The carpeted shopping area was filled with two racks of T-shirts, a metal shelf containing household merchandise (such as baby oil, paper towels, and glass cleaner) that all sold for a dollar, and a small book area along one of the walls. In the corner opposite the door were two glass display cases placed perpendicular to each other that, together with a wall and a partition, created an enclosed area for salespeople. In the cases were baseball hats, beepers, and jewelry. The partitions that separated the shopping area from Queenesta's office and the manufacturing area were six feet tall; the bottom half of the partitions were plastic, while the top were glass. That allowed anybody working behind the partitions to observe the entire store.

During September, when she and Shayna were living with her mother, Queenesta had searched for a place to live and a location for a new store. She was able to arrange for an apartment and a shop in the same building. The prospect of living and working in the same building galvanized her to seek a $1,000 loan from Les Papillons' emergency loan fund, put down her deposit with the landlord, and get current on her payments to Chicago Pagers, a beeper wholesaler. Several days before opening, she registered her new business and lease in her own name.

Restarting her business was difficult. There was the issue of merchandise—she had virtually none left. The only way to get through the period when her income from beepers would not meet her store rent of $500 would be to take in subtenants. As fate would have it, Victor was facing a crisis of his own in September.

His landlord was raising his rent from $700 to $850, and he would have none of it. In fact, he was tiring of holding seminars and book-signings, and saw his future in manufacturing kufis. His daughter Sheila had become a talented seamstress over the past year, and he soon had another woman working for him as well. Between the two young women and Victor, they could produce hundreds of kufis per month, and demand was growing.

Victor was also looking to get out of the book business. When he'd opened West Side Books in 1990, it had been the only store on the West Side selling black-oriented books. By the fall of 1994, there were six. By then, much of his income came from other mer-chandise, such as clothing, household goods, and jewelry. In any case, he figured that he had made good money for a couple of years but that now, with the book market saturated, it was time to get out. When Queenesta told Victor about her new location, he pro-posed that he come in as a subtenant. He would be willing to contribute his display cases and shelves from his old store if Queen-esta would let him liquidate some of his stock of books at her store. This suited her fine, and they made arrangements and raced to be ready for an October 1 opening.

Early in October, a man Victor knew became Queenesta's sec-ond subtenant. He wanted to sell dollar merchandise from one display cabinet and a metal shelf. Queenesta thought it might not appeal to the younger crowd she was targeting—baby lotion and sponges are more likely to be bought by adults—but it was rental income, and she jumped at the opportunity.

One chilly, windswept day in mid-October, Omiyale phoned Queenesta at the store and asked her how things were going. "Oh, slow, I guess. But it's coming along, you know," she said. The conversation was brief, but Queenesta appreciated the call. She and Omiyale had become closer in recent months. Omiyale kept telling her to focus on the positive side of what had happened—now she lived where she worked, Nixon was out of the picture, her business was hers and hers alone, and she had not lost all that she had learned in the past two years. Omiyale had been impressed with the store when she came out to see it, and told her so. "You're better off than you ever were, Queenesta," Omiyale would often say that fall, "and someday you'll see that more clearly than you do today." The more she said it, the more Queenesta believed it.

Yet there was still a sadness about Queenesta as she sat in her store that day. Her dispute with Duwondes Nixon had become a rather public one. She didn't like having to defend herself before friends, acquaintances, and even complete strangers about things dating back to her childhood and her relationship with Shayna's father. Moreover, all of the conflicting advice she was getting confused her. She decided to stay away from Nixon. There were moments when Queenesta blamed herself for the entire mess; belatedly, she concluded that if she had been more cautious and patient, she might have been able to keep the Hip Hop Shop and its merchandise. Moving in with Nixon, she realized, had been more risky than she'd thought at the time. But she was a proud woman who didn't like to share her self-doubts with many people. Mostly, she wanted to lay low while she got herself back on her feet. Naming the store Q's was part of that—remaining somewhat anonymous to the public while showing people who know her that she, and not Victor or any other man, was in charge.

"Hey," Victor called out to a visitor sitting on a couch next to Queenesta's desk, "don't you think it's amazing?" Victor, smiling mischievously, was standing in his manufacturing area, which was littered with fabric, scraps, sewing machines, and flyers. "Don't you think it's amazing that Queenesta landed on her feet? After all that happened, here she is in a store, she's opened it, and she has two tenants. What do you think?" Victor McClain admired and respected Queenesta. For all his rough edges, he was big enough to be able to joke about how their roles had been reversed.

Before the person to whom Victor had directed his question could answer, a customer walked in the door, and Queenesta rushed out to help him. By the time she returned, Victor was busy sorting through fabric, his question long since forgotten.

During his campaign for the presidency in 1992, Bill Clinton suggested that Muhammad Yunus should win the Nobel Prize and that, if elected, Clinton planned to start a thousand Grameen-style micro-enterprise programs, organizations like WSEP, in the United

States. This, combined with the prospect of an overhaul of the health care and welfare systems, and the possibility that changes would be accomplished in a manner that took into account the needs of the self-employed poor, gave many people familiar with the micro-enterprise field reason to hope. Furthermore, members of Congress ranging from liberal Democrat Tony Hall to conservative Republican Fred Grandy were talking about the need to encourage self-employment as a path out of poverty.

Three years into Clinton's term, some of those hopes have been realized, while others remain stalled. Yet no one can deny that presidential attention has opened doors for micro-enterprise programs. But exposure is a double-edged sword; it has also given critics of the approach new opportunities to articulate their doubts. How these critiques are answered in the next few years, both in foundation-sponsored seminars and in places like Queenesta's store and the Lindblom Park Field House, will go a long way toward determining whether U.S.-based micro-enterprise programs in general, and Grameen-style peer lending projects in particular, are short-lived fads or something more substantial and important.

There are three areas where legitimate challenges can be made to the viability of micro-enterprise programs, and they revolve around the issues of cost, impact, and scale.

By several measurements, the "products" that WSEP offers its clients, including the Full Circle Fund, are expensive. It costs WSEP more than $1 in administrative expenses to lend $1. This is much more than it costs Grameen and other successful projects in the Third World to lend. To date, interest earned on its loan portfolio covers only a small fraction of WSEP's (or the FCF's) institutional costs. Few programs in the United States can claim to be doing much better. Yet some successful projects in developing countries have been able to reach the break-even point. Even taking into consideration sometimes exaggerated claims of cost recovery and questionable accounting practices, it is undeniable that micro-enterprise lending programs based in the Third World, including those that use peer lending, are able to come many times closer to profitability than those in North America and Europe.

Given the cost structures in the two regions, one would be surprised were it otherwise. In Bangladesh, a university graduate with a master's degree who begins work at Grameen Bank earns less than 3,000 taka ($75) per month, including benefits. This is roughly equal to the average loan size of first-time borrowers. In WSEP, an entry-level employee with a master's degree will earn more than $3,000 in monthly pretax income, including benefits—roughly four times the average amount of a first-time loan. Moreover, were Grameen to drop its entry-level salary by 20 percent, it would still get thousands of qualified applicants; were WSEP to do the same, it would have difficulty filling its positions.

The criticism that programs like WSEP are too expensive misses several other crucial points. First, it fails to recognize that when successful programs like Grameen were in their youth, and when the field of Third World microlending was new, most programs lost considerable sums of donor, government, and foundation funds. Many still do. Only as the best programs matured did people even begin to talk about breaking even after all subsidies were withdrawn. (Before that, many simply marveled that a nonprofit organization could cover a substantial percentage of its costs.) By using strict criteria for what constitutes income and expenditure, Grameen experienced its first truly profitable year in 1994—seventeen years after the first loan was given out.* Only through thousands of cycles of trial and error by field staff, continuous attention to cost-cutting, and the growing capacity of borrowers to absorb larger loans (while requiring less supervision) was it able to achieve this. Most other projects in developing countries that have made a profit in a shorter time span have done so without significantly involving extremely poor clients. Thus, to expect the programs in industrialized countries to break even when they and their field are relatively young is to expect more out of them than was expected of their forerunners in the Third World, which did

---

*Even when using these strict criteria, which exclude income Grameen has received from investing some of its idle funds, by the middle and late 1980s it was operating near the break-even point and the losses were largely attributable to the establishment of significant numbers of new branches as part of an aggressive expansion program. (New branches, like new businesses, tend to lose money for a few years while progressing toward profitability.)

not have to deal with First World wages, regulations, and welfare disincentives. Even so, newer, leaner programs such as the Coalition for Women's Economic Development in Los Angeles—modeled on WSEP—have cut costs per dollar by more than half in recent years.

Perhaps it would be fairer to compare programs like the Full Circle Fund with training programs, government transfer payment schemes, "workfare" programs, and enterprise zones in terms of cost-effectiveness. If, dollar for dollar, WSEP can increase the poor's income or get people off welfare rolls—and onto the tax rolls—more efficiently than other interventions, then it will have a legitimate claim on public and philanthropic resources. Preliminary data collected by the Aspen Institute indicate that when held to this standard, WSEP and similar programs meet and exceed the standards set by many other poverty strategies. For instance, the Institute claims that the cost per job created in six micro-enterprise organizations averaged roughly $4,000, about one-third as much as some traditional employment programs.

If these agencies, like the projects in developing countries, can slowly reduce costs and increase revenue so that they come closer to the break-even point, all the better. Some newer projects, such as the New England–based Working Capital, have been able to learn from the experiences of the older ones and are achieving impressive progress toward profitability. But to call for discontinuing support for these programs, as some policy wonks and people in the philanthropic community have done, by holding them to a higher standard than the projects with which they are competing for resources seems foolhardy.

Another criticism of peer lending programs is that they have not been able to attract significant numbers of poor entrepreneurs to participate in them. And some claim that the default rates experienced by these programs will be unacceptably high. By the end of 1994, WSEP had made loans totaling nearly $1 million to some 500 women. Of this amount, two-thirds has already been repaid and another $50,000 has been collected in interest payments. All but about two dozen loans have either been paid back or are outstanding and are being repaid more or less on schedule. These numbers are neither embarrassing nor overwhelming. Certainly they are not in the league of Grameen's 1.9 million borrowers or even the 25,000 that a four-year-old program in El Salvador has reached. Many North American programs, including some modeled after Grameen, have not even been able to achieve the modest figures reached by WSEP; a few have hardly been able to attract any clients and have experienced high delinquency rates. Critics take these findings to suggest that peer lending programs have little to offer them in their attempt to start or improve their business. Others question the wisdom of encouraging the poor to be self-employed in the first place, and use programs with high default rates as evidence.

These arguments, however, fail to recognize that during Grameen's first four years of operation it barely reached five hundred people. In fact, at the conclusion of the Jobra stage in late 1979, many of the borrowers who had joined were leaving the program or were in default. But Yunus and his students learned from their mistakes in Jobra as they set up operations in Tangail. That second phase progressed faster, although this was in part due to their taking some shortcuts, such as including large numbers of male borrowers—shortcuts that led to a repayment crisis that was subsequently solved in the mid-1980s. What Grameen's own experience demonstrates is that even in Bangladesh, a program's early years, particularly when the field is new in that country, are rarely characterized by large numbers of participants and perfect repayment. In reality, the early years serve primarily to educate the staff of an organization through a laborious process of experimentation. If, in the course of that process, people like Zorina (the beggar woman from Jobra) or Thelma Ali are able to benefit, all the better. And this is precisely the experience in North America, where the more successful programs are learning from their experiments and the best of the new programs are setting a new standard for repayment and participation in the pilot phase. As Yunus realized in Bangladesh, business at new branches begins slowly and later grows as the first borrowers experience success and people hear about it. In Asia no less than Chicago, the vast majority of poor women approach credit programs with trepidation. It takes some time to gain their trust.

In truth, even if the implementing agencies perfect their approaches over the next several years, there will need to be some larger policy changes if peer lending is going to reach large numbers of low-income people in North America. Breakthroughs will be unlikely to occur unless some headway is made in changing the zoning, social welfare, and health care policies that currently work against the self-employed poor. Indeed, it is a wonder that so many women have already tried to leave welfare by joining these programs despite the fact that they gave up, or risked giving up, a monthly check and health benefits when they did so. It is only slightly less remarkable that so many others have opted for self-employment (supported by programs like WSEP) over welfare after they lost their jobs. Unless the incentives are reversed, so that work is more rewarding than welfare and so that self-employment is a viable alternative to wage employment for people who want it, it would be naive to think that these programs will grow exponentially, as they have overseas.

But grow they will, if only modestly. And if the policies are changed, they may become larger than anyone can now imagine. Indeed, it would have been difficult to predict in 1980 that in a disaster-prone country with a moribund economy, a pilot project with a decidedly mixed record of success would, over the next fifteen years, grow into a financial institution serving more than two million people, lending more than $1.5 million every working day, earning enough to make a modest profit, and training people from dozens of countries spanning five continents to reproduce its success. There are reasons to believe that the approach may be on the verge of a similar period of growth in the developed world. The micro-enterprise movement in the United States, in particular, has come a long way since its first pilot projects were launched in the late 1980s. During the process of trial-and-error experimentation that followed, a great deal has been learned about how to adapt an antipoverty strategy that originated in the Third World to the realities of impoverished communities in developed countries.

In an effort to accelerate the process of refining the approach and lobbying for policy changes that would benefit poor entrepreneurs, organizations pioneering the micro-enterprise approach in North America have formed a coalition called the Association for Enterprise Opportunity (AEO) that has already held a series of successful conferences. On several occasions, Muhammad Yunus has participated in AEO's deliberations, providing technical advice and moral support. If Mary Houghton, Connie Evans, and others who launched the micro-enterprise movement can build on what has been learned and accomplished already, they may yet demonstrate to America that the best way to help poor people may be neither by expanding nor curtailing their welfare benefits but by greatly increasing their access to investment capital through a Bangladesh approach that emphasizes solidarity, personal responsibility, and the value of traditional survival skills.

The sun was shining now, though Thelma and Janet Johnson, Omiyale's sister, hardly noticed it. They had arrived before dawn to set up their tables at the new Maxwell Street Market. At 7:00 A.M., they were already helping customers who had walked into the Fourteenth Street viaduct, one of two that was part of the new bazaar. The vendors' tables were partially illuminated by fluorescent lights whose casings were covered with several years of accumulated dirt. Wind whipped through the tunnel, often leaving tablecloths and merchandise fluttering in its wake. Thelma wondered what the wind conditions would be like in December and January.

Two teenage girls walked up to Thelma's black wooden coffee table and inspected the berets and hair wraps on the table. The hair wraps were still popular; she let them go at three for $1, having bought them for $2 a dozen from a Korean wholesaler on Clark Street. The Tunisian oils had been moving slowly since she moved to the new market; she had encouraged her regular customers to stock up in August, the last month of the old bazaar, and had sold nearly $600 in oils then. Still, she brought the oils to the bazaar, hoping that the old customers would find her when they ran out; she had put her stall number on her business card and given it to them. She also hoped to be able to build up a new customer base here.

The girls bought $4 worth of hair accessories, and as they walked away Thelma called out, "Thanks a lot, and tell your friends about me, ya hear." It was 7:25 A.M., and she had already made $45. Her trusty leather purse was slung around her torso and was filling with quarters and small bills. She was suffering from a head cold, and was thinking about buying some chicken soup from a vendor on Canal Street, the new market's main drag that ran perpendicular to the two viaducts.

Thelma left her table with a friend and walked toward Canal Street, passing several vendors she knew and two she didn't. This market isn't so bad, Thelma thought as she came out from under the viaduct. The sunlight felt warm on her skin, but it forced her to shield her eyes, as she'd been under the viaduct since 5:50 A.M. It's a different type of traffic, she thought, more white and Hispanic, less black. But different doesn't always mean bad, she knew. She looked to her left and saw Marshall Zimmerman. He was doing fairly well selling shoes, and during the week he was selling videos on a street corner near the site of the old Maxwell Street Market. Down a little farther, just out of sight, was Marmadu, the Senegalese purse vendor with whom she was friendly.

The old market had died a soggy death on August 28, 1994. A few activists tried to instigate a protest but had had little success. "The vendors and their customers," the *Chicago Tribune* explained the next day, "had known for months that a squeeze play by Mayor Richard Daley and the University of Illinois at Chicago was going to wipe out the market. If there was any fight left in them, there was no sign of it." Within days, the few vendors' shacks that remained were torn down, a handful of protesters were removed, and most of the area that had constituted the bazaar was fenced in and bulldozed. Weeks later, broken asphalt wedges jutted into the air at the same sharp angles they had assumed in the early days of September. So urgent was the university's need for the land that they left it alone for several months after having hurriedly made it unusable to the vendors and customers.

On September 4, the new market opened. As expected, it had manifest disadvantages compared with the original. There was room for only four hundred vendors, less than half as many as used to crowd into the old bazaar. Vendors were forced to pay higher fees ($15 each week for small spots like Thelma had and $35 for larger spots in which the vendor could park his car), were prohibited from selling certain goods (for example, food) without the appropriate license, and were not allowed to sell certain other merchandise (such as X-rated videos) under any circumstances. Business was down for most vendors. Parking was difficult for customers to find, and the location had no history and was unfamiliar. Fewer people came and they tended to spend less. And, most important, the raucous and irreverent edges of Maxwell Street had been smoothed, its naked capitalism covered by unfamiliar clothes.

Yet the new market was not without its redeeming features, and as the weeks passed, business slowly improved. The original plan for the reconstituted bazaar, drawn up by a New York consulting firm that was paid $80,000 for its efforts, was to transform it into a New England–style yuppie market. Activists and vendors protested, and the city ordered that the plan be redone. Later versions were more in keeping with the spirit of the original Maxwell Street, and once the market was inaugurated, a few of the city employees who were charged with overseeing it relaxed some of the regulations, further enhancing the bazaar's charm and character. Welcome additions to the new market included portable toilets, trash cans, and Dumpsters. By October, even vendors who claimed their sales were off 70 percent were saying, "It's not so bad. We'll give it a try. It'll need time to develop. Let's see."

The poor, as they have throughout history, adapted to the whims of the establishment and were doing the best they could—not because they are more magnanimous than wealthier folks, but because they have no other choice. The new market was inferior to the old one, but not so inferior as to make it useless to them. They continued to need money, and there was still money to be made—albeit less than there had been before.

Thelma stayed. It was her most consistent source of income after the summer festivals were over. Janet also stayed, her dream of owning property alive and well. Omiyale, who arrived at 7:55 A.M., kept coming, too. On this day, she was selling old inventory, her cookies, and a few of her African imports.

As Thelma returned to her stall, a customer came up and bought some dish towels from her. Another bought a wood carving of a Thai temple for $20. Some teens came by and toyed with a lighter in the shape of a gun. When someone wanted to buy some tools but only had a $100 bill, Thelma brought it to Lewis, who sold used books and records, for change. He had it, but wasn't sure the bill was genuine. Another vendor inspected it closely and pronounced it okay. Lewis promptly pulled out a wad of tens and twenties and made change for Thelma.

Down at the other end of the viaduct, Omiyale was bringing out the last of her merchandise from her car and setting up alongside Janet. There were children's two-piece outfits for $4 that she had picked up for $1 at a going-out-of-business sale, an adjustable knee brace, a cardboard box full of butter cookies, a Halloween costume, and a few pairs of mittens. For the next hour, she and her sister did a brisk business.

Omiyale sold two children's outfits and several packages of cookies. A few people opened the knee brace and looked at it, but none would part with $15. She offered it for $12 to one woman, who then decided against it after hesitating for a moment. Omiyale felt sure it would go for $10—$5 more than she had paid for it. As three Mexican women crowded around Janet's table, a car-parts vendor from the other side of the viaduct came and bought six packs of butter cookies.

Other vendors were among Omiyale's best cookie customers. Indeed, when she wanted to unload one hundred packets in a hurry, she always went down to the stores near the site of the old Maxwell Street Market and sold them there, even on weekdays, even after the market closed. Rarely did she return with anything except small bills and an empty cardboard box. During the fall, she would often bake in the morning, sell fresh-made cookies warm in the early afternoon, and hold a house party to sell her imports in the late afternoon. Somewhere in there she would return calls to Colete and Leverta Pack, pick up butter, flour, and sugar, fix meals for her family, and pick her grandchildren up from school. It was a busy lifestyle, but she was keeping up with her payments and making good money. In October, she was working on a roller-skating party for December that would raise money to retire the debts of two defaulters in her center.

Thelma, Omiyale, and Janet would remain down at the new Maxwell Street until late that mid-October afternoon. By then they had made more than $300 between them. Janet saved most of her profits for the down payment on the house she would buy one day, and Omiyale put hers aside for her plane fare to Africa. For Thelma it meant another payment on a sewing machine she had put on layaway. She hoped to have it in her apartment by December, so that she could spend the winter months making children's kufis and other Afrocentric clothes to sell at a small number of winter events she attended in the South, at the Black Women's Expo in March, and throughout the following summer. She was also considering taking a loan of $24,000 from the Small Business Administration through WSEP. Doing so would mean spending most of the warm months on the road doing events. The idea frightened and excited her, and as she returned home at six o'clock that Sunday afternoon, she was deep in thought, trying to decide whether to take the risk. Perhaps the Almighty Allah, she concluded for the time being, would give her a sign to guide her. Until then, she would keep to her tried-and-true formula—borrowing, investing, earning, and reinvesting, with most of her merchandise retailing for $3 and under. It was not exactly glamorous, but she often enjoyed it. Most important, it helped pay the bills. And that, after all, was what mattered.

EPILOGUE

During the year since I finished writing this book, I have kept abreast of developments in Kholshi and Englewood and with Grameen and WSEP. For the most part, the progress of the women themselves and of the institutions they are associated with has continued in the same halting but impressive manner that it had during 1993 and 1994. Despite continuing though largely nonviolent struggles with her husband, Amena built up savings and assets by continuing to raise livestock and expanding her vegetable garden to virtually every inch of land around her hut. Devi joined with other net-weavers in the Haldar *para* to sew a huge net that was then sold for more than 10,000 taka during the beginning of the monsoon. Shandha and Nonibala continued as before, while Fulzan settled into her newly purchased homestead plot with her husband and children. Sadly, in August her older daughter died from a snake bite.

A series of events unfolded during the monsoon that profoundly affected the branch. On the night of May 29, 1995, a meeting was held in Munshikandi, a village near the Zianpur bazaar. Local elders—mostly politicians but also a few religious leaders and moneylenders—convinced a large number of husbands of Grameen borrowers in the village to stop payment on their loans. Among the arguments the elders used was that Grameen was un-Islamic and that protests would force the Bank to lower its interest rates. In reality, the elders were acting primarily in their own self-interest. As a few would admit later, disrupting the relationship between Grameen and its borrowers would revive their moneylending businesses and increase the number of destitute women willing to be servants in their households.

The campaign was successful at first. On the day following the meeting, the branch experienced its first missed installments since it was founded in 1987. Instead of finding women borrowers in the Munshi-kandi centers that morning, the bank workers found husbands and village elders presenting grievances and demands. Grameen employees responded that policy changes were made by the bank's board of directors, a body on which borrowers served; changes were possible but would take time. Later that same day, bank workers went directly to the houses of some of the women and spoke to them. The men, however, stood firm: No changes, no installments. The following day, the elders informed the bank that they would no longer allow any direct contact between the staff and the women. When the bank workers attempted to go to center meetings anyway, they were stopped on the village paths by the elders and their henchmen, who sent the Grameen employees back to the office. Within a few weeks, this conflict spread to virtually every village in which the branch had centers. The local Member of Parliament as well as an opposition leader who planned to challenge the M.P. in the coming election spoke out in favor of withholding payments. The branch's repayment rate temporarily plummeted to 8 percent. Periodically, letters from borrowers arrived at the branch office; they would explain that the women wanted to repay but were afraid to. In Kholshi, Amena and Shandha were the last borrowers to back down.

As the manager and bank workers searched for a solution, a severe flood hit the area. Soon after the waters receded and the monsoon rice was replanted, another flood struck. After that flood abated and rice was planted for a third time, an unprecedented third flood occurred. In many ways, this disaster was more severe than the "flood of the century" that had hit the nation in 1988.

The local Grameen employees huddled with their supervisors in Tepra and Dhaka to devise a strategy to get the branch back on track. First, word was spread that Grameen would distribute money from the borrowers' disaster savings fund, which had been established after the flood of 1988. When borrowers came to the bank office to collect their share of nearly 200 taka each—this was a trip few husbands were willing to oppose—the link between the bank and its borrowers was reestablished. At the same time, Grameen took legal action against those who were preventing bank workers from traveling to the centers, an act that had its intended effect: intimidating the intimidators. By October, virtually all center meetings were being held again, and repayment rose to nearly 50 percent, despite the floods' devastation; in Shanda's center it was nearly 100 percent. By December it was clear that the branch had weathered two simultaneous attacks—one from the enemies it had made in the community, the other from nature.

In Chicago, Thelma's business thrived, particularly during the summer months. She resisted the temptation to take a large Small Business Administration loan, at least for 1995. Omiyale progressed toward completing the courses necessary to get her baker's license and sold a lot of cookies. Glenda continued working for Westcorp and making jewelry, while Geri found another full-time job after Fort Smith, his store having been vandalized five times, closed up his retail business to concentrate on manufacturing and wholesaling. Queenesta's business as well as those of her tenants grew impressively, considering their modest beginnings, and Shayna transferred to the North Side grammar school that her mother had attended.

Still, a cloud hung over the group's achievements in 1995. Queenesta was able to make only token payments on her loan, usually $25 per month but occasionally as much as $100. As a result, lending to members of Les Papillons was temporarily suspended. Relations among the women became strained. At times it seemed as though the circle might dissolve, but it never did. Instead, the women struggled together to make their businesses thrive without loans from WSEP and to raise the money to retire Queenesta's debt.

The Grameen Bank and WSEP experienced similarly fluctuating fortunes in 1995. While the threat of the Islamic fundamentalists to Grameen and Bangladesh as a whole receded, other groups opposed to Grameen attempted to incite borrowers to revolt against the Bank in branches throughout the country. In most branches the effect was negligible, but in others it was more substantial—at least for a few months. In the course of putting out these brush-fires, Grameen's board of directors approved several policy changes that addressed issues that had, for a time, provided anti-Grameen activists with powerful weapons to organize borrowers and—particulary—their husbands. Of course, the 1995 flood didn't help matters any. In general, however, the process of borrowing, investing, earning, and repaying continued apace in the 35,000 villages where Grameen operated.

The Full Circle Fund experienced growth—in numbers of new circles formed and in success stories, but also in late payments. In the Lindblom center, the oldest and largest in the program, nearly two dozen new borrowers joined circles in 1995, while overdue loans ballooned to $10,000. Like Grameen before it, the FCF began to struggle with isolated cases of default after having passed its initial years with virtually 100 percent repayment. Fortunately, many borrowers who had experienced crises followed Queenesta's example by paying back whatever they could afford even if it was less than what they had agreed to pay. A few, however, had more or less given up. Motivating those women to rejoin the fold was a challenge that Colete and other FCF staff faced during 1995 that would continue into the following year.

As these internal issues played themselves out in WSEP, Grameen, and hundreds of other organizations providing microcredit, there were a series of breakthroughs in the effort to reach the millions more poor people. Hillary Clinton's visit to Grameen in April 1995 raised the movement's profile significantly. The United Nations Conference on Women in Beijing in August 1995 brought to thousands of policy-makers and activists the message of microlending as a way to empower women. When Muhammad Yunus was featured by Peter Jennings on ABC World News Tonight as "Person of the Week" at the time of the conference, millions more learned about microlending.

In addition to increased publicity, institutional support for the movement grew. The World Bank, after years of quiet hostility toward Grameen, created the Consultative Group to Assist the Poorest (C-GAP), a semiautonomous institution whose goal was to channel at least $100 million to microlending programs in third-world countries. After some initial wrangling, Yunus threw his support behind the effort and was chosen to chair a high-level committee of advisers that the World Bank created to guide C-GAP. If managed wisely, C-GAP could catalyze a dramatic expansion of existing microcredit institutions and the creation of new ones.

In an effort to capitalize on this momentum, in early 1995 microcredit providers and advocates began preparing to hold a Microcredit Summit in 1996 to map out a strategy to reach with small loans 100 million poor families in the third world by the year 2005 and to expand the reach of programs in developed countries. Their leadership in the movement recognized, Muhammad Yunus and Connie Evans were chosen to join a small group charged with planning the summit and soliciting the participation of corporations, banks, governments, the United Nations, the media, politicians, and the general public.

In October 1995 I had an opportunity to meet with Muhammad Yunus. During our discussion, he reflected on the challenges Grameen was facing. "During the next decade," he said, "I will be working to ensure that the Microcredit Summit's goal is met. In the case of Grameen, we will be facing problems related to getting bigger, older, and inefficient. It is an inevitable process—the aging process. But while some organizations become old at three years of age, others serve a useful purpose for fifty or one hundred years. If we get old fast, other, more efficient organizations will take over.

"You see, it is not the organization that is important; it's the service. In our case, you are talking about credit for the poor. And credit for the poor has very deep roots, and they will continue to sprout. Even though Grameen Bank may not exist tomorrow, credit for the poor will not leave. It will flourish. It is an irreversible process."

THE SIXTEEN DECISIONS

1. We shall follow and advance the four principles of Grameen Bank—Discipline, Unity, Courage, and Hard Work—in all walks of our lives.
2. Prosperity we shall bring to our families.
3. We shall not live in dilapidated houses. We shall repair our houses and work towards constructing new houses as soon as possible.
4. We shall grow vegetables all year round. We shall eat plenty of them and sell the surplus.
5. During the plantation season, we shall plant as many seedlings as possible.
6. We shall plan to keep our families small. We shall minimize our expenditures. We shall look after our health.
7. We shall educate our children and ensure that we can earn to pay for their education.
8. We shall always keep our children and their environment clean.
9. We shall build and use pit-latrines.
10. We shall drink water from tube wells. If it is not available, we shall boil water or use alum.
11. We shall not take dowry at our sons' weddings, nor shall we give any dowry at our daughters' weddings. We shall keep our centre free from the curse of dowry. We shall not practice child marriage.

12. We shall not inflict any injustice on anyone, nor shall we allow anyone else to do so.
13. We shall collectively undertake larger investments for higher incomes.
14. We shall always be ready to help each other. If anyone is in difficulty, we shall help him or her.
15. If we come to know of any breach of discipline in any centre, we shall go there and help restore discipline.
16. We shall introduce physical exercises in all of our centres. We shall take part in all social activities collectively.

Formulated in a national workshop of one hundred women center chiefs in Joydevpur (about 30 miles north of Dhaka) in March 1984, the Sixteen Decisions might be called the social development constitution of Grameen Bank. All Grameen Bank members are expected to memorize and implement these decisions.

CONTACT ADDRESSES
FOR ORGANIZATIONS MENTIONED
IN THIS BOOK

Consultative Group to Assist the Poorest (C-GAP)
c/o The World Bank
1818 H Street N.W.
Washington, D.C. 20433

Grameen Bank
Mirpur 2
Dhaka 1216
Bangladesh

Microcredit Summit
c/o RESULTS Educational Fund
236 Massachusetts Avenue N.E., Suite 300
Washington, D.C. 20002

RESULTS
236 Massachusetts Avenue N.E., Suite 300
Washington, D.C. 20002

South Shore Bank
7054 S. Jeffrey Boulevard
Chicago, Illinois 60649

Women's Self-Employment Project
20 N. Clark Street
Chicago, Illinois 60602

NOTES

CHAPTER 1

11 "All human problems": "Worm's Eye View: Interviews with Women of the Grameen Bank," Alexander M. Counts, editor, RESULTS Educational Fund, Washington, D.C., 1992, p. iii.

17 "... the program was not": Chittagong University Rural Development Program, *Annual Report (1978–79),* Chittagong, 1980, p. 9.

18 "The historian Pliny": Iftikhar Ul Anwar, "State of Indigenous Industries," a chapter in Sirajul Islam, ed., *History of Bangladesh: 1704–1971 (Volume 2),* Asiatic Society of Bangladesh, Dhaka, 1992, p. 273.

18 "the Paradise of Nations": James J. Novak, *Bangladesh: Reflections on the Water,* University Press Limited (in association with the University of Indiana Press), Dhaka, 1994, p. 75.

18 "Money is so plentiful": Haroun Er Rashid, *Geography of Bangladesh,* University Press Limited, Dhaka, 1991, p. 141. The traveler was Sebastian Manrique.

18 "When at some distance": Iftikhar Ul Anwar, op. cit., p. 278.

19 "one-third of all cotton textiles": James J. Novak, op. cit., p. 75.

19 *gomasta* quotation and information on Agency System: Iftikhar Ul Anwar, op. cit., pp. 275–77.

19 Information and statistics on the decline of the textile industry: Iftikhar Ul Anwar, op. cit., pp. 297–302.

20 Information on famine, famine codes, and 1943 famine: Mosharaff Hossain, *The Assault That Failed: A Profile of Poverty in Six Villages of Bangladesh,* UNRISD, Geneva, 1987, pp. 11–13; and James J. Novak, op. cit., pp. 55–58.

21 "moth-eaten state": Rehman Sobhan, *Bangladesh: Problems of Governance,* University Press Limited, Dhaka, 1993, p. 79.

21 "the greatest rural slum": Larry Collins and Dominique Lapierre, *Freedom at Midnight,* Simon and Schuster, New York, 1975, p. 114.

21 "The state language of Pakistan": Badruddin Umar, "Language Movement," from Sirajul Islam, ed., *History of Bangladesh: 1704–1971 (Volume 1),* Asiatic Society of Bangladesh, Dhaka, 1992, p. 437.

22 "[When I returned] I was brought": Anthony Mascarenhas, *Bangladesh: Legacy of Blood,* Hodder and Stoughton, London, 1986, p. 10. Reference to Rakhi Bahini is from the same book, p. 37, and the information on the 1974 famine, including the quotation in the *Guardian,* is on pp. 43–44.

25 Background information on the mismanagement of deep tube wells can be found in Chapter 19 of Betsy Hartmann and James Boyce, *A Quiet Violence: View from a Bangladesh Village,* Zed Books, London, 1983. The information about Tehbhaga comes from interviews with Yunus, Dipal, and Latifee, from interviews with farmers and others conducted on a trip I took to Chittagong in July 1989, and from H. I. Latifee, "A Report on Nabajug Tehbhaga Khamar," Department of Economics, Chittagong University, Chittagong, August 1980.

30 Statistics on worsening Bangladesh poverty come from Mosharaff Hossain, op. cit., pp. 28–33.

CHAPTER 2

47 "[Zorina] came to know": Jowshan ara Rahman, "Jobra: The Grameen Bank Project," *Shishu Diganta,* April 1980.

CHAPTER 3

This chapter relies exclusively on firsthand observations and interviews.

CHAPTER 4

97 "When I was a child": from a speech by Muhammad Yunus, "Anything Wrong," Grameen Bank, Dhaka, 1990.

109   Average family income statistic: Isabel Wilkerson, "Graduation: Where 500 Began, 150 Remain," *New York Times,* June 13, 1994, pp. 1, 9.

110   Information on Englewood in the period 1850–1920: *Local Community Fact Book, Chicago Metropolitan Area, based on the 1970 and 1980 Censuses,* edited by the Chicago Fact Book Consortium, Chicago Review Press, Chicago, 1984, pp. 172–75.

110   "The Englewood area": "Englewood: Hot Gang War Spot," *Chicago Daily News,* April 26, 1968. Statistics on demographic change from *Local Community Fact Book,* op. cit., pp. 172–75.

111   "All hell broke loose": William Recktenwald and Colin McMahon, "Deadly End to Deadly Year," *Chicago Tribune,* January 1, 1993, p. 1.

118   Information on the rate of black business ownership: Jawanza Kunjufu, *Black Economics: Solutions for Economic and Community Empowerment,* African-American Images, Chicago, 1991, p. iii. The information concerning how much black consumers spend on black business is on pp. 53–55.

119   "the so-called model minorities": For information concerning immigrants' economic success in the United States, see Ivan Light, *Ethnic Enterprise in America: Business and Welfare Among Chinese, Japanese and Blacks,* University of California Press, Berkeley, 1972; Ivan Light, "Immigrant and Ethnic Enterprise in North America," *Journal of Ethnic and Racial Studies,* April, 1984, pp. 195–216; Ivan Light and E. Bonacich, *Immigrant Entrepreneurs: Koreans in Los Angeles, 1965–1982,* University of California Press, Berkeley, 1988; and Balkin, *Self-Employment for Low-Income People,* Praeger, New York, 1989, pp. 51–68.

122   Historical information on Maxwell Street: Ira Berkow, *Maxwell Street: Survival in a Bazaar,* Doubleday and Co., Garden City, N.Y. 1977, p. 10.

CHAPTER 5

This chapter relies exclusively on firsthand observations and interviews.

CHAPTER 6

147   Chicago history through 1919: St. Clair Drake and Horace R. Clayton, *Black Metropolis: A Study of Negro Life in a Northern City,* University of Chicago Press, 1993, pp. 3–77.

149   "It was undeniable": Nicholas Lemann, *The Promised Land: The Great Black Migration and How It Changed America,* Knopf, New York, 1991, p. 41.

152 Chicago history from 1919 through the 1960s: Drake, op. cit., pp. 3–77; and Mike Royko, *Boss: Richard M. Daley of Chicago,* Plume, New York, 1971.

154 "the largest public housing project": Lemann, op. cit., p. 92.

156 "After 1970": William Julius Wilson, *The Truly Disadvantaged,* University of Chicago Press, Chicago, 1987, p. 3. The statistics in the next paragraph are found in the same work, p. 21.

156 "Wednesday found criminal activity": "Overnight Violence Leaves 1 Dead, 8 Hurt," *Chicago Defender,* November 18, 1993, p. 4.

157 "[There is a] sense of worthlessness": Cornel West, *Race Matters,* Vintage, New York, 1993, p. 27.

157 "should be dreaming": Marian Wright Edelman, "Violence Crushes Youths' Dreams," *Chicago Defender,* November 15, 1993, p. 12.

CHAPTER 7

173 Discussion of foreign aid under Mujib: Rehman Sobhan, *The Crisis of External Dependence,* University Press Limited, Dhaka, 1982, pp. 166–201.

174 Study on aid industry information: Rehman Sobhan and Syed Hashemi, "Beneficiaries of Foreign Aid," in Rehman Sobhan, ed., *From Aid Dependence to Self-Reliance: Development Options for Bangladesh,* Dhaka, University Press Limited, Dhaka, 1990.

174 "In the world of aid": James Novak, op. cit., pp. 5–6.

182 Yunus speech to World Bank: Muhammad Yunus, "Hunger, Poverty, and the World Bank," Grameen Bank, Dhaka, 1993.

CHAPTER 8

192 The pro–Maxwell Street pieces in the *Sun-Times* were written by Raymond R. Coffey. They were "UIC Expansion Plan: Does It Make Sense?" July 16, 1993; "Maxwell St. Ready to Fight Local Bully," July 18, 1993; and "UIC, City Created Maxwell St. Mess," July 20, 1993.

192 Harold Washington Library meeting: interviews with people in attendance, and Ethan Mitchell, "Opposition Mounts to Maxwell St. Shutdown," *Chicago Defender,* December 1, 1993, p. 1.

195 Balkin report on financial losses: Steve Balkin, Alfonso Morales, and Joseph Persky, "The Value of Benefits of a Public Market: The Case of Maxwell Street," Roosevelt University, Chicago, July 1993. The quote from a young vendor is from p. 19 of this paper.

196 "Specific types of programmatic activities": Steve Balkin, Alfonso Morales, and Joseph Persky, "Why the University of Illinois Is Wrong," mimeographed, February 1994, p. 4.

201 Drop in crime information: Fran Spielman, "Community Policing Area Leads City's Crime Drop," *Chicago Sun-Times,* January 21, 1994, p. 14. The information on the drop in crime in Englewood comes from Julie Irwin, "Murders Plummet in Englewood," *Chicago Tribune,* March 1, 1994, p. 1 (Chicagoland section).

CHAPTER 9
This chapter relies exclusively on firsthand observations and interviews.

CHAPTER 10
239 "For 120 years": Isabel Wilkerson, "Change Threatens a Legendary Street Bazaar," *New York Times,* March 23, 1994, p. A14.

239 "Ready to Rumble? Step into Council Chambers": John Kass, *Chicago Tribune,* April 14, 1994, p. 1.

240 *Post* and *Economist* articles: Megan Garvey, "The Last Sale of a Faded Urban Market," *Washington Post,* April 12, 1994; "Goodbye, Maxwell Street," *Economist,* April 23, 1994, p. 31.

241 "Nobody ever went": John McCarron, "On Maxwell, No Need to Circle the Wagons," *Chicago Tribune,* August 22, 1993, section 7, p. 3.

246 "the predicament of welfare mothers": Jason DeParle, "Welfare Mothers Find Jobs Easy to Get But Hard to Hold," *New York Times,* October 24, 1994, p. 1.

246 "[The] removal or reduction of poverty": David Gibbons, ed., *The Grameen Reader* (second edition, revised), Grameen Bank, Dhaka, Bangladesh, 1994, p. 47.

247 Discussion of business use of personal credit cards: "Some Cash-Poor Firms Just Charge It," *Chicago Sun-Times,* July 27, 1994, p. 54.

247 Discussion of unemployed males turning to self-employment: D. S. Evans and L. S. Leighton, "Self-Employment Selection and Earnings over the Life Cycle," Washington, D.C., U.S. Small Business Administration, Office of Advocacy, 1987, quoted in Balkin, op. cit., p. 35.

247 "Show me a welfare mother": Donald R. Katz, "Where Credit Is Due," *Investment Vision* magazine, August/September 1991, p. 54.

248　Discussion of U.K. and French programs: Balkin, op. cit., pp. 105–8. Job Corps information: Amy Kazlow, "Corps for Troubled Youth Now Finds Itself in Trouble," *Christian Science Monitor,* February 2, 1995, pp. 1, 8.

250　"Several thousand of them": Kunjufu, op. cit., p. 15.

250　"Free blacks in antebellum America": Balkin, op. cit., p. 71.

250　Information on Freedman's Bank and DuBois quote: Balkin, op. cit., pp. 71–74.

251　Census Bureau statistics on black firms and business ownership among different ethnic groups: Andrew Hacker, *Two Nations: Black and White, Separate, Hostile, Unequal,* Ballantine, New York, 1992, pp. 108–9.

251　Information on black net worth: *State of Black America 1994,* National Urban League, New York, 1994, p. 20.

251　Information on blacks' consumption: National Urban League, op. cit., pp. 51–84; Nancy Ryan, "Marketing to Black Consumers," *Chicago Tribune,* June 9, 1991, section 7, p. 6.

CHAPTER 11

This chapter relies exclusively on firsthand observations and interviews.

CHAPTER 12

This chapter relies exclusively on firsthand observations and interviews.

CHAPTER 13

309　Yunus speech: "Grameen Bank: Does Capitalist System Have to Be the Handmaiden of the Rich?" keynote address delivered at the 85th Rotary International Convention, held in Taipei, Taiwan, June 12–15, 1994, published by the Grameen Bank, Bangladesh, 1994.

316　Statistics on Shaymganj from interviews and inspection of loan ledgers and forms at the branch. Muhammad Abdul Rohim was particularly helpful in tracking down these statistics.

CHAPTER 14

333　Cost-per-job-created estimates: Interviews with Peggy Clark, of the Aspen Institute, and Rona Feit, a consultant formerly with the Corporation for Enterprise Development, a Washington, D.C.–based think tank.

333   WSEP statistics: "1993 Microenterprise Briefing Packet: Facts and Figures on Seven U.S. Microenterprise Development Programs," Self-Employment Learning Project, Washington, D.C., 1994, supplemented by updates contained in my correspondence with the Aspen Institute and WSEP.

ACKNOWLEDGMENTS

This book was nearly five years in the making; it should not be surprising, therefore, that the debts incurred in writing it have been substantial. The women who are featured in the book, and in some cases members of their families, their friends, and colleagues, have devoted themselves to it for nearly two years. The women in Chicago, for instance, agreed to keep a diary during this time and to share its contents with me. Furthermore, there are women who went through the process of telling me their life stories but who do not appear in this book.

The idea to structure the book along the lines that I did, and to include the women from Chicago so prominently, came from my gifted agent, Joel Fishman. His editorial comments on the manuscript, as well as on the original proposal, were excellent. On many occasions he went beyond the call of duty for me. The people at Random House were a pleasure to work with. Ian Jackman, my editor, worked tirelessly on taking the flab out of my early, and rather verbose, drafts while retaining what was right about them. He is the finest editor a young writer could ask for. Ann Godoff provided sage advice and reassurance.

A number of my friends and colleagues agreed to read the working manuscript and give me their comments. They include Steve Balkin, Dipal Chandra Barua, Karen Doyle, David Gibbons, Alan Gold, Sam Harris,

Nick Langton, H. I. Latifee, Sharon Mason, Susan Matteucci, Bob Philips, Jennifer Robey, Khalid Shams, Helen Todd, and Lynn Walker-McMullen. Muhammad Yunus read the chapters as they were being written and provided valuable feedback. But among this group Steve Dewhurst stands alone, for the amount of criticism he provided, the good humor it was wrapped in, and the speed with which he made it available—usually faxing it to me in Bangladesh within twenty-four hours of receiving a batch of new chapters.

In researching this book, it was necessary to conduct scores of interviews. Among those who agreed to talk with me were Muhammad Shah Alam, Absar Ali, Muhammad Jobbar Ali, Lutfa Ali, Shashona Ali, Thelma Dean Ali, Venita Allen, S. M. Shamim Anwar, Assaduzzaman, Krishna Das Bala, Steve Balkin, Dipal Chandra Barua, Aduree Begum, Amena Begum, Firoza Khatoon, Fulzan Begum, Nurjahan Begum, Rasheda Begum, Rukia Begum, Supi Begum, Zomella Begum, Zorina Begum, Lynnette Boone, Pam Bozeman, Gwen Burns, Kazal Chowdhury, Peggy Clark, Stacy Craighead, Mary Dean, Tiziana Dearing, Fred DeLuca, Geraldine Dinkins, Hkeem DuPart, Omiyale DuPart, Connie Evans, Gopal Ghosh, Nonibala Ghosh, Oloka Ghosh, Colete Grant, Odette Gueringer, Amodini Rani Haldar, Devi Rani Haldar, Shandha Rani Haldar, Lynn Hardy, Della Harris, Glenda Harris, June Harris, Queenesta Harris, Mary Houghton, Muzammel Huq, Muhammad Jakaria, Janet Johnson, Sukor Kasim, Muhammad Abdul Khashem, Dulal Chandra Kor, Joanne Kyle, H. I. Latifee, Cawa Levi, Wanda Little, Victor McClain, Susan Matteucci, Muhammad Munaf Mia, Belvia Muhammad, Muhammad Abdul Mustafiz, Duwondes Nixon, Jewell Pates, Debra Payne, Thelma Perkins, Jannat Quinine, Harun ur Rashid, Claudette Redic, Alma Jean Richardson, Muhammad Abdul Rohim, Gheeliyah Rojas, Rebecca Rosofsky, Muhammad Samsuddin, Shabnum Sanghvi, Khalid Shams, Carol Simms, B. J. Slay, Fort Smith, Muhammad Abdul Mannan Talukdar, Steve White, Gary Williams, Muhammad Yunus, and Marshall Zimmerman.

A number of people and institutions contributed to this project. The staff at the Harold Washington Library and the Chicago Historical Society were extremely helpful during my frequent visits. The staff and volunteers of RESULTS, where I worked from 1989 to 1992, were (and are) a source of inspiration. The Wallace Genetic Foundation and the Fund for Innovation and Public Service provided funding that enabled this book's initial research to be conducted. Several books influenced my thinking on the issues addressed herein. Prominent among them were *The Promised Land,* by Nicholas Lemann; *There Are No Children Here,* by Alex Kotlowitz; *Black Metropolis: A Study of Negro Life in a Northern City,* by St. Clair Drake and Horace R. Clayton; *Bangladesh: Reflections on the Water,* by James Novak; and *Among Schoolchildren,* by Tracy Kidder. Barbara Charbonnet, Sam Harris, Nick Shatzki, and Lynn Walker-McMullen led a fund-raising drive to buy me the computer on which this book was written. Randal Castleman and the late Robert McCardell, English teachers of mine at the Horace Mann School, taught me how to write. Duane and Mary Wainwright, my in-laws as of June 1994, were patient and supportive while their prospective son-in-law spent his engagement with thousands of people (most of whom were women) but rarely with their daughter. Salehuddin Azizee, one of Grameen's two in-house professional photographers, spent long hours taking pictures. Mir Akhtar Hossain contributed his time and effort to many of the logistical requirements of producing the book, as well as his warmth and friendship during some trying times. Masud Isa assisted by providing statistical analyses of Grameen, and the computer unit he oversees, headed up by Naznin Sultana, helped me out of many a jam. Carol Petersen, her son Dan, and Jim Dickert were gracious and generous hosts during all six of my visits to Chicago. Above all, there were Connie Evans and Muhammad Yunus, who not only contributed their time and expertise, but allowed me to have unlimited access to their organizations as I researched this book.

My parents, Robert Counts and Carolyn Fox, and my stepparents, Norma Hakusa Counts and John Fox, gave me the confidence and courage to attempt such an undertaking and considerable moral and material support once I began. And tying it all together, my wife, Emily, played the roles of editor, coach, friend, patient fiancée, wedding planner, and (at long last) supportive spouse while I struggled through the research and writing processes.

While these people and many others contributed to this book, I alone am responsible for its contents.

ABOUT THE AUTHOR

ALEX COUNTS, a former Fulbright
scholar in Bangladesh, has worked
for nonprofit organizations, including RESULTS and CARE, since grad-
uating from Cornell University in
1988. A native of New York City, he
now lives in Dhaka with his wife, Emily. This is his first book.